THE PRICE OF EXPERIENCE

© Caryl Eshleman

THE PRICE OF EXPERIENCE

CLAYTON ESHLEMAN

Black Widow Press is an imprint of Commonwealth Books, Inc., Boston, MA. Distributed to the trade by NBN (National Book Network) throughout North America, Canada, and the U.K. All Black Widow Press books are printed on acid-free paper, and glued into bindings. Black Widow Press and its logo are registered trademarks of Commonwealth Books, Inc.

Joseph S. Phillips and Susan J. Wood, Ph.D, Publishers
www.blackwidowpress.com

Cover Design: Kerrie Kemperman
Typesetting: Kerrie Kemperman
Cover art by Leon Golub, *Blue Sphinx,* 1988, acrylic on linen, 305 x 378.5 cm.
Carnegie Museum of Art, Pittsburgh.
Frontispiece photo by Caryl Eshleman
Author photo by Tom Wallace

ISBN-13: 978-0-9856122-0-7

Printed in the United States

10 9 8 7 6 5 4 3 2 1

ACKNOWLEDGEMENTS

Some of these pieces originally appeared, often in earlier versions, in the following magazines and literary blogs: *Caterpillar, ActionYes, Poetry News: Beyond Baroque Literary Arts Center, Sulfur, AWP Writers Chronicle, Rain Taxi, The Jivin' Ladybug, Jacket, APR, Callaloo, Nomadics, New American Writing, The Black Herald, Tributary, Cerise Press, Montevidayo, Cover, Alligatorzine, Volta, Poems and Poetics, Broome Street Review, They Will Sew The Blue Sail,* and *Big Bridge.*

The first of the "Three New York Stories" was read by Paul Auster on NPR and published in his collection of stories and anecdotes *I Thought My Father was God,* Henry Holt, NYC, 2001.

Some of the material in the second of the "Three New York Stories" appeared in Daniel Kane's *All Poets Welcome: The Lower East Side Scene in the 1960s,* University of California Press, Berkeley, 2003.

"Paul Blackburn's Parallel Voyages" appeared in *The Parallel Voyages,* selected by Clayton Eshleman, and edited by Edith Jarolim, SUN-Gemini Press, Tuscon, 1987.

"Organized Nomadistorms of Broken Oases" appeared in *Cartographies of the In-Between,* edited by Peter Cockelbergh, Litteraria Pragensia Books, Charles University, Prague, 2011.

"Erratics" first appeared as the chapbook *Erratics,* Hunger Press, Rosendale, NY, 2000, ed. by J.J. Blickstein; in a revised form it appeared in *My Devotion,* Black Sparrow Press, David R. Godine, Publisher, Boston, 2004. It has once more been revised for its publication here.

"An Anatomy of the Night" was published as a chapbook by BlazeVOX, Buffalo, NY, in 2011.

My gratitude to Ron Padgett who read the first and penultimate drafts of "An Anatomy of the Night" and made very useful editorial suggestions, nearly all of which I accepted and incorporated. Padgett's participation in my working through the multiple strategies involved in realizing this poem was a true gesture of comradely display.

For Robert Kelly and Jerome Rothenberg,

fellow Argonauts

What is the price of Experience do men buy it for a song
Or wisdom for a dance in the street? No it is bought with the price
Of all that a man hath his house his wife his children
Wisdom is sold in the desolate market where none come to buy
And in the witherd field where the farmer plows for bread in vain

It is an easy thing to triumph in the summers sun
And in the vintage & to sing on the waggon loaded with corn
It is an easy thing to talk of patience to the afflicted
To speak the laws of prudence to the houseless wanderer
To listen to the hungry ravens cry in wintry season
When the red blood is filld with wine & with the marrow of lambs

It is an easy thing to laugh at wrathful elements
To hear the dog howl at the wintry door, the ox in the slaughter house moan
To see a god on every wind & a blessing on every blast
To hear sounds of love in the thunder storm that destroys our enemies house
To rejoice in the blight that covers his field, & the sickness that cuts off his children
While our olive & vine sing & laugh round our door & our children bring fruits & flowers

Then the groan & the dolor are quite forgotten & the slave grinding at the mill
And the captive in chains & the poor in the prison, & the soldier in the field
When the shatterd bone hath laid him groaning among the happier dead

It is an easy thing to rejoice in the tents of prosperity
Thus could I sing & thus rejoice, but it is not so with me!

—William Blake, *The Four Zoas,* Night the Second

TABLE OF CONTENTS

I

II

III

IV

V

VI

I

A NOTE ON CAROLEE SCHNEEMANN'S *FUSES*

Wondering how to begin a note on these stills from Carolee Schneeman's first film, three years in the making, I came across a copy of *Yugen 7* and leafing thru it found some blues chorus lines of Bessie Smith's:

> Bought me a coffee-grinder, got the best one I could find,
> So he could grind my coffee, 'cause he has a brand new grind.
>
> He's a deep-sea diver with a stroke that can't go wrong,
> He can touch the bottom, and his wind holds out so long.

There is that kind of joy in Carolee Schneeman's work. *Fuses,* the film, runs 18 minutes, running in & out of a man & a woman's life together, their bed as the life-source of the house they inhabit which is among trees, cows, sky, a car and beach, these instances as a laurel of which the love-making is the root, openly, only root as open; he is her hero, she loves his body & the camera/hand caresses both of them, diving onto bed, lolling, frenzied, to which a cat is also witness, or better, friend, & sits or crawls in the window or car, almost at times as the man & woman's animal nature at peace within itself. The idea of this film, if there is one, seems to be that great peace, or clear light, that some inhabit through releasing everything. There is a fluid drive, a melting & a gorgeousness glowing in & about this film that does not come from frustration, or perhaps an older underlying thesis about art that for hundreds of years has assumed that the artist kept his other forever warming up in a bullpen. Often when an artist says the art is my life, he sadly means, implicitly, that the art realized the life which was not realizable in itself. *Fuses,* which is impregnated with combustible matter, could only have been made real through a life constantly realized. This is Carolee Schneeman's blend, & many will bless her for having shown so much of what everyman in his heart of hearts is.

[I published this Note on Fuses to not only acknowledge the film but to introduce six stills from it in the second issue of Caterpillar *magazine in the spring of 1967. One of the stills featured James Tenney's erection looming up in semi-darkness with two spots of light on the glans giving it ghostly eyes. Another still on the cover of the magazine, tilted vertically, shows Schneemann and Tenney, I think, in orgasm. I dropped off copies of the issue in various NYC bookstores and was amazed when only a week later I received phone calls asking for more copies of the issue. Soon I realized that* Caterpillar #2 *had appeared at the same time that the first flurry of sex magazines and newspapers, like* Screw, *had hit the bookstores and newsstands, and that because of the Fuses material customers had purchased it as a sexually-oriented magazine.]*

THE MOISTINSPLENDOR

For Ruth Hirschman

Introduction: I first took LSD intentionally in the late spring of 1965, while living in Bloomington, Indiana. I write "intentionally" because I have for years suspected that Joanne Kyger put LSD in my tea when I dropped in for a visit primarily with Gary Snyder at their home in northwest Kyoto, in 1963. Gary was not home, so Joanne offered me a cup of tea. After leaving the Snyder/Kyger house on my motorcycle I began to hallucinate and ended up circumambulating Nijo Castle. At one point I looked up and saw a huge red spider testing her web. I have written about this experience elsewhere on several occasions, so I won't go into detail about it here.[1] *The red spider vision impressed me at the time as an active realization of the strange sensations I had felt reading César Vallejo's poem "La araña" ("The Spider") in 1958 while a student at Indiana University in Bloomington. In Kyoto I had been praying for a vision to confirm that I had made the right decision about dedicating my life to poetry. I knew nothing about LSD at this time, other than what one heard about it in the news, or hearsay. Gary and Joanne had told me that they had been given some "acid" by Timothy Leary and proposed that I try it. I said no, as I was having enough psychological difficulties at the time without exacerbating them, I thought, with LSD.*

So in the spring of 1965 in Bloomington, Daphne Marlatt, her then husband Alan, and I decided to take LSD in McCormick's Creek State Park, about 10 miles away. After we took the LSD, I wandered away from them:

---

1 See pp. 55–57 and 117–119 in *Companion Spider* (Wesleyan, 2002), and the first section of "Erratics" in the present book, which includes a translation of the Vallejo Spider poem.

I took off my clothes, sat down in the woods, and just looked around, watching the sun through my held up arm in which I could see the blood flowing. Daphne and her husband were one hundred feet away, and I suppose Daphne crossed my mind as I felt up the grass and watched my nakedness with peaceful astonishment. I was in a pause, somewhere between ordinary awareness and an awareness that tipped over into a state in which consciousness was free to pass through anything that inducted it. Or to put it another way: the subconscious, highly stimulated, had become projected onto whatever "scene" it shone on—it mixed sunlight with the blood flowing in my arm showing me directly what I sensed was there. I had become more receptor than actor. Masculinity had taken a backseat to adolescent formations of a wanderlust that was erotic but not erectional or charged.[2]

An hour later, I found myself inside an old semi-destroyed barn. I lay down on my back and stared at what was left of the insides of the roof. My first wife Barbara's face appeared (as if the roof remains were a screen). She had Chinese eyes and long shimmering black hair. She opened her lips, as if to kiss, and blood began to trickle out of her mouth. The blood increased to the point it looked like a kind of waterfall and in the stream an infant appeared, dancing in the blood.

This was certainly the high point of this experience and today I don't recall what happened after it. Two weeks later we found out that Barbara was pregnant.

We moved to Lima, Peru, that fall, as I was obsessed with getting a look at César Vallejo's typescript for the Poemas humanos *which I had started to translate while in Kyoto. We were living on a little*

2 From "Under the Spell of Red Berries," an Appendix to "Tavern of the Scarlet Bagpipe" in *Anticline,* Black Widow Press, 2010.

street called Domingo Orué when our son Matthew was born. At that point I was checking my Vallejo translations with Maureen Ahern who lived outside of Lima in a hamlet called Cieneguilla. Maureen's husband, Johnny, who worked in Lima, would give me a ride out to their place after work; Maureen and I would work together the next day, and the following morning he would give me a ride back to Lima. The week after Matthew was born it turned out that Johnny was unavailable and so I did not leave with him for the countryside. That night Barbara began to hemorrhage. I made a towel-bed for her on the floor but after a few minutes when the blood started to tumble out of her in jello-like waves, I realized that if I did not get her to a hospital immediately she was going to bleed to death. I raced out of our apartment and ran through the halls of the building across the street, screaming for help. A door opened, a doctor came out, we bundled her into the back of his Volkswagen and sped to the nearest clinic. A piece of the placenta had remained in her. We saved her life, barely—but I shudder to think what might have happened had I gone to Cieneguilla as planned.

It appears that something in me knew back in Bloomington that Barbara was pregnant and that something also knew that she was going to hemorrhage after the baby was born. Such defies common sense. But since I projected the vision, how else explain it? And since the infant was dancing in the streaming blood, I guess that something also knew that Matthew was going to survive!

I took LSD four more times and on two of these occasions extraordinary experiences again occurred. Before I present the poem "The Moistinsplendor," written at the end of 1967 while under the influence of LSD, I want to revisit the crucial moment during the last time I took LSD, with Caryl, who later became my second wife, in 1970. Over the past two years I had relationships with two other women. I was still angry about the end of both relationships and confused as to how I really felt about Caryl. In 1972, when Caryl and I were living in Sherman Oaks, California, I wrote a complicated and complex poem called "Coils" (the title poem of a book published by Black Sparrow Press in 1973) in which I tried to grasp what had taken place in that last LSD experience. The poem is too long to quote in its entirety here; I cut in near its end, at a point in which I am in conversation with Yorunomado, a psychic companion I had generated while working on Vallejo translations in Kyoto:

I turned to Yorunomado now by me by my mother's bed—
I asked him to assimilate her body, that she be buried at
the center of my poetry; yet through his eyes I saw her alive
& fine,
around 50, sitting up in bed, with a pitcher of wine on her
night-table.
She offered me wine from her bed, passing me a glass of it
as I left, looking into it, then ran! The bodies of numberless
dead. "The burgundy," Yorunomado spoke, "is loaded, a
piece of
her placenta is stuck inside you. Go back to the 59th line of
Huitzilopochtli's Vision—you are still desiring your mother,
thus I cannot assimilate her. The wine you take from her is
afloat
with bees & flies, a brew, not a wine, a witch is still alive in
your mind." I flew back to the 59th line, found the
Plymouth still
parked off 86th Street in the woods behind the golf-course,
my
teen-age werefriends milling around while one by one we
took
turns inside. I could not immediately understand why
this scene was stillborn in my mind. "There must be a total
transformation," Yorunomado said—"there is something
in your present life keeping this scene intact. As long as it
remains intact you will dream your mother is alive. And as
long
as she is alive, I cannot receive her." I think I know where
this leads,

I told him, why you have brought me again to fall 1950
Indianapolis, for as I look at this Plymouth I see another car,
a Volkswagen Caryl and I rented a Sunday in the spring of 1970,
drove to Harriman State Park & ate acid in the woods.
Filled with that poison I began to shout for Hollie, my "new" Marie,
the person I had chosen, after meeting Caryl, to love, but love
as self-torture. Before Caryl, I was screaming for Hollie—
why are you not here? Up to that time I had responded to Caryl
only with my body. In my mind I still saw woman as femme fatal
on one hand, housewife on the other. Caryl and I came back to the car
at dusk, parking-lot filled with picnicking Puerto Ricans.
Caryl had her camera; we started taking pictures of each other
over the back of the Volkswagen—once looking through the lens
I saw Caryl—saw Caryl—not La Muerte nor a slave
but an exasperated sweating woman who was original!
She was not the image of woman I had absorbed in my mind.
She was not superficial, she was fresh.
At that moment I felt my woman image divide, & fall to the ground, a broken mask—

The poem then continues to work through several strands of self-imposed mythological complications to reach a point in which I write:

the whole of creation lifting into the glowing night azure sky
over the intense Okumura Garden where I stood amazed
watching my
image separate from me, & by the persimmon where
stretched
the pregnant red spider's web Caryl appeared, I love you
I cried, I love you with all my life, you are Caryl
& you are what counts...

Writing later about what one felt or saw while under the charge of LSD is a lot different than writing while one is under *the influence of LSD. Near the end of 1967 in NYC, I decided to see what would happen were I to write a poem on LSD. I do not recall how much I took. While I was writing, I also drank two bottles of red wine. I set myself up at my desk in my loft at 36 Green Street, at 8 PM and I typed on my old IBM electric typewriter, with a few brief breaks, until around 3 AM.*

My comrade Robert Kelly at times comes off rather badly in the poem. I was struggling with my respect for his poetry versus my anger at his having agreed to distribute my first book, Mexico & North *which was published in 1962 while I was in Japan. Kelly kept most of the copies that I sent him in his house. The book remained undistributed for several years. He sent me a box of my books in 1969 and we finally came to terms with what had happened. Today I consider him to be a dear friend.*

I feel ambivalent in 2011 about reprinting "The Moistinsplendor." While certain shifts strike me as jarring and charged, the poem's tropes constantly dissolve into the rushing undercurrent of chaotic sensations. However, I still believe that the poem's drive to praise that slashes its way through layers of murky self-conflict is one of poetry's primary goals. It is certainly a poem of its era, complexed with stabs at and positings of "enlightenment."

One challenge of the experience was to get completely out of it and still be with it. The poem's opening gesture, "bough out," embedded with its counter-pun, "bow out," carries in nucleus much of the poem's projection-destruction.

My girlfriend at the time was a woman named Marie Benoit who was obsessed with Scientology and Macrobiotics. She was forever playing games with me while rather obtusely I kept trying to break through to her.

On one level the poem is a struggle to think against erasure. At the moment I would seem to focus on something, the drug kicked it into a kaleidoscopic maze. My experience with LSD was that it operated mentally like the amusement park ride called the loop-the-loop. I found myself constantly wildly swinging between what appeared to be an imaginative insight and having the insight pulled inside out and being slapped in the face with it. When a line suddenly looked peculiar or dumb I would immediately write down the next thing that came to mind. There was no revision. I had the feeling, as peculiar as it may sound, that by drinking wine while I wrote that I was grounding myself and keeping the LSD from whirling me into a lockjaw abyss.

My son Matthew was nearly two at this time. I had left his mother in the summer of 1966 and while I had subsequently tried to act responsibly in regard to both her and him, I also felt contrite about what I had done. His birth and the vision of the baby dancing in blood figure obliquely in the poem. Friends who are mentioned include: Frank Samperi, Keith Lampe, Leon Golub, Nancy Spero, Carolee Schneemann, Jim Tenney, Donald Phelps, Jack Hirschman, Jerome Rothenberg, Michael and Doris Heller, Elaine Summers, Armand Schwerner, Nora Jaffe, Jack Boyce, Joanne Kyger, and Larry Meyers.

Louis Zukofsky, an acquaintance, had refused to contribute to the first issue of my magazine Caterpillar *because I had left my wife. After reading my translation of César Vallejo's* Human Poems, *he informed me that Vallejo was too sick to write poetry. So I had an ax to grind with him.*

I have no memory as to how the Emily Dickinson poem slipped into the fray. I suddenly recalled it, and it partially disintegrated in the combustion of my moods.

Soon after it was written I read the poem to Hugh Seidman and Michael Heller. They stared at me as if they were worried about my sanity. I also read it the following summer to Michael McClure in his San Francisco apartment. At the end of it he proclaimed: "Clayton, this is your Declaration of Independence!"

As I mentioned above, there were no revisions. Even spelling errors were left in. This is the text that appeared in the 1968 double #3/4 issue of Caterpillar. *In his essay, "American Poetry Since 1950: A Very Brief History," from his anthology* American Poetry Since 1950 *(Marsilio, NYC, 1993), Eliot Weinberger described the contents of this issue as follows: "Ryunosuke Akutagawa's last writings before his suicide; articles comparing translations of Catullus and Rilke; Gary Snyder's journals as a forest ranger including Buddhist sutras and American Indian songs; poems by Robert Kelly incorporating imagery from the Kabbalah, the Maya and the history of astronomy; a poem on a shipwreck in the Great Lakes that ends up with the Cro-Magnons; photographs of child napalm victims; Jerome Rothenberg's invocations of the prewar Poland of his parents; a long poem by Eshleman written entirely under the influence of LSD; an essay on phonetics that ranges from Sanskrit to Middle English to current slang; a translation of the Martiniquean surrealist Aimé Césaire; writings on nutrition by the Japanese founder of Macrobiotics; an essay on the comic strip* Little Orphan Annie; *paintings by Leon Golub; and Lorine Niedecker's detailed evocation of local flora, among other contributions."*

*

bough
out

never so full
as at that moment in Japan
dusk in rock
churned ribcage
storming at the base of a tooth.
                    Plugged
up

sea darkening
wild geese cry far white
Bashō

at Niemonjima
island
at full myth,

dear island
bough out like a hand
brail cereal

that's carried me 6 years
in the heart of Yorunomado
can sing

Kansing
unknown province of
the heart mind
at loins will work Job
how beautiful the sky is
blue clouds at dusk
piling white over Chinatown
loaded
packhorse
can sing

Wontsing

beckon in the year   .

Kansing Wontsing
in
on
sensed at one

dark side of mountain
north side of stream
starlight forever in Marie's breast

at napetide
the gratitude
brimming with no one's
ever loved me
gives
bladder so happy
thanks
a farewell pee
hunched on the toilet
little fish

that I could love
someone so different from me
in
on

forever
enton yuzu
working out over years
utter enlightenment
the light one carries
the light of the moon
in
on

Marie
alone

my second birth

cuttlefish oranges
torture mill

in aqua lights
fuchsia grapes
dear rice
douzed cliffs

& spread about me the wonderment of his toys
that he is no locust husk
this son, I've
not climbed out of him
soft millfly arace in starlight

in her breast
is her breast
in
on

my hand
brail cereal

          you give
someone something
soft millfly arace in starlight

it happens so fast
as I bathed him
Matthew to my cheek
moy moy as Mastrioanni
como estas padre
the tone of the moon in
on
me

Marie
alone

utter enlightenment

will give you brown rice
sauteed
dissolve armor
Ohsawa
Reich
my new ones
are my oldest ones
a man is a woman is a man

cased steers
no longer
will I be haunted
by the blood of those
I have devoured is Job
at mercy of Marie
is not alone

moon
in
on her

O lovely creature
change
because I could not stop for love
she kindly stopped for me
her Carriage
can look at you
Carnage apricots
I believe in your lion-form
Vietnam fullraped
gnawed at tooth
waters forever in the slings of rocks

& hold just myself
my mortality
as I settled into your Carriage

We slowly drove
for I had put away my haste
my labor and my leisure too for
why am I changed,
how has this been the year of my change
1967
idiot ciphers
all part of one body
but a fleck
as Reich saw stars guppy
his Adam?

Is it as Frank says
when we get to the other side the river has disappeared
is Generation swallowed up in Regeneration is
O my utter enlightenment
cuttlefish

moon
in
moon
radish
consumed

is unconsumed
giving
is

my wife
my citadel
her Carriage

holds just ourselves
Duration
spread about me in wonderment
Decay

I want to be happy
orga orga
to exorcise Donald Hall from all of Richard's letters
Job

in lion-form
suffering real
pleasure
pain
for we do not drink from one wine
intwisted Rilke
Hitler
but of the ages
thyme in sage
we get
thru moonlight
ginger
felt her stomach
coming erect
loved raw pulsing erection
tongue up in
vagina taste
of your diaphragm in my nose
bough
out
pine led out by the children walking
Frank
whose most hated
word clerk
comes home to
brood
unending cycle
in
on

my shoulders
that light is in
on
that light is in
on that
light is in on
stone
that this year I've sensed
cuttlefish
vat of feeling
in apricot
on pit
in pit
on semen
exp;oding
podal
podal

it is
Marie
alone

for the first time in my life
at lion power
mother father all is redeemed

& spread out around me a woman's face
Barbara's cheeks of rice
Chinese eyes
in the form of Barbara's face
Do not doubt the poem
Black Mane
flowing over me
Anima
surrounded by eyes upon eyes a peacock omiyagi
utter enlightenment is Matthew's toys

that they are there
that you are here
that I am here
separate
together
there is no blame
in
on
the point at which

    I TOUCH YOU!
island opening
O cunt cunt cunt & again cunt
with rollers and steamers & hot dyes & oranges & walnuts
raped rise in the young girl's lattice
My selfhood still in love
will always be in love with violence it is fire
my wife
citadel
it is fire

policeman's face
young girl
cascading Rockerfeller
Salvation tortured Army
all man

is all men
one body
do not hurt Marie
like you hurt Barbara
one time you are here
the elect
if
in

on
drives you,

teach
another
nothing

Marie
alone

give
bough out
minister
wrenched out
each day at noon
fucked into the day
day fucked into me
the daylights
I will blow out of you
roar over love's body
when I was born Leo rising
violence is only in *unheard* of acts
hearing loves all stamina
gives lives in
on me, wrench
locked at the base
of my neck,
screwed like a desk to the earth
accept it
roar pouring thru you
day fuck into me
Yo
ro
no
ma
do

Ni
e
mon
ji
ma
Yoru
no
mado Ni
e
mon Ji
ma Yoruno
MadoNi
Emonjima

Conjunct
Spheres identical
Pass out into the night

Because I could not stop for Love
She kindly stopped for me
The Carriage held but just ourselves
Mortality

We slowly swung—She knew no haste
And I had put away
My creation & my happiness too,
for Her necessity—

We passed procreation, the need thereof, where Children strove
like Oxen in a Ring,
We passed the Fields of Growing Life
We passed Conception's Sun

or rather—He passed us—
The loft grew quivering & chill

For only on my Knees, my Body—
My Courage—only Skin—

We rushed into a House that seemed
A Swelling of the Ground—
Its Pipes were scarcely visible—
The Heartline—in the Sound—

Since then, there're no longer Centuries—and yet
Each Moment feels longer than the Day
I first surmised the Plumber's Joy
was Bursting in Lead—

§ § §

second birth
pain
of reprisal

that the prize
is a power over,
is the property

of Property,
succinct
member,

Robert Kelly
the pain
righteous

not giving up
what I know I
am right to,

booty,
an act of retaliation
against

Kelly
enemy
since

he is
likewise
unmoved.

Chess
in chest
tansu

worms
carried
as is Matthew

from Japan
carried from
curried

house to house
all falls to
paring

Robert   Kelly
or take it as
tomato   eggplant

How can you
not love
any man's genuine

talent,
given
this

fact?
How can you
love

but love
as open able
not as a door

stuck to   open
organ
as eye is

open when it
wants
it always wants

at
root the cry
his hand

his brail
cereal,
back to

his back thru
toy fair,
all let go is

alway a toy
fair in the face
of the chance

to get back
at that
back,

that spurned you,
dorsal
in your soup,

Blake has it tho
enemy not
to be forgiven

until he confesses
his wrong,
mercy

is that I do not need to
think of you
tho you wronged me

you sick enuch.
Is
that where it is?

Lampe
on
5th

hairflowed
out from under
his weakness

burnished
during war,
I would not

question
his weakness
given my

delight at
his resurgence,
it is
yes,   resurgence

the shade
of your
eyes before my face

my father your face
outlined in fire
feeding your mail into

the pit
your cookout back
fire place,

place fired
your presence

buckeye timeless
blue clouds over Chinatown
white over Indianapolis
flames licking your profile
sunlight at flames you
feed
into the fire
in
on
Matthew in
me on
meow

we only write
regular stanzas
when not in love,
love
is
energy the life of the body total confrontation in the act
creation Matthew
father at my face
flames anger enough to be changed
when Matthew came into the world
I saw that all of man's images of world creation & apocalypse have
their seedbed,
or where I first
saw Barbara in creation
along a bank
violets cornflowers over way beyond us
we stepped along
I was at her mons veneris
when I was closest to her
can that be true
it is so much against the force of my argument that I cld
be most touched by her thru the force
of a place thru her presence,
and was
her slit open
Matthew snarled at neck
torn away from Niagara,
their creation
in man at pod break
blood all violence
enegenered
engendered
it breaks forth
yellow river blood river Po Wabash Annandale
as our arms are up into it
washing or at armlengths away from a beast

in her
that it come towards us
does not injure us

this is more than man can bear

Penis
in Vagina

Trust in
God

our only home
our homelessness is our utter enlightenment

that I cld be back
in you father
wld make me feel
better abt Kelly

but that all
the past is
all
the past

I'm
only here
cobra
leaned into daybreak

I am
either a
friend of myself

or
nothing,

blood
is not clear
moon
in
on
me
loves Cage
Lorca equally,

is it this not
forgetting
that is the moon,

source
of Marie
alone?

I mean,
that the hesitance in the act
is as real as
act,

is act,
wash basin
held to moon

sloshed
grindered foetus
at

roadside Indiana
it's not
what else cld
he have done

but that he is
here
holding the thing in his hands,

as if he answered

    It grows greener
redder, in sun
light, flames,
his temple vein is
more, now, a lobe
blue over bone
  the softness
therein felt
partially rot
thus not terror

Kelly is just
as sacred
and just
as scared
as

you are,
aoi,
blue

bfren
green
aoi

inter
us,

dad wadded

cast against   the lattice
pebbles
cast   against the lattice

§ § §

I am happy I am alive
& am happy you are alive
Christ in 3
    that I speak of you
that that happens is holy
& what got this poem going is
I find I've been speaking of Robert
saying Yes, the AXON DENDRON TREE
write 5 more.

        that I wash Matthew
laid over my leg
asshole
less than navel,
that we are more
here than
out of.

        that I wash Grace Paley's legs
which must be tired from marching,
that I might do very well
to get down and kiss them,
for it would mean nothing more than
bough out does to grass up
or Robert Nichol's legs
mean to all the poetry in his soul,
or Ronald Johnson's legs
are also used for carrying

that each word he writes
is everything he can give,
and he is holy
but no more no less
than an IBM typewriter.
Life does not stop
at the cock
                    nor begin with it,
all act or voice of genius comes from people
and goes toward people, immediately or transmitted
by incessant breezes, by the reddened smoke
of tense promises not held.
          How
much do I have to give?

Marie grinning.
Was
that a mistake?

We never know.

bough
out

never so full
as at that moment in Japan
remember everything.

flickering off & on
a xmas tree bulb
in the chest of Marie's

photo over my head
she is drawing back
is my destiny aligned with you?

I think it is,
    I am so full
if you will
    not just
turtorue me I will
    never stop flowing
believe that I only
want to plant
fuck,
kill,
watch the sunrise,

                it comes in waves
gemini over gemini
under the Marine's butt
stoke in Fuherer
will only be raised,
                may
only be
touched
in the forest
fire of
his humanity,

for if he wld
fall in shadow,
Leon,
he wld die,

this seed
that needs a bone-
withering blast to openit,

so much to
be opened,
Leo

in pride,
soft fire
how

can words
ever be more than
soaked in earth
of absorbed
in rock

in wife .
in citadel .
that

which is my material
absorbed in my cry
cri in lattice
joan

caterpillar Jerusalem

O HAVE ME
rock
at friendlength
swept away from the conflict
at waterfall there was no waterfall
reconstruction walked away
nightfall in the inn
stood on the beach leaving you higher
wrapped ropes sound off island on island
climbing to be away from you away from you
on shore wanting you chipped in rock
SEA
DARKENING
WILD

GEESE
CRY
FAR

white
crest
of the hour

I waited for you
you did not come
pater
in mudfly,

Xrist
what do I
have to say to atone
for my aiming of

Hirschman,
twins yoked
by archer,

laugh
in
on laugh

conexis
of pain & pleasure,
it will come here slowly
as that's the way its always been.
believe

in archer,
who led
you here

WILL LEAD YOU HENCE,
The cries of men to be born
O Aires sweep
me away from her

in
to Ni
E
Monjima,

and that I know now Niemonjima
the sand of a piece of furniture spinning thru my organic
Yoru,

how life's
dance finds
its dance
in the poem,

the whole thing
is to bow out
Lead
me into Lead,
end

seizure.
Job
at peace with flock
inner
worms in ricebowl.
now you know
you wanted to be away
from her
Washed Cabbage
Rice
Spirits.

Alphabet
Blocks

Penis
Yoru

Everything that happens to you is what you are lacking
He who can embrace his antagonists is the happiest man
Give everything with greatest pleasure & thanks
Health is nothing but a good
   equilibrium established between those two antagonistic sys-
      tems
on
in

bough
out

neither title
you are
   no longer interested in yourself.

kill
   still
in measure,

   paranoia
lights flashing
at the rim,

 crab giving birth.
obsidian,
   fucking & killing
still
identity,

at the base of
the mind one piece.
Gorgon
    measure.
        That you

still believe
you are a killer,
                      if
Reich
means
anything

you
must experience
this difference,
     as if in the muscle
of the poem
this contraction
   keeps you
still
     at identity.
turban
titty
tarftan,

but nothing makes any sense
  til you get at this once thing
Turban
Titty
-a-la-tarftan

Tribe
   out of the soundi
  enegnerding you.
Engeneering you

Kneading you
  Guts held
as if by a Fist
at floor
at floor
  to admit
its sick?
That the tit is a turban of guilt
that the turban winds back into the tit
wch is your consciousness
    banked in shit
Stomach
  Still
Banded
  Against
NightCrawler

     IT DOES NOT
MATTER WHAT
     YOU EAT,

  experience your brokenness
that the thunder in your head
is the graft between
       righthand littlefinger & #4
connected to
the cramp in your left leg,
severed Xrist body
you carry erect
  in Full Health
   in Wonder at his Things
    abt you.
Good lord,
  be gentle to
     everything you touch,
as you are.

Everything you touch
As you Are.
  Xrist
Wrecked
   Health
Around you.
CRAB

 in Stellar Crown
SEA SLUG
  the shit of your own decision.

I had wanted to take
 this whole fuselage with me thru acid wine sleep
come down

Job
is still
Job,

man
cant
be budged in his sufferings,

   STOP EXPERIENCING YOUR BIRTH

aort
aorta of pain
otal
 intaglio
otakeim
cave
help
me in,
blood

it is only the innards
remain
but forever.

torture leaves
trunk Nixon
freed of cancer

otum
OTUM
get up
into yr sphere,

mating leo
scorpion
he cant find where to put it
she wants to cut it
STOP THAT BULLSHIT
aort
aorta
otal
O Fiesh!
O FIESH!
Clean'em, clean'em, gettim outa you,
all that Hebrew bullshit, all
that animal, all that
whitetrampshit
niggersniperfire
cleanit out
fuckitouta aorta
o you unclean mistle
you fithy penis
fuckitoutayou
git all that LeRoi Jones outa you
you clean mistle
you clean snipafire,

rapt
 in jellum,
napalm
 wreath,

all that
shitin you
 that this machine
is part of the

god masticating you,
 enwreathed
in jellum,
 jizzom
jazz
 sticky on
all that

force in your gut
 for such thin hands
funk, all
 that squirm youd lika bloe
 in their Face,

squirt on page,
the majesty
 & the depth
of my
 misery plumbed
Sink Tread

 OUR MASS
TURBINED
 INTO MAREEEEEEEE,
flunking
you,

fuckit outa you,
fuckit outa you,
our Lady
  in our Sea
ops groind
oru
eating,
    at the base of the tree
there aint no Artaud thing to rehearse
no Louis eating Celia
  wiredjawed retriever
locked in its curse,

       lower level,
to aim
       at who are human,
now regenerated
youd suckoff Zukofsky
who wld suckoff you
     means you no

longer play by their games.
   G i v e n   all you know
you still
        are given,

you cannot
  give,   really,
let fantasy beconsumed

O Xrist,
  what we all want is peace
                                        more
than understanding,
what is this all about
my neck

caught in Mixtla
Xrist
beyond ALL propriety
is NO PROPRIETY
NEEDS
Anyone who puts any laws rights to it
is already
Urizen,
O LET THE SHIT
FLOW
Xmas Night
means
CrossBeam
Tarnsih
in
on

A POETRY OF TOTAL REDEMPTION
I
X

that for the world
you are
poet,
po
et,
total release
seeing that the wood grain
is even now passing like clouds,
you wanted to come & make on in
Now that the world is changed

If I cant
say something
directly as a human
being

to you,
TO YOU,
WHY
I'll just cancel myself out,
Xristos mixed in spirit
rock in dusk
dusk in pinnacle
this is why I've held off
rock in dusk in dawnlight pinnacle
THAT THESE
LAST HOURS FORM
A CONNECTION
WITH JIM TENNEY
& CAROLEE SCHNEEMANN
IF I AM GOING TO BE DEVOURED
I WANT TO BE DEVOURED WITH CREATORS
I WILL NOT
GO WITH ANY
LESS THAN
I AM

b a s t a ,
the best wine,
orto
gostollion perefinee
ortam
ortam
prot
oust as prow
ha hha haha hhhhhhhhh
This is a kristMass
DECK THE HALLS

Out old Fustum out Zukofsky
Out ole Blakam
outole M 2

old code for
ortam

stand as you
experience it
island
at nightfall
dawn
on
in
to
hooked
crawler,
into

AGHGHGHGH
whipped into you worpspheed
the machine running close to my ear
the audience can hear
the sound of my reels,
island
GLORY OSTRAM
Glory of my islands filled with stars
hooked
into nightCrawler
Torn Out
Glory Unto the New Year
They Were Grasphsing
Goats Around itsh Peakssh
Glory
on
in,

we climbed the island
at morning-rise
we had not been able to ocaso

at night
Old sun ached in
all its tourns,
O shit
who cares
fucked in who is wfoofed in
GLORY
TO JOHN CAGE
you were simply
trying to make peace with her
you were trying to get up her hill
you were trying to sleep
and to fuck her, you were
& you were and you Were
O GLORY
into the New Year
O fiber
bamboo prying the N F L g i rl's face apart
HOW LONG CAN YOU WITHSTAND
THE TOTAL
ORTAM
GLORY
ALL MAN & WOMAN RESTORED TO LION FORMS
ORTAM
GLORY
to Matthew
glory to Carolee
glory to Jim
glory

glory glory Marie
O glory glory Marie
O manytim2s

red mountain
Rothenberg

trudged up
how beautiful to see
my friend's face,

glory to Michael
glory to Doris
glory to Bennet
glory to Oda
glory to SAUL
ODASAUL
glory odasaul
glory michaeldoris
michaelodimas in splendour
IS CHRISTMAS
starlight sprinkling
chao chao ole Job
wipe off the ledger

as forever
my song
awakened me from my dream,
that Donald Phelps is a weightless angel
o mercy & power
for Donald Phelps in his Lion Form
for that the oranhrtree ankes on Hirschman
Collie Lavender Starlight
on
in

O MiadenForm for Otan Otan
Yorunomado
Ni

eMonJiMa O O anke me
ANK ME ANK ME
Glory Island on in Rising Splendour Moving

Fustianfear WeightlessAngel
FUSTY STILL THERES SUMTHIN FUSTY BOUT YR
Gory glory
New Birth at
midyear
Leonancy
ortalostangostanchancey
moving beauty chao chao
Glory
HALLELULAH ELAINE
GLORY
MICHAEL DORIS
HLLER SOMMER

AGUA moving FUSCHIA
always forever in ELAINE
Leonostratancy
OrtonGollia
Barbara in Lion Form
Matthew in Lion Pisces Form
OrtonGolia HALLELUHAH AFLAME
orton meastrod
cho kon
GLORY
MICHAELDORIS
HELLERCHILDINSOMMER
OrtonGollia in the Neuflame
OrtonGollia Meastern Splendour
AuroraBorealisMeastronSplendour
glory
GLORY VILE SPIRITUM DEPART
EXITUS CUERPUM DORIS
OrtonFlaileaNeuflameMeastromSplendour
Marie in Archer Fish Illuminatum
OrtonFlaileaNeuflameNewFlameMeastomMyFeast
Meal O Fish Issuillustratam

BoughOut
  o o o my eggnoodles
o my earth
fed up tidieumsplendour
At midnight at noon
fucking around in the peaks
Ha Hah O Nora's Splendour
 whipped into the roar
on
in

on
in
O Night
Before Xmas
XMAS
Hallelujah Robert Kelly
OrtonGollia Oaks in Splendour
that we wanted
    her
that we received her
ORTONGOLLIA
OAKS IN SPELDOUR
ORTONGOLLIA CHRISTFIRE
Glroy OriOriOriolumAmbus
GLORY TO THE CHRISTFIRE OF LARRY MAEYERS
PAULBLACKBURNSARAH
BARBARAMATTHEW
O glory of the tunnel that is the flame
O glory for Armand who is Jerry who is
ALFRENZIED
 secretly Hirschmann
  secretly Eshleman
ahh HA HA HA HA HA HA
openly Hirschman
aflame Sagitarius Christ

caut in boughs
OTAN KRISTEEL BENTIN FLAMES
OTAN KRISTEEL BENTIN FLAMES
BARBARAMATTHEWNIGHTINFLAMES
GLORY FRIENDSHIP
LOVE
MARIEPTUMHIRSCHMAN
MARIESTUMHIRSCHMAN
GLORY GLORY GLORY
GLORY GLORY GLORY
LIFEGUARD
LATTICE STOCKEDIN SALVA
KRISTAN,

ALPSMORTTON
GRACED GRACED GRACED
GLORY TO THE NEW FORM
ORTAN MAGNOLIA OSTON SPLENDOUR
WHICH IS HIS NAME
FOREVER MORE
Is Named Matthew Named in Coronation
on
in
her
on
in
her
CANOES INWCH WE ALLR WINNERS
ALSTONGARRULAR
ON
IN
HER
On
In
JackJoanne
ORIF SPELDENROUR

HA
 HE IS RISEN
  HE IS RISEN
OrtalgoftenNisenSpldour

ARIGATO!

***

A Night
Before Xmas
eve.
 NYC. 8 p.m. – 3 a.m. 1967

THREE NEW YORK CITY STORIES

In 1958, while still a student at Indiana University, I began to drive to New York City over vacations and holidays, and like countless aspiring artists before me, to "knock on doors." Allen Ginsberg came to the door of his Tenth Street flat and told me that he would talk with me if I would buy him a hamburger. I did, downstairs in the luncheonette, and he talked nonstop for an hour about Shelley and Mayakofsky. Then he told me to go meet Herbert Huncke and tell him Allen had sent me. I knocked and was met by a gentle face from the pit who invited me in to a living room in which several people were silently camped out on battered furniture. "We're cookin a poem, man," Huncke said, "com'ere." He led me into the kitchen and opened the oven door. There it was! A typed poem on a sheet of paper turning brown around the edges in a hot oven. Huncke closed the oven door and shuffled back into the living room, me following. Still no one said anything. After hanging around for a few moments, I decided that I wasn't hungry, and slipped out.

*

In 1967, I paid Joanne Kyger and her companion Jack Boyce $750 for the key to a second floor loft at the corner of Green and Grand Street. Jack, a painter with carpenter skills, had fixed the loft up with basic amenities; the rent was $65 a month paid by check to the landlady who lived in Yonkers. A Scot named Ed Iglehart, who grew his own marijuana in dirt-filled bathtubs and sold hashish pipes on Wall Street, lived on the third floor. Jack Smith was our super! He had the top two floors, or, actually, he only had the fourth floor since he had destroyed most of the fifth floor, except for a two foot area that extended from each wall that he would shoot from. He grew marijuana on the roof and I think he shot most of *Flaming Creatures* there. He was an incoherent but utterly benign person. At one point he took months or possibly years of junk from his loft and piled it seven or eight feet high on the sidewalk in front of our building. Somehow it caught fire and we were all awakened early one morning by the fire department putting the fire out.

Jack had no money at all and once a month he would put up announcements on walls in Greenwich Village announcing a Lobster Moon Pageant the coming Saturday night. Kids visiting NYC from New Jersey would see these announcements and some would drift down to Green and Grand and climb the stairs to Jack's fourth floor—where they would be met by Jackie Curtis or some other transvestite friend of Jack's. There would be one jug of cheap red wine on a table and some paper cups. As for the "Pageant," the ones I saw mainly involved Jack and Jackie having an argument over how to be photographed. The kids would have spent their $5 and gradually got bored and wandered down the stairway.

At this time I was involved in an anti-Vietnam War group called Angry Arts and was one of those in charge of the poets' activities which, for example, involved renting flatbed trucks and putting on readings while holding up large photos of napalmed Vietnamese in Harlem (where we were welcomed), at Queens' shopping centers (where we were attacked), and once before the Metropolitan Museum of Art (quiet curiosity). We heard that Andrei Voznesensky was going to be reading at the uptown 92nd Street YMCA, and since we knew that the war would not even be mentioned there, we invited Voznesensky to read downtown with us at Fillmore East to call attention to the downtown poetry community and provide a unified voice against the Vietnam War. We called the event a Three Penny Poetry Reading (after Brecht's Three Penny Opera), and several thousand people attended.

About twenty of us read with Voznesensky. I was the master of ceremonies, wearing a white raw silk suit. At the beginning of the reading, the poet Piero Heliczer came up and said: "I want to read." I told him that there was no way at this point to include people not on the program. This pissed him off and he retreated backstage and proceeded to get drunk during the nearly three hour reading. Jackson Mac Low was the last reader. He was standing up on the stage holding up a filthy, tattered American flag he had found in the gutter that day, proclaiming, when Heliczer rushed out with a bucket and tossed its contents into, he intended, the audience. However, most of it—water and piss—went into the faces and cameras of the Shirley Clark camera crew, in the orchestra pit, filming the reading. David Antin and I, each from a different direction, went after Heliczer and in the dark backstage we each whopped him a few times.

The following afternoon, someone knocked on my loft door. It was Heliczer who, friendly as could be, held out his hand and introduced himself. Smith had invited him to stay with him and Piero was introducing himself to people in the building. He apparently did not recall meeting me at all, so I informed him that we had met last evening, before *and* after he had thrown a bucket of piss water into the Clark camera crew. "Oh man," Heliczer exclaimed, "don't you realize that I performed the only Surrealist act of the evening?"

*

I had been on a macrobiotic #7 diet for months, eating only raw brown rice and tea, and sleeping four hours a night, with the clearest mind I have ever had. It was the spring of 1969, when truth seemed stranger than fiction. I decided to buy my girlfriend Caryl Reiter something pretty for her birthday. We walked to a boutique that no longer exists on MacDougal, just south of 8th Street. I sat on a sofa in the center of the store while Caryl tried on dresses. Immediately a stranger, also trying on dresses, began to pose before me, asking for my opinion about this or that dress. She would flounce around, disappear, then return with more poses and banter. Finally Caryl came back and said she had not found anything. "Where's my hand bag?" she asked. I looked down next to the sofa. "My god, she took it," I yelled. "Who?" Caryl asked. Without explaining, I told her to wait there, and took off.

At this time 8th Street, between 5th and 6th Avenues, had a number of women's boutiques and I figured this thief was in one of them, setting somebody else up. I also figured I only had one shot at her, so I loped down 8th Street, trying to guess which store she'd be in. Without thinking, I turned into one, and walked straight back to a row of dressing rooms, picked one, and pulled the door open. There she was, going through Caryl's wallet. "I'm on Methadone," she cried, "don't turn me in! Just take the wallet, everything's still in it. I left the hand bag in a basket near where you were sitting." "If you are telling the truth, there's no problem," I said, and holding her by the collar, marched her back to Caryl's boutique, on the steps of which Caryl greeted us with astonishment. The hand bag was there, so I let the woman go.

ADHESIVE LOVE

Embracing, fervently embracing, in the embrace itself the bud of imagination is born, as if one were asleep before, suddenly as excitement mounts mind is stimulated, yet this stimulation is felt moving toward orgasm as a part of the physical excitement itself,

it is the creation of the world,

the closed triptych of *The Garden of Earthly Delights,* the earth swaddled in fog, the light blue uroboric fog,

orgasm opens the triptych to.

It opens to—

Orgasm is not the interior painted surface, but orgasm will rain down on that little bud trembling up to mind, trembling up through the entire body in the fervor of embrace, and after the triptych opens, after I lose control of myself in you, cry out and throb, discharging the phantom of myself, the triptych is open, I lie back, softly head against your sweet breast, my eyes closed I dream into it, the orgasm so intense that I dream awake, often I see a green glade, figures moving about, fields, bright blue skies,

or if my eyes are open

what would otherwise be visual are words, sometimes from nowhere, words I have never spoken, formations, gratitudes, or word I have thought about, phrases, near-poems, infused, covered with a wonderful gauze, I smell your sweet breasts, doze, forgetting and remembering.

But of course when I arise I begin again—I could say the poetry was in those moments of blissful reverie, that what is written down is tragic because it is always in some way an attempt to recover the very instant of inspiration when the image or formation is most bud-like—and that is true for the individual soul. For the individual soul the magnificence is in that rain of embrace contacting the little bud of mind reaching up wanting O wanting to be touched—it is that touch that tells a man or a woman I AM—tells them *There is something more here than this pleasurable or aching biology. What I call my body or my biology is but a fleck of what I am—*

And that reassurance must be given in the bone.

It cannot come just as idea, as another's experience—and when it does come we have a great proud experience, we feel ten feet tall, we fit nowhere, and then we awake into another consciousness: that ten foot arrogance, that great proud dwelling, is just that—is our individual soul, and if we live by it, if we try to live by it we are as Gulliver in a world of little people—and to have the soul AND to see beyond the having of it, to have it and to see most other people for the little people they are—this is the beginning of compassion—it is unbearable, and the budded soul is trapped by the very consequence of *perception outside itself*—for if it stays within itself, knows it is soul, is wetted in fervent embrace and remains there, it becomes moldy and eventually rots; for to be wet is to grow, and the growth is out of the bed, man woman like vine, or any combination of lovers, a great double vine loaded with the vegetation of knowledge slowly climbing, great muscled creeper, green and demanding, out of spore, out and out, until the original pulsation achieves itself, flowers.

So the writing down, the making of art at large, is not really tragic once one sees that the act is accountable to *more than the individual soul.* For from the viewpoint of my desk the imaginative bud given in embrace turns into fantasy; that is, I am here now, with all my desire, in spite of everything, to say I am—*without you.* If you and I, Caryl, get it fully in bed, if the love is genuine and gratifying, then I do not long back to the bed from the desk—but if the bud did not ignite there, O what a misery it is to be here! What an awful revision, what a re-making and re-making, that collapsed image of creation as masturbation, the poor self-denying soul praying, in effect, God at least let me get it off here in my head! And it is out of such denial in the place of biological spore that most of what we recognize as wit or cleverness, "literature," in contrast to poetry, comes. The "academic," the "formula poem," that which feeds off other artists' genuine experience, all that sad rippling extension of the genuine stone plunked into the pool—but not the stone's own ripples—no, more as if occasionally a stone were to be plunked in and go straight about its business to the bottom, and these ripples were waiting over there in the pond grass and came out gently sucking at the stone's centrific power.

*

I believe man and woman kind are coming into a time of extraordinary fulfillment and push into the human future. I believe that we can now understand, perhaps for the first time, although the individual soul has dreamed this understanding throughout the ages, perhaps for the first time to understand Walt Whitman's distinction between amatory and adhesive love. Whitman does not say much about the distinction; his emphasis is on the latter in such a way that some of its meaning lies in man to man love, in what has been to this time called "homosexual" in contrast to "heterosexual." The word "amatory" has the ring of the western love-tradition, or amour etc., that we associate with men and women. The word "adhesive," on the other hand, seems to mean more, evoking for me as well a sense of coherence, a word dear to the creative process.

I came to this distinction of Whitman's reading an interview with Allen Ginsberg in *Gay Sunshine* newspaper and I see in Ginsberg's new book, *The Fall of America,* that he has repeated this Whitman statement (a footnote from *Democratic Vistas*) under his dedication of his book to Walt Whitman. What struck me the hardest about the quote is that 50 years ago it would have been read within the shell of a tradition that today seems to have cracked, and thus the words ring of a profound insight into our present state:

> It is to the development, identification and general prevalence of that fervid comradeship (the adhesive love, at least rivaling the amative love hitherto possessing imaginative literature, if not going beyond it) that I look for the counter-balance and offset of our materialistic and vulgar American democracy and for the spiritualization thereof.

> Many will say it is a dream and will not follow my inferences: but I confidentially expect a time when there will be seen running through it like a half-hid warp through all the myriad audible and visible worldly interests of America, threads of manly friendship, fond and loving, pure and sweet, strong and life-long, carried to degrees hitherto unknown, not only giving tone to individual character and making it unprecedentedly emotional, muscular, heroic and refined, but having the deepest relation to general politics. I say democracy infers such loving comradeship as its most inevitable twin or counterpart, without which it will be incomplete, in vain and incapable of perpetuating itself.

In the newspaper article, Ginsberg then quotes from another footnote, to the Preface of the 1876 edition of *Leaves of Grass,* in which the word "adhesive" again occurs:

> —this universal democratic companionship, this old eternal yet ever-new exchange of adhesiveness, so fitly emblematic of America—

"Amatory" love is a state of love in which not only are man and woman at war but so are man and man, and woman and woman. "Adhesive" love implies a sense of the human in which love in its variations and forms becomes the *adhesive force* of all relation.

Of course what "adhesive" is, exactly is, is deadly difficult to define—quite possibly none of our present ideas as to what love is are capable of grasping it—the main thing I keep in mind while thinking about it is that it is human and not sexual. One approximation might be Blake's "The human is four-fold, the sexual three-fold," which is Blake's distinction between the third level of archetypal consciousness, Beulah, or erotic love, and the fourth (and in Blake's work, the highest) level, which is Eden, or creative love. The problem with all causes is that as such, as cause, they imply an effect which is bound up with the cause itself i.e., equal rights, or a share of the existing power structure. One feels sexually imprisoned, say, and locks into a cause to seek sexual freedom. Yet sexual freedom does not end with even erotic fulfillment, and those who set their water-mark as "sexual freedom" inevitably end up defending it as an end, and thus pruning their vines short of their own potential for growth.

Yet if what is "adhesive" does not stop at what is "sexual" it most certainly includes it, takes sexual fulfillment as base, or compost. For it seems to me that the great great error of what we understand as history has been to uphold the spirit at the expense of sexual fulfillment, to drive a wedge between the erotic and the human, to say in effect that if you take your truth from one you are therefore at odds with the other. Spirit should be an increase or rebirth out of sexual gratification, not an alternative to it.

We see Van Gogh, for example, on the burning dusty road outside Arles at summer noon, trudging along with his easel and paints, his feet seem to melt into the road itself, they seem to become a glue he is pulling himself out of, against, in order to move at all, for Van Gogh was, as many others have been *burdened with* the "adhesive"—his desire was to fulfill his spirit, and thus the spirits of others, through his art—he brought a terrible power to his art, which is essentially the reason it exists with such force in the human psyche today, terrible in that, like César Vallejo, he needed to paint (or in Vallejo's case, to write) *in order to be human*—and thus his leap, or more aptly his explosion, was directly from what he was given, his mortal birth, directly into creative love without the intervention of erotic fulfillment. Van Gogh burns like a roman-candle; it is one fast explosion of fire and sparks, 10 years, over 700 paintings, over 1500 drawings, one smoking surge without the intervention of *other*—and bam he is over like that! I am not making any kind of ultimate judgment on the value of Van Gogh's art when I put my feelings about his life this way—I am attempting to see him as heroic, for one reason, because he was operating in a tradition of "amatory" love in which the heart of love has walls of steel—

For Van Gogh is part of a heroic tradition that is now just beginning to emerge as a form, a tradition that might be sighted as: *art as redemption based on the antithesis of sexual versus spiritual fulfillment,*

and the evil of this tradition is that the division is repeated at every juncture of human relation. The Van Goghs of the world escape suddenly from the trap and die as outsiders overnight—why? Because the trap is like the Queen and they the bee—they got out, but their genitals were torn off, left inside her, and with a gaping hole under one's gut, with a tortured burning hole of deadness in the biological place of the *Song of Songs* a man or a woman can exist just so long, and at what expense, at what pain!

So the horror of the "amatory" is that out of its own genital deadness it sets up, most often via religion, an infinite string of "ones" in each variety of life, on the putrid assumption that a person is one self, is not a congeries of selves, each trying within one person like bees locked in a bottle to escape into what the bees vaguely see as sunlight, air and the garden—

i.e., creation to be named God

which is the chief spike driven all the way through the human spirit, nailing it in the idea that men are closer to blessedness than women, and not only that, but all life other than the human has no blessedness in it at all,

and there you have the hierarchy, that the closer creatures are to not even people but man! the closer they are to deserving consideration and life. However, if one thinks about this madness for just a moment, one can construct an argument in the opposite direction that allows just as much if not more mystery into the idea of a world:

> The A-shi-wi, or Zunis, suppose the sun, moon, and stars, the sky, earth, and sea, in all their phenomena and elements, and all inanimate objects, as well as plants, animals, and men, to belong to one great system of all-conscious and interrelated life, in which the degrees of relationship seem to be determined largely, if not wholly, by the degrees

of resemblance. In this system of life the starting point is man, the most finished, yet the lowest organism; at least, the lowest because most dependent and least mysterious. In just so far as an organism, actual or imaginary, resembles his, it is believed to be related to him and correspondingly mortal; in just so far as it is mysterious, it is considered to be removed from him, further advanced, powerful, and immortal.

The point is, that I stand in such a depth of ignorance, that to say a man is closer to Creation than a slug makes no more sense than to say a slug is closer to Creation than a man. The beauty of this Zuni thought is that it allows a flow both ways which in the way I would like to take it would suggest an interdependent circuit of being, the changing and the timeless both "holy" in that they are alive,

yet this reading of primitive "adhesiveness" only seems to go so far. I mean, I may want to consider the slug, and not rip it off, but what do I do when the tiger includes me as part of its eating?

I may adore the emblematic beautify of the tiger, as say D H Lawrence did and may fight that sense of life that wishes for the tiger to lay down with the lamb, but I must build a protection from the tiger if I live in the bush, must separate myself from it and thus from its power, as well as the power of the mosquito, the power of the sun, the power of the rain, as well as the power of the dry earth, and thus through a series of separations that may take only five or six generations I have a very thorough *inside* and *outside* set up and am beginning to dream the spirit of creation to be "human" like myself.

This is an eternal reoccurrence; it is happening with great imagination on the left hand panel of Bosch's *Garden of Earthly Delights* where a rather spooked robed priest takes a naked woman's hand, the two of them watched by a naked man sitting by them on the ground; he watches them with a kind of bland interest, making no move to interfere. In my imagination I see that a few moments, or centuries before, he was standing in this glade holding the woman where the priest is standing now; as if he fell back, and his place was taken by the robed man. In this sense, the priest is a tendency in humankind manifest in the Christ or patriarchy; the Adam and Eve of equal exchange replaced by self-conscious Eve and robed priest—

yet in this very moment first creatures are crawling out of a dark pool, the water black yet the walls sunlit and salmon-colored, winged fish, 3-headed serpent birds, a cat with a mouse by the ear, a hooded kind of duck-fish reading a tiny book afloat in the pool,

Christ has appeared / the end is in sight

yet it is also the moment of emergence,

Where I grew up, Indianapolis, one Catholic teenage "sport" was to drive downtown after dates on Friday night, pick up "queers," take them out to the country, and as soon as they'd suck the guys off, beat the shit out of them, and take their money.

At that point the human psyche cries out,

another creature crawls out of the throbbing eye in the vise,

I am stunned that within my own age I could be witness to what the McCahill brothers did to other people in Indianapolis 1952

and see the rebound, the sudden pressing forth of that aspect of the human, the homosexual, demanding to take its place in the mystical alphabet of *human being,*

but is there ever an end to this expansion / contraction?

Because as Wilhelm Reich pointed out there is a biological principle at work in the storm cloud as well as the amoeba as well as a person which can be identified as peristaltic, and which achieves it acme of excitation in the human being at the moment of orgasm.

Are we to be governed by this principle on all levels of interaction, that is, is this the first and ultimate image of the experience of the universe?

It is crushing to feel a slow slow clarification taking place yet to also feel that the clarification has always been taking place, and that what one feels as "new" or "now possible" is at root the inexhaustible yearning of the imagination for a liberation it knows nothing of, but which seems as I sit here at this moment to travel forever in a dream-time, in which all that is imagined could be visited—

For the green glade and the obscure figures moving as I lay by your side this morning, breathing in the sweetness of your breast, are not in my deepest hopes "metaphors for poetry,"

but a sighting of where I would like to go with my entire body and soul where everything that had ever lived would be living,

yes, where there would be no gravity or opaqueness or ministers of separation, the shaman dream, to visit the "land of the ever-living,"

that harpsichord of yearning upon which Carlos Castaneda plays, in himself as well as in us, that he met a man who actually had made a hole in the material universe,

yet my friend Robert Kelly says it does not matter whether Don Juan is real or not, whether someone named Juan Mattus exists or whether Carlos imagined him, and at the time Kelly said that something powerful in my mind protested, No I said, if Mattus does not exist then those books are just more of what we have always had,

imagination compensating for our essential impotence and ignorance confronted with existence.

This afternoon I see Kelly and I are both right; to break the wall down is to imagine nothing, the fact that the wall is before me forces me into my mind to imagine what is beyond the wall—yet to stop there is to live in my mind, for there is another force in me that wants to tear down this wall to enable another friend, Paul Blackburn, who I watched die two years ago, to escape from the trap in which we are all buried—

What kind of maniac would I be if I said Paul is as present in his books as he was when he was alive with his books?

And yet, and yet, the treadle of the "cohesive" at work, that slow slow sense of increasing clarification which moved me to think early this morning,

when I opened the Bosch I expected to see him way ahead of us, at least in the center panel of the triptych—

I came to *The Garden of Earthly Delight* lured by the possibility that the human species is approaching the moment in which the action, the intermingling, actual intermingling of the kingdoms, will occur—

where men and women will make love to fish and berries,

where songbirds will feed human babies,

where a collie fucking a young woman will be a pleasant scene,

where a boar tearing a man apart will be an ecstasy not penalized by putting a fence around the boar,

and then I looked at the Bosch; I was amazed by how much I had imagined. In this great intermingling center panel

there is not even any fucking,

most of the people look vaguely bored,

no erect penises, no passionate eyes,

and the whole business of sensual dalliance leading to the hell of the right hand panel was again upon me,

the slow rot of sensual dalliance, the staying in bed, the setting of an upper limit in Beulah, *the garden of love,* with the consequent plunge into the Ulro, sterile fusion of self of night and fire and machinery, demons of unfulfilled desire climbing up ladders out of the body gone to rot in it's own wetness.

Caterpillar #20, 1973

A NOTE ON LELAND HICKMAN'S TIRESIAS I: 9:B: GREAT SLAVE LAKE SUITE, MOMENTUM PRESS, 1980

I bow to Hickman's grueling and powerful honesty and ability to sustain an affirmation in spite of an impish, flaccid, near-murderous sado-masochism that is flayed into the language itself. His monolithic drive is really something to pull off today, for the echoes are Hopkins, Thomas and Ginsberg, with a William Carlos Williams-like attention to material detail, and an engaging sense of Charles Olson's use of Maximus in *The Maximus Poems.*

So there is the power of the kicking Coltrane-like stanza heaves at the same time a slug creature pulls itself along an endless urinal of sexual hunger. Hickman's work on the father is undoubtedly the most thorough since Olson, less mythic, and much more open to background, especially child sexuality.

Hickman slightly misquotes Olson on page 43, turning the former poet's "The poetics of such a situation / are not yet to be found out" into "poetics of this situation not yet figured out." On a superficial level, the meaning here is obvious: Hickman has been beaten by his father into being a homosexual and he has not yet figured out how he can beat his "queerness" into poetry. On a more far-reaching level, the reader should look up the Olson source (*Maximus Poems IV, V, VI,* p. 79) for Olson has just stated, before the quoted lines, "that no event / is not penetrated, in intersection or collision with, an eternal / event." In regard to Hickman's poetry, this statement gives the poet a fathering justification for Tiresias, his archetype, as a deepening of each contour of his personal hell.

Relative to this book, Hickman's Tiresias remains ambiguous, rather lop-sided—that is, in contrast to Eliot's soothsayer, "throbbing between two lives," the archetypal shadow in *Great Slave Lake Suite* is so totally male that the occasional female appearances are wraith-like, and detached from the Protean-Pan armored cock which seems to me to say again and again that

Hickman is haunted not by a hermaphrodite but by something much more horrifying—that, whipped into his father's cock, forced to become his father's half-born member, he is obsessively magnetized to the maleness of nature; for at no point in this poem is there a sense of male/female reciprocity or equality. On a few occasions we are offered fleeting, torn shots of his mother, and the weakest, most labored writing in the book is an elaboration of two women the poet was impotently (I gather, in the largest sense) involved with, and one is even referred to as a muse. I think Jeanne and Ginny have a place in the *Suite,* but only as pathetic reinforcers of Hickman's failure, other than in this magnificent poem, to emerge from "dadspace."

Great Slave Lake Suite is twisted upon itself in layers, and its cable holding the bridgework in place is a snake/penis/worm/maggot complex that Hickman initially sounds in his use of Hexagram #18 from the *I Ching: work on what has been spoiled by the father.* The Chinese character for the hexagram represents a bowl in whose contents worms are breeding. Other than the presence of decay throughout the poem, as a kind of maggoty elegant weather, in the second of the two childhood/adolescent narrative sections, Leland discovers actual maggots under the skin of some fish his grandfather had given his mother to fry.

Impossible to over-emphasize the extent to which Hickman's "queer fused rasa" *contains* the man's self-destructiveness, and his terrible compulsion to destroy his "blue temple" (his etheric or subtle body, what the Egyptians called the Ba). Did he see two snake parents coupling, tear their image apart and in infantile rage take on what Herodotus called "the female disease"? Or did he choose, as an astral body, this Lee and Eleanor to discover in his fetus-ship that his mother's soul had been destroyed by a battalion of fathers, and the womb that he was nurtured by was essentially a casket?

There is a spongy condition to *Great Slave Lake Suite,* a springy condition, steel-like and oddly vernal. It makes me ask the kind of questions I mention above. Or do I draw upon this rather minor mystical aspect of this book as a heterosexual who can never quite come to terms with the drained basin of homosexual john-light starkness?

At the bone of things where we are born and where we die there is no sensuality, and the sexuality is closer to hunger than it is to procreation. Odysseus receives from Tiresias the most ancient possible instruction, and the one most worth having: "do not anger the sun." And this Hickman son, in his intelligence, comes intact through the darkness and the water beneath the world, and may draw a mortal caught in that darkness out with him again into the light.

Poetry News, Beyond Baroque Literary/Arts Center, May 1981

THE ANSWER MAN

For Ron Padgett

1952: we'd meet at 7 AM in the downtown Kirby office. Since I knew how to play the piano, they asked me to knock out standards like "Margie," whose lyrics had been exchanged for Kirby hype:

"Kirrrr-bee, I'm always thinkin' of'yuh Kirrrr-bee"
(then quickly since it didn't match the beat)
"you-are-the-only-vacuum-cleaner-I-adore"

Then we lugged our kits out the door and drove to one of Indianapolis's lower class white neighborhoods (blacks never made payments, we were told). For outposts, we used diners where we'd fill several booths. The guy I rode with that summer had a milkshake first thing, with a raw egg added to make him "come good" that night.

After coffee, the canvassers fanned out. Would the lady of the house like to be called on a chance basis to win a prize on the Kirby Quiz Program (WABC, 91.5 on your dial)? Nearly all said yes. The canvasser then asked if she was familiar with the Kirby Home Renovation Outfit. When she shook her head no, he explained that the Kirby folks liked winners, and did not want to call people who could not answer questions. Would she mind if the Kirby Answer Man dropped by and gave her a list of questions and answers?

"Hello, Ma'am, I'm the Kirby Answer Man," and as she stared at my three-foot-high kit, I'd move in around her, drop to the floor and start assembling. I had an expensive, lifetime-guaranteed machine to sell, which I knew would out-perform any machine she had in her home, especially tank types. I'd sprinkle some dirt under a rug and suck some of it through. Sometimes there was only a throw rug or two. Then I'd immediately have to make "the bedroom move."

As instructed, I would ask: "Do you mind if I demonstrate on your mattress?"

Going into the bedroom usually made for some tension. One salesman claimed he'd screwed both the mother and the daughter and then sold both of them Kirbys. I'd strip back the covers to the bottom sheet which at 9 AM would sometimes still be warm, with hairs and other body signs. I'd attach a square of white muslin to the exhaust outlet with a big rubber band and vacuum the sheet. Mr. Distlehorst, the Kirby franchise owner, had told us that most mattresses doubled their weight every ten years. Then I'd unband the muslin and place it on my out-spread palm. It usually held a silver dollar-sized cake of greasy gray stuff on it which I'd raise uncomfortably close to the woman's face and, as instructed, ask: "Do you know what this is, Ma'am?" After her "no," I would say, forcefully: "This is BODY SLUDGE"—and after a pause: "Ma'am, you could fry an egg in this!"

The egg line always got them, but very few would sign a contract on the spot.

When I could see that I was striking out, I'd go for a second appointment that evening when the old man would be home. Now, men are harder to sell than women (they do not even see dirt in the way women do), but evening had one big advantage: the Closer. He was Distlehorst's right-hand man and, unlike the other salesmen, had been with Kirby for a long time. He'd work the field by himself during the day, then hang around during the evening for a 10% bonus on our sales. He was a real weasel, with all sorts of tricks, lies, and pressures. He could cut right through a couple's resistance if he spotted a gleam of Kirby "need" in their eyes.

The Closer would work the husband until he finally said Ok she can have it IF she can figure out a way to pay for it out of her household allowance. Then the Closer would lean forward and say: if I gave you this great machine for nothing, would you be willing to come down to the office once a week and sign a book thanking us? After she said yes, the Closer would tell her that her payments would come to less than her bus fares.

Near the end of that summer, I sold a machine to a woman who was so poor she had no rugs at all. I got a lot of praise for that, and thought I was hot shit for a week or so. But then a log rolled over, and I saw another shade of white, the odor of poverty, the dirt and grime Kirby was dependent upon. Who were these people? *These people.* Who was I, to do this?

1985

Broome Street Review, 2012

II

OUR JOURNEY AROUND THE DROWNED CITY OF IS

Introduction: This composite work of poetry and prose is based on a travel journal, written out in notebooks while traveling in France, July and August, 1985. Our first week in Paris I did not write at all, but once we reached the town of Les Eyzies de Tayac in the Dordogne, a captivating speech by Hart Crane filled my head and I wrote daily for an hour or two for the rest of our trip.

After a week in Les Eyzies de Tayac, we headed north along the coast, spending two boring days on the Ile de Ré. Then, via Nantes, we entered the Brittany peninsula. Over the next three weeks we drove into and around it, paying special attention to the megaliths in the Carnac area, the fissured cliffs of Finistère, the ominous Arrée Mountains, and the beautiful pink granite coast of the Bretonne Corniche.

In spite of my attempt to get everything into the journal that counted, there were inevitably some precious moments that got away. One such moment was a visit to the tiny and intricately-engraved cave of Gabillou, near Mussidan in the Dordogne, accompanied by Dr. Jean Gaussen, who has been the cave's owner and guardian since 1955. Another was discovering a mysterious box on our table in the outdoor dining area of the Hotel Cro-Magnon in Les Eyzies de Tayac when Caryl and I came down for dinner one evening. In the box was a signed first edition of the Abbé Henri Breuil's Four Hundred Centuries of Cave Art, *which the Abbé had offered to Jacques and Christiane Leyssales, the owners of the hotel, on his last visit there near the end of his life. The Leyssales now offered the book to us.*

In Paris, at the start of our trip, the poet Michel Deguy had suggested that we visit the Breton poet Guy Etienne, who lives in Châteaulin in Finistère. We did, and were received simultaneously as strangers and friends. Etienne is a psychiatrist who has elected to write poetry in Breton (which is not his native tongue) and, I have been told, has added to the vocabulary of that endangered language. When he and his wife Gizella discovered that we appreciated good wine they opened their "cave" to us, and over two evenings we tasted rare wines that only exist today in the cellars of serious collectors like the Etiennes.

I see the fugal preoccupations with the Neolithic menhirs and dolmens in the Carnac area as links between the Upper Paleolithic world of the decorated caves and modern art history.

Yorunomado and Niemonjima, figures in my personal mythology, first appeared in my work in the 1960s and roamed at large in Coils, 1973. Based on the name of the coffee shop in which I translated César Vallejo while living in Kyoto (1962-64), Yorunomado ("Night Window") was released from my solar plexus during the act of seppuku in the poem "The Book of Yorunomado." His female counterpart Niemonjima is based on the name of an island off Futomi visited by Bashō and celebrated by him in his poetry.

The title of this work is based on the following entry from the Michelin Green Guide to Brittany:

> The town of Is. – *At the time of good* King Gradion, *about 6 BC, Is was the capital of Cornouaille; finds claimed as belonging to Is have been discovered in Trépasssés and Douarnenez Bays and off Penmarch Peninsula. The town was so beautiful that according to a Breton tradition the inhabitants of Lutetia, seeking a name for their own proud city, chose Par-is ("like Is"), whence the name: Paris. The town was protected from the sea by a dyke, opened by locks to which the King always carried the golden key.*
>
> *His daughter, the beautiful Dahut, also called Ahès, who led a dissolute life, met the devil in the form of an attractive young man. To test her love, he asked her to open the sea gate. Dahut stole the key while the King was asleep, and soon the sea rushed into the town. King Gradion fled on horseback, with his daughter on the crupper. But the waves pursued him and were about to swallow him up. At this moment a celestial voice ordered him, if he would be saved, to throw the demon who was riding behind him into the sea. With*

aching heart the King obeyed and the sea withdrew at once, but Is was destroyed.

For his new capital Gradion chose Quimper; this is why his statue stands between the two towers of the cathedral. He ended his days in the odor of sanctity, guided and sustained by St. Corentine. As for Dahut, she turned into a mermaid, who is known as Marie-Morgane and, by her beauty, still lures sailors to the bottom of the sea. Everything will stay exactly as it is until the Good Friday when Mass is celebrated in one of the churches of the drowned city. Then Is will ceased to be accursed and Morgane will no longer be a siren.

*

A VISIT FROM HART CRANE

As I sat adoring Les Eyzies' ochre-colored limestone cliffs, Crane began to speak: "The shark that ate me was not a hammerhead but a self-savaging cruising the hunger-filled waters of North American soul. But you may imagine my light topcoat twisted around a shark, as if it were a Rodin Balzac, wearing my coat as a cloak, on a rise of the ocean floor below the *Orizaba* that 1932 noon. *There* is an image for our Midwestern souls! To offer it, I had to abandon my work on Hermaphroditus, which involved constantly circulating between 'male' and 'female' poles—the man as double of the woman, the woman as double of the man, a roller-rink my soul glided, never racing to win until it woke into poetry and faced those monsters: the Covering Patriarch and the Cherub of Narcissism, 'guardians' of that hole between desire and its fulfillment. The Cherub is an infantilization of the soul, helpless crying, abandoned in the grotto the Patriarch 'covers,' in mockery of the cobra spreading over meditating Gautama, his ally and root support from depths in which serpent and person are daemonically entangled, where images are winding windows and I am loosed in that pattern that Zinsser and I spoke of..."

His voice faded and I momentarily lost him in geographical confusion: did Zinsser offer his prophecy to Crane at that point in ocean later re-crossed with Peggy Cowley? Somehow "loose yourself within a pattern's mastery or go on to undeserved doom" seems the locus of Crane's leap, the noon after the day he tried to *lose* Peggy in Havana. They were to meet in a restaurant—Crane (according to Cowley) never showed up. Perhaps some part of him wanted to abandon her there and to sail on without her—but she made her way back to the ship. What has this to do with his suicide? For years I thought that after connecting with a woman, Crane discovered he could not *maintain* the connection—that he was doomed in spite of having been given "the independence of my mind and soul again, and perhaps a real wholeness to my body"—doomed again and again to drunkenly seek merger with himself in the figure of an alien man, that in spite of any woman the old pattern would reassert itself. That is why he leapt. In my dream last night, Crane was intact—though only 2 inches tall, reclining on a glass shelf in what appeared to be the Hart Crane Museum, a homunculus in the muse of my dream, homunculus and muse, a merger.

"No," he spoke again, "I could have continued my work for years, could have been thrashed until old age, lost my ears, even my organs, had not the 'connection' as you call it with Cowley *polarized* my work into clearly male and female contraiety. The spectre of fulfillment, of gratification, is intolerable. Those of us who wind about the never-finished Hermaphroditic body cannot tolerate that sensation of birth that swings like massive vulvar bells through heterosexual screwing. Its sensation, joyful and corrugated with dread, lifted my tower from a sunless workable gloom into a daylit presence and in that moment it snapped in two. It was my natal daemon, covered with the vermin of our Midwestern compulsion to *realize ourselves* in intercourse, that drove me before death's altar in that land where more than one gringo has gone to *exercise his skeleton*. I went to the stern trying to understand why I had said goodbye to her, why all my life I had been saying goodbye to that hideous bell tower whose breasts in a phallic retort were compacted in the face of things—in the human expression of a snake, in the serpentine look of a man. My man in Havana, my man in Hell, my white serpent father whose breasts I failed to draw forth. I stood by the rail and stared into the poetry that had driven and sustained me. Suddenly everything stopped. I was out of time in the fortress of the Cherub. The *Orizaba* was perched on one very tall rotten wave and, as if miles below, a dazzling light appeared, as if this were my 'opening night,' as if to die is 'World Premiere.' And then the Cherub of Narcissism was at my ear: 'You are no further along your path than in the instant when you were conceived. You are merely my play, which I re-stage and re-celebrate with limousines and furs.' And the Covering Patriarch hissed: 'It makes no difference how you carry on—*we'll only talk about you when you're gone*.' I hurled myself into that mindless ditty, to shatter its lantern mockery, its sinister pointing out to the night that 'the real show' is bodies winding out those plush caves in which psyche is, in fact, to be bled..."

He paused long enough for me to ask: your Dionysus, with a Nazarene core, is a full company of bit parts as he flames and sparks at the stake. In what sense is his "target smile" "unmangled?"

"The 'I' must go unpruned and be allowed to elaborate its tendrils. Since I could not 'shoulder the curse of sundered parentage,' I sought a Hermaphroditic grafting. I refused my parents' nature in favor of a vision that included crucifixion *and* pagan multiplicity. Dionysus never *was* mangled—his being takes place in parts, or minute orders, 'divine particulars,' yet 'the bottom of the sea *is* cruel.' For the Protestant, always under curfew, the underworld is infested with criminal elements, thuds of Capone, Manson buttraped as a child whose later martial hysteria wrote its 'helter-skelter' in living flesh. As a Protestant, I was always on that 'sundered' leash when I went down into the image hive, but that was part of my vision too: to wander under Dionysus and to suffer Dionysus in the flesh. Because of this I allowed my sense of line to be governed by Tate and Winters. Only the voicings *rising in writing* I know now are not estrangements. Winters often visits me in this place. In death his soul has become mellow and most open. I see him wandering a nearby vale, chewing peyote, reading Artaud, his flesh neatly stacked on his skull…"

Again he paused, and I caught myself starting to ask: but Hart, how *are you*? A question I realized would burden him with human relationship—for he was truly neither well nor ailing, but in my hesitation he vanished, to become a resonance in the hanging vines, the red geranium pots, the overarching mimosa whose lime and pink tipped blossoms swayed as *if*—an "as if" empty enough to enroot the following notion: as poets we are, forever, in Ariadne, divided—divied up, re-quarried, her fodder, thus her dividend, her divided end, a double *and*. "Whispers antiphonal in azure swing," voicing reversing voicing, ocean reHearsing the casket that has "always" just tumbled out of our mouths.

July 20–21, 1985, Hotel Cro-Magnon

*

Three tigers padding about their three circus cells
attended by a gypsy whose dirty dead feet,
as if the ankles were nailed, hang crossed.

Unlike apes or people, the tigers don't
touch the bars, but turn, as if
on the axis of their own boundary marking.

Don't forget the animals the battered tip box commands.
Tonight, in lurid poolroom light,
these tigers will be led through a cage tunnel

to earn their keep. These tigers
know their Buddhism, whose Nirvana-
principles are inherent in their tread.

Outside La Flotte, Ile de Ré

*

GISANTS

In Nantes, François II curbed &
keenly cut in sculptured white stone,
his hands pressed in prayer, like a shark fin cutting
  the roily cathedral air.
Marguerite de Foix, even more polished, as if oiled,
duplicates his gestures—or is he duplicating M's?
Two "gisants" in gender duplication, cut to resemble their
  prayers to remain! And to think
anyone could be cut from this stone—by a deeper gouge here,
  a peasant,   3 gouges across the face, a suicide…
In stone then, it must be said,
resides the latent expression of everyone.

F and M guard themselves with cherubs, a greyhound, angels.
They know, as they cruise the nave,
how arbitrary their rule was! How their hunger
  to be remembered   must be reinforced by
our hunger   to step inside
                their *temenos,* & swim with them
  in spirit,   carnivorous,   nuptial,
  to the throb of the organ   against
the organs of the worshippers, at attention,
                    as they too make & unmake
shark fins with their upended end-facing hands!

Cathédrale St.-Pierre et St.-Paul

*

FIGUREHEAD

To enter the 2nd floor gallery of the Maritime Museum
is to be stopped by a thirteen-foot woman.

"A tempest liberated me
from dragging across the ocean floor.
The left side of my body was torn apart,
my forearms snapped off. I freed myself, surfaced
on the beach of Tharon, 1920.
You see where the sailors touched me
after licking their fingers before boarding.
Thousands of fingers wore my yoni away so that you, fresh
pilgrim, if you have the nerve, may thrust your finger deep
into my touch-hole... But 'good luck'
for what? Pity for those baking tins of blacks
fitted in spoonwise behind me,
pity for their shackle-
raped wrists.

Here, with bleached African tiara,
teredo-riddled stumps,
I greet you."

Nantes

*

Sunday, 10 PM,   part of our hotel room projects into Nantes,
a tender lampshade half   floating in the rain-spotted air.
Marsh of wheels on Place Duchesse Anne,   a yellow ambulance
peers through,   the cobblestones Spinoza-near,   gleaming nail-
heads,
"eternal,"   Freud-near,   spanked into the distance a huge
caterpillar grazes rue du Château,   disappears into its own feet.
You rest in bed reading Alice Miller's *For Your Own Good.*

Clouds of infant curiosity,   the building force,   close in on
  you.
What did happen at 0?   At 1?   Only the infant can report
his fish bowl experience with his massive Belgian mother,
the scabbard hand of her Watusi daddy—the "roles" are the
  EYES
in the head of owl Minerva,   wisdom an interior shrine,   but
  always
within sound of the clashing,   smashing   child gates…

White tar in drying black luminescence…
Ah the old pond
One can understand why it persists—
to know in *furu ike*
that *frog* and *plop*
are predictable,   & good,
of course, *ah!*   Before or after
old pond…

Now after breakfast, writing down my dream in a dimly-lit nook: A new man in the office. Another man and a woman employee saw him go to into the bathroom with an erection, so they sent a new woman employee in to have sex with him there. She was to report to the other employees, but instead she and the man fell in love and made love all the time. One day the man was called into the office of the other two employees and told that he was fired. He was outraged, for he'd done nothing wrong. He found out that he had been filmed with other employees, all of whom, except him, made awful faces and noises when asked about love. Only he had affirmed love. "And you're going to fire me for that?" Then his lover came in and introduced him to a new woman employee. "I think she can be of great help to us," his lover said. So the man went with the new woman employee into another office. Finding each other attractive, they decided to have sex. He began to finger her and found that she had a string hanging out of her vagina—at this point I began to come and ejaculated very slowly it seemed.

As I woke, I recalled a dream before this one: my mother was lying down and rubbing her breasts with ice cubes. I asked her if I might do that for her. As I was rubbing her very small breasts with ice, I realized that I was rubbing her with my initials and that we had been having intercourse for years, and how strange it was that anyone would think there was anything wrong with this. She smiled at me—was about sixty, aging but very attractive. I then recalled Olson's obsession in "The Song of Ullikummi," with Kumarbi fucking the "huge rock" (as well as Olson's retelling of the Algonquin myth of the woman who "marries" the mountain); at this moment, it seemed clearly Oedipal, and that whenever there is a hero having intercourse with a big impersonal force, it is probably Oedipal. I then recalled that I had been repeating, over and over, for the past several days: "He does not negate anymore," a phrase which I associated with Dionysus. I had been asking the god to release me from negation (specifically, criticism of others, especially of Caryl). I had come to feel that what I had needed to learn via negation had been learned, and that negation could now be abandoned.

I fell asleep again and found myself driving an old car with a complicated gear shift, which was very tall and went way up, nearly to the roof of he car when I put it in 2nd gear. A man came to look at the car and explained the marvelous gear shift. He tried to work it and the window broke…

Then Caryl and I were living in a large house in which M and his family, as well as M's brother and his family, were living. Caryl left, and both men took me into their confidence: both had mistresses. The brother kept his in a cocoon-like tent in the cellar. We all got down on our knees to look at her. She was blonde, very pretty, and not disturbed that we were looking at her. I went upstairs and found that M had introduced his children to his mistress. They were all sitting around talking. Caryl returned and I explained what was going on. She said: "We should leave." I said: Not yet; let's spend at least the rest of the night here.

Again I awoke and continued to think about incest. It seemed that my mother had been returning *ill* in dreams for years *unsatisfied* with my failure to recognize that not only did I desire her but that I had been "in desire" with her for years. And that in being with her in dream all these years I had birthed myself by her and now was my own father. This suggested to me that the "Oedipal project" has not mother as goal, but parthenogenesis, in imitation (male imitation) of the early matriarchal mysteries of birth, when no connection was made between pregnancy and intercourse. Men want to inhabit *that* power and they go through mother to get there. This made me feel that everyman's goal is mother as gate to pass through into a vision of himself as truly independent—and affirmative? I realized that my desire to end negation had been set in motion by feelings in the early 1970s: having loved Caryl and having been loved fully by her, I could happily die now. To accept dying and to abandon negation seemed yoked, a double perspective that would enable the soul to have a lot of room to move around in. So that large house in the last dream has souls in change—fellow inhabitants viewed as living in transition.

(While waiting to order lunch)

Two skeletons entangle my own—
the one of Red Bones is very old, permeated with menstrual,
  matriarchal ochre.
The one of Black Bones is very burnt, very anguished with altar
  consummation—
it yearns to be packed & posted by my own of White Bones.
From this triple viewpoint, I am whole, a joke the Triple
  Goddess tells to her selves,

a football huddle of wives whispering of waves and filth,
of whales and sills,   for whom each word is a scream,
  & the spaces between:
iron hooks dangling sirloin & tendon streamers in a granular
  wind...

L'Hôtel et Auberge du Château

*

KERMARIO

One needs to be a samurai
  to stride between these menhirs,
a held-in belly man
a stomach-centered
    heart-lowered person

People move   hidden from
  thigh down,   they seem to float
the lanes,   there is a sense of a whole
tatter,   a wide
    physical slump the stones enweb
as if netting *place,*
  its net worth
  its gross weight
    en vrac
loose,   bulky
  Leviathan joints

I have bound my lower belly with placental ties
have placed my heart there,   have targeted
  self   at the mid-point of earth & sky,
I move like an orb-weaver, a Noh ghost,
the Neolithic pot-belly I fire
    to bear my stone child

The cave is out!   Like an inverse light!
   Pieces of Car   drying
         in moon & day light,
chicots,   in the breeze of the field's
                                   mouth,

tons
on
one
tone:
stone

its oath,
its oracular
stowage.

*

KERLESCAN

The open   loaded
field

Neanderthal muscle,
      a return of
"the repressed" struggle
      against opacity,
that wall of weather,
      overcome by
      Cro-Magnon—

It resurfaces
   stegosaurian plates
      fins lifting up
         from *holed* earth,

the shapings of the cave
emptied out,
the interior organ design
excavated—

aligned rinds,
culls of the custodian
mother,
her teeth—

indentated ground.

Thistle & heather, ferns,
for ground company—

welts of lichen,
granular saffron
wounds
rescabbed—

I write
from the lectern of one piece of Car,
Ker, the Carmenta
scattered

in this static, rampaging field,
as if the cave were a whirling millstone, as if
muscular goddesses in maddened distraction were tightening
& unloosening the Upper Paleolithic hub,
Laussel dividing into multiple divinities, Lascaux exploding,
Les Trois Frères, Altamira, Niaux, Combarelles,
Font de Gaume, massive undifferentiated cores
whirling into children of the mist, nebulae of marshes,
meres, springs,
into towns & cities, Demeter-spores of childbirth—

The cauldron interior of the cave that had contained
swirls of animal life,   this purgatorio with dragon-fly incubi,
  darters of divinational dreams,
has,   in the mind of the earth,   gone to seed!
The amoebic hybrid congeal,   never a "center" but a physical
  syllogism,   has erupted into a 3000 part argument,
the cowrie did it,   or was it Carya,   the walnut tree?

Kerlescan,   you are not only dedicated to Ker, but to Kore,
  Q're,   Car-Dia,   Cerdo,   Carna,
your great-grandkids are carnivals & charms,   karma,
  cherubs,
the kernel thanks you,   charity erects 3 standing stones,
because of you we have cereal,   Ceres,   we are carnal,
close kindred,   there are cardinal points,   cairns,
the kern or sacred womb vase out of which the grain god was
  born,
Kerlescan,   where the matron menhirs tipple,
where they still wiggle their tentacle towers,   big mama
  breakwaters,   they alleluia in place
while the root canals whistle along.   At times
they converge into a cromlech to evoke an animal band:

the lion is seated   sawing away at his zebra harp,
a bull is covering his Leda drum, a snake is playing
the human spine as if it were a chakra clarinet,
the eagle is swaying over her weasel phone which cries more
  fiercely than Illinois Jacquet!
They play the *kerubn,*   their fabulous muzzles combining,
for the Cherub is not a plump infant with an arrow
nor a demon with a flaming sword,   but the insignia of
the grotesque melodies of this world brooding and incubat-
  ing us.

Carnac is a telluric instant of Car's consternation,
the menhirs drive like distracted miners off into the menace of
  the sunset,
they waver in lines,   memories of the winding path,
rudimental bell towers impounding the skeletal leashes to
  everyone's
  Matterhorn,   that impulse to *up and away!*
KA,   curl in the infant lip, gum pressing forth as the first
  storm cloud appears over a nipple,
O terrible new soul,   fern drifting onto a sleeping dragon's
  out-lapped tongue,
to stand knee-deep in the flamey plush of this tongue,
a moment later the irked mouth reforms,   ka becomes ka-r,
  currr,
open ka seeking closure,   at the end, his vehicle lost, Olson
  moaned "my wife   my car..."

These long stones represent nothing,   as do Zen monks,
they draw me in to their shed-in-time shawls,
they bear on their granite the menstrual stains of dusk,
& as the moon conceals herself forth,   they seem to advance,
Noh ghosts baffled on the rise of that bridge between worlds,
fluttering the imaginal silk of midnight gore,   sticky with
  karma,
mulberry-stained leather armor peeling from the rotted bones
  of former stories, on their way to the ark of etymologies!

One is a poet for an instant   upon breathing in
  the fumes from one's combined cauldrons,
I've swallowed the millstone of my father,   no special feat,
the trick is to re-imagine him, think of him as a bean,
then to go with the grinding.   Car, nut nymph or Caryatid?
Tree trunk or column?   Are these menhirs axles or pestles?
The grinding takes place in the tomb,   Caer Sidin,   the maze
  castle of Ariadne,   revolving because the souls of those
crushed under these menhirs are maggots weevilng,

compost the moon whitens with its scour,
the top of the pestle is the Corona Borealis,
Caer Arianrhod, the Cretan Goddess, wife of Dionysus.

To be a man is to be divided, stretched between one's tomb
& one's star, part of me is a prisoner in Caer Sidin,
the animal mortar, I am the Beast trying to move Beauty
through the sorgum of my eyes, glint of Caer Arianrhod
in my iris implosions, deep very distant Caer Arianrhod,
Crown of the North Wind, as a poet my *cor* (heart) is under
Cerridwen, I am of cerdd, grain & the inspired arts,
the feast of Lady Carnea is June 1, my birth & web day
in the lost Thirteenth House of the Spider.
As *cerdo* (craftsman) I have eaten *cerdo* (pig),
my character goes back to *carato,* from *qirat*
(bean), to Carnea: pig meat & beans, I have swallowed my
father's attempt to enwomb & to be reborn,
I raise my *keras* (horns), cuckolded by the power of Charybdis,
as a door I am the son of Cardea, from *cardo* (hinge),
by these forces
am I permeated,

anima is *pneuma,* the soul a storied fart.

*

In Christianity, the stone is the death impulse; in Blake it is death and Satan, because it cannot be redeemed. The physical world: a rock, within which all secular life is vegetal. Rock as egg, out of which we doomed sinners stagger. I prefer to think of the stone as grotesque, as the *inherent grotesque.* It has no beginning, no end, is in its own way perfect, solid, not an imitation of anything else. It bears the manganese and ochre of my prehistory like nothing else. It is ominous because I cannot milk it. Nor can I see through it. But it will support my record, will not wither. While it is heartless, it is true. True in the sense of being a truce, a stable limbo, a kind of tree onto which I can scratch spirals (to express patterns), or use to cover my dead (thus a lid, for mother earth's even more grotesque cooking pot). Because it endures, it is suspect, especially since its longevity exceeds our perceptual sense of change. We stand it by our dead—and why have we not called it a wombstone? It signals that they are here, filling our present, the bridge over which we cross what we do not understand. Even the abyss is stone-like in that it is charged with the ferocious weight of our ignorance.

Because it cannot be converted in the Christian sense but can be made into stable or home we should be grateful to stone, we should invite it in, offer it the best seat by the fire. To spend an evening with stone is a chilling, rewarding experience, ambivalent, accurate to the vise of life and death. Hold a small stone in your palm for a while. Curl your fingers around it and wait—10 or 15 minutes. You will feel your own weight, I think, as I have felt mine, in a more accurate sense than scales can measure.

To be inside stone, as in a cave, is even more grimly refreshing. And to notice a menhir which has paused before one, with its shoulders lowered as it grasps its iron skirts, before stepping over where one might have been, is a lesson against stasis, a lesson leaned against what one can never begin to fill: space, the floating paradise of solitude, the nailheads of the stars which, were we to fly there in stone boats, would reveal themselves, I believe, as fiery menhirs, really "long stones," whose extents are pure extension, the kind of enrooting that inspires infants to cup their megaphones and shout for milk on Mars.

Mané Lud

*

Stone is heartless, hardest, enduring. We have identified our source in what endures, in what it is in notness, in not us, in block. Unredeemable stone. You bear our record after we scratch it into you. You are no one but you are not Paul Celan's no-one god, the Auschwitz anti-heavenly zero. No, stone, you are good, no one good, unqualified good, the Oz of goodness, Tlaloc with her cistern eyes, eyes not eyes, which spook us when we spot them in knotty pine, in the socket circles of light that flash in knuckle-rubbed eyes upon waking—

toward that eye-filled head
we kneel & crawl,
toward the eye-filled body,
the ovary chimney with its two sweeps,
toward the double zero with its roaring, immobile tide

rockface, silent nickelodeon

Mané Kerioned

*

Menhirs appear to repeat themselves, to fall in line. When they are part of a grave, the walls of a burial chamber, they are sometimes engraved with repeated crooks, or labyrinthine arcs, goddess oculi, the hope of the dying placing their eye necks on our living lines. As if Upper Paleolithic meanders, finger traced in wall clay or cut with silex in the rockface, had been bent, and bound, arched, cathedraled, placed in atonal rhythm, out of each, against each, deadending each, died pools, a rippling stasis, the way life emerges and exits.

Charles Olson suggested that poetry is the turned blow of place, or the ability to twist the blow that one's own place has reverberated in one.

The mazes engraved in the Gavrinis orthostats emphasize blockage or movement in looping tunnels that have no entrance or exit. They anticipate cathedral portals and volutes. As arches within arches they remember the 30,000 year old vulva in La Ferrassie, where the curl of the fleshy stone is so soft that the receptivity of woman is established, and held, for the entire life of the earth.

Gavrinis

*

At Rondossec, a bright-orange wrapper named "Pindar." An all too American roadside. I kick the paper aside, and stooping, hunch my way to the end of another Gallery Grave. Is it puberty? Something in these skeletons of communal tombs is close to my boyhood—first sense of death? Death as the twist in puberty? Peristalsis of the awakening, contracting body? At bird's eye view, Gallery Graves look like schematic caterpillars, close to Wilhelm Reich's caterpillar contraction/expansion drawing of sexual energy. The "passages" waver or slightly twist, undulate, toward their "head" or bulbous mushroom-cap-like end chamber. Add kids jumping up and down on the capstone. But this is life at the ruins, no? What should I have expected—"Winter sunset at Kermario?" Or do I think of them as caterpillars because they are not temples? Stunted works, creepings forth from a tremendous loss, hinge of the Neolithic, point at which one feels a crucial amount of feminine psyche invested in the earth, to get agriculture going, with the counter-motion, that it was also to be dispersed, as psychic energy did not seem to be from what I can "read" on the Upper Paleolithic cave walls. These exteriors (stone skeletons, out in the daylight, available to all) are not only treated differently than, but felt differently than the interiors of protected, decorated caves. These dolmens live like tolerated gypsies in the fields.

*

YORUNOMADO'S END

Back at Kerlescan,
flame of my book & hands,
steady breeze,   6:30 PM
        1 August 1985
The history of stone is
the history of human ignorance.
A dolmen by the sea,
a darker opening than even the sea provides,
30 feet of galleried stone,   to end as if
we ended that far from   the waves we rose
out of.
            There is an elder king
                bound & carried
by several men into this gallery grave by the sea.
He can no longer excite & satisfy the queen,
his name is Yorunomado,
  he glimpses the last light of his life
as they drag him in under
the dolmen,   into box-like
  dark & ignorance,

as if his impotent vigor shed
would reproduce in the ground, as if
the earth needed Yorunomado's
bones to thrive,   to press forth
golden genista & bright purple heather in spring—

            They have burned
his corpse,   tamped his ashes into a posthole
at Kerlescan,   priming for
the menhir to be swung down onto,
    s a c r e d   a s h

so that the stone resting on
the ash of an elder is a sprout in death,
they pack manure around the loaded hole

          & so the stones of Kerlescan
                wander off
            in place,
the sun's westward flight
  draws dark up their sides,
these stones,   or fingers in death row,
  cowled stones,
planted against the furrow of the mother,
so hard is she at 5000 BC.

As the mystery of her being that out of which an all emerges
  congeals,
as the elder king is replanted by a young man,
  she grows *dur*—
but no word as dense as *menhir,*
              exploded subliminal
                   unity staggering
back somewhat in line
so that all life becomes memorial…

Into the phallus carve the limit,
carve the trajectory of Yorunomado's death & burial—
into the limit carve the labyrinth.
No way now to go beyond full circle.
Into the circle carry his decapitated body
around the cromlech 8 times,
before placing it on a centric pyre—
out of the dolmen by the sea
red flows down to the lapping,
every path we walk
   the ghost of such a flow.

*

"Professor of anonymity,"   I murmured,
circling the menhir in a field near Pontivy,
"all paths turn upward,   right as well as left,
all paths   detours as we ascend   through ourselves
  wandering away from our deepening feet—

menhir   lighthouse   belted by a sea of diamond-back green,
menhir   nighthouse   refusing tomb of your long stone blade."

*

The wind-bent
    pines of Quiberon
green & rust pins,
    tight hardened cones,
twisted inland
        schoonered away from shore,   shaved,
whose blackened air shears east,   even
in their gash-tarred
            branch vaults they veer

Some low branches have crawled in the air 30 feet from their trunks
  & dangle   crutch-
             aloft

*

Ragged file of 5 menhirs on a meadow's rise,
from what goddess comb   these remaining broken teeth?

Noh ghosts paused on that suspension bridge between worlds

Testicle-breasts,   weights by which night was
  once sounded
before the angel's wing was turned into a scythe
& the world-end winds bottled as ma & pa.

near Plouharnel

*

LES PIERRES PLATES

I crept down Les Pierres Plates' gallery, noticing on the passage stones engravings that looked like bent snakes, gouged cupules in the non-snake spaces—stopping places for wandering souls to drink? Les Pierre Plates seems to be an early purgatorio with little "maps" on its passage stones for the newly-dead. Perhaps for the souls too that sweep in from the sea…

I was approached by a local teen-ager who hung out at the site with a flashlight. He whined "Do you want information?" pushing his light at the tourists (since you have to have one to study the engravings). I needed a strong light (having only a penlight), but said No, not wanting to be beholden to him. Was he an Ira I later wondered, a figure upon whom one projects all of that which is unacceptable about oneself? "And Los embraced his Spectre," Blake wrote. His full humanity, I understood, let it flow into the art, as another aspect of what is. But I was so physically repelled—plus he did not care about Les Pierres Plates. He was only there for money. Squatting by the entrance as I crept out.

I wanted to remain, by myself, slightly inside, to get a feel for the sea from there. He knew he was not going to get a tip out of me, so my presence slightly inside—as someone taking the place seriously—a few feet from his waiting place, with no fresh tourists around, seemed to piss him off. He edged back in, hunched up next to me, and with his face inches from my own, half-snarled: "Did it please you, mister?" I said nothing. So he repeated the question, several times, all over my face. The only response I wanted to make was to tear out his cheek. Then we both saw new tourist legs, and he scurried away with his flashlight...

In the spectrum of things, it was not much to suffer his breath or his cheek. But it leaves an impress, lightening Les Pierres Plates, weighting 5 PM, August 3, 1985.

*

"To remain is everything," Kerlescan spoke,
"inert & splendid, splayed out beneath the stars,
in Nirvana state, free of human genital tyranny—
the Artaud-state par excellence, organ free,
impacted with human god-curiosity, the ensigns of
conditional entry, where the arachnoid world of nature
weaves around us the ripe continuum that
humans row through, their boats high in the air,
their oars stilts that never move,
the navigator leaning earnestly forward behind his wheel
as if there were a course to choose...

We are in vertical pause,
our goddess Ker
your cherished core.

Here's a koan: what is the sound of
The Raft of the Medusa?
—as the human eels
coil in the salt,
and reach, as we stones never do,
for Fool's Udder,
as if they could churn
Morgane la Fey out of a cloud!"

Kerzerho

*

POSTCARDS FROM CARNAC

Dear Eliot & Nina: this pack of menhirs spotted regrouping around midnight August 1, 1734 BC. As they dolmenize the landscape breaks out into vitriolic bloom, moon green. Everything for an instant on the same band of laughter. The dolmen body is the first cello, goddess body, whose transcepts are buttocks, breasts, wind, bones, a fugal lesion, a kind of larval streetcar nosing about in the fields of night, a vacuum cleaner that for a change cleans the vacuum from the spinning mind of the earth. Zesty abrazos…

Dear Bill & Yoshiko: in case you hadn't realized it, this is the squid face of the goddess who watches over our sleep & dreams in Morbihan. She is the sky support & rather glum recently with all the rejection we are flushing into ocean & sky. Anyway, here we are, talking with dolmens, on a constant wild menhir hunt. They see us & flee, like abashed fairies into their covens, or convents, of rock…

Dear Mike & Priscilla: if you turn this card upside down, you can see the menhirs actually move as they often do here late at night, playfully rearranging themselves into skeletal diagrams (for are they not the *joints* of that universal body that was lost once & for all in the Neolithic?) Or are they axle parts, gagged spokes of that hub we've *never* lost, about which we walk no matter how straight we think we proceed? Cordial regards from the Vale of Truncated Questions…

Hennebont, Château de Locquénolé

*

YORUNOMADO IN THE UNDERWORLD

In the Arrée Mountains, "the *youdig,*
  a gulf forming the entrance to Hell,"
swirls of fog blowing mist
between Huelgoat & Brasparts,
          boulders like military emplacements,
in the vale: "a great peat bog called the Yeun Elez"
  & the nuclear station at Brennilis—
              extinction *is.*

Yorunomado appears in the masked air,
a spinning barber pole, bearing
his animal in his arms. Niemonjima receives him.
Into her convolutions he whirls,
of his life maze she rubs out one half.
If he can remember himself & dance his memory
she will accept the animal in lieu of him—

                as we saw at Pont-Aven
the village dancers working round-dances,
peristaltic hand-held convergences,
dilations, caterpillar energy patterns displayed
in traditional garb,

          at Pleyben, Christ does not move,
all the stations of his life & death are portrayed,
he is mottled, yellow-lichened granite,
a grass sprig shivers in the dark rain
before his clasped hands...

The Christian mouth of Hell is packed with sinners.
The Celtic "*youdig*" is folds of invisibility.
Can we remember ourselves as we circle
the outer ceremonies that would seem to strip us of
  mental mirrors?

On the far side of any experience
comrade souls await us.
The animal Yorunomado bears is the one we lost
when the first seams of boundary distinctions were sown.
Yorunomado goes to the abyss with an image,
I bear the traces of my pets in my body's unlived lines.

                    Far below this road
Yorunomado is struggling to recall
the erased aspects of his life maze,
                              he has an image,
thus a chance. He knows who he is to be damned with—
he drags a clump of moss from the granite Christ,
squeezes it out like a sponge into Niemonjima's slavering
   jaws. The brimmer lubricates the devourer,
energy has no center. The image is
a concave black mountain bristling
                    on sea-urchin alert—

          Into this image he pours
the silicon of memory,
                              in the *youdig*
there are only swirling, devouring stripes,
my hair fell to the 16th Street barbershop floor,
I saw it glide into the street,   my father,
the buck & a quarter cut,   all are swirling down into
earth's vast reservoir of
                    paratactic appetite. Niemonjima
   is ravenous,   she wants the perfectly
organized path to be impacted
   in every act.

*

AT CAP RAZ

                    mush white
webby gleaming
gull-puckered rocks—

Bodies of the drowned are cranked by water cords into
    "the devil's chimney" "the Hell of Plogoff"
once there they are dismembered,
    "inspected" like sacrificial timber
 by the rocks.

As I move through Finistère
I dream more pungently,   omen-bountiful with
the ancient dread emanating from the Eurasian continent's end.
Sudden showers sudden sun,
voids boomed with waves
pitchforking gulls   (which squeal like mice.

The lightning is haruspex
it rains   malign.

*

By houseside or doorstep,   village after village,
clumps of hydrangeas,   sickly granite-white
   with baby-blue pinkish hues.
Burgeoned grave décor. Death bulbs.

Finistère

*

In Hotel de la Plage,   from the dining-room bay window,
vista of wide, flat sea…   To the left the rampart of a hill:
  a massive dead caterpillar,
its lanes twisting with worm fur,   pine turrets,
rovings & twirls,   from time to time it shudders,
a hibernating pillar corpse,   an organic wall—

the surf lace flows,   blowsy oyster frill
fern-blue flattery,   ripe,   staid,
anal flavors,   uroboric orals.

Ste.-Anne-La-Palud

*

Behind the Christianized menhir,   a 10 year old boy &
  older sister smoking… I recalled Octavio Paz's line,
"En lo alto de la piramide los muchachos fuman marihuana"

& Judy Joyce offering me a cigarette, on a school night no less,
  behind Fairview Presbyterian Church—
as if there's something about a "sacred spot" that makes us want
  to smoke there.

near St.-Duzec

*

At the end of a rutted farm wagon-way, the gallery grave, marked on a local map, angled away from a rotting wagon covered with vines. Bridal. Xochipilli! In one capstone: a depression filled with baptism. The gallery grave, on its last slab legs, also smelled of cattle. As I squatted inside, Robert Creeley's words, "death can still propose the old labors" rephrased themselves as: death can still propose the oldest flavors…

near Kerguntuilh

*

APOTHEOSIS

Where clouds
temple the horizon, realms of whitened
light enfolding
vast inorganic fruit. Grandeur:
unfurling arabesques
that confirm parthenogenesis.

The bay is swooned with streaks of cobalt, jade,
"granit rose," pink & black speckled rock
dolmen-contoured in soft
lifting heaps, or saucers—
their ridges, furrows, lobes or lobbies invite the early
Dali of imagination, and in this light,
the pink & black meld to tawny rose, living rock,
rose rock!
One need go no further for satisfaction with the earth.
"Nature is imagination itself."

Seamless, the day is *sloth & ray*
moving under the language film
as breasts, or turtles

Breaking through enthusiasm, *enthousiasmos*
"possessed by the god," language,
beautiful chains of surf reaching
the apex of their heave
reswarm this tawny rose to reveal
the saddle of Persephone flecked by Zeus

Trégastel

*

The rapidly changing skies, sudden bursts of rain cut almost immediately by sunbeams, seem to stimulate dreaming. Last night I crept up a stadium-like embankment to watch tai-chi-like dancers stretching their bodies into extraordinary shapes. As I watched, they discharged a large black and red locomotive into the sky. It sailed, landed heavily, bounced out of sight. I turned back to the dancers now launching rockets—six at a time—they shot toward me, veering into what looked like train-switch mechanisms where they were re-aimed by six large human figures. The action kept speeding up, set after set of rockets, with frenetic activity on the part of the switchmen who received and re-aimed them at machinegun speed. I watched in awe as the action became a phantasmagoria of color and movement. Someone beside me said very loudly: THIS IS THE HUMAN BRAIN. My eyes were ringing when I awoke...

Trébeurden

*

In the dining room at Manoir de Lan-Kerellec, the tape of a 1930ish piano running through "sentimental favorites" offered me real bewitchment. Caryl knew some of the words, sang them, the music went on and on in my head: *Dearly Beloved.* The particular combination of major/minor modulations enthralled me like a foreign language poem in a dream that one can magically understand, but only in the dream, never after. *Dearly Beloved* was a sound text that I had once understood and now it mocked my inability to call myself forward through it. On one level it was just another tune of the times, a little corny, too sweet with a bit of rancidity about the edges—but on another level, a black purling lagoon of sound, a siren melody...

Now, a day later, it has continued like the spectre of a singing fly. My mother had stacks of sheet music from the 30s and 40s, and sang daily at the piano. I recall being in my room and hearing her, out in the living room, alone, singing her love songs. In a way she was singing to me (for she brought me into her music world by starting me on neighborhood teacher piano lessons at six years old), and to my father in the slaughterhouse downtown, but she was also singing words that enabled her to express some of the romance in her soul that otherwise had no language or object. But I do not recall her singing *Dearly Beloved.* And now the song has the sensation of a card passed on by the head waiter in an elegant bistro from someone on the other side of the room who the recipient cannot make out. The card is blank, of course, or the message, if there is one, is in a foreign language, and as I continue to listen to the music in my head, it coalesces into a violet pearl on a tiny gray velvet pillow that I have kept under my hearing, right below my hearing, for so many years...

Trébeurden

*

ST.-MALO TO DINARD BY FERRY

Back of a frail man in a breeze-trembled, short-sleeve shirt, pissing against a seaweed-blackened wall. As he finished, & turning around exhaled a fret of smoke, I reheard Keats' line, "The trembling hare limps through the frozen grass."

On the floor planks of the ferry
Caryl noticed a "ladybug bus"—
          Our Lady of the Underworld
   out for an afternoon crossing.

          [Last night: the open, enraged
mouth of a Zambezi crocodile on hotel room TV,
a real "mouth of the universe" roped so easily by clever
  crocodile farmers,

the enraged mouth of the earth, so powerful, so mindless &
  so vulnerable—
seeing it was *tragedy,*   like a Beethoven stroke, or
Vallejo by a warming afternoon beer, Montparnasse, fall 1937,
or the feet of Fabre, around his observation table,
  wearing a groove in the stone floor]

Against the rain light,
  slate
          & a waving hollyhock
whose mint green bud end twists beyond the flower.

Below Pointe du Moulinet,
pollen-colored lichen,
a chaos of tar brown rocks…
                                        most difficult to say
the appearance, let alone the being, of shore water
as it opaques out, transluces in

melusina   *melusina*

          below the island of Bé
            the drowned city of Is.

On a small "Place," littered with ladybug corpses,
a middle-aged couple, on a bench, necking.
As we cross, their mouths do not release.
His cheeks pulsing, like bellows.

*

Then I dreamed my way to Henry Miller, who was now the interior guardian of Les Combarelles (not the cave guide, but the guardian who dwells within, who from the outside appears to be caged, but from the inside is the one free of fear). Once we were tucked in the rock, Miller said: "you've seen a grown man cry, haven't you?" Yes, I answered. "Well," he laughed, "have you ever seen a grown man *squeeze his infancy out his eyes?*" Then he made his face very round, put his palms against the sides of his head and pushed hard: elephant trunks emerged from each eye and waved around. He released his hold, the trunks withdrew. "When you learn how to do that," he said, "you won't have any more problems."

But seriously, I protested... "Serishly smearishly," he returned, suddenly fierce. "I offered my 4 year old daughter to a madman once... there was a terrible massacre, but she survived, in fact all my daughters did. Now they tend the suffering boat people stacked like cordwood outside Les Combarelles."

The last time I saw Miller he was going home, at dusk. He passed by as I was sitting at the side of the road. He had a Howdy Doody expression on his face, and as he passed, I noticed that the back of his head had a face too, a serious, pale, medieval virgin, who spat a shower of pomegranate seeds into my questioning expression.

> PS: I forgot to add that while we were tucked in the
> rock, Miller also said: "A man's genitals are the culprits
> of his fate. First they strangle his tongue, then his anus,
> then they withdraw deep into his groin to watch the
> "light show," having suspended, as decoys, penis and tes-
> ticles, to mesmerize the women who otherwise might
> try to save him."

St.-Servan-sur-Mer (St.-Malo Sud), 13 August 1985

[Sections from this journal appeared in New American Writing #29 *and* Big Bridge #15.*]*

III

The quintessential Paul Blackburn poem ("Affinities II" would be a good example) is visually speaking more like a sketch (Franz Kline was his favorite painter) than a work in oil. Lines are brisk, deft strokes resulting in mobile half-stanzas, particle-stanzas, slightly assymetrical, that tilt the poem on. Whether in Barcelona or in the New York City 23rd Street "Bakery," the Blackburn persona is generally off-stage, activated by desire, an observer scoring nodes which the reader can connect to constellate relationship-oriented patterns. The tendency is to seek out value, or as Blackburn himself puts it in one poem included in *The Parallel Voyages,*[1] "the whole and the flowing," but he is also fascinated by the extent to which humankind is derailed, and redesigned, by a ritualistic emotional and material interface. The content of this quintessential poem is spare, idiomatically erudite, and only marginally introspective. It frames itself as it tracks its own material, resulting in a page design that is quite mobile, with weighted, balanced lines and word clumps:

Affinities II

Why do gulls like
to sit in the sea
only when there are waves, when there
is ground swell?

1 This essay, now with minor revisions, and a few additions (including the two poems I quote, which are not from the collection the essay was written for), introduced Paul Blackburn's *The Parallel Voyages,* edited and annotated by Edith Jarolim, with drawings by Ellen McMahon, SUN-gemini Press, Tucson, 1987. At the end of that Introduction I commented on some of the previously unpublished Blackburn poems I had collected from the UCSD Special Collections Library and included in *The Parallel Voyages.* I have not reprinted that section here.

And never will
when it is smooth?
Must be they take pleasure from
the motion of wave
as I do,
the lift and ride and rise, the swing
down the trough, climbing
effortlessly
the next crest.

Best to sit in the sun afterward, tho,
on rock,
watching the rollers break, spill-
slide up the beach,
letting spray fall back its jet
upon wet rocks, brown legs, the next
against the sun.
We never learn
to distrust such motion, Carroll.

I recall your long legs
tumbling in such a sea
at Bañalbufar that summer,
white
body reddening
taking its first day's sun
with brown face set on top with already
thinning hair.
Caring, steadily caring, for ideas alone
had not kept you from trying to rise
to your feet, smiling against such a sea,
the surf cracking you back to a sitting
posture against the stone
beach, the sea sliding around you
no god to help you, only your stalk-
white, reddening legs

could lift you timed in the face of it.
No god there that afternoon, Carroll,
only our powers, not yours, our demons
sea . sun . wind-squall
among us found a balance.
It was your own.

This winter sun
streams across my legs and chest, flashes
across the crashing surf-line.
A fisherman comes down with a heavy line and
drags it out its length along the beach,
heaving
each portion out
into the surf
until it's a snake part in, part out of water.
He washes, not too carefully
the oil slick off it . Long rope
it takes him a long time . He finishes finally
and sticking to rock
avoiding the sand he
hauls it again to the top of the sea-
wall and coils his rope
to dry in the sun,
slows his coiling to talk to a friend
gives the line a last turn
the work done.

When will we learn
so naturally to
quit, when what we have to do
is done?
Or that the print of rough stone,
rock
set deep in the flesh of the palm,
my own or yours,

see what we will in reading it, patterned
                palms . pyramids . cuneiform
                        tablets, a cross, some
small starched waves or winging gulls, the shell,
                        the flower
                we see or think we see . there
no matter
we trust and fear
this movement, that god,
                        will disappear
                                inside this quarter-hour?

Málaga, Winter 1956–57

"Carroll" is the poet Paul Carroll.

Note Blackburn's "floating period," which pauses the thought or image and at the same time continues the line's movement. I have always suspected he picked it up from the eccentric punctuation in Ezra Pound's Cantos worksheets (standardized in the New Directions collections).

Such a poem, it turned out, could only accommodate a limited amount of variation and materials that challenged its procedure. Anything that drew the poem inwards, that, in effect, unmoored its outer connections, seemed like sabotage. While there are some excellent poems of the early 1960s in which this frame is under great tension and bending to accommodate disintegrative psychological pressure ("The Sea and The Shadow" is an example), by the mid-60s Blackburn could no longer count on it as an organizing pattern. While it occurs from time to time in the "Journals" of the late-60s, it must fight for time and space there in a context that is increasingly given over to trivia and daily factual mapping.

The work of the mid-60s is to a great extent about Paul's failure to come to terms with himself as a man, or to weather the transition from being a young, accomplished poet to becoming a mature poet with a sustaining pattern out of which to work. While Paul may have had complicated defenses in the social world, he had few in his poetry. In contrast to the self-contained pieces of the mid- and late-50s, which are models of opening, developing, and resolving a poem, the mid-60s work is amorphous, meandering and preoccupied with daily and historical events in a reportorial way. The specific and resolved poems are somewhat dated repetitions of earlier modes. Be this as it may, Blackburn's fate is being worked out during this period, and any ultimate and genuine evaluation of his life and his poetry must take the mid-60s carefully into consideration.

In the early spring of 1963, Paul wrote most of the long "Selection of Heaven" and his fusion of New York City observation and Greek myth, "The Watchers," two major works which, in the light of what he later produced, can oddly be thought of as summations. After these two peaks, references to alcohol, bars, bums, sensations of social or sexual rejection and impotence mill about in his writing. In a curious and touching way, the poem itself becomes a vagabond, without schedule or resting place. While Sara Blackburn, his second wife, is seldom mentioned at this point, she appears to be the companion figure who, according to Paul at least, is rejecting him.

There are fits and starts of word-play oriented poems, and some pieces that juxtapose seemingly unrelated patches of experience (e.g., "Hesper Adest" and "You Light It"), both modes of which could, under different circumstances, have been developed to stake out new grounds. Something deep and central in Paul has come unhinged and the poem has become a murky lamentation rather than a tool to get at and come to terms with the problem. At accurate indication of what has happened can be gauged by comparing "The Watchers" to a 1966 poem organized in a similar way, "the procedures." In contrast to the former poem which bristles with alertness, the speaker in the latter piece is unengaged and seems to be writing to pass the time.

Blackburn's decline in this period might well be pondered by younger writers coming to poetry now out of a William Carlos Williamsesque idiomatic tradition which has been filtered and softened by the "confessional" poetry of the late-50s/early-60s. On one hand, Blackburn stayed "open" by not locking himself into a set of values that would have determined what he affirmed and what he rejected. On the other hand, his failure to do so, made him extremely dependent upon the facts of daily existence in the harsh, impersonal labyrinth of New York City. Had he been tougher, more self-dependent, and more aggressive in directly expressing his feelings, he might have come through his "mid-life crisis," completed his troubadour translation project, and developed a sustaining vision based on his work in the mid- to late-50s.

However, the facts, according to the poetry, seem to indicate that Paul's sense of creative worth was exceptionally contingent upon sexual acceptance, very overtly in the case of women, and very covertly in the case of men. His antennae were lust-sensitive, and many poems are organized explicitly around an anonymous or intimately-known person who aroused him. As he approached his 40s, this point of imaginative ignition increasingly misfired, or did not spark at all, to the point that the pain of loving (himself as well as others) appears to have engulfed sexual gratification. In the chasm that began to appear as this single power gave way and divided was a morass of unresolvable childhood unhappiness.

In her Introduction to *The Collected Poetry* (Persea, NYC, 1985) Edie Jarolim writes that Paul and his slightly younger sister lived with his mother's "strict and elderly grandparents" in Vermont between his fourth and fourteenth years, while his mother, Francis Frost, recipient of the 1929 Yale Younger Poets Award, was in New York City trying to earn a living as a writer, and living with a woman companion. According to comments that Robert Creeley has related,[2] Paul was regularly whipped by his maternal grandmother. The image of a small, brutalized fourteen year old Paul rejoining his mother in New York City in 1940 and via her encouragement becoming, as she did not, a major American poet and translator, is so redolent with Oedipal consternation that I begin to think that the host of anonymous women whose sexuality drifts in and out of his poetry (as well as his wonderful troubadour translations, which he could never to his satisfaction complete) is Paul's reversed version of Isis and Osiris, in which it is the female figure whose body is scattered and the task of the poet-son to vainly attempt to reconstruct her via endless sallies into the moment of desire.

In this context it is worthwhile to think about what looked at superficially appears to be a heavy load of machoism in Blackburn's poetry. Women are often signed, or identified, as sexual targets, and his seeming dependence on women for self-affirmation empowers them with overwhelming, sometimes menacing, psychic size. The humorous "takes" (from a patriarchal viewpoint) are in one way escape-valves to let out some of the pressure such size builds up. But it is more complicated than this. There is, for example, a cluster of images making use of traps and nets (the purse-seine in the poem by that title, "the net of lust" and "that silken trap" in "Call It the Net") that evokes Blake's poem, "The Crystal Cabinet." Unlike the speaker in Blake's superb lyric, who is brought to understand that intercourse per se is not going to yield an apocalyptic vision, Blackburn never seems to get clear as to the limitation, meanings, and specific mental rewards of sexual union—or is able to develop an alternative set of values that lie outside its crisis.

From the late-50s on, he seems to turn and twist, a dreamer in its nets, as if in the grip of an inhibition so intense that the source of the anguish (homosexuality?) cannot be identified, let alone addressed.

---

2 See Creeley's brief Preface to *Against the Silences*, Permanent Press, London & New York, 1980. While the editor Robert Vas Dias states on the back of this book that it "comprises the last manuscript remaining to be published which Paul Blackburn conceived as a separate and unified book," he informs the reader in a Publisher's Note that he has eliminated a third of this manuscript from the book. Vas Dias also states that "no title has been assigned to the collection," while assigning to it the first half of a poem title, "Against the Silences of Staircases." Without "of Staircases," "Against the Silences" is "poetic" in a way that Blackburn always avoided. Blackburn himself referred to this gathering as "the black binder," which seems to me to be the most appropriate title for the collection—which should have also been published entire, as Paul left it.

An indication of the extent to which sexual fulfillment is endlessly complicated occurs in the splendid "Purse-Seine," when the "sea bird," in context a gull-man-penis, facing the rising hips of the other, "hits the mast in the dark and falls / with a cry to the deck and flutters off." These lines occur at the threshold of penetration, and immediately after the "bird" strikes this peculiar "mast," we read: "Panic spreads, the / night is long, no / one sleeps, the net / is tight…" In "Call It The Net," a poem written five years later, in 1964, the speaker "imagines a young woman / lying on her back at the intersection / third Ave., and 8th St.," and as he continues to both titillate and vex himself, he writes:

> It is a threshold I cross, no
> longer an intersection, the bird
> hidden in the shirt upon the chest
> torn . the eye
> swells in the head
> bird flutters and falls into the sea of eyes
> She was so beautiful
> Bird and sun are holy take the head
> tear it open and set it like a
> melon upon the threshold

Taken together, these two related passages suggest to me that Blackburn has projected a phallic intensity ("the mast") upon the vagina, with a loss of potency before penetration can take place. Subsequently, in the above passage, he fantasizes that he is castrated, and offers the street-woman object of his fantasy his genitals as a sacrificial gift. Given that Blackburn's first and ongoing projection of the creative self is the gull, which is envisioned as the poet's own childhood body as well as the numinous word riding the wind, or lines, of inspiration,[3] the implication of these lines is nothing less than devastating. The sexual act becomes the sacrificial grounds where language, the poet, his identity and his sexuality are drawn and quartered.

"Lust is unpredictable," he wrote in a poem dated June 21, 1963, in which a stanza describing an angry black woman on the A train appears in a context that otherwise has nothing to do with her. The next week or so, Blackburn wrote the shocking "Birds chirp listlessly in the heat," now published in *The Parallel Voyages,*[4] which lets the reader in on what he believes women would do if they really had their own way with him. The terror implied by such writing is so extreme as to become somatically entropic. If the reader thinks that I am exaggerating, let him read "Crank It Up For All Of Us, But Let Me Heaven Go" in the *Collected Poems.* It is one of the most perfectly executed and genuinely disturbing poems in American literature.

---

3 From the late 1940s through the early 1960s, Blackburn's poetry is graced with continuing bird, most often gull, appearances. Some of the key poems in this respect are: "Cantar de Noit," "The Birds," "The Lanner," Winter Solstice," The Purse-Seine," "The Summer Window," "In Winter," and sections 1 and 6 of "The Selection of Heaven." He once wrote to me in 1963: "Dear Clay, Never look a gull in the eye, love, Paul."

4 I founded *Sulfur* magazine at the California Institute of Technology in Pasadena in the spring of 1981, and the first eight issues were edited there, published by the Institute, with a commitment of deficit funding for five years provided by President Goldberger. In 1983, I was informed by Goldberger that Caltech's name had to beimmediately struck from *Sulfur* because of the following incident: he had been using discretionary funds from the Weingart Foundation in Pasadena to support the magazine, and at one point showed the Weingart Board of Trustees a copy of *Sulfur* #4, which included twenty-two of the Blackburn poems included in *The Parallel Voyages.* Apparently, someone from the Foundation picked up the issue, leafed through and settled on "Birds chirp listlessly in the heat…" which he read aloud to everyone at the Board meeting. He then told Goldberger that *Sulfur* was pornographic and that their funds were no longer to be used to support the magazine, and that they wanted Caltech's name removed from it. Goldberger told me that as much as he disagreed with the Trustees' response, he had to honor it because of the Weingart Foundation's huge yearly donations to the Institute. Goldberger, quite honorably

Keeping in mind the issue of machoism that I raised, I would like to suggest that there are at least three kinds of sexuality in Blackburn's poetry, only one of which is offensive from my viewpoint (which is one that believes in reciprocity between the sexes). The first kind is of the dirty joke variety, with Blackburn ogling ass on the subway or identifying anonymous women on the basis of their sexual "equipment." While such poems as "Clickety-Clack" and "The Once-Over," are well-written examples of this kind of humor, they in no way represent the range and complexity of Blackburn's sexuality or poetry at large, and it is a shame to see him represented in anthologies by them.

A second kind is the turgid sexual despair that Paul attempted to reveal, or unravel, in the kind of poems that I quoted from earlier. Whatever sexism there may be in these multiple images of gulls, women, nets and masts, is overwhelmed, to my reading, by Blackburn's self-inflicted short-circuiting, and I can only lament that he suffered so much in this way. I am moved, not put off, by his hesitant, always somewhat thwarted attempt to express the core of his compulsive self-revulsion.

A third kind of sexuality, and certainly the dominant one for the first half of Blackburn's writing career, is an admiration and tender respect for what might be thought of as femininity in all forms. This motif is sounded again and again, as contact with women, animals (generally cats—the occasional dogs seem to indicate a negative male presence), and plants, and appears to envision a feminine principle as the force that provides the world

---

I felt, offered to make good on his original five year deficit funding commitment to *Sulfur* via other sources, so that the magazine could continue either on its own for a while or until it attracted a new sponsor. While the Blackburn poem is genuinely shocking, it is hardly pornographic. That a single poem by this shy, unassertive poet was sufficient to nearly eliminate a literary magazine on grounds of censorship in 1983 should keep us all alert to the fact that while things seem to change, "the sexual revolution" etc., on another level they remain stuck, and the same.

with growth and beauty. When Blackburn is under the sway of this persuasion (generally in his apartment, in contrast to out on the street or in the New York City subway), he is fair-minded, masculine, and extremely sensitive. The reader who draws back at "The Once-Over" should be willing to read "The One Night Stand: An Approach to the Bridge," in which there is a scene that many American men and women who grew up in the 40s and 50s experienced, suffered, and seldom happily resolved:

The One Night Stand : An Approach to the Bridge

Migod, a picture window
both of us sitting there
on the too-narrow couch
variously unclothed
watching sky lighten over the city

You compile your list of noes
it is incomplete
I add another
there is no anger
we keep it open
trying,
shying
away, your all
too-solid body melts, revives, stif-
fens, clears and dis-
solves, an i-
dentity emerges, disappears, it is
like watching a film, the takes dis-
solving into other takes,
spliced suddenly to a closeup
The window tints pink
                                        I wait
We sleep a bit . Your
identity goes and comes

it is never for me,
it is never sure of itself
                                        I wait, you
ask too much of yourself, why
of the moment, why
is your fear of feeding off other people? Must
you always feed off yourself
and find it unreal food you eat, unreal
water you drink from the source of yourself, un-
real liquor you take from the hand of a friend, and
never grow gloriously drunk, but stay
eating yourself
finding the fare thin,
stay in a dark room holding
uneasily, in an unreal hand
a thin man's unreal cock who stays
and grows more unreal to himself?
                                        We both sleep.

New day's sun
doubles itself in the river
A double string of blue lights
glares to mark the bridge, the
city huddles under a yellow light
the sodium flares
gleam under oblique
sun's double in the stream,
                                        I wake
ready, make my move.
"You'll make me pregnant" you murmur
and barely audible, "I'll die"
neither will stop me
your legs are open
I am there at the wet edge
of life, the moist living lips

It will not do
I have been at this life's edge
and hurt too many hours
It will be all me for a moment
then all you
Identities will dissolve
under this new act, or
six quick strokes
you move once
toward me, say
one word, even
moan, I will be finished
done
dissolved
become real, alone, no
it will not do
You are no victim and
I no rapist hero, I can
still, I
I stop at the life's edge

Later
we are too real
separate, try
to recover
dully, our-
selves gone out
The coffee does not warm
there is an orange sun in the river
there are blue lights on the bridge
Animal tenderness and
sadness is all we salvage, is
all the picture window
mirrors and maintains

[1961/1962]

What to say? There is no other poem from this period (or perhaps in American poetry at large) remotely like this. The speaker's decision in favor of respecting his "date's" sexual fears, and not pressing himself onto, and into, her, is genuinely evocative of Paul Blackburn's respect for others at large.

I have drawn out these three differing attitudes toward sexuality to point out that they represent such a complex *and* complicated web of ambivalences that they cannot be simply passed off as macho. To read Blackburn on these matters and to think what they humanly mean makes me wonder what we would think of T.S. Eliot, Wallace Stevens, and Ezra Pound if, in their poetry, they had been as honest as Paul Blackburn about their sexual relationship to themselves and to their women and wives. The poetry of Blackburn represents a kind of halfway house in regard to the extent of the thrust into his fantasy life and the extent to which he was able to excavate the kind of ore that is precious to those of us who continue to believe, as has been attributed to Marx, that anything human is not alien.

It would be appropriate to evaluate Paul Blackburn's poetry in the company of his own entire generation—not just the haphazardly-identified "Black Mountain" associates (Levertov, Dorn, Creeley, Oppenheimer etc)—but of those American poets born between 1923 and 1929, who began to make their mark in the mid- to late-50s. In this sense Blackburn's company would also include Dickey, Simpson, Koch, Ammons, Merrill, Ginsberg, O'Hara, Bly, Ashbery, Merwin, Wright, Spicer, Levine, Sexton, and Rich. I would say that with the possible exceptions of Ginsberg, Ashbery, O'Hara, and Rich that Blackburn is a match for any of these poets, and were a reader to assemble the best 100 pages of each of them, and do a comparative reading, that Blackburn's 100 pages would be definitive and unique, an original energy that is not elsewhere duplicated or backgrounded e.g., he is not the lesser example of any other poet, his best work is not secondary. Here, for whatever it is worth, is a list of the poems by which I feel he should be centrally identified:

The Birds
The Lanner
The Search
Pancho Villa…
Bañalbufar…
Plaza Real with Palm Trees
El Camino Verde
The Letter
Ramas, Divendres…
Alaméda

Affinities II
Atardecer
El Día Viene…
Brooklyn Narcissus
Hot Afternoons have been…
The Purse-Seine
Definition
The Net of Place

The Sea and the Shadow
The One Night Stand…
Ritual I
The Mint Quality
Bryant Park
Phone Call to Rutherford
Crank It Up…
This Is Not the Same…
Pre-Lenten Gestures
#1, 7, and 17 from The Selection of Heaven
The Watchers
Here They Go
At the Well
Call It the Net
Faces I
Sunflower Rock
The Voices, It's Cheap
The Touch

*

Between the years 1959 and 1966, Paul Blackburn and I had an active personal as well as literary friendship, much of which took place while he was in New York City and I was in Kyoto, Japan. Kyoto, in the early to mid-60s, was a kind of mecca for a small group of American writers and artists, including Gary Snyder, Joanne Kyger, Cid Corman, Will Petersen, Frank Samperi, Philip Whalen, with occasional visits by Alan Watts and Allen Ginsberg. Paul seemed to notice that our presence there represented a new alternative to Paris as a base where foreign materials could be drawn into American art.

In his poetry as well as in his correspondence, I seemed to be on Paul's mind more than the other Kyoto Americans, and some of the gifts I sent him (in particular, a *happi* coat mentioned in "Doubles: It's a Cabin" which he wore until it disintegrated) turned up in poems, as well as news from my daily life. A tape on which I described the images tacked upon the wall over my work area, along with a reading of Hart Crane's "The Harbor Dawn," led to Section 5 of "The Selection of Heaven," and material describing workmen in the ravine (behind the downstairs area of the Okumura house where we lived in 1962) warming their hands over fires they had built in oil-drums stimulated Paul to bring noticings of similar scenes in New York City into "Ritual IX: Gathering Winter Fuel." The conjunctions of hands and fire was also symbolically worked into "Crank It Up For All Of Us…," one of the poems Paul read on a 1963 tape sent to Kyoto that stunned me and consequently help me break through a block that had paralyzed me for over a year.[5] His last mention of Kyoto appears to have been in the "24 . II . 64 / Note to Kyoto," in which he expressed the age-old spring desire to get roving again, in his own case to leap back to Paris and Barcelona.

Paul was a loyal and comradely correspondent during these years, exactly the kind of slightly older friend that a young uncertain poet needs—not a mentor, let alone a master, but someone with a little more life and literary experience who is willing to set forth his views and let the younger person make of them what he can.

Paul was the first person to make me aware to what extent my creative blocks had to do with a swelling up of unassimilated childhood material, and of the extent to which participating in a full present life had to do with working through such material. In 1963 he married his second wife, Sara Golden, and spontaneously I started to write a poem celebrating their marriage. As I worked away on it, the problems in my own first marriage tore through

5 There is a more complete description of the effect of this poem on me in my essay, "The Gull Wall," most recently reprinted in *The Grindstone of Rapport: A Clayton Eshleman Reader,* Black Widow Press, Boston, 2008.

the fabric, so I set the Blackburn poem aside and tried to concentrate on my own difficulties, into which churned so much materialfrom the past that before I knew it I was working on a poem that attempted to bring my past life to bear on all that had happened to me since I had started writing poetry and come to Kyoto. This still unpublished four hundred page poem, "The Tsuruginomiya Regeneration," was used as a quarry for the some of the sections in *Coils,* published by Black Sparrow Press in 1973.

It has now been over fifteen years since Paul's death, and not a week has gone by that I have not thought of him. It seems on one level that the fate of our friendship was in the stars, that we were to be magnetized and then demagnetized by currents that rose up through us. Our closest years took place continents apart and appeared to be balanced not only on the age difference (nine years) but on my youthful and Paul's more mature uncertainties. This incongruity was very workable when we were apart, but when I moved to New York City in the summer of 1966 and started the groundwork for the life that I have been building ever since, while Paul, from about 1963 on, seemed to be losing his grip on much that was dearest to him, the vectors of our drawing apart were set in motion. I was not invited to dinner at the Blackburns during the entire first year of my separation from Barbara Eshleman. During the summer of 1967, Sara had an affair with Hunter Thompson while she and Paul were in Aspen, Colorado. Sara returned to New York City before Paul did and begged me not to tell him when he returned where she was living because she was afraid that he would physically attack her. When Paul did return, with a broken arm from a bicycle accident, I told him that I did not know where she was living, and he decided that this meant that I had had an affair with her myself (which I had not). I probably did the wrong thing by not telling him, since my primary loyalty was to Paul and not to Sara. This misunderstanding nearly destroyed our friendship and while I continued to see Paul from time to time in the late 1960s our relationship was that of acquaintances, not friends.

Cutting through how we felt about each other was how we felt about ourselves as men and as writers in a world that never lets us take anything for granted. Thinking about Paul now makes me realize how tough, how nigh impossible it is, for American artists of different generations to have lifelong friendships.

1987

[This essay appeared on Tributary *blog in 2011.]*

"As if they just rolled out of bed and started writing." Wouldn't it be amazing if they could—on the class-room floor, in pajamas, a kind of finger-painting, the rush of colors right before waking...

But no, as novices, we have to drag in elaborate machinery, different-sized vises, and then to find someone—a Vallejo in my case—who will screw the jaws tight. At the high noon of apprenticehood, we look ridiculous, a Rube Goldberg crucifixion ("I'm only playing," we believe the vise-tightener will say—but consider the faces on Bosch's mockers surrounding Christ).

Those jaws—our shackle suits? Our irons are: we need to reach impediment to call upon the strength to move, to discover just how much we want to move. What, if any, are our resources?

In a decade most of us will be stacked around Stonehenge, bales of barbed-wire. Something to protect ruins.

But for now: "My name is not Houdini—nor Samson. My name is, if the tightenings are right, and my strength mental—my name has not been done before. I am the first poet to pull clichés from his body like leeches, to transform chains into unfilled-in blanks, to realize that the vise-tightener is not merely myself nor a master other, but my desire for imagination, which I begged to move."

If it did, it approached the novice as what he was not, with the marked-up map face of an Auden. "Then Los embraced his Spectre," as if the crucified apprentice is one so deeply in love he never disentangles. There he is, on any corner, giant scorpion jaws half-closed about his head, his helmet, or herohood, out of which he is peering at a gash of autumn, his dictionary lavishly open in his arms, a thin, reddish *carotene* river, "as near to you," the scorpion hisses, "as the Styx."

1988

LEON GOLUB AT BARBARA GLADSTONE

Four large (120 x 150") paintings that are a breathtaking imaginative advance on Golub's body of work. The strongest of the four—"Blue Sphinx"—is a masterpiece. I will describe it in detail after explaining what I mean by an "advance."

In the early 1950s, Golub began to paint sphinxes, a few of which can be seen in reproduction in the Donald Kuspit monograph (*Leon Golub: Existential / Activist Painter,* Rutgers University Press, 1985). While a few of these sphinxes are lovely muse-like female creatures (the poet Jack Hirschman reproduced one on the cover of his first book, *A Correspondence of Americans,* Indiana University Press, 1960), most of them, in Golub's context, have lost their Greek mythological referentiality, and are symbolic of Golub's struggle to emerge as an artist with his own vision of man. For example, in "Siamese Sphinx I" (1954), a head placed over the animal's rump seems to be excrementally twisting its way out, while the frontal head grimaces at the viewer as if it were giving birth.

The other Golubian image to keep in mind while contemplating these new paintings is that of the mercenary, the principle "character" in the large, dramatic paintings which emerged in the late 1970s (e.g., "Mercenaries I," 1979). In contrast to the sphinxes (and Gigantomachies of the 1960s), the mercenaries locked Golub's art into our time. In such paintings as "Interrogation II" (1981), Golub depicts torturers at their work who appear to be aware that we are watching them. So, slightly larger than we are, they turn to us and wink or give us the finger, as if we were a clientele watching chefs in a see-into kitchen prepare our dinner. The interplay that Golub establishes in such paintings is rich with psychological entrances and exits—lubricious, intransigent, and condemnational. Donald Kuspit has called "Interrogation III" (1981), in which two mercs are torturing a bound and blindfolded naked woman, "the greatest feminist picture ever made by a man."

The mercenary has become for Golub a kind of keyhole through which to view scenes from Salvador, South Africa, and, in this current show I think one could argue, the streets of New York City. I didn't take notes while I was at the show, so other than "Blue Sphinx" (a b/w of which I requested from the gallery), I am writing from memory. One painting is a slashing rush of men dashed by an over-painting that evokes rainy street neon glare. The other three paintings frame single figures, all "sphinxes:" "Yellow Sphinx," Wounded Sphinx," and "Blue Sphinx." In all of these there is a rush of color, neither representational nor austere, that is quite surprising, even lush. For people who only became aware of Golub in the early 1980s, after the Susan Caldwell show attracted so much attention, I would guess that this almost gorgeous effusion of color would seem bizarre, or at least hard to contextualize. For those of us who have followed Golub's careers from the 1950s on, such color can represent a bringing forth of sensual display that has been prefigured and touched upon from the beginning.

"Blue Sphinx," as I said, is the kingpin of the show. If you keep in mind what I said about Golub's sphinxes and mercenaries, you will be able to follow the move he has made with both of these previous figures. To put it simply, a merc head has been soldered to a sphinx body. I write "soldered," as there is an intentional lack of harmony, no blending, between the two, and both merc and sphinx have gone through subtle transformations in the constructing of this new image. The merc head is that of an anguished military man—and it is painted in a lurid whitish green that evokes a deadly disease lit up from within. The animal body is more that of a dog than of a mythological creature, with an unusually long and powerful right foreleg/forearm that juts toward the viewer (recalling the executioner's arm pressed vertically down on the neck of Saint John the Baptist in Caravaggio's "The Beheading of Saint John the Baptist"). The "dog man" is crouched somewhat like a line-man right before the ball is snapped in a football formation—at the same time, "he" seems to be slightly rearing back, in alarm at our seeing him—or is this an illusion, based on the asymmetrical tension in the figure? Some horizontal strokes suggest a ground, or street, and to the right, so blurred as to seem mostly erased, is a Greek column, with a support that cuts back behind the figure. This is what is left of the Greek vision today? Hard to know, for the glaring, slippery blue background, highlighted by smears of white, evokes Manhattan, a wet neon street scene at night, with perhaps the East River behind the figure.

The "Blue Sphinx" is also the 1988 street person, living as an animal might, stripped of the outward indications of humanity, yet poised, with ferocious animal body, defying us. And the "Blue Sphinx" is also the merc come home to roost, as if what he represents (an up-dated version of the Japanese "ronin," or "wave man," a masterless samurai warrior tramp with day-to-day allegiances, going with the flow) has now imagistically joined with the homeless, suggesting that what American society has pushed out onto the street is no longer the traditional bum or beggar, but a force that is rippling with poisonous power. On another level, one can propose that "Blue Sphinx" is a vision of our exported rapacity now beginning to loom in the faces of our own street people. The fear and anxiety in the sphinx's face mirrors my own anguish as I contemplate America's unexpressed grief in the targeted and resonantly backgrounded image the painting presents.

1988, Cover magazine

There is a poem based on this painting in Anticline, *Black Widow Press, 2010.*

NOTICINGS 1

Like most readers I read new and older books together, often relative to my own research projects. What follows is a very heterogeneous list of recent books and slightly older ones that I've read with interest over the past six months.

Re: Upper Paleolithic research (an ongoing project over the past decade): Hans Peter Duerr's *Dreamtime (Concerning the Boundary between Wilderness and Civilization),* Blackwell, 1987, is packed with up-to-date information on the flights, potions, and intentions of the shamans and witches who cross back and forth between boundaries. Duerr, a kind of scholar-Castaneda, provides a well-written (and translated, by Felicitas Goodman) 139 page text, accompanied by 231 pages of footnotes, and an 86 page bibliography. The book is best read by having two copies open side by side, so one can shuttle back and forth between text and notes. While in the Dordogne this June, I picked up a copy of Lya Dams' *Les Peintures Rupestres du Levant Espagñol* (Paris, Picard, 1984), which appears to be the first illustrated survey of decorated Spanish rock shelters, over 200 of which have been discovered with nearly 8000 paintings. Robert McCully's *Jung and Rorschach* (Spring, 1987) applies Jungian ideas to Rorschach's plates by examining Upper Paleolithic images and also includes an appendix on Adolf Eichmann's Rorschach protocol.

Wolfgang Giegerich's essay, "The Nuclear Bomb and the Fate of God" (Spring Annual, 1985), led me to James Hillman's "Wars, Arms, Rams, Mars: On the Love of War" (*Facing Apocalypse,* Spring, 1987), which led me to Richard Rhodes' *The Making of the Atomic Bomb* (Simon and Schuster, 1986), a well-written history of the development of the bomb, which is also a chronicle of the development of physics in the first half of the century. Here is Rhodes' description of the first explosion, at Trinity, July 16, 1945:

> Time: 05:29:45. The firing circuit closed; the X-unit discharged; detonators at thirty-two detonation points simultaneously fire; they ignited the outer lens shells of Composition B; the detonation waves separately bulged, encountered inclusions of Baratol, slowed, curved, turned inside out, merged to a common inward-driving sphere; the spherical detonation wave crossed into the second shell of solid fast Composition B and accelerated; hit the wall of dense uranium tamper and became a shock wave and squeezed, liquefying, moving through; hit the nickel plating of the plutonium core and squeezed, the small sphere shrinking, collapsing into itself, becoming an eyeball; the shock wave reaching the tiny initiator at the center and swirling through its designed irregularities to mix its beryllium and polonium; polonium alphas kicking neutrons free from scant atoms to beryllium: one, two, seven, nine, hardly more neutrons drilling into the surrounding plutonium to start the chain reaction. Then fission multiplying its prodigious energy release through eighty generations in millionths of a second, tens of millions of degrees, millions of pounds of pressure. Before the radiation leaked away, conditions within the eyeball briefly resembled the state of the universe moments after its first primordial explosion.

While I am uncomfortable with the ramifications of her argument, I found Andrea Dworkin's *Pornography (Men Possessing Women),* A Perigee Book, 1981, compelling and powerfully written; Dworkin is capable of a muscular, fugal prose that lifts its argument like laminated layers before the reader's eyes. And although I enjoyed Barbara G. Walker's *The Skeptical Feminist* (Harper & Row, 1987), especially the chapter "Kali Ma," I found it a much lesser work than her monumental *The Woman's Encyclopedia of Myths and Secrets* (Harper & Row, 1987), which is the first encyclopedia I have read straight through, at "thriller" pitch. Recalling her information-packed pages on "Menstruation," reminds me that Grove Press is doing an American edition of Penelope Shuttle and Peter Redgrove's *The Wise Wound (Myths, Realities, and Meanings of Menstruation)* this fall. This wonderful book first appeared in England in 1978 and has been more or less unavailable for the past seven years.

Many *Sulfur* readers are familiar with Charles Olson's *Letters for Origin,* published in 1969, which contains an edited but representative portion of his letters to Cid Corman, from 1950 to 1956. Now we have Volume I of *Charles Olson & Cid Corman: The Complete Correspondence, 1950-1964* (National Poetry Foundation, 1987), edited and annotated by George Evans. It is a terrific correspondence, as engaging as the Olson/Dahlberg correspondence (which we ran in *Sulfur*s #1–3), but with Olson in the role of mentor this time, roaring at young Cid Corman, as, partially via Olson's vision of culture, Corman edits the first series of origin magazine.

Sulfur readers who enjoyed the sections of Clark Coolidge's "Book of During" (in numbers 14, 16, and 17), will probably also admire *Mesh* (In Camera, 1988), the improvisational movement of which is, like the earlier prose work, solidly soldered to Eros. The two poems of August Kleinzahler in *Sulfur* #20 are collected in a handsome little book, *On Johnny's Time* (Pig Press, Durham, England, 1988), with a cover photo by Ben Watkins (whose work appeared in our #22). Gustaf Sobin's *Voyaging Portraits* (New Directions, 1988) seems to me to be his finest collection; Sobin's word placements, visually and aurally, are masterful, and for those interested in reading about his work, Paul Christensen has published two first-rate essays on Sobin in *Parnassus* #14 and *Temblor* #7. There is at last a new translation of Lorcas's *Poet in New York* (Farrar Straus Giroux, 1988), by Greg Simon and Steven F. White, and while it is not encumbered with rhetorical improvisation, as was Ben Bellit's earlier version, it still is not the version that many of us have hoped would be done. The opening line of the opening poems—"Cut down by the sky" for "Asesinado por el cielo"—carries in nucleus the timidity and off-centeredness of the translation. I cannot evaluate the quality of the translations in regard to Janos

Pilinszky's *Crater* (London, Anvil Press, 1978) or Tomaž Šalamun's *Selected Poems* (Ecco Press, 1988), but I am thinking that *Sulfur* readers who were engaged by our Hungarian section in #21 would find both Pilinszky (a Hungarian who died in the late 1970s) and Šalamun (a Yugoslavian, very much alive) of interest. Pilinszky, translated by Peter Jay, is bone dry but with the odd fits of black humor that are part of the uniqueness of the Slavic imagination. Šalamun, translated by a number of people but mainly by Charles Simic, is superficially the opposite of Pilinszky—but his wryness and sensual humor is larded, at it were, with bleakness and desperation.

Lastly, I heartily recommend *A Kayak Full of Ghosts* (Capra, 1987), Eskimo tales gathered and retold by Lawrence Millman, whose little introduction is a gem. Gruesome, beautiful, violent, and scatological, these tales propose, in effect, an Eskimo Grotesque. Here is "Arviaq and the Worm:"

> There once was a woman named Arviaq who could not get with child. Her husband was a short little man with no strength in his loins. He told Arviaq: "If you want to be a mother, go find yourself a worm. They're much nicer than children, anyway." And so Arviaq found a worm and placed it against her breast as if it were a little child. She nursed it until she ran out of milk and then she nursed it under her armpits. Soon the worm began to grow large. And the larger it grew, the thinner Arviaq became. All her blood was flowing into her offspring. And all her love too—often she would spend the whole day at home, fondling and kissing the worm. At last it was large enough to crawl around the village. This did not make people very happy, because it had sharp teeth and a rather unpleasant disposition. One day the head-man and a few others took their knives to it. Spurts of blood as high as a house shot up from its body and the worm shriveled back to its orig-

inal size. Poor Arviaq watched all of this and afterwards beat her head against a rock, crying: "My dear little child, my dear little child."

Told by Ib Brodersden, seal hunter,
Angmagssalik, East Greenland.

Sulfur #23, 1988

CALL WHO ISHMAEL?

A painter friend of mine, Irving Petlin, once came up with the following book idea: write to a wide range of writers and artists and ask: at whose door did you knock after you decided you wanted to be an artist? What were the consequences of your having knocked?

In August, 1936, the twenty-six year old Charles Olson knocked on thirty-six year old Edward Dahlberg's boarding house door in East Gloucester, and because of a misunderstanding was kept waiting for several hours before Dahlberg brought him in. This initial mix-up is, in hindsight, darkly prophetic of their twenty-year mentor/apprenticeship relationship, and has led to a book[1] that in my opinion every young writer should memorize in his bones. This correspondence makes me wonder if there is any way to get around this rite of passage that says, in effect, if you think you survived the father/son struggle, think again: in its revival, your future as an artist and as a man is at stake.

Relatively compact, at 230 pages, the correspondence does not include all the letters the two men wrote each other (more of Dahlberg's letters survive than Olson's), but no matter: as is, it is a harrowing record of the psychodynamic drama in which an older artist believes he enables a younger one to give birth to an immortal work which will change the latter's life but in some crucial ways always remain the property of the mentor. Because of this "gift," the two can never become equals, even if the apprentice demonstrates that he has become his own master. Why? Because the demonstration of such mastery will inevitably, for the older figure, represent a betrayal of what he stands for. Furthermore, for the

1 *In Love, In Sorrow: The Complete Correspondence of Charles Olson and Edward Dahlberg,* edited with an Introduction by Paul Christensen, Paragon House, NYC, 1990. This review appeared in an issue of the *AWP Writers Chronicle* the same year. Concerning knocking on doors: see the first of my "Three New York Stories" in this collection.

apprentice to become his own person, he will have to thwart the mentor by denying him the right to continue to exert power over his soul. Since Olson and Dahlberg are both major mid-century authors (who do their finest work[2] after the collapse of their relationship), it is especially fascinating to enter their labyrinth in which each man, at various points, plays the role of Ariadne, Theseus, and the Minotaur.

The story is essentially tied to two books: Olson's *Call Me Ishmael* (1947) and Dahlberg's *The Flea of Sodom* (1950). Joined by a common enthusiasm for Melville (who hovers over the drama like a great atavistic spirit), both men first came into conflict over Dahlberg's stylistic domination of Olson's first version of his book on Melville. In 1940, Olson stopped writing altogether for several years because he could not yet subordinate Dahlberg's influence to his own vision and language. He returned to the project in 1945, quickly reworked the manuscript (without any contact with Dahlberg), and might very well have never been involved with Dahlberg again had not the latter written him an apparently congratulatory letter upon discovering the book's publication. Near the end of this letter is the following remark: "I am, as you know, an Ishmael in solitude." What this will turn out to mean is: not only did I give you everything that is good and true in *Call Me Ishmael,* but I am more deserving to be called Ishmael than you are, Charles, and thus in a double sense the book and its title are mine.

Edward Dahlberg's letter is dated April 9th. Eight days later (Olson having not yet responded), Dahlberg writes one of the most outrageous letters I have ever read. Because Olson has not immediately thanked his benefactor, he is guilty of "churlish silence," of "becoming dainty and effeminate about [his] time."

---

2 Dahlberg's masterpiece is *Because I Was Flesh* (New Directions, 1966). While a number of his books are out of print, a fine introduction to his essay style is *The Leafless American,* reprinted by McPherson & Co., 1986. Olson's two essential books are *The Maximus Poems* and *The Collected Poems,* both published by University of California Press.

While Dahlberg boasts of having "word-flogged" Charles Olson into rewriting the book (there is no evidence of this), of having taken Olson "unto [his] identity," Olson is accused of being "perverse," of having "sinned against [his] nature," of possessing a silence "brewed in that foss and marsh where muddy and defiled shadows abide," of having "spilled [his] spirit like the defiled seed of Onan," and of being bound up in "Sodomy… and the ache for a united Babel of the world." Claiming to be the true author of the book, Dahlberg implies that he has, at the same time, inseminated a feminine Charles Olson and (via such anal sadistic images of the muddy foss) buggered a masculine version of the same person. This is clearly a non-win situation for Olson (who has elaborately dedicated a crucial chapter of *Ishmael* to Dahlberg), and it is amazing to me that he doesn't tell Dahlberg off and have done with him. It is only after a second lambasting from Dahlberg four days later (in which Olson is accused of "harboring in [his] intestines, the Laodicean serpent that hungers for the Jew's liver") that Olson somewhat stiffly manages an indignant reply. Dahlberg then cries out that he has been reviled ("Why do you revile my sputum?"). Strangely enough, while Dahlberg continues to complain, attack and fabricate endless chains of homophobic, Biblical-layered, uroboric images, Olson stays interested and takes the beatings.[3]

Within the year, what will turn out to be the reversal (and ultimately the end) of the correspondence is set in motion: Dahlberg writes to Olson that he has completed "a small volume about the size of Ishmael." This is *The Flea of Sodom,* which Olson will

3 I wonder: had Olson cut himself loose from Dahlberg after the initial irrational attacks, might he not have handled Cid Corman as roughly as he did in their correspondence? Corman subsequently wrote a number of arrogant and demeaning letters to me (as well as to many others). I dealt with this situation by turning Corman into a character in my poetry and had my way with him there. See my essay honoring Corman's positive effects on my life and work, "What Brought You Here Will Take You Hence," in *Archaic Design,* Black Widow Press, 2007.

initially praise privately but finally refuse to publicly address. Desperate for attention in general, and, in particular, for a confirmation of the book's hatred for America (and one could almost say, for life at large), which he knows Olson opposes, Dahlberg crams their entire relationship into this single monolithic demand that Olson must publish a review of the book. As Dahlberg in letter after letter ornately and baldly pleads for a public response, we feel Olson weighing the book's merits and faults and via elaborately stated procrastinations extricating himself from Dahlberg's power. He finally states that he opposes Dahlberg's doctrine, which he describes as a "personally-contrived hell."

In Edward Dahlberg, phobias, self-pity, rhetorical power, pessimism, and mythology are so richly fused that getting letters from him at this time must have been like opening your front door to find the ocean pouring waist-high into the house. Has any other writer ever so elaborately surrounded another with pleas for attention as in the following:

> So if you will not do the critique, but insist on interring the book in some Sidonian mound near the marge of Pillars, where mariners take their dories with lamentation and trembling, going first ashore to pour libations to the Nereids and to offer prayers to the Trident, the Serpent of Sais, and to Poseidon who blesses the oar, before passing through the Gates to noxious Lethe, then may you in a moment of blasphemous inattention write a lettuce eunuch adjective like Waldo Frank! But after this torment, may you then return to King Aeolus, to the source of the WINDS; for there the MUSES chant, as they sit on the purple kelp, and heed the lowing of the sea-calves going to their oceanic stalls; and after you have composed a perfect quatrain, may you then admit that a friend buries his friend with the same myrtle, cypress, and Plutonian spade and implements as his enemies.

Under the coiling of such sentences is an impossible situation: Edward Dahlberg wants you to feel sorry for him while he beats you up. Thus Charles Olson, who is capable of formidable, rhetorical prose,[4] is always kept on the defensive, and it is perhaps that kind of relentless curtailment that ultimately weans him from Dahlberg. In this correspondence, he comes off as the lesser writer of the two, but as I suggest above, he never has a chance to show his stuff as Dahlberg is simply not interested in Olson *as himself.* In fact, he trashes Olson's first collection of poetry as infected by Pound (thus compounding Olson's son-ship: I am the author of your prose; Pound is the author of your poetry), and ceaselessly praises and repraises *Ishmael.* After a several year hiatus in the early 1950s, Dahlberg picks up the correspondence, ostensibly to help Olson get published, but fundamentally to dump old issues on him again. The final handful of letters read like ponderous, black soliloquys, neither man even hearing the other any more. Dahlberg has the last word, ending the final letters, "in love and in sorrow," from whence the title of this collection.

Paul Christensen's twenty-page introduction is first-rate, and written out of a complex and knowledgable feeling for both men; it is so good, in fact, that it really introduces the reader to Dahlberg and Olson as writers. I find Christensen's handling of footnotes, however, problematic. Given the incompleteness of the correspondence, there are many gaps and references that need annota-

4 For Olson in full-flight as correspondent, look into the nine published volumes of the *Charles Olson/Robert Creeley Correspondence,* published by Black Sparrow Press, or into Volume 1 of the *Olson/Cid Corman Correspondence,* published by the National Poetry Foundation. For Olson essays, see *Human Universe* (Grove Press, 1967). There is a small section of Dahlberg letters to various correspondents in *The Edward Dahlberg Reader* (New Directions, 1967). Dahlberg's extensive correspondence with William Carlos Williams and Alfred Stieglitz (at Yale) has never been published.

tion (George Butterick's handling of the Olson/Creeley correspondence comes to mind here). Christensen injects some information into the text between brackets and leaves other things out.

Regardless of this, the book is a dark gem, and for this reader at least opened up the psychosexual abyss that is generated in such relationships. Maybe the novice would do better to restrict his apprenticeship to the great dead, who cannot write letters to him or ask for anything in return. But the great dead are no picnic either. Psychosexually, such exchanges take place in cemeteries and pantheons. As we pry open the tombs of the Olsons and Dahlbergs, Kali Ma hides in the bushes with her cups, gongs, and cleavers, licking her lips. She can hardly wait for the evening raga to begin, six feet under.

[*AWP Chronicle,* 1991, with minor revisions]

NOTICINGS 2

First off, congratulations to Keith and Rosmarie Waldrop, of Burning Deck, who, with the publication of Barbara Guest's *The Countess from Minneapolis* and Julie Kalendek's *The Fundamental Difference,* have completed their third decade of publishing hand-printed contemporary poetry. How many books must they have published? 300? Given the fact that both editors have full careers as poets and translators, this publishing service to the community of poetry is truly extraordinary. In every generation, there are a handful of people who make the transmission of poetry possible—as Michel Palmer has written: "without Burning Deck and a very few others, experimental poetry would, simply, not exist."

In *The Discovery of the Art of the Insane,* John M. MacGregor has written the first history of the art of the insane in English, beginning with a discussion of the situation of the mentally ill in the 1700s, as well as the later Romantic obsession with the insane as visionary heroes (which we still honor, without yet understanding much about it). MacGregor's well-researched work (studded with amazing paintings and drawings, and handsomely produced by Princeton University Press) moves through Surrealism (some astute distinctions between Artaud and Dali, for example), Jean Dubuffet and Art Brut, which over the past couple decades has broadened into Outsider Art. I was disappointed to find no work by or discussion of Friedrich Schröder-Sonnenstern, whom Edouard Roditi has championed as one of the greatest of the Surrealists.

Like others of my generation, I first discovered the work of Norman O. Brown in the mid-1960s, upon the publication of the second book of his now completed trilogy: *Life Against Death* (1959), *Love's Body* (1966), and *Apocalypse and/or Metamorphosis* (University of California Press, 1991). Constellating literature, philosophy, history, psychology, and politics, Brown is our greatest living theorist, a writer of the same amplitude, if different directions, as Arnold Hauser and Northrop Frye. Brown's break with the discursive, systematic form of *Life Against Death* in *Love's Body* indicated that he had found a way to practice "poetry" as "the scholar's art" (Wallace Stevens). In that book, subject-oriented chapters ("Liberty," "Trinity," "Nature," etc) processed facets of an ongoing argument as it passed through their domains, in quote-packed stanza-like paragraphs. *Love's Body* moves as poetic intuition, with precise, analytic cores rippling out, fusing and/or interlacing, so that realized feedback and Brown's own insights braid into a multi-currented serial structure. With the new book, the trilogy looks like Brown's "divine comedy," in which *Apocalypse and/or Metamorphosis,* utilizing styles and formats from both previous volumes, becomes a kind of thinking man's paradise. Brown's brief reply to Herbert Marcuse's critique of *Love's Body,* in the March 1967 *Commentary,* deserves to be reprinted (along with other uncollected talks, notes, and essays). Here is a paragraph from it:

> From politics to poetry. Legislation is not politics, nor philosophy, but poetry. Poetry, art, is not an epiphenomenal reflection of some other (political, economic) realm which is the "real thing": nor a sublimation of something else which is the "real," carnal "act." Poetry, art, imagination, the creator spirit is life itself; the real revolutionary power to change the world; and to change the human body. To change the human body: here is the crisis, *hic Rhodus, hic salta;* which, as Hegël said, is to be translated "here is the Rose, here begin to dance." To begin to dance, who can tell the dancer from the dance; it is the impossible unity and union of everything.

If Brown was a major discovery of the 1960s, Weston LaBarre's *The Ghost Dance* (recommended by Gary Snyder for its chaper on Upper Paleolithic cave art) was a similar largesse in the mid-1970s. In 1985, LaBarre (born two years earlier than Brown, in 1911) published a kind of annex to the 676 page *The Ghost Dance,* called *Muelos: A Stone Age Superstition about Sexuality* (Columbia University Press—I recently discovered the book in a discount catalog). In 140 pages, LaBarre tracks the longevity and ramification of this superstition from the oldest rituals we are aware of, in the Upper Paleolithic, through Christian, Renaissance, and Victorian history. He summarizes this complex in the following way:

> Bones are given by the male parent, and bones can magically reconstitute the whole animal. As the main storehouse of bone marrow, the brain is the source of semen, via the spinal cord. The supply is limited. The fertility of the head is assimilated to cosmic fertility of the sun, rain, lightning. Fire, light, lightning, and seed are all aspects of the same holy male mystery. The fertility of humans, wild animals, and fields can be increased by collecting severed human heads. Fat-marrow and bones are appropriate sacrifice to the immortal spirits, the eternal gods. Immortality also consists in the "continence" of the muelos-seed, achieved in various ways. Adult manhood is not the result of endogenous forces but must be obtained form outside through a variety of methods, including homosexual acts. Virility is secreted with semen, in all ejaculation of whatever kind; virility can thus on occasion be made a gift. Loss of manhood, power, and ultimately life itself results from the "spending" of the life-force, which is a finite capital.

Like the Waldrops, Cid Corman has served the community of poetry, as publisher, editor, and translator, for some 40 years. Here I will only touch on some of his contributions before passing on to what might be the most unusual "selected poems" ever assembled. Corman started *origin* magazine in 1951, and was the first to offer a significant amount of pages to Olson, Creeley, Bronk, and Zukofsky, to name four of the now major figures who, when they appeared in *origin,* were hardly published elsewhere. Corman is also an odyssean letter writer (his response to a letter seemed to arrive within hours of the letter being mailed), and his correspondence with Olson, like Olson's with Dahlberg, is a dark spectacle of mentor/apprentice strife. *Origin* has appeared in four series, a total of 74 issues, spanning (with some breaks) thirty-one years. The first two series (34 issues) are brilliantly edited and taught me how to edit a literary magazine. The last two series are less formidable, as over the years Corman has narrowed and purified his view of what is significant in American poetry (he has always been more open to the new, the experimental, in foreign poetries).

Corman is also one of the great translators of our times. His work with Kamaike Susumu on Bashō achieved the finest translation ever done of haiku poetry (*Back Roads to Far Towns*, Mushinsha-Grossman, 1967, now a White Pine Press reprint). He was one of the first, or *the* first, to translate and publish translations of Artaud, Celan, Sanesi, Scotellaro, du Bouchet, Daumal, Daive, Ponge, Jaccottet, and Kusano Shimpei. He has also done many pages of Montale (they are superb), Char, Perse, Dadelsen, Hitomaro, Chuang-Tzu, and recently Phillippe Denis. While there is an understandable variation in quality, the over-all quality is as high as any poet-translator of this century. In many instances, Corman's versions are the only ones available—though "available" must be qualified, as many of his translations remain in issues of *origin* (which had a print run of 300 copies per issue). Someone, obviously, should do a 500 page Corman Selected Translations. What a gift this would be for a young American poet.

Corman's career as a poet is more difficult for me to assess. Over the past forty years he has published more than sixty collections, many of them quite tiny, with only a few (such as *Sun Rock Man* and *Livingdying*, both New Directions books) widely distributed. Under these conditions, Lapis Press's 1990 boxed two-volume *Of*, beautifully produced with bold calligraphy by Sam Francis, is certainly welcome. It comes to 1500 pages, and one opens it expecting to find a lifetime's work. It turns out that *Of* represents a selection from, roughly, the first two-fifths of Corman's career. I say "roughly" as one must guess: there is no chronological or previous publication information offered. As an old Corman reader I know that many of the poems have appeared before, some in *origin,* and some in contexts—Corman's years in Matera, Italy, for example, the subject of *Sun Rock Man*—that are damaged when excerpted from, especially when the poems are not identified as a being from an earlier book.

For a first time reader, the presentation must be baffling. Each volume contains five sections (based, I believe, on Noh play categories), and each begins with a cluster of translations (fragments as well as entire poems), out of which Corman's own poetry appears to rise (clouds of dust on the horizon, out of which a single rider is seen). The relation of author to author's translated texts is shockingly complicated by the fact that all of the translations are treated as Corman poems—at no point are Homer, Sophocles, Catullus, Tao Ch'ien, Villon, Rimbaud, Mallarmé. Bashō, Rilke, Ungaretti, Char, Montale, Celan, Artaud, Scotellaro, and Lorine Niedecker (!) identified as original authors (and these are just the ones I noticed—I am sure there are more). Wanting to be fair in bringing this matter up in a review, I wrote Corman. Since his response is pretty astonishing, I will quote it at length:

> When Sam Francis first called me, from Tokyo, almost exactly 4 years ago—the first words were: "Cid—I want to do all your work!" And my reply, pronto: "Sam—you don't know what you're saying: I'm the most productive poet in human history (the fact)." Anyway it prompted *Of*: which was never, despite catalogue, given out as a "selected poems"—tho any book of mine cd be called that. ALL my books are edited with a care, unique I suspect, in the annals of poetry. It took me 6 years to EDIT: SUN ROCK MAN. But when I did Volume 1—even before I completed it—I realized it had to be 2 volumes—and then when I had done the 2—and Sam was mulling the printing of them—slowly—I realized the book (ONE BOOK) had to be 5 volumes. And that's what it will be. (No PATERSON or MAX or CANTOS biz.) Each volume about the same size, about 750pp. That represents less than one half percent of my work—and that's putting it on the heavy side. (On my

desk—I plan to photograph it in due time—the mss towards the final 3 vols are piled up. If they were in a single pile they wd reach literally from the desktop to the ceiling of this room. Jap. ceilings, as you know, aint very high. 1000s of poems. And those represent already a culling. From which the 3 vols. will come.)

The work will have covered, in effect, some 50 years of writing. And the book works in ways that are unique. Despite the ultimate 3500pp—the book reads, as you can already see, "easily" (my poems, of course, tending to be short). And even a child wd find much pleasure. Once you have read thru—got the feel of how it goes—you can open anywhere and read backwards or forwards. The opening sections are always Others' work. This is equally true of earlier books of mine— though very few seem to notice… If I had published *Of* (by myself, as I will be doing these final 3 vols) my name wdntve appeared in the book or on it at all (apart from being another character in it: even you are in it). It draws on all literature and everyone I know or have known who has touched me in one way or another: I'm simply (as Blake knew and I think you know) the medium.

Identifications are easy to work out: I give ample cues, when they are not outright. But they are NOT essential. The words are… I'm not testing the reader, or critic: I never test anyone—not my style: I just offer the best I know. In the best way I can. As I've often said: If you can improve any work of mine by changing a single word or comma etc—go to it—and you are free to claim the poem as your own. I can't be stolen from: all is given.

Well. If this "ONE BOOK" of 3500 pages represents less than one half percent of Corman's poetry (over fifty years, going back to before 1940, when Corman was fifteen years old), this puts the total production at over 700,000 pages, or 14,000 a year, or 40 pages a day. If this is so, Corman must not only be the most productive poet in human history—he must also be the first to write non-stop for fifty years, including while eating and asleep. The underside of Corman's claim is of course that no one knows or can know. I wonder if Little Joe Gould is trying to get our attention from the grave…

If Corman does issue the next three volumes anonymously, some of the apparent hubris will be taken care of. However, his justifications don't bear scrutiny. He knows very well that signing one's own name to the work of others was not what Blake had in mind when he wrote that the authors were in eternity. Blake signed his own name to all of the art and writing that he produced. The thought that one would find in a Blake collection, via Corman's logic, poems by Chaucer and Milton presented as Blake's own is unimaginable. Blake meant that he was the medium through which poetry spoke; not the poet who erased other authors' names as their poems passed through the editing into his own book. Corman also evades the issue by offering us the right to change and then claim as our own his (own?) poems. Gee, thanks, Cid—are we to be grateful for this license? He must think we can't write our own poems as he presumably can. As a matter of fact, in publicity copy that Corman offered Lapis Press, he did include his own name and identified the "book" as "poems selected from a lifetime and reaching beyond." Does this mean poems from the other side? Or poems by other poets?

Furthermore, there are no attempts at cues or identifications other than what the contents of the translations themselves offer. Perhaps Corman has in mind letters from Bronk and Samperi that are cut into Corman stanzas/poems and that, at the end, include the original letter-writers' names. Private letters have become objects d'art "of" Cid Corman. What, basically, is the point of a translator usurping authorship? As a matter of fact, I don't think anonymous publication solves this problem. Corman by this act presumes that original author and reader should be unconcerned with who made what art. He wants us to believe that we are egotistic in expecting author identification, and that, in taking all other authors' names off their work, in his book, but his own (or even with his own), that he is not.

Sulfur #29, 1991

VALLEJO'S SUCCULENT SNACK OF UNITY

One of the most striking portraits of César Vallejo comes from the Peruvian novelist Ciro Alegría who was one of Vallejo's students when the young poet worked as a grade-school teacher in Trujillo in 1915. Alegría was only six years old when he first laid eyes on Vallejo:

> César Vallejo—I've always thought that was the first time I saw him—had his hands on the table and his face turned toward the door. Below his abundant black hair, his features showed deep and definite lines. His nose was energetic and his chin, more energetic still, jutted out like a keel. His dark eyes—I don't recall if they were grey or black—shown as if there were tears in them. His suit was old and rumpled, and his white shirt collar was closed by a carelessly-looped little tie. He began to smoke, continuing to look toward the door through which came the bright light of April. He was thinking or dreaming who knows what. From his whole being flowed a great sadness. Never have I seen a man who appeared more sad. His grief was at once secret and visible, and after a while it infected me. A certain strange and inexplicable pain went through me. Though he seemed at peace, there was something deeply ripped apart in this man that I could not understand, but that I felt with the quick, alert sensitivity of a child. Suddenly, I found myself thinking about my birthplace, the mountains I had crossed, the life I had left behind. Studying my teacher's face a little more, I decided that he resembled Cayetano Oruna, a peasant on our hacienda, who was called Cayo. Cayo was taller and more robust, but their faces, both with an expression that was between solemnity and sadness, were very similar. This man Vallejo struck me as a message from the earth. I kept watching him. He put out his cigarette, pressed his fore-

head, ran his fingers through his dark hair and returned to his thoughts. His lips twisted into a painful contraction. Cayo again. But Vallejo's personality was disquieting even just to see. I was very perturbed by then and began to suspect that, from so much suffering and from literally radiating sadness, Vallejo had to have something to do with the mystery of poetry. He turned slightly, looked at me, and we looked at each other. The other students were reading their books, so I opened mine. I couldn't see the words and wanted to cry..."[1]

Young Alegría must be thinking back to a sierra peasant to connect with his mysterious teacher because Vallejo is from the sierra, and in demeanor and manner different from the coastal Peruvian. Vallejo's indigenous situation is complexed by the fact that both of us grandfathers were Jesuit priests from Galicia, Spain, and both of his grandmothers were Chimú Indians. Under his revolutionary warping of the Spanish language, one feels a *cholo* (a person of mixed Spanish and Indian blood) struggling not only with identity but with a resentment against the Spanish language itself, a colonial imposition on an indigenous people. In his first book, *Los heraldos negros* (1918), Vallejo, in fairly conventional verse, had made a few gestures using Inca terms and themes. Such gestures disappear in *Trilce* (to my knowledge there is only one Quechua word in the book), while at the same time Vallejo's indigenous personality becomes more manifest through the atmosphere of sadness, solemnity, and austerity in the poems themselves. The last line of the last poem—"Sing, rain, on the coast still without sea!"—appears to refer to the Peruvian sierra, where there is indeed no sea, but where the awesome mountain ranges may feel "coastal" relative to the Peruvian lowlands, desert, and jungle—areas with considerably differing cultures.

---

1 Alegría's commentary on Vallejo is partially reprinted in the Colección Archivos edition of Vallejo's poetry; the full text can be found in *Cuadernos americanos* 3, No. 6 (November–December 1944): pp. 175-191.

***

Trilce's title is a neologism and the gate guardian of the book. This masterpiece of international modernism has its perilous, heroic predicament embedded in its title, and sewn, via the title, like filaments, into the work itself.

The story goes that Vallejo had originally called the book "Cráneos de bronce" (Bronze Skulls), and had planned to sign it with the pseudonym "César Perú" (perhaps in the spirit of Anatole France). At the last moment, friends convinced him that the pseudonym was a mistake; however, the first pages had already been printed, and the author was told that the cost to reprint them would come to *tres libras,* a small amount, but money he really didn't have. His friend Juan Espejo Asturrizaga recalls: "Vallejo repeated 'tres, tres, tres,' several times, with that insistence he had for repeating and deforming words, 'tresss, triesss, tril, trilsss,' He got tongue-tied, and in the process 'trilsssce' came out… '*trilce*? *trilce*?' He paused for a moment and then exclaimed: 'O.K., it will carry my own name, but the book itself will be called *Trilce*.'"

Other commentators have conjectured that the word was formed by fusing *triste* (sad) with *dulce* (sweet). While there is no reason to believe that Espejo made the story up, I believe that the poems contain internal evidence that attests to the neologism's conceptual status, which is involved with the meaning of the book at large and goes considerably beyond an impulsive deformation of words. In his memoir of Vallejo's Peruvian years, Espejo constantly offers anecdotes and recollections as explanations for the meaning of poems that remain utterly enigmatic in spite of his commentary. His anecdote explaining the origin of the word "*trilce*" is in the same spirit.

A more thoughtful response to the formation of the word was made by Henry Gifford who, with Charles Tomlinson, translated a dozen or so poems from *Trilce* in the early 1970s. Gifford writes: "For '*trilce*,' Vallejo compounded two numerals, *trillon* and *trece,* a trillion and thirteen. A truncated trillion is held prisoner by the ill-chanced and broken thirteen. Or, perhaps, like the arm of the Venus de Milo in another *Trilce* poem, it should be seen rather as uncreated, subject to the 'perennial imperfection' of life."

Gifford does not support his numerical observation with evidence from *Trilce,* but the evidence is there. In an early version of XXXII which appeared in a Lima newspaper in 1921, the last line read:

¡Tres trillones y trece calorías!...

It is possible that at some stage of revising/completing the book, Vallejo spotted the potentially new word in this line, and, pulling the *tril* from the left side of *trillones,* and the *ce* from the right side of *trece,* coined "*trilce.*" And while the *tri-* and the *tre-* of the two words signify "three," it is fascinating to notice what happens to that three, and to the zeros, when *lones* and *tre* are shed: *tril* signifies a one, followed by an ambiguous number of zeros (since before it can complete the eighteen zeros found in the Spanish *trillon*—which in American English means "quintillion," not "trillion"—it is truncated and hooked onto *ce*). And by eliminating the *tre* from *trece,* Vallejo had made use of only the latter part of the word, which signifies ten (like the English "teen" in "thirteen"). Thus written out as a number, "*trilce*" looks something like this:

1,0000000000000000... 10

While it *evokes* threeness, there is no actual three in it. Instead, we have a ghost of threeness, and a mass of indefinite zeros, with the one of trillion bounding the left, and the one of ten nearly bounding the right—a word, in effect, that is without interior determination.

So, how might we contextualize "*trilce*"? In XVI, we find that the poet seeks to "galloon [himself] with zeros on the left."[2] Since the greatest part of the zero mass is on the "tril" (left) side of "*trilce,*" such a line suggests that Vallejo may have been aware of the title idea—if he had not already coined the word himself—when XVI was written (in 1919, according to Espejo).

In XXXVIII, we are informed that a mysterious crystal "has passed from animal, / and now goes off to form lefts, / the new Minuses." Again, "the new Minuses," especially of or on the "left," could very well refer to the nebulous zero mass of "*trilce*."

The word "left" first appears in the book at the end of the very cryptic IV: "Heat. Ovary. Almost transparency. / All has been cried out. Has been completely waked / in deep left." While *en plena izquierda* can be translated in a number of ways (in full left, in the heart of the left, right in the left, at the height of the left), contextual considerations back up this translation of the phrase. This is not a high nor a full left, but a deep one, with an indefinite extension that is negative, of the underworld, as opposed to positive, of height or heaven.

At the end of XXXVI—Vallejo's *ars poetica*—readers are commanded to "Make way for the new odd number / potent with orphanhood!" Surely this new odd number is "*trilce*" itself, word and title, Vallejo's own Via Negativa, with orphanhood (suggested by the ones) stranded in a milky way of zeros, or, to turn the meaning slightly, "*trilce*" as an orphan potent because self-conceived, and belonging to the world of poetry, not to the world of numbers that we use to block out time.

***

Once potency and orphanhood are associated with "*trilce*," we find ourselves in the thick of the book, immersed in Vallejo's complex relations to his two power sources, his mother and Otilia Villanueva. Much of the burden of *Trilce* is the transformation of a mother-son, via a lover, into an orphan-poet who has fetal and phallic status at the same time. To think of the two orphan ones in a milky way of zeros can be to sense the speaker in the

2. For an alternative reading, see the note on this line in *The Complete Poetry of César Vallejo* (University of California Press, 2007), p. 630.

mother of the left and, at the same time, in the lover of the right, charging the title with the strife of the book itself.

The major psychological pressure in *Trilce* is the vise of sex and death. Through certain eating scenes, entangled with elegiac mother sensations and acute erotic registrations, the tomb/womb space of the mother is explored as the body of a lover is caressed and, by implication, consumed. In its deep structure, *Trilce* achieves its freedom-in-tension by incestuously breaching the wall that divides masculine energy between being a son and being a lover. When such a wall breaks, a new, terrible heaven and hell pervade consciousness.

To be a self-created orphan is quite an accomplishment, but to *be* an orphan, regardless of how one became orphaned, is a severe limitation: one is dependent, with no protection or advantage, and in this sense one is certainly not free. *Trilce*'s uniqueness is shaped by a sense of self-isolation, as if to attain such uniqueness it had to cut itself off from the precursor support-system of Latin American and (by way of translation, in Vallejo's case) French Symbolist poetry of the past. This book seems at once deprived and new, emaciated and fresh. Such words as "potent" and "orphanhood" jar in a way that evokes André Breton's term, "exploding/fixed," for the Surreal image.[3]

3 Vallejo was of course unaware of Surrealism when writing *Trilce* (the first Surrealist Manifesto was published in Paris in 1924). While in Europe, he mainly showed contempt for Surrealism, viewing it as a literary game tied in with decadent Western capitalistic society—see César Vallejo, *Autopsy On Surrealism,* Tr. by Richard Schaaf (Curbstone Press, Willimantic CT, 1982). Susan Sontag's remarks on Antonin Artaud's incompatibility with Surrealist theory, however, are applicable to Vallejo: "The Surrealists are connoisseurs of joy, freedom, pleasure. Artaud is a connoisseur of despair and moral struggle. While the surrealists explicitly refused to accord art an autonomous value, they perceived no conflict between moral longings and aesthetic ones, and in that sense Artaud is quite right in saying their program is 'aesthetic'—merely aesthetic, he means." *Antonin Artaud: Selected Writings,* Tr. by Helen Weaver (Farrar, Straus and Giroux, New York, 1976), p. xxviii.

Vallejo's nostalgic portrayal of his mother juxtaposed with his severe, shapely treatment of the ruins of his experience remind me of certain paintings of Arshile Gorky—in particular the early "The Artist and His Mother" set next to the late "The Liver is the Cock's Comb." In Gorky's life, fifteen years separate these two paintings, and one feels the slow, dreadful advance into the self that the journey between the two represents. Another aspect of *Trilce*'s uniqueness is that, written in a period of less than four years, it juxtaposes thematic narratives—the poetic equivalent of the early Gorky painting—with dense, empty-and-lush lyrics, whose multiple directions are compatible, writing-wise, with Gorky's late canvasses. While it would be going to far to say that *Trilce* contains multiple personalities, the stylistic differences (scrambled throughout the book so as to appear without pattern) are so great that the reader may feel, in passing from poem III to IV, for example, that he has turned the page of Robert Lowell's "Skunk Hour" to find Charles Olson's "La Préface."

In XIX, Vallejo speaks of the necessity of burning all bridges. *Trilce* is filled not only with burned bridges, but with intact ones, or one might say: with models of what is being burned. The most striking writing in the book is involved with fracturing the referential functions of communicative language in a way that anticipates "projective verse" and "language poetry" by a number of decades. Some of the book's potent orphanhood, then, consists of a two-way movement between the inside and the outside. There are interiors, in which the act of writing generates associative clusters released from temporal and special obligations, and exteriors which, via sketches of childhood, romance, and jail confinement, establish a documented life. The exteriors create frames in which an interior freedom is discovered and contested (unlike Artaud, Vallejo does not make a shambles of the reality principle—his transgressional crossings are always discreet). And while poems III and IV offer a real sense of the book's oppositional poetics, such friction more often than not exists as fibers or circuits that tangle within individual poems, or even stanzas. *Trilce* may be the first twentieth-century poetic text to propose an intensely gregarious and autistic doubling that sets forth a coherent picture of the creative personality.

***

In *Trilce,* the only free being is "the free beast / who takes pleasure where he wants, when he can" (XIII). While the speaker envies "the beast," his supposed ability to express sexual desire spontaneously, he also understands that as a man he is neither sexually nor imaginatively free. On an imaginative plane this is so because Vallejo believes that too much of his life—which in XXXIII is said to extend back via the womb into infinite Vedic time—has passed before he became conscious that he had a life at all. It had passed, it will not return, and it cannot be redeemed. For Vallejo, the hour of birth is also the darkening of the light. In XLVII, he tells us that for the infant groping in his crib for something to take hold of, it is "already one o'clock."

To believe this is to give mother and early childhood an enormous size (thus the vast zero depth of the left side of the "*trilce*" formation). It follows that without imagination, life is a predetermined depression unto death. Even with an extraordinary effort of imagination (imagining, as Vallejo does, that he has yet to be born), only a truce, or holding-pattern, can be attained. Under these circumstances, the artist is tempted to sell himself the notion that through poetry itself one can be free. Such a view is solidly renounced in LVII. Vallejo calls this suspect freedom "Harmony," with its attendant henchman, perfection. Much of his *ars poetica* (XXXVI) is involved with fighting for coherence while marshalling an argument against being taken in by an idealization of our relentlessly imperfect, odd-numbered, state.

***

We must now look at some of the numbers which bounce, spill, and roll, sometimes alone, sometimes in clusters, through *Trilce*'s seventy-seven poems.

Four evokes confinement and restraint. When it is located in the company of three, it ceases to be simply negative and becomes formal boundary, or to borrow William Blake's term, "the circumference of energy." In poem IV, we find: "The whole song / squared by three silences." Tercet silences evoke the Trinity, but since Vallejo felt that the Trinity had been emptied of significance, Father, Son, and Holy Ghost are depicted as three zeros. I have mentioned how threeness is enghosted in the word "*trilce*" itself. If the book has a single, diaphanous waver, it is in the way that it nods toward a childlike yearning for the spiritual significance of the Trinity, and also nods away, toward us, to question the veracity of all traditional systems.

A more packed, and negative, use of three/four appears in poem X. It may be useful to quote this short passage, to invite the reader to confront Vallejo's thoughtful obliqueness rather than pass over it as poetic effect:

> How whales cut doves to fit.
> How these in turn leave their beak
> cubed as a third wing.
> How we saddleframe, facing monotonous croups.

One way to read this might be the following: the doves, or meek ones, tailored on the basis of the whales' notion of size, continue to tailor themselves on their own (the poor man becomes his own policeman and does not break the shop window to get bread for his starving family); they treat their beaks as merely another aspect of their anatomy, not an outlet for protest, let alone song and poetry.

In *Trilce,* the move from three to four—"cubed as a third wing"—is always a retreat. The result of this mistaken and constrictive process is to mistake the saddle for oneself, to turn oneself into a seat for others. To do so is to face the ass not only of the rider, but of the viewpoint to which one has allowed oneself to be magnetized. In reading this stanza, it is crucial to notice that Vallejo has turned *arzón* (saddleframe) into a verb. If one does not notice this, one may read it as "to saddle up" (as other translators have done), which will ruin an appropriate reading of "facing monotonous croups."

While there are occasional hints of alchemical lore, I think the basic sense of number in the book originates in response to physical experience which is set against the extent to which life is numerically framed and hexed. Vallejo was the youngest of eleven children. His mother was forty-two when he was born. As the youngest of the eleven, he seems to have been acutely aware of the burden of the four youngest children on his—by Peruvian sierra standards—aging mother. The four youngest find themselves abandoned as a little group at dusk in poem III, and in XXIII—the first of a set of poems to receive the weight of the mother burden to be transformed—the same four are seen as gaping baby bird beaks waiting to be fed. They are then immediately reidentified as his mother's "beggars." In the fourth stanza, Vallejo finds himself nearly paralyzed by the thought of swallowing the last morel of food fed to him by his mother, who has been identified at the beginning of the poem as his "estuous oven" as well as the "yolk" of his "sweet rolls." She is thus responsible for his form as well as for his content. Nourishment is fundamental to the ontology of *Trilce,* but before saying more about it, a few other things should be mentioned in regard to number.

The oppressive sense of four is reinforced by the one hundred and five day incarceration at the end of 1920. XVIII is dominated by "the four walls of the cell." In XXII, the speaker is pursued by "four magistrates," presumably the tribunal of judges who wanted to return Vallejo to prison.

Two is more ambiguous than three or four. It is the sign of repetition and fruitless duality, and of mother and son, lover and lover. Doubleness seems to have several possibilities in *Trilce*: it can stale and repeat itself (XV), press into trinity (V), or multiply out evenly to become "the thirty-two cables" of IX or "the three-hundred and sixty degrees"—a clock face around which two hands continually end up facing each other at frozen attention—in LII.

Aside from the title itself, the feminine space of zero is first sounded in V, where it "wakes the 1 and makes it stand." And the roman numeral V itself would have indicated femininity to Vallejo, as he makes erotic use of the letter "v" in IX.

Three is the most mobile and playful of *Trilce*'s numbers: it appears as the yonic triangle (XI), triples to become the nine months of gestation (X), appears as a three-year-old girl (XX), expands to "999 calories" (XXXII), and becomes the yin/yang symbol—69—of the transformational coin in XLVIII.

However, three is always shadowed by the spectral threeness of the book's title, a massive deflation of Catholic confidence. The prayer world of both parents is just that: hope without presence. But Vallejo is still touched by this world. Given his surgical mind, I find it moving that he acknowledges nostalgia and even sentimentality as still-active childhood habitations. When certain Christian figures appear, they are usually decapitalized like the "two marys" of XXIV that dethrone Mary into a secular company, which by implication can occur again and again throughout time. The lover in LXII offers his "mossy and cold-benumbed nos" as knee rests for the other—not Jesus—"in the seven falls of that infinite slope." The suggestion that ordinary people reenact Christ's Stations of the Cross, and the prayer to "saintgabriel" to "make the soul conceive" (XIX), look forward to the poems Vallejo will write years later in Paris, where dying, rimmed with life, is at once sacred and secular.

***

Reflecting on a long, rich life in 1983, Kenneth Burke commented, after criticizing D.W. Winnicott's psychoanalytic model for turning the child into a "Momma's boy": "I didn't think from what I read of Winnicott that he brought out the necessary making of a division. For instance, to me this is the great beauty of

Baudelaire's poem, "La Geante," that poem of crawling over a woman as a giantess, like a mountain. The genius of the poem is in its way of confusing the distinction between the maternal woman and erotic woman."[4]

Burke seems to be praising Baudelaire, at least in the poem, for refusing to make the distinction. On an unconscious dream level, we never leave our mothers. We are pulled from the maternal womb into that of the firmament (Blake's "Mundane Shell"), and in that sense we wander wombwise tombward as long as we wander/breathe at all.[5] There is something revolting about this to Western man; against cyclical return (death, the first pact life makes with itself), he has posed the fantasy of personal immortality, devastatingly tied to sexism and its amplification, war.

Some of the ambivalence toward freedom in *Trilce* is an ambivalence toward the mother's size (and, in contrast, toward the lover's lesser stature—if the mother is associated with the zero depth of the left side of "*trilce*," the right side, with its diminutive ten, belongs to the lover). Shadowed by outer mother dark, Vallejo fails to achieve a reciprocal relationship with any of the several lovers who move in and out of *Trilce*'s image of "the other." The lover is viewed as a figure involved with constructing a marriage trap (LIX), with the implication that to be married and, even worse, to become a father, is to be finished as an imagination. When the lover is not viewed as a pathetic seducer, she appears

---

4 All Area #2 (spring 1983): p. 30.

5 See the chapter "Nature," in N.O. Brown's *Love's Body* (Random House, NYC, 1966) for a trenchant meditation on the extent to which we never leave the mother. Brown writes: "All walking, or wandering, is from mother, to mother, in mother; it gets us nowhere. Movement is in space; and space, as Plato says in the *Timaeus*, is a receptacle, a vessel; a matrix; as it were the mother or nurse, of all becoming. Space is a sphere or spheres containing us; ambient and embracing; the world-mothering air as atmosphere. Also a chaos or chasm, a yawning pit, a devouring mother. Without form; void; and dark. And then there is light walking in darkness: the son-sun-hero in the mother-dragon night."

as an anonymous sexual engine. Such evasions of courtship as one finds in XXXIV, XXXVII, and XLVI, make for the flattest reading in the book. On the other hand, the pieces driven by a death-anxious, sexual mesh (IX, XXX, XLIII, and LXXI, for example) are keen and plangent.

The most dramatic poems in *Trilce* deal with mother as source (XXIII), mother as absence (XXVIII), lover as mother substitute (XXXV), family—mother included—as asleep forever (LXI), and mother as the immortal dead one (LXV). This group, flanked by the two groups mentioned above, create the deep structure of the book; these are the tectonic plates on which the entire surface sits and shifts. The five poems concerning the mother operate as a cycle: leaving the source, having adventures away from it, and returning to it, burdened and somewhat enlightened. XXXV has one quite revealing stanza, and since it falls at the far point of Vallejo's circular arc away from and toward mother, it is worth looking at now:

> Lunch with her who might be
> serving the dish that we liked yesterday
> and is repeated today,
> but with a bit more mustard;
> the absorbed fork, her coquettish radiance
> of a pistil in May, and her worthless
> modesty, for no reason at all.
> And the lyric and nervous beer
> watched over by her two nipples without hops,
> of which you shouldn't drink so much!

The third or fourth time I read this stanza I blinked, suddenly grasping its last three lines, hearing the phrase "nursing a beer" in an entirely new way! Literally, he is drinking a beer facing her across a table, aware of her breasts. But the lines really say that he is drinking from her nipples, and once that is noticed, one glances back up the stanza noticing that the eating imagery is a playful, if devious, veneer of the couple's sexual relationship. To call this oral copulation does not go far enough: the speaker portrays himself as both as nursing infant and a sexual adult.

Against these lines I want to set a stanza from XXVIII. The story here, told by Espejo, is that the poet had been eating from time to time with the Espejo family. One day when Vallejo was coming to lunch, the family had to eat early and leave, so Vallejo arrived to find the table with his lunch on it, but no one there to eat it with. Vallejo's response:

> How could I have had lunch. How served myself
> those things from such distant plates,
> when my own home will have broken up,
> when not even mother appears at my lips.
> How could I have had a nothing lunch.

Several insights can be drawn from the juxtaposition of these stanzas: eating and drinking with the lover is the bridge by which the nourishing mother is maintained as a psychic source of energy. Because drinking with the lover is experienced as an upper displacement of coitus, Vallejo's fetal life is recontacted. Partially being in lover is relived as totally being in mother. Again the two ones, afloat in the multiple zeros of "*trilce*," come to the fore, the larger mother mass to the left, the much smaller lover unit to the right.

While Vallejo's stance in these poems is one of self-empowerment, his energy bristles with the forbidden. He is involved in the dangerous game of defending against what he is also attempting to induct. Such attraction/repulsion is signaled, at the simplest level, by the continual mentionings of coming and going, entering and leaving, or opening and closing.

As long as Vallejo can behave as a son himself, the divisive Oedipal wall will remain breached, and the flow of transformational imagery will continue. Much of the book's uniqueness and obscurity occurs through Vallejo's shifts to maintain access to psychic incest while defending against his awareness of doing so. Certain poems—XXV is a wonderful example—are thus very coherent and very obscure. The flow is contingent upon sonship. At the point when the son must face becoming a father, turning lover into mother and being replaced by an infant (the marriage contract, in effect), depth recedes, and the poetry risks becoming flatly social, exchanging its paradise for reportage governed by memory and linear event.

***

It should now be clear that the word "trilce" does indeed contain a trinity. There is not only the ghost of the Trinity, but new players in the three roles: Mother, Lover, and fetal/phallic Vallejo. In this vision of himself, he is the orphan who renders odd and potent the number that without him would be all zeros.

When Vallejo was born his father was fifty-two. In contrast to his wife, the father hardly appears in *Trilce*. But two of his four brief appearances are remarkable. In XXVIII, he is referred to as asking "for his postponed / image, between the greater clasps of sound." I think there is a birth image neatly semi-concealed in these lines: rather than praying (which he actually did before every meal), he is seen by Vallejo as asking to be delivered, his birth (with forceps?) having been postponed by his poet son.

The father's last appearance takes place in the great elegy for Vallejo's mother (LXV). The mother in death is seen as a living pantheon, whose "arches" are so holy that only the most humble can enter her. "Even my father," he writes, "to go through there, /humblest himself until less than half a man, / until being the first child that you had." The tone coaxes the reader to take these lines in a sentimental way, but what is happening is hardly sentimental: Vallejo is denying his father's manhood and reducing him to merely another of the mother's children. Via the emphasis on smallness, the father is equated with the poet himself, the youngest (now) of twelve. Incest as the image turbine of elegy! The material worked through in LXV gives the poet the green light to finish the book, and the family, as such, never again appears.

Trilce's resolution is made possible not only by the tunnel-work constructed by breaching the incest prohibition, but through the development and resolution of a number of other thought-units which appear and reappear fugally throughout the poems. In the first ten poems, a kind of combined-object of problems to be taken up occurs. It includes 1) the poet's discovery while in jail that much of one's life is spent facing one's own ass,[6] 2) the collapse of the pre-Darwinian world, 3) the struggle to avoid repeating dead initiations, 4) the contingency of male upon female, 5) the marriage trap, 6) the intersection of the sacred and the secular, and 7) the family romance. I merely mention here what could be thought of as *Trilce*'s "bundle of burden" because the reader is entitled to the difficulty and pleasure of engaging what Vallejo does with it. Some moves peter out, while others develop and become substantial in the book.

One example: the discovery in the opening poem that life is involved with sifting shit, or negation, for possible bits of gold, is immediately focused by the speaker, raising up "from behind, muzziled, imperturbable / on the fatal balance line." The first attempt to revise this predicament occurs in VIII, where Vallejo proposes to run through (as if with a sword) his own front, so as to be "left with my front toward my back." That is, instead of literally turning away from one's backside (since in a sense one cannot), why not sublimate it into a more cogent form? What now has become a motif recurs in X, "facing monotonous croups," and again in XIV, "those buttocks seated upward." In these instances, Vallejo does not appear to know how to offer the problem more imaginative value, but he keeps it present, an ikon to ponder. Then, in XL, the "shadow" suddenly rears up "completely frontal," sug-

6 For an intricate and extended commentary on the opening poem in *Trilce* see "A Translational Understanding of *Trilce* #1" in *Companion Spider* (Wesleyan University Press, Middletown CT, 2002). Since writing that essay I have revised my translation of the first two lines of the poem. For the final version of #1 see *The Complete Poetry of César Vallejo.*

gesting that front and back have ceased to be in opposition. They fuse in LXIX: the sea is envisioned as "an edition standing, / in its single leaf the recto / facing the verso."

Once the mother is accorded dead and immortal status in poem LXV, it is as if *Trilce* breathes a joyous sigh of relief, quickens its pace, and through a series of chromatic balancings—contradictions no longer felt as such—moves briskly toward LXXVII, the final poem, in which hail, rain, fire, coast, and sierra become the keys to a simultaneous descent/ascent, the powers of poetry. On our way to LXXVII, we pass the recto facing the verso, stone as "benefacient pillow," everyone smiling at César Vallejo as he urges the living to love the living, and his lover's voice informing him that every bit of him (fetally too?) is inside her. Their hands become reciprocal, and intercourse turns into a flurry of brilliant-colored gamecocks. It is time for this orphan, who has now justified his earlier claims of potency, to rejoice over his shot not of whiskey but of water. The amount of sweetness present is too much even for a shroud. As another "ay" triumphs, only absurdity is found to be pure, and, facing the absurd, in a gesture that recalls the alchemical *rubedo,* the poet's "excess" (transmuted guano from the opening poem?) begins to "sweat golden pleasure." Suddenly all childhood discipline is envisioned as having taken place to enable Vallejo to "compose" himself. As that isolated line falls at the end of LXXIV, the having to compose himself as a schoolchild becomes the permission to have composed himself as a book. The poet who rejoiced as an orphan now state the essence of orphanhood: being dead without ever having been alive. I read this as a farewell to the totality of his background. The quite Blakean conversion of opposites into contraries with which *Trilce* ends offers a severe developmental contour to the book and releases it into itself without flattening its complexity into a single, idealized perspective.[7]

My comments on *Trilce* should not be taken as definitive or summational: rather, they are what I have been able to dig out of the text while translating it. I have attempted to set before the reader the extent to which the book's title appears to invade and permeate the poems, and how, in turn, its poles of mother and lover generate much of the emotional circuitry through which, around which, against which the orphan self in the poems steers his way. I have intentionally avoided discussing the book in terms of current critical jargon which, if cogent at all, only seems relevant once the book is understood on its own terms as much as is possible. My desire here, then, has been to give the reader some railings, and foot holds, but not in any way to reduce the arduousness of the climb. I have read hundreds of pages of criticism of *Trilce* in Spanish, and have used it mainly for linguistic cues. I have resisted making use of often quite speculative interpretation as a guide in actual translating. What remains to be done now, in English as well as other languages, is an evaluation of *Trilce* (and the rest of Vallejo's poetry) in a context that includes such poets as Lezama Lima, Borges, Girondo, Moro, Huidobro and Neruda. While the most striking features of *Trilce* are of Vallejo's own

---

7 When I had basically completed the translation of *Trilce* that appeared in the 1992 Marsilio edition (the definitive version to be found in *The Complete Poetry of César Vallejo* is the third published version of the text), I had the following dream: a black-haired woman in charge of a kitchen gives me a food package. She says: just don't learn how it was killed. I can see through the translucent wrapping a large crab gripping the breast of a chicken that appears to still be alive. Both are immersed in liquid. My companion and I take it to our place, which is under gang siege, difficult to get into—one has to enter a building surrounded by hostile addicts and thieves. We get the package into the building and to our kitchen and study it. The chicken seems to be passing an egg through her body, as if giving her life to bear this egg, which is red and glows, as the crab flexes, with its claws sunk into the chicken's breast. I fear the egg is all blood, or has no containing wall. My companion receives the egg and treats it like a treasure. We both watch the huge chicken, out on the kitchen floor now, pulsing in an agonizing way, as if she wants the egg back! The crab is gone. Only the chicken (size of a large turkey), cavernous, dilated, opening and closing, trying to draw something back inside that is gone forever...

making (one early commentator stated that in *Trilce* Vallejo invented "surrealism" before Surrealism), it is also clear that the book was not conceived in a total void. In this sense, a study of Vallejo's borrowings from certain French Symbolists—in particular Rimbaud and Mallarmé—and from the early twentieth century avant-garde would help us understand how, before leaving Peru, he was responding to the beginnings of international modernism. Ultimately, Vallejo's poetry must be viewed within the sphere of twentieth-century world poetry, a millennial retrospective that would set him alongside Rilke, Eliot, Mayakofsky, Apollinaire, Holan etc. To do so, I feel, would indicate even further the range of *Trilce*'s trajectory from a poetry unique for its time to a poetry that in certain respects is still a bit beyond what English-speaking readers can understand and assimilate today.

[From the first two editions of Trilce, *with an Introduction by Américo Ferrari, published by Marsilio (NYC, 1991) and Wesleyan University Press (Middletown CT, 2000), with minor revisions, 2011.]*

NOTICINGS 3

It seems fundamentally wrong that the first Caribbean Nobel Prize in Literature did not go to Aimé Césaire. This is not to knock the poetry of Derek Walcott who did receive the Prize, but to once again insist that there is a quantum leap between a body of work that is accomplished and a body of work that is unique. Thinking about this, I went back to André Breton's essay, "A Great Black Poet," written in 1941, after Breton, visiting Martinique on his way to exile in America, discovered a section of "Notebook of a Return to the Native Land" in Césaire's literary journal, *Tropiques.* Breton's words still ring absolutely true to me in 1993, and I quote a paragraph here as a modest testimony to Aimé Césaire, now entering his 80th year:

> And the next day, Césaire. I recall my first quite elementary reaction at finding him of a black so pure and even more unnoticeable at first because he was smiling. Through him (I already know it, I see it and everything will confirm it later), human essence is heated to a point of maximum effervescence in which knowledge—here of the highest order—overlaps with magical gifts. In my eyes his emergence, and I do not mean merely that day, in a form sheerly his own, takes on the value of a *sign of our times.* Thus, defying single-handedly an era in which we appear to be witnessing the general abdication of the mind, in which nothing appears to be created except for the purpose of perfecting the triumph of death, in which art itself threatens to congeal in obsolete schemes, the first revivifying new breath capable of restoring confidence comes from a black. And it is a black who handles the French language in a manner that no white man is capable of today, And it is a black who guides us today into the unexplored, establishing along the way, as if by child's play, the contacts that make us advance on sparks. And it is a black who is not

only a black but all of man, who conveys all of man's questionings, all of his anguish, all of his hopes and all of his ecstasies and who will remain more and more for me the prototype of dignity.

(Tr. by Annette Smith and Clayton Eshleman)

Readers of *Caterpillar* may remember *#15/16* in which 80 pages of the poetry of Stephen Jonas (1921–1970) appeared. Jonas is still not well known, so it is a pleasure to notice that Joseph Torra's fine magazine, *lift,* has done a double issue (*#10 & 11*), on Jonas's poetry, with responses by Gerrit Lansing, Cid Corman, John Wieners, David Rattray, and Raffael de Gruttola, among others. This issue is $9, and can be ordered at: 10-Rear Oxford Street, Somerville, MA 02143.

The Horse has Six Legs (an anthology of Serbian Poetry), edited and translated by Charles Simic, Graywolf. Over one hundred poems by 20th century Serbian poets, among whom Momcilo Nastasijevic, Rade Drainac, Vasko Popa, Ljubomir Simovic, and Aleksandar Ristovic appear outstanding. The jewel of the book is Popa's "Little Box" series. Oddly, there is no sense of a political landscape, no writing that would seem to prefigure the present Yugoslavian catastrophe.

Evening Train is Denise Levertov's best collection of poems since the early 1970s, and its publication by New Directions is accompanied by her *New & Selected Essays,* which includes a fascinating and moving essay on her relationship with Robert Duncan. Levertov has now assimilated Williams and Rilke so thoroughly that her poetic lines move with a flexibility and openness rare in any poetry.

Peter Quartermain's *Disjunctive Poetics: From Gertrude Stein and Louis Zukofsky to Susan Howe* (Cambridge) will be reviewed in *Sulfur #33* by Keith Tuma. I mention it here as the chapter on Bunting sent me back to Bunting's *Collected Poems,* and when I opened the book, a little postcard, published by the Basil Bunting

Poetry Archive, 1990, fell out. I am sure the Archive will not mind if I quote the contents (Bunting's advice to student poets in Newcastle, in the early 1970s):

I SUGGEST

1. Compose loud; poetry is a sound.
2. Vary rhythm enough to stir the emotion you want but not so as to lose impetus.
3. Use spoken words and syntax.
4. Fear adjectives; they bleed nouns. Hate the passive.
5. Jettison ornament gaily but keep shape.

Put your poem away till you forget it, then:

6. Cut out every word you dare.
7. Do it again a week later, and again.

Never explain—your reader is as smart as you.

In 1991 Jahbone Press in Los Angeles published *Lee Sr Falls to the Floor* by Leland Hickman. Unfortunately, there is no accompanying information as to whether this is the rest of Lee's poetry (before and after *Great Slave Lake Suite,* Momentum, 1980)—and if it is, I am astonished, as Lee often referred to a long work-in-progress, "Tiresias," of which *GSLS* is identified as only "I:9:B" (that is, where is I:8? I:9:A?). To further confuse matters, six of the twelve "elements" in *GSLS* are reprinted in the Jahbone book, without their dedications. As some *Sulfur* readers know, Hickman more or less stopped writing poetry while editing and setting type for the ten issues of *Temblor,* surely one of the most magnificent one-man efforts in literary magazine editing. But previous to *Temblor,* I am under the impression that Lee worked for year on "Tiresias," and if the working papers are still existent, I suspect they would be very interesting to see.

For Henry Miller fans, a really first-rate collection of essays has recently been published: *Critical Essays on Henry Miller,* edited by

Ronald Gottesman (GK Hall & Co.). Along with fairly-well known pieces by Mailer, Rexroth, Lawrence Durrell's letter on receiving *Tropic of Cancer,* Kate Millet and Jay Martin, there is a previously unpublished review of *Cancer* by Ezra Pound, a poem to Miller by William Carlos Williams (published in a limited 1945 Bern Porter edition), and an engaging tribute by Robert Creeley. From a letter by Isaac Bashevis Singer to Bertrand Mathieu: "Although I don't write in his style, I cherish him as a writer and as a friend of everything which is genuine in the art of writing."

I have only written three book jacket blurbs in my life—for Blackburn's *Collected Poems,* Rothenberg's *Khurbn,* and most recently, Karen Kelley's *Her Angel* (Singing Horse Press), which for my money is the most exciting first book in some time. This is the beginning of a kind of poetry N.O. Brown was arguing for in his masterpiece, *Love's Body.*

Over the past few yeas, I have collected some half dozen books on the Mexican Día de Muertos (Day of the Dead), in which the dead are welcomed in homes and cemeteries, with various foods and offerings, end of October/beginning of November. My hunch is that this is one of the oldest human festivals, with roots in early Neolithic agrarian culture, in which revenants are appeased as well as greeted, at the crest of harvest. The Mexican version is layered with pre-Columbian and colonial imagery, some of which comes from the European medieval preoccupation with skulls and skeletons. Among the books on the subject I have found, most of which are mainly collections of photographs, one is quite serious and thorough: *The Skeleton at the Feast,* by Elizabeth Carmichael and Chloe Sayers (U of Texas Press). It sensitively includes a number of interviews with artists and craftsmen whose altars, sugar skulls, sugar paste animals, candelabra, and papercuts are among the finest made in present-day Mexico. This past fall, Caryl Eshleman and I spent a week in Oaxaca over the Day of the Dead period. As might be expected, American Halloween, with its plastic and rubber low quality goods, has invaded the traditional stalls in the markets.

Nancy Peters, the editor of City Lights Books, should be congratulated for her editing of the "War After War" issue of *City Lights Review* (#5). Excellent pieces on the so-called Gulf "War" by Chomsky, Boal, Lamborn Wilson, Solomon, Indiana, Huston, Lubin and Blankfort. Of the books I have read on what Chomsky refers to as "international terrorism on a colossal scale," Jean Edward Smith's *George Bush's War* (Holt) is the best. Besides being an excellent chronicle of Bush's deft manipulation of other nations under obligation to us, Congress, and the media, the book is a meditation on the dangers of arbitrary executive power. I also recommend Stephen Brockman's "The Cultural Meaning of the Gulf War," in the spring 1992 issue of the *Michigan Quarterly Review.* Of related horror is *Four Hours in My Lai* by Michael Bilton and Kevin Sim (Viking), "the fullest account ever published of the most infamous war crime in American military history."

As a kind of vast, ontological update on Upton Sinclair's *The Jungle,* Jeremy Rifkin's *Beyond Beef: The Rise and Fall of the Cattle Culture* (Dutton) contains information that pervades many aspects of current planetary ecological peril. From Mithraic myth:

> From the bull's body sprang all the plants and herbs that men now find useful. From the spinal cord sprang wheat, the staff of man's life, from the blood came the grape vine and wine, the sacred joy of life.

From the first official description of the devil (447 AD):

> a large black monstrous apparition with horns on his head, cloven hoofs—or one cloven hoof—ass's ears, hair, claws, fiery eyes, terrible teeth, an immense phallus, and a sulphurous smell.

From a contemporary description of a slaughterhouse workstation:

The kill floor looks like a red sea… warm blood bubbles and coagulates in an ankle deep pool. The smell sears the nostrils. Men stand in gore… each night the gooey mess is wiped away…

Sulfur #32, 1993

A NOTE ON MEDUSA'S SOURCES

The Greek iconography of the Medusa's face includes "bulging or glaring eyes, gnashing tusks, a protruding tongue, and snake-like hair." In some versions, she also has "grossly foliated skin, the absence of corners in her mouth, and single or multiple dots on her forehead."[1] This syncretic image is, I suspect, only the surface of a palimpsest with earliest scratches in the Upper Paleolithic (thus from this viewpoint, the Perseus story is a late addition). Here are some hunches and sightings about the construction of the Medusa's lethal face.

It is possible to imagine the snakes encircling the face as the winding corridors of a cave, and the tusks or fangs, in the center of the face, as the ghosts of those dreadful encounters where in total blackness and at times far from the cave entrance, a human met a huge cave bear or cave lion.

To set a fanged beast mouth into a woman's face is to associate women with "predation." Barbara Ehrenreich argues that Cro-Magnon women probably participated in "drives" of big game animals, and acted as butchers and bearers once the animals had been slaughtered.[2] In this regard, the Spartan name for Artemis (who may have originally been a bear or lioness, and of Upper Paleolithic antiquity) is Artamis, meaning "cutter" or "butcher."[3]

While most Upper Paleolithic hybrids are male (with bison or bird heads), there is a lion-headed 30,000 year old statuette from Hohlenstein-Stadel, Germany, that is probably female (the genitals are difficult to identify, but there is clearly no phallus). At this point

1 A. David Napier, *Masks, Transformation, and Paradox,* University of California Press, Berkeley, 1986. See chapter 4, "Perseus and the Gorgon Head."

2 Barbara Ehrenreich, *Blood Rites,* Metropolitan Books, NYC, 1997. See chapter 6, "When the Predator Had a Woman's Face."

3 Barbara G. Walker, *The Woman's Encyclopedia of Myths and Secrets,* Harper & Row, NYC, 1983. See the entry for "Artemis."

in time, the animal had only been partially differentiated from the human image (the Greek Medusa subordinates animal parts to a basically human head). The dots on the Medusa foreheads may indicate the lion's superciliary tufts of hair above the eyes.

Another link between women and hunting predation may have involved menstruation. There was probably no way to camouflage bloody discharges then as there is today. It is also believed that prehistoric women synchronized their periods which also closely matched the 29.5 day cycle of the moon. According to Ehrenreich, "it may have seemed that women's cycles control the moon, or else that the divine presence that is the moon expresses itself through the bodies of human females."[4]

Thus the Medusa's fanged face may also contain a bleeding vagina, suggesting an origin for the superstition of the "vagina dentata." On a vulvar level, the snakes evoke pubic hair encircling a site of possible castration in which a phallus has been replaced by the fangs responsible for the rending. I also think of an octopus here, with its snake-like tentacles encircling a powerfully-beaked mouth (the Medusa and her sisters were said to reside on the shores of Oceanus).

Another explanation for the Medusa's snakes is to be found in Penelope Shuttle and Peter Redgrove's *The Wise Wound*:

> A.P.H. Scott points out that during an eclipse of the sun, during which the menstruation of women was thought by Pliny to be particularly dangerous), the moon's shadow rushing towards you across the land ripples with the refractions of the earth's atmosphere like snakes. The solar corona can also be observed wriggling like a crown of snakes round the moon's shadow, if you use smoked glass. However, we have also seen that it is a common cultural

4 Ehrenreich, p. 105.

> image of menstruation that a woman is bitten by a snake-god who comes from the moon. The moon sloughs herself and renews, just as the snake sheds its skin.[5]

A Cro-Magnon child's terror at seeing not only its hunter-mother's bloody hands but also her bloody vagina circulates upward through the centuries to become a snake-wreathed slaughterface, impacted with holy dread—as if the gate of life were revealed to contain a carnivore mouth.

1998

Montevidayo, 2011

5 Penelope Shuttle and Peter Redgrove, *The Wise Wound,* Penguin Books, London, 1978, pp. 263–264.

THE FIRST STROPHE OF AIMÉ CÉSAIRE'S *NOTEBOOK OF A RETURN TO THE NATIVE LAND*

This morning I would like to engage the translation of poetry by scrutinizing the charged opening strophe of Césaire's *Notebook.* I will first comment on some of the strophe's key words and present Annette Smith's and my translation of it. I will then consider two differing translations of this strophe: the first is from John Berger and Anna Bostock's translation of *Return to My Native Land* (Penguin Books, 1969); the second is by Emile Snyder, from his version of *Return to My Native Land* (Présence Africaine, Paris, 1971).

Annette and I had the advantage of having these two previous translations to inspect and to differ with; from our viewpoint our translation does not represent a definitive or unchallengable version. It is simply the best we could do in the late 1970s. Since then we have made changes in our translation of the *Notebook* several times. The version of the opening strophe presented here is to be found in *Notebook of a Return to the Native Land,* Wesleyan University Press, 2001.[1]

I am critiquing Berger/Bostock and Snyder to help the reader evaluate word choices and strategies in translation. Annette's and my theory of translation can be put very simply: to make a translation that is as accurate as possible to the original as well as one that is up to its performance level. These two pursuits are often not compatible. To translate accurately, especially literally, often results in a wooden English/American version. So translators constantly fudge or reconstruct, taking liberties, as it were, with the

1 This article was originally given as a lecture to a seminar at The Naropa Institute, in Boulder, Colorado, June 2000. It was published in a 2002 issue of the *AWP Writer's Chronicle.* For this presentation of the piece, I have eliminated a couple of paragraphs not directly pertinent to the strophe under examination.

original. Many of the translations of poetry that I have any familiarity with significantly distort the original and offer something that is neither an accurate version nor a poem that could be considered original—as Robert Lowell's *Imitations* once were—in the second language.

Aimé Césaire's poetry is an especially good test of a translator's abilities. It is metaphorically dense, and packed with technical and arcane words, as well as some neologisms. Césaire's syntax is also complex and to render it faithfully and intelligently sometimes involves acrobatic strategies on the translator's part.

Here is the opening strophe of *Notebook of a Return to the Native Land* in the original French:

> Va-t'en, lui disais-je, gueule de flic, gueule de vache, va-t'en je déteste les larbins de l'ordre et les hannetons de l'espérance. Va-t'en mauvais gris-gris, punaise de moinillon. Puis je me tournais vers des paradis pour lui et les siens perdus, plus calme que la face d'une femme qui ment, et là, bercé par les effluves d'une pensée jamais lasse je nourrissais le vent, je délaçais les monsters et j'entendais monter de l'autre côte du désastre un fleuve de tourerelles et de trèfles de la savane que je porte toujours dans mes profondeurs à hauteur inverse du vingtième étage des maisons les plus insolentes et par précaution contre la force putréfiante des ambiances crépusculaires, arpentée nuit et jour d'une sacré soleil vénérien.

Here are translations of some of the key words in this opening strophe:

Vache—cow; in slang it can refer to a policeman and is close to our "pig"

Larbin—pejorative term for a valet—a flunkie. In other contexts it can refer to the dress of particular servants in which case it is not pejorative.

Hanneton—cockchafer, a beetle that is destructive to vegetation.

Gris-gris—an African term for a charm, amulet, or talisman. Webster's defines it as "an African Negro talisman," thus while it is not in common use, it exists in English.
Punaise—bedbug.
Bercé—past tense of "bercer"—to rock, as a baby in a cradle.
Nourrissais—past tense of "nourrir"—to nourish or to suckle (an infant); also to feed people, animals; to foster (plants or hatred).
Delaçias—past tense of "delaçer"—to unlace, to loosen (a corset); to undo (shoes).
Tourterelles—turtledoves.
Trèfles de la savane—savanna clover.
A hauteur inverse du vingtième étage—at inverse height to the 20th floor. The idea here is that the speaker's depths ("profondeurs") are as deep as the 20-floor houses ("maisons") are high—undoubtedly a reference to towering apartment houses with penthouses owned by the rich in Martinique. We tighten the phrase, rendering it as "height-deep as the twentieth floor."
Arpentée—past tense of "arpenter"—to survey, measure (land); in another context (e.g., "arpenter le terrain") to stride over the ground.
Sacré—past tense of "sacrer"—to curse (as well as to anoint, crown, or consecrate).

Note that this strophe consists of three sentences: two short commands, followed by a long, looping sentence made up of eight phrases.

Here is our translation of this strophe:

> Beat it, I said to him, you cop, you lousy pig, beat it I de-
> test the flunkies of order and the cockchafers of hope.
> Beat it evil gris-gris, you bedbug of a petty monk. Then
> I turned toward paradises lost for him and his kin,
> calmer than the face of a woman telling lies, and there,

> rocked by the flux of a never exhausted thought I nourished the wind, I unlaced the monsters and heard rise from the other side of disaster a river of turtledoves and savanna clover which I carry forever in my depths height-deep as the twentieth floor of the most arrogant houses and as a guard against the putrefying force of crepuscular surroundings, surveyed night and day by a cursed venereal sun.

The reader will note that in the first line we had to make some adjustments that while they do not alter the meaning, they depart from a literal translation. Both "flic" and "vache" are slang for "policeman" (with the latter a bit more insulting). "Gueule" is an animal or fish mouth that when applied to human beings is often translated as "mug" or, in context, "trap" (like "shut your trap"). "You cop, you lousy pig" stresses the oral nature of the challenge.

Let's now look at the Berger/Bostock translation:

> Get away, I said, you bastard of a cop, swine get away. I hate the livery of order and the fish-hooks of hope. Get away foul ju-ju, bedbug of a monk. Then I turned to dream for him and his lost ones' paradises more calm than the face of a woman telling lies. Rocked there on the breath of inexhaustible thought, I fed the wind, set monsters free and heard a river of turtle doves and savannah clover rising on the far side of disaster: a river in my depth as deep as the brazen twentieth storey is high; a river to protect me against the corruptions of dusk that are paced day and night by a damned venereal sun.

Although there are a lot of things that can be questioned here, I will only concentrate on material that seems clearly distortional. For example, while "Va-t'en" can be translated as "Get away," such a phrase implies a gesture that I don't think Césaire is making. And "swine get away" doesn't strike me as spoken. There are other tonal discrepancies in the translation that could be addressed.

On a more serious level, the second part of Césaire's first sentence (which becomes a new sentence in this translation) offers "livery" for "larbins" and "fish-hooks" for "hannetons." It seems clear to Annette and me that Césaire is addressing people with the word "larbins" and not the uniforms they are wearing. As for "fish-hooks," it appears that Berger/Bostock have misread "hannetons" for "hameçons" (which does mean "fish-hooks"). At the end of their third sentence they translate "moinillon" as "monk" which is only partly correct, as "monk" is "moin," and moinillon" is "little monk," or possibly, in this context, a pejorative term for a monk, such as "petty monk."

Berger/Bostock's fourth sentence (which is the beginning of Césaire's third) adds the word "dream" ("to dream for him") which does not exist in the original. The addition complicates a phrase that is quite clear in the original. Césaire is saying that he turns toward paradises that are lost for the French colonist (a kind of combined cop/priest), not that, as Berger/Bostock have it, that he is dreaming "for him and his lost ones' paradises." In Berger/Bostock's fifth sentence (the original at this point is still building up momentum in its third), "breath" is an inadequate translation of "effluves" which combines most effluvium (or emanation) with discharge. Here the word seems to stress the speaker's being rocked by an implied dream of paradise (which he opposes to Martinique's social stagnation).

I think the reader will see that Cesaire's long, winding third sentence has been seriously altered by Berger/Bostock. The word "river" is arbitrarily repeated twice after imposed colons. After the third "river," Césaire's powerful phrase, "the putrefying force of crepuscular surroundings" (which is simple to translate) has been rewritten as "the corruptions of the dusk." Lastly, "arpentée" has been translated as "paced."

My hunch is that Berger/Bostock, on the basis of the "fishhooks" error, employed a lot of guesswork in their translation. To avoid such errors—and to track down words not to be found in the dictionaries that Annette and I consulted—I met with Césaire twice in Paris, each time bringing a word list to go over with him. On a third occasion, Annette and I met with him after having completed a penultimate draft of our translation. At that point we had reduced our problematic word list to about a dozen words, and we rejoiced when we left his son's apartment, having finally solved all of our word problems. In a few cases, Césaire had to reconsult French-African dictionaries that he had not looked at for decades.

The other version of this opening strophe is by Emile Snyder, a now deceased French poet and translator who lived for many years in the United States. It was through Emile's translation of Césaire's prose poem "Lynch 1" that I discovered the poet in 1960. While Emile's English was fluent, conversationally speaking, he was still translating *into* a second language, which is much more difficult than translating a second language into one's first. Here is Snyder's version of the strophe:

> Go away, I said, with your mug of a copper, your mug of a pig, go away. I hate the flunkies of order and the beetles of hope. Go away, you evil charm, little punk of a monk. Then I turned toward heavens lost to him and his own kind, heavens more calm than the face of a woman who lies, and there, lulled by the effluvia of endless thoughts, I fed the wind, I untied the monsters and heard rise from the other bank of disaster, a river of turtle-doves and the clovers of the savanna I still carry deep inside me at inverse depth of the twentieth floor of the most insolent houses and as guard against the putrefying power of ambient twilights, surveyed day and night by a cursed poxy sun.

Snyder has tried to match word for word most of Césaire's first line. The phrasing is somewhat awkward (one cannot imagine an infuriated Martinican shouting this line at a cop), and with "copper," we have a dated British word for "cop." "Cockchafer" is generalized into "beetle" (Césaire is always extremely specific regarding fauna and flora; here the cockchafer's destructiveness to vegetation seems to be a key element in the word choice). "Punaise de moinillon" is rendered as "little punk of a monk." Snyder prided himself in being up on American slang, and here you have an instance in which his hipness, as it were, led him to substitute a rhyme for a more accurate rendition.

I would also question translating "paradis" as "heavens"—especially since the word has heavy Christian overtones (which "paradise" does not), and also since Césaire's writings contain many anti-Christian images. Snyder repeats "heavens" in the following line, proposing that they, and not the speaker, are "more calm than the face of a woman who lies."

It strikes me that "endless thoughts" deflects the crucial implication of "une pensée jamais lasse" (our "a never exhausted thought"). For us, the implied meaning here is the speaker's refusal to give up his dream of paradise (or freedom) that is the engine of this strophe (and much of the forty page poem that follows).

The rest of Snyder's strophe, with a few exceptions, is passable. "The clovers of the savanna" is a little awkward; "ambient twilights" lacks the force of "crepuscular surroundings;" and "poxy," while evocative of venereal diseases, could refer to other pox diseases, such as smallpox or chickenpox. A strong cognate like "vénérien" is hard to improve on.

A NOTE ON RODIN AND UPPER PALEOLITHIC CAVE WALL ENGRAVINGS AND SCULPTURE

Cro-Magnon hand lamps made certain aspects of wall contours suggest animal and human anatomy. A significant number of engravings, paintings, and high relief wall sculpture employ natural formations. It may have seemed to these early explorers that animals (and, less often, humans) were partially embedded in, or emerging through, such walls, and that such presences only needed the assistance of some human-made lines or carving to be completely there. Since the animal was sighted as partly submerged in stone, imagination, reinforced by actual modeling or engraving, could bring forth its form. If a wall was "with animal," then some Cro-Magnon mid-wifery could help it give birth.

In certain marble and bronze-cast sculpture by Rodin the figures inspire the fantasy that they were existent in the rock (or metal) itself, and that the sculptor's work was to cut away the gangue (marble in a rough state) around them. In finished form, they appear to still belong to their gangue or plaster origin. For example, in *Christ and the Magdalen* (1894), legs disappear into foundational rock. The work itself resembles the solidity of rock formations. Visions of grottos, or ancient caves, animate the viewer's imagination.

The Sirens (1886—bronze) undulate within their metal as if projections of the wave-like background that binds them, as if they were projected forth from it, while still being a part of it—as if the wave spoke itself into siren form and then flowed back into a seamless swing.

In *The Creation of Woman* (1894—marble) a female form seems to be kissing the paw/hand of an amorphous tree-like shape, phallic and anatomical, that rises up out of a marble base, like a plant surging forth.

The figure in *Meditation* (1896—bronze) is armless, and its head is half-buried in bronze background, which is gnarled and swirling into the figure's forehead, as the figure attempts to lift itself up out of the rooty bronze base. Meditation as a compromised reverie, still infested with the grounds of our being, the matter out of which the primate rose and which accompanies us in thought and physical subsistence.

Andromeda (1885—marble) is half-coiled, half-collapsed into herself atop the rock in which one of her legs is buried. She floats on the rock like a soft moon, gelatinous, radiant, in contrast to the rock's unhewn contours, yet of it, deposited on it and, at the same time, emerging from it.

In *The Hand of the Devil* (1902—marble), fingers reach out of the chaos of marble, as if out of snow, cradling the human, the wrist chopped, with a knot of rough marble like a bone stub. In shifting marble snow this sleigh-like hand, with its enfolded human cargo.

Rodin, of course, began with blocks, wax, or plaster, in contrast to limestone cave walls (or tusks or antlers). But like the sculptors of Cap Blanc (a rock shelter outside of Les Eyzies in the French Dordogne) especially, some of his forms appear to be embedded in the raw material, with the suggestion that one of the artist's tasks is to hew and release them, partially, into view. In both cases, some of the matrix remains, as if being itself is never free of its primal and engendering collisions.

[Note: over the years, we would meet our group for our tours to the Ice Age painted caves in southwestern France initially in Paris, and on several occasions we took these groups to the Rodin Museum there. I handed out this piece to them before going to the Museum so as to tie Rodin's sculptural forms into aspects of Upper Paleolithic wall sculpture. 2001.]

SOUTINE IMPACTED

I saw my first Soutine in 1963 in the Ohara Museum of Art, in Kurashiki, Japan. It is now identified as "Hanging Duck," painted around 1925. Seeing this "thing" was so riveting that I remember nothing else in the museum. It was a hybrid fusion, at once a flayed man hung from a pulpy wrist and flailing, with gorgeous white wings attached to his leg stumps, and a gem-like putrescent bird, hung by one leg, in an underworld filled with bird-beaked monsters and zooming gushes of blood-colored and sky-blue paint. For the forty years since, I have kept Soutine's art in heart and mind.

In 1993, Maurice Tuchman, Esti Dunow, and Klaus Perls edited *Chaim Soutine (1893–1943) Catalogue Raisonné* (Benedikt Taschen Verlag, Cologne), a boxed two-volume collection of 780 pages. A magnificent advance on all Soutine books and catalogues up to then, it included newly discovered paintings (and rejected some mediocre pieces as fakes, which have been used over the years to criticize Soutine's standing). I celebrated devouring this collection by writing a twenty-two page poem, "Soutine's Lapis," included in my book *From Scratch* (Black Sparrow Press, Santa Rosa, 1998).

Now Tuchman and Dunow have assembled *The Impact of Chaim Soutine* (Hatje Cantz, Cologne, 2002, $45), a 168 page book based on a 2001 exhibition at the Galerie Gmurzynska, also in Cologne. Its purpose is to deliver visual and verbal proof that Soutine significantly influenced "some of the most influential artists of the second half of the twentieth century"—in particular, Willem de Kooning, Francis Bacon, Jackson Pollock and Jean Dubuffet. The book has only a dozen or so pages of text (some of which contains a Soutine chronology), and is mainly filled with statements by artists and art historians juxtaposed with five de Koonings, three Bacons, four Pollocks, seven Dubuffets, and sixty-six Soutines (eight of which are recently discovered). The somewhat melodramatic and forced format is underscored by the back cover art: the four quarters of a grotesque face are each details from paintings by Soutine, Bacon, Dubuffet, and de Kooning.

In "Another Way of Seeing," an essay in the March 2002 issue of *Harper's* magazine, John Berger writes: "More directly than any other art, painting is an affirmation of the existent, of the physical world into which mankind has been thrown." Later in the essay, we find the following paragraph:

> Soutine was among the great painters of the twentieth century. It has taken fifty years for this to become clear, because his art was both traditional and uncouth, and this mixture offended all fashionable tastes. It was as if his painting had a broken accent and so was considered inarticulate: at best exotic and at worst barbarian. Now his devotion to the existent becomes more and more exemplary. Few other painters have revealed more graphically than he the collaboration, implicit in the act of painting, between model and painter. The poplars, the carcasses, the childrens' faces on Soutine's canvases clung to his brush.

Soutine always worked from a model, whether it was a bunch of houses in a hillscape, a beef carcass, or a human being. Like Caravaggio, he never drew. His "existents"—especially while he was in Céret, France (1919–1922)—besides being his focus are also projection-spooked. Whatever Soutine looked at there seems to have pulled wads of childhood nightmare out of him. His Céret landscapes are not only in earthquake rumba mode, but pixilated with a very personal, anthropomorphic hysteria. Houses often have grotesque expressions—something between a house and a terrified human face. Some houses even twist into humanesque shapes—they cower in clumps, like frightened children or crawl up onto the "backs" of their neighbors.

Céret is strangely enough Soutine's extreme point. Had he been willing to abandon his "existents," he might have become an abstract expressionist. But he recoiled from his work at Céret (later destroying a significant amount of it), and his post-Céret painting (1923–43) is a kind of crab-wise retreat into traditional painting. To put it this way is a little misleading because some of the later portraits, the beef carcasses, most of the hanging fowl, the ray fish, and some of the last landscapes at Civry and Champigny are wonderful, bold achievements—yet none are as audacious or as intuitively fearless as the Céret work. It is as if John Coltrane played free form jazz as a young musician and then, after a few years, improvised off standards for the rest of his life.

Berger mentions that Soutine was traditional *and* uncouth. He was also adroit *and* clumsy. With portraits, he seems to have locked libido-wise onto certain parts of the sitter environment, and to have dismissed others. Faces and bodily postures can be uncanny, but backgrounds are often muddy messes, and hands can be almost comical. Tuchman and Dunow blow up two hand details in *Impact*—out of respect, I suspect. The fingers look like careless swipes or like deranged worms attempting to take off. These dualities are part of Soutine's essence. A more physically-driven painter than even Pollock, he seems to have worked in a frenzied, semi-trance, attached to his "existent" like certain American Indian initiates were attached to hooks through their chests to the "sun." When Soutine is "on," he produces paintings that are peristaltic, semi-metaphoric, absurd, brilliant, poignant, and unforgettable.

We must now look at how effectively the authors have demonstrated Soutine's influence. Painters who are simply the sum of their influences are easy to deal with in this regard, but why bother if they have nothing of their own to offer. Specific influence is much more difficult to determine in the cases of painters who have made use of many predecessors, all of whom are blended in, some more, some less, with their own originality. The four painters said to be impacted by Soutine are, with the possible exception of Dubuffet, major 20th century figures whose best work is absolutely their own. In juxtaposing their paintings with those of Soutine, one almost needs an Artaudian nerve scale to determine the extent of Soutine's presence.

De Kooning openly, and incisively, acknowledged his admiration for Soutine, calling him, in 1977, his "favorite artist." De Kooning's *Woman as Landscape* (1954–1955) is filled with impulsive Céret-like moves. The crazed, cartoonish smile in red, smeared where "her" genitals might be, is very much in the spirit of some 1920s Soutines. Another de Kooning, *Woman, Sag Harbor* (1964) is reproduced facing a 1923 *Street at Cagnes* by Soutine, whose undulant vertical yellow street looks also like a headless female body in profile. Outside of this "woman" patterned work, I don't find much of Soutine in de Kooning's paintings. They have no "existent" in any sense outside of de Kooning's own self-seeking, which increases in vacuity and aimlessness as he ages. There is a drift in de Kooning that is unimaginable with Soutine.

The late British art historian and Bacon-conversationalist David Sylvester is quoted to the effect that Soutine's paintings had "a crucial influence on Bacon's work between 1956 and, say, 1957 as they had on de Kooning's from 1951." I take it Sylvester had in mind the series of van Gogh portraits, or such paintings as *Man Carrying a Child, Study for the Nurse in the film Battleship Potempkin,* or *Study for Figure IV,* all of which were done in these years. Yet none of these paintings are reproduced in *Impact;* instead, we are shown Bacon paintings from 1962, 1965, and 1978. Since Sylvester knew Bacon's work in great detail, recording over a hundred pages of interviews with him between 1962 and 1974, it seems to me that one should begin with his proposal and work out from there.

Bacon's portraits are significantly beholden to Soutine, although their distortions are more bravura gesturings than anatomical warpings. His decadent statement, "I wanted to paint the scream more than the horror," is presented twice in *Impact* (as are some other statements and two Soutine paintings). The first time it is presented in bright-red oversized type on a page otherwise blank facing an opened-up, flayed Soutine rabbit: no relationship to a scream. The appropriate Soutine to juxtapose with Bacon's statement (obviously referencing the famous Munch *The Scream*) is on page 99: *Side of Beef,* which can be read as a flayed man in profile, head arched back, mouth gaping. The failure to find appropriate paintings to back up quotations is a problem throughout this book.

Jackson Pollock is more enigmatic than de Kooning and Bacon relative to Soutine influence. Pollock's early influences are well-known (Benton, Beckmann, Orozco, Picasso). Soutine is not among them. *Impact* reproduces four Pollocks: *Head with Polygons* (1938–1941), *Eyes in the Heat* (1946), *Full Fathom Five* (1947), and *Scent* (1955). There are a few Pollock paintings from the 1930s, such as *The Flame* and *Composition with Figures and Banners* (both dated 1934–1938), that suggest Pollock had looked at the Céret paintings. However, *Head with Polygons* is not one of these and its inclusion, in this context, is puzzling. It is presented twice, as a matter of fact, the first time turned at a 45° angle (perhaps to make some point that evades me).

From 1946 on, Pollock's work is relentlessly abstract. On page 67, the art historian William Seitz is quoted. He writes that Pollock pushed "values inherent in van Gogh and Soutine to an ultimate conclusion." I have already mentioned that in Céret Soutine stood on a precipice beyond which was some new form of abstract expressionism. But he did not make that leap, for to have done so would have meant giving up his "models," his grip on reality. Pollock never appears to have used a model (though there is one very early self-portrait), and his movement from the old to the new is the opposite of Soutine's. From my point of view, the fluffy white disintegrating patterns in the late *Scent* (which Frank O'Hara wrote was painted in homage to Soutine) have nothing to do with the essence of Soutine's work.

On page 28, the authors compare Soutine's excessive demands on his models to Pollock's painterly immersion. It seems like an irrelevant comparison.

Dubuffet, as is well known, came into painting at mid-life inspired by "art brut," and created a kind of sophisticated "primitivism" that is often childlike and humorous. To me he seems closer to Jean Michel Basquiat than to Soutine. Unlike Soutine, Dubuffet seems to approach the making of art from a Dadaist contempt for artistry and tradition. His world is one of mythic smears, melting geometric patterns, and the banal aswarm with itself.

On page 40, one reads: "The raw power of Dubuffet's early *Corps de dame* series… may have been prompted indeed by the fleshy meat paintings that Dubuffet knew (as the artist stated to Maurice Tuchman in 1968)." Since Tuchman is one of the authors of *Impact,* why does he present information in this form? If Dubuffet made such a statement, why is he not quoted? If such a statement has been previously published, why is it not cited? Note Soutine is not mentioned in the quotation.

The book design of *Impact* leaves a lot to be desired. No sources are given for quotations. There are ten photographs of the artists in the book by themselves or in their studios. All appear to have messy studios. Does this ally them to the supposedly untidy Soutine? For contemporary relevance, the painter R.B. Kitaj is quoted to the effect that he attempted to draw Soutine's one painting of a nude. Facing the quote is a reproduction of *Female Nude* (1933), a sad and moving painting that is completely consistent with everything we know about Soutine (and it is utterly different than any of de Kooning's "women"). Since the Kitaj quote does not contribute to the book's thesis, how explain its presence? The Soutine nude needs no justification for inclusion. Finally, the "open-ended juxtaposition" format is, in my opinion, much less effective than including an extending analytical essay or two. However, I think Tuchman and Dunow would be hard pressed to make convincing personal arguments for significant influence in these four cases.

I don't think any of these approaches is the proper one if the goal is to gain Soutine a wider audience and increased status in the art world. Such a goal should be based on his uniqueness, on what is inimitable in his painting, on what sets him forth as one whose body of work makes a statement that is not subservient to any other painter. This is the Soutine that I "met" in Kurashiki, a Soutine capable of engaging the presence of common things and common people like no other 20th century artist. This is the Soutine whose conflicted "existent" give and take is immune to all imaginal appropriations.

Rain Taxi, Fall 2002 [with minor revisions]

DAUMIER MOMENTS

Monumental nymphs in zebra light pursued by satyrs as if by saber blows.

"The First Dip," up to his unlit penis in pond water, with moon-white belly, a child wades, partially suspended by his father's sausage arms.

Under Cezanne, Daumier's bathing poor.

Dragging, ragged lance of fugitives, pushing hiltwise under a hard rose cowl of light.

Faces like roller-rinks of shifting planes, sneers bubbling with slime satisfaction, arched brows over eyes poking out like spotted eggs

Below an old lawyer, hunched rockwork on the Palace of Justice steps, a snob drifts.

Interlocking wrestlers: a Siberian mammoth-tusk hut.

Wrestleresquely, a man gathers a child into a kiss.

Daumier seems to have been interested in everything.

A destitute and famished woman drinker, with both hands suctioning a cup.

Saltimbanques departing. The nearly naked skeletal child grips a collection box. His clown father stoops clutching a chair, his garb.

Stooped gentleman in bowler scrutinizing prints. Stale light drifts the loaded rack. Is man not more alone for having draped himself with the world?

Old Quixote, a semi-recumbent wrestler, in bronze-amber light, reading.

Hoisted via Daumier's bones, the Jolly Roger through which all humanity blows.

2003

A NOTE ON ANTINOFF'S "SPIRITUAL ATHEISM"

In his two-part essay [APR May/June and July/August 2006], Steven Antinoff, in a very thoughtful way, proposes committed meditation as a way and anti-way of breaking through a plethora of problems that plague all sorts of people. He presents himself as one who has obsessively based his life on an extremely grueling meditative regime. He indicates that although he has experienced his goal, he has not realized it.

While Antinoff clearly respects many artists and writers, he remains ambivalent about the extent to which art resolves loneliness, ego entrapment, the longing for fulfillment, totality and infinity, and being confronted with the void (also variously discussed as the abyss, the gap, and the wound). Since he eschews religiosity, salvation and its analogues appear irrelevant to his argument. In fact, since all the stages of meditative practice are metaphorically described, and since he says the problem cannot be resolved artistically (art being the primary realm of metaphor), fulfillment for him (in terms that I can understand) seems to be either a kind of ineffable sensation that blocks out the exterior world, or the description of a kind of art that does not exist.

In his use of his own and others' metaphors to convey meditational states of mind, Antinoff is somewhat like an artist describing his work. The difference between him and an artist is that the artist has a product that symbolizes the creative process itself. Antinoff in the hundred or so pages of his essay only offers a description of otherwise (as far as I know) unrecorded years of passage. I think he would argue that making art involves a means without an end. That is, "end" in the sense of achieving some mysterious solution to living and dying. When an artist walks away from a just completed work, he is as much a part of this world, with all its problems and horrors, as he was before he embarked on his creative project, and he returns to a state of mind very close to that with which he began his project. I finish Antinoff's essay with the feeling that his form of meditation is directed toward a publicly invisible end, and that it is based on publicly invisible means. He does mention that he has written an unpublished novel called *The Atheist's Monastery.* Perhaps he has addressed some of the process missing from his essay in this work.

Were Antinoff to walk up to me and say that he has freed himself from "life-and-death," my response would be to touch him, to remind him that he has a body, thus was born, and having been born will die. When César Vallejo writes in *Human Poems:*

> What's got into me, that I'm neither alive nor dead?

he is not announcing that he is beyond being alive or being dead, but is in a limbo, or an abyssal state of self-contradiction (which William Blake would describe as being in his "specter's power"). What Antinoff describes, to his horror, as "crystallized anxiety" is an realm I feel that such writers as Vallejo, Beckett, and Kafka, have opened up the insides of and presented the anatomy of its various interiors.

It may be that Antinoff feels that bringing in class, poverty, social oppression, in particular American imperialism, is beside the point of his focus. I wonder, because the most meaningful artists, in my opinion, hold open to the exterior world, and by suffering it in their work enable their vision to take on a human dimension that is denied to one who is completely self-goaled. Antinoff's evocation of "monastery" in the title of his novel suggests that in his long quest he has basically been in retreat.

Most of the facets of the problem noted above are addressed by certain poets. While they do not sublimate them into an "ordinary mind" that is at once "vast and boundless," they incorporate them into structures that, via what N.O. Brown has called "a protean flux of metamorphosis," engage freedom and an adherence to otherness.

Antinoff writes that loneliness begins in knowing that "I am I." As if against this isolation lock, Arthur Rimbaud proposed that "I is somebody else." Or: I is the undiscovered self, an operative in the abyss, or subconscious realm. Non-being can be conceived of as source, not just sheer absence. The swarm of terms that humankind has generated to approach the abyss may go back to Upper Paleolithic imagination: in one object carved out of reindeer antler an erect phallus appears to grow out of a vulva at the base. The vulva seems to produce the phallus. To put it idiomatically, *this is a hole that grows into a pole.* Other mythologems for this force are the First Parents in coitus, the two snakes copulating seen by Tiresias, and the uroboric snake (in effect a hole pole).

Another trope on the artist and the abyss came to me in the mid 1980s while writing the poem "Deeds Done and Suffered by Light:"

> ...over the cobweb orchestra
> there's an ice
> conductor,
> forget the orchestra,
> conduct the pit!

In *Conductors of the Pit,* a collection of my translations, I have identified as "conductors of the pit" such poets as Antonin Artaud, Vladimir Holan, and César Vallejo who write a poetry *in extremis,* a poetry that goes for the whole and attempts to become responsible for all the poet knows about himself and the world.

Rather than viewing "blocks" as something that happens to one on a quest (such as "writers' blocks"), Antinoff sees them as self-created formations that represent an advanced stage of the drive for fulfillment. I mainly experience blocks at the point in a poem when I am pushing toward closure, seeking to be up to and beyond my limits, going for an ultimate process-generated perception. Suddenly there is the sensation: "I can't see through this," or: "there is no resolution to this." Not being able to see through the matter at hand reverberates as all matter, the power of the opaque which I project out of my own opaqueness. In a letter from October, 1882, Vincent van Gogh wrote:

> What is drawing? How does one learn it? It is working through an invisible iron wall that seems to stand between what one feels and what one can do. How is one to get through that wall—since pounding against it is of no use? One must undermine the wall and drill through it slowly and patiently, in my opinion.

I think that both Antinoff and I would agree that both artist and meditative quester must figure out how to abandon the literal, egotistic, mind/body dominated world for a performance space that is totally metaphorical, where everything is something else. There is no path, or as Chuang Tzu, quoted by Antinoff, wrote: "Truth is a pathless land." In my poetry that often means that, in contrast to the traditional narrative poem, no advance move can be planned. If I think of a good "last line" I know it is only the next line. Each image is its own barrier and its own breakthrough.

Unlike Antinoff, I do not seek to jettison ego in the creative process. My ego becomes a hovering super-ego watching the creative I, a focus manager conducting the intersecting conscious and subconscious realms. Vicente Huidobro once wrote: "Invent new worlds but be careful of what you say." It is the creative I that invents; it is the super-ego that must spot bullshit when it is masquerading as imagination. The realities of the spirit are in love with critical intelligence.

I took a special pleasure in Antinoff's quotation from Paul Tillich's *Love, Power, and Justice:* "A life process is the more powerful, the more non-being it can include in its self-affirmation, without being destroyed by it."

Affirmation is only viable when it survives repeated immersions in negation. At the point one says: I am an American artist, one inducts the Hydra of news, in which what is true and what is untrue, what is necessary and what is human, all compete as head lines. Such is outer negation with its acidic rivulets of guilt. Inner negation, far more complex, plays the abyss off against one's own hedged gestation and decay. When the pre-Columbian ball court of the dead surfaces, partially flooding the ivory tower, there is tremendous congress. Each next line is a last line compelling another.

APR, 2006 [with very minor revisions]

ADRIENNE RICH'S *TELEPHONE RINGING IN THE LABYRINTH*

Adrienne Rich's new book (Norton, 2007) is written from the viewpoint of a poet who, now in her late 70s, feels over- and underwhelmed by the global and domestic weight of the American imperium. Her writing is charged with residual aptness and alertness. Unlike much "late style" poetry, her intellectual formulations are still attached to social experience. That, plus her way of being thoroughly political without adopting a posture of being for or against, but humanly—in Vallejo's sense of that word—involved, suggests that in *Telephone Ringing in the Labyrinth* she may have figured out a new way to create a "book of a soul contending."

Hers is a voice awed by the galaxies we human beings thankfully have no access to, and stunned by what people are doing to life on earth (there is a poem about a kangaroo set on fire by someone that simply frames the burning creature, without commentary).

For Rich, "the thin-ice present where we're balancing here," other than for some grateful and moving gestures to her partner of many years, no longer provides nourishing fundament. "Words gather like flies above this carcass of meaning." Revolutionary zeal is a thing of the past: any optimism now is a kind of living debris, evoking memories from what I take to be her 1967–1974 period—times "tense with elation," "a world echoing everywhere." Basic pleasures like spring water, mown grass, and food from a local market are tentatively shored against "the great machine coughing out the pieces, hurtling on." I write "shored," invoking T.S. Eliot's "shored against my ruins" but that placement is probably too massive for what is happening in *Telephone Ringing in the Labyrinth.*

This resonant title evokes a number of things: the poet herself attempting to communicate with antiquity and hearing no response. Labyrinth as laboratory into which antiquity is calling with no one picking up. Ringing as the scar of *was* on the labyrinth's wall. Motel transiency as a kind of spectral evocation of the labyrinth, where the Minotaur has been reduced to "a horned beast made of mist." I sense an implication here that human kind would be better off *in* the labyrinth, in hair-raising conjunction with Minotaurs and endless winding paths, than outside of it—that it was an error TO GET OUT. "Out" being our present-day, demythologized world where:

> Silent limousines meet jets descending over the Rockies. Steam rooms, pure thick towels, vases of tuberose and jasmine, old vintages await the après-skiers.
>
> Rooms of mahogany and leather, conversations open in international code. Thighs and buttocks to open later by arrangement.
>
> Out of sight, out of mind, she solitary wrestles a huge duvet, resheathes heavy tasseled bolsters. Bed after bed. Nights, in her room, ices strained arms. Rests her legs.
>
> Elsewhere, in Andhra Pradesh, another farmer swallows pesticide.

The procedure in this keen little prose poem is cog-like, logical. Underpaid women make possible the five-star ski lodge life of the super-rich. But don't start feeling sorry for them, because they are "well off" relative to the 25,000 Indian farmers who, driven into abject poverty by World Bank "structural adjustments" (meaning having to purchase yearly genetically-engineered seeds which drives the farmers into unpayable debts), have committed suicide over the past decade. In such a piece, the poet's eye drills down through pomp and its immigrant carytids into the "dreamfaces blurring horrorlands: border of poetry."

Some of Rich's lines offer evidence like a smudge on a wall, more a trace of history than growth. Other lines, like:

After the burnt forests   silhouettes wade
  liquid hibiscus air

carry a precise conjunction of language and feeling.

Donald Rumsfeld's words "You go to war with the army you have" (cited in a footnote) is repositioned as the poet ponders maimed veterans with prosthetic limbs:

Ghost limbs go into spasm in the night.
You come back from war with the body you have.

Later in the book, as if in unpitying sympathy with the maimed as well as her own mortality, such "ghost limbs" become:

Is there a ghost-in-waiting?
Time to bring that one in.

There is now in her poetry a disavowal of any writing that would let the reader off the hook of his own lostness—that is, to throw him the carrot of an explanatory exit (possibly the reason that neither Iraq nor Bush are mentioned). Antonio Gramsci's viewpoint, as expressed in his prison notebooks, she implies, might now be spoken by a poet as a citizen in an exile constructed with information bars and beserk navigational positionings.

Because of her age, Rich has little futurity to gamble with. She's out on a beach of sorts, watching the tidal steel build, "rebuilding daily the sand city." Paul Celan's eyelid floats in.

Rain Taxi, 2008

IV

LECTURES ON THE ICE AGE PAINTED CAVES OF SOUTHWESTERN FRANCE

In the spring of 1974, my wife Caryl and I rented a furnished apartment in a farmhouse outside of Tursac, in the French Dordogne. We soon discovered the painted Ice Age caves in the region and after Hallam Movius Jr., a Harvard archeologist who had worked in the region for decades, arranged for us to visit the Lascaux cave, I decided to mount what Charles Olson has referred to as "a saturation job" on the origin of image-making as it could be discerned in the caves of the Dordogne, Lot, and Ariège regions. I completed my work in 1999, after many visits in these areas both to caves open to the public as well as privately owned caves for which special visitation permission was required. Jean Clottes arranged visits to several very important caves in the Ariège, including the great Tuc d'Audoubert which the owners, the Bégouën family, only visit once a year. I arranged six visits to the original Lascaux cave, and on my last time there was given permission to spend a half an hour in the Shaft inspecting the most engaging narrative "scene" in Upper Paleolithic image making. In 2003, Wesleyan University Press published Juniper Fuse: Upper Paleolithic Imagination & the Construction of the Underworld. *As I write this Introduction this afternoon in the fall of 2008, Wesleyan is in the process of producing a second edition of my book.*

In 1981 and 1983, Caryl and I took small groups of people to visit some of these caves. After doing the tour on our own twice, we decided it was too much work to publicize and handle all the hotel and restaurant reservations on our own and we did not set up another tour until 1996 when Eastern Michigan University sponsored us. Gary Snyder came along that year as guest lecturer. In 2000, Ringling School of Art and Design in Sarasota, Florida decided to sponsor us on an ongoing basis (mainly thanks to Nancee Clark, the Director of Continuing Education there). We have now done seven tours with

Ringling, and Dale Pendell, Wade Davis, and Robert Creeley have joined us as guest lecturers. For many years, Mathilde Sitbon has been our extremely valuable French coordinator and tour assistant.

Each year we have taken our groups of twelve to eighteen people to a half dozen caves (including the Lascaux facsimile, the original having been closed to the public for many decades). Like all visitors, we must go with a guide who mainly, in French or English, points out and comments very briefly on the images. In order to prepare our groups for these visits I wrote up lectures for each cave and gave them to our groups usually right before we left our hotel for a particular cave. Over the years I have edited and, in some cases, expanded these lectures, adding information from new books on the subject when appropriate.

Besides Juniper Fuse, I can especially recommend for people who are planning on visiting these caves (all of which are open to the public, although the number of visitors is increasingly limited for preservation purposes) two books that have been around for some time: S. Giedion's The Eternal Present: The Beginnings of Art (Bollingen, 1957) and André-Leroi Gourhan's Treasures of Prehistoric Art (Abrams, 1967). Both of these books are out of print, but can be found online. I also recommend the Michelin Red Guide for hotels and restaurants and the Michelin Green Guide on the Dordogne for cave locations and visiting hours. A car is necessary as all caves are in the countryside

The first of these lectures introduces our groups to the world of the Upper Paleolithic painted caves. The second one describes the Laussel bas-relief wall sculptures in the Bordeaux Musée d'Aquitaine. Lectures three through seven introduce the six caves that we always visited: Rouffignac, Combarelles, Font-de-Gaume, Lascaux (the facsimile), Cougnac and Pech Merle. To these lectures I have added two on small, minor caves in the Dordogne that we visited occasionally: Bernifal and St.-Cirq. On two occasions we bused four hours south of the Dordogne to the Ariège region and visited the caves of Gargas and Niaux. These are both, in their own ways, very impressive caves, so I have added my lectures on these as well.

APPROACHING THE CAVES

When we enter a cave, we leave the world of bird song and blue sky for a world of constricted darkness that can fill us with a mystical enthusiasm.

The caves we will visit not only have some of the earliest image-making of humankind but their own limestone personalities: what we recognize as stalagmites, stalactites and draperies, may have struck Cro-Magnon people as earth organs. The shifting contours of stone walls, with their cracks and ridges may have suggested animals partially emerging from, or disappearing into, such walls.

We will visit two prehistory museums, the prehistory section of Bordeaux's Musée d'Aquitaine, five caves and the Lascaux facsimile. The original cave has been closed to the public since 1962. Until 2001, a few professionals and dignitaries were allowed to visit Lascaux for forty-five minutes, four days a week. During the research for my book, *Juniper Fuse: Upper Paleolithic Imagination & the Construction of the Underworld,* between 1974 and 1999, Caryl and I visited Lascaux six times. Because of a white mold outbreak in 2001, and more recently black spots the size of human hands in a significant number of the paintings, the original cave is now closed to everyone. For reports on the Lascaux situation up to 2008, go to www.savelascaux.org.

The Musée d'Aquitaine has a small prehistoric collection, including four wall sculptures from the Laussel rock shelter, the most famous of which is known as "the Venus of Laussel." I will discuss these works when we visit the museum. Our second museum is the new National Prehistory Museum in Les Eyzies. Some of the focus here is on evolution, so we will begin our visit there with one of the museum's guides. I will later make some comments on a few engraved slabs from nearby rock shelters that represent some of the earliest known image-making in the Dordogne. After our visit to the Lascaux facsimile, we will visit our third museum, Le Thot, which has, in facsimile, some paintings from the cave that are not part of the Lascaux facsimile.

Concerning the caves: I will give a lecture on each cave before we visit it, including the Lascaux facsimile, and in these lectures, along with my talk on "Cave Art Theory" (from my book), I will hope to offer you a "crash course" (as we used to say in the 1960s) on Upper Paleolithic image-making in the caves of the Dordogne and Lot regions. After each lecture, we will then, sometimes all together, sometimes in small groups, visit the caves themselves—always, as required by French law, with a French guide, most of whose comments will focus on what we are seeing on the spot. Our travel coordinator, Mathilde Sitbon, will offer interpretations in English of the guides' remarks when the guide does not speak English.

I encourage all of you to take notes, and to write down thoughts occurring to you during my lectures or in the caves themselves. Near the end of our trip, all of you will have a chance to express your feelings about what you have experienced.

Were we to spend hours in cave dark, we might have the sort of experiences that Barbara McLeod did, during long sits, in the caves of Guatemala and Belize (I quote from a paper she wrote about her cave experiences in *Juniper Fuse,* pages 133–135). For some, like McLeod, the cave's sensory isolational atmosphere is experienced as spirit-filled, even as hallucinogenic. For example, grotesque and hybrid cave-images suggest a fusion between consciousness and subterranean "entities." It is as if the soul of an all-devouring monster earth can be contacted in cavern dark as a living and fathomless reservoir of psychic force.

Our cave visits should give us a chance to reflect on how it might have been for Cro-Magnon men, women, adolescents and children to explore them. There is evidence that all ages and sexes visited the caves. The image-making we will see ranges from the childishly crude to the extremely sophisticated. We can imagine that many images, or wandering lines, were made spontaneously, sometimes without hand lamps in total dark, while others indicate planned artistic projects, including the heating of pigments, shading, perspective, and, in Lascaux's case, scaffolding.

Here are a few pertinent remarks by the Canadian literary scholar, Northrop Frye:

> In Paleolithic times the liveliest and most spirited paintings of animals were made in caves under incredibly difficult conditions of position and lighting. Doubtless there was some aesthetic motive at work to create a work of beauty, but this would be hopelessly inadequate to account for painting in such conditions. We can add such words as 're-ligion' and 'magic', but the fact remains that the complexity, urgency, and sheer titanic power of the motivation involved is something we cannot understand now, much less recapture.
>
> The nearest we can come to putting such motivation into words, I think, is to say that the bison and bears portrayed were a kind of extension of human consciousness and power into the objects of greatest energy and strength they could see in the world around them. This is the real function of what appears in words as metaphor: the assimilating of the energy, the beauty, the elusive glory, latent in nature to the observing mind. I speak of 'the mind' as though it were the mind of a separated individual, but of course the community out of which the individual artist emerges guides his hand and controls his speech....
>
> Then again, in the cave drawings we see animal forms with human eyes looking through them, and suspect that we are really seeing a sorcerer or shaman who has identified himself with the animal by putting on its skin....
>
> At the bottom of the primitive in literature is a totally metaphorical world with no consistent distinction of subject and object. Space in such a world is, like dream space, anywhere but nowhere in particular.

And here is a statement by the experimental filmmaker Stan Brakhage that also strikes me as pertinent to the realm that we are about to enter:

> Imagine an eye unruled by man-made laws of perspective.... Our whole structure of visual thinking is based on man-made laws of perspective.... But imagine an eye unprejudiced by compositional logic, an eye which does not respond to the name of everything, but which must know each object encountered in life through an adventure of perception. In other words, everything you see you have to be having an immediate adventure with it. It's not canned in any sense. How many colors are there in a field of grass to the crawling baby unaware of green? Imagine a world alive with incomprehensible objects...shimmering with an endless variety of movements.... There's not a moment of stillness anywhere.... Imagine a world before the beginning was the Word.

Brakhage's comments suggest an explanation for the superimposition of one form over another, as we will see in the Black Fresco at Pech Merle, in some of the engravings in Combarelles, and in the Rotunda at Lascaux, where ponies and cows are superimposed across the legs of the giant aurochs.

Here is some basic information concerning prehistory and the painted caves:

Gouged lines, zig-zags, scratches, and ochre smears on stone now appear to have occurred at different places on the earth during the Lower Paleolithic (2 million to 100,000 years ago). It is not until the Upper Paleolithic, at around 35,000 B.P. (meaning, "before the present," the present being 1950 when radiocarbon dating techniques were perfected), that figurative images in association with signs occur.

Upper Paleolithic people are referred to as Cro-Magnons. They looks exactly like we do. The first Cro-Magnon skeletons were discovered in 1868 in a rock shelter of that name in Les Eyzies de Tayac, where we will be spending seven days. Cro-Magnon means "big hole." So we are the descemdemts of the Big Hole People, a term with eerie vibrations in our times.

We can call this image-making "art" as long as we allow for the probability that it did not mean to its makers and viewers what art means to us today. It must have included magical, initiational, and utilitarian aspects that lie outside of our aesthetic considerations.

There are now estimated to be over 320 "decorated" or "ensouled" caves in Western Europe (160 in France, 130 in Spain, 25 in Italy/Sicily, 3 in Portugal). Parietal—or wall—art mainly consists of signs and animals. Such are engraved with flint blades or brushed on or sprayed using manganese, charcoal, or ochre mixed with cave water.

The horse and the bison are the two most depicted animals, usually a side view in outline. Dangerous animals, such as rhinoceroses, lions, bears, and mammoths, are seldom depicted—with the exception of Chauvet, a cave in the Ardèche.

There are no backgrounds or ground lines, and very few narrative scenes. Most animals are presented in isolation.

Many activities that are important to us today are not depicted: there are only a few questionable scenes of intercourse, one possible birth scene, no depictions of people fighting, and—it is important to state—no hunting scenes.

Human figurations occur much less than animal depictions, and they are less complete, often schematic, and are, if they have heads, faceless, or "masked." The most imaginative, from my point of view, are the hybrids (human body with bison or bird heads), which may reflect a proto-shamanism and thus the beginnings of the kind of mental travel that becomes poetry. Women are depicted more often than men. The most oft-repeated female images are the so-called "Venus" figurines, some 140 of which have been found, from southern France, across Germany, and into Siberia.

Decorated caves do not appear to have been inhabited or used as burial grounds. Refuse sites, called middens, are usually found outside, near cave entrances. Thus the notion that such caves were "sanctuaries," or sites of initiation and introspection, is quite reasonable.

Lighting was generated by flickering wicks in oil-pooled stone hand lamps. There is seldom any evidence of torches.

The primary painting ingredients—black manganese, red ochre, and charcoal—were mixed with cave water for pigment consistency.

Evidence for genuine antiquity makes use of any or all of the following: parts of paintings covered over and sealed by layers of ancient calcite; objects or paintings covered by archeological deposits; depictions of long-extinct species; stylistic affinities with organic surviving materials from which radiocarbon estimates can be obtained; engravings covered by micro-crystals; painted lines containing miniscule areas of eroded material.

The earliest radiocarbon dated painting at this point is a charcoal rhinoceros in Chauvet, dated in 1995 at 32,400 B.P. This datation, based on research from a single laboratory, has recently been disputed by some scholars.

For Hamlet, the question was: to be or not to be. I would propose that it was in the Upper Paleolithic, in the caves' womb-charged, absence-saturated dark, that Cro-Magnon may have realized that the real burden was to be and not to be. For looking at a horse drawn on a stone wall, he or she must have realized that the animal that was not there WAS THERE.

While inside the Combarelles cave in 1970, I had the intuition that image-making was motivated by a crisis in which Cro-Magnon people began to separate the animal out of their about-to-be human heads and to project it onto cave walls (as well as onto a variety of portable tools and weapons, often made out of the animal themselves).

In other words, the liberation of what might be called "the autonomous imagination" came from within, as a projective response on the part of those struggling to differentiate themselves from, while being deeply bonded to, animals.

Shamanism, or what might be more accurately termed proto-shamanism, may have come into being as a reactive swerve against this separation continuum, to rebind this new human being to the fantasy of a paradise in which humans could converse with animals and thus, if only momentarily, make contact with the world before the separation continuum.

The religious historian Mircea Eliade proposed in his book, *Zalmoxis: The Vanishing God,* that the oldest myth we have access to today might be that of the "Cosmic Dive." This is a creation story of an animal who dives into the depths of the primeval sea to bring up the stuff of which the earth is made. This creature with mud on its paws or claws may be a metaphor for a Cro-Magnon shaman with red ochre on his hands, stuff not simply brought up, but utilized on a wall in cave depths. We now know that the mixing agent for ochre and manganese was cave water. Thus this "oldest myth" may be a cosmogonic tale based on the origins of image-making. See pages 207–209 in *Juniper Fuse* for more thoughts about the "Cosmic Dive."

THE LAUSSEL BAS-RELIEF SCULPTURES

Halfway up a slope above the Beune River (a tributary of the Vézère; we will have dinner at the Moulin de la Beune in Les Eyzies, by which the Beune flows) is a one hundred yard long rock shelter, some five miles from Les Eyzies, which for thousands of years was a dwelling place for various Cro-Magnon groups. There is good evidence that this shelter was also a fertility shrine inasmuch as it included a group of stone blocks with five human figures and at least five more blocks with phallic and vulvar engravings.

The principle bas-relief figure is known as the Venus of Laussel. She is one of the first efforts (during the Gravettian period, roughly 25,000 years ago) to depict the human figure in relief and may be considered as the prototype of the Great or Mother Goddess. However, I must also mention that the Venus figure in the Chauvet cave, discovered in 1994, is probably 5000 years older.

The first description of the Venus of Laussel is given by Dr. Lalanne, the Dordogne physician who was her discoverer, in 1911. He writes:

> It is a statuette carved into a block of hard limestone; it represents a nude female, holding in her right hand the horn of a bison. The figure is 46 cm, (17 inches) tall.... The head, though largely disengaged, presents no traces of a face. Despite this, one can observe that it was carved in profile.... The neck is clearly defined and elongated.... Two long and pendulous breasts, oval in form, grow beautifully out from her chest.... The right arm falls naturally beside the body but the forearm is raised to the height of the shoulder where the hand supports a bison's horn. The whole body is polished except for the head.... The statue was originally painted red.

To this description I can add: the horn has 13 notches which might represent the 13 lunar months of a year. It could also be an obstetrical calendar or a musical scraper. The traces of red ochre, at the time of discovery, were confined to the left breast, lower stomach and the area chipped out between the body and the right arm, possibly indicating menstrual symbolism. The figure may be pregnant or just obese; however, the reverential placement on the belly by the left hand suggests to me pregnancy.

Sigfried Giedion, in *The Eternal Present: The Beginnings of Art,* writes:

> The figure and the block are inseparably interlocked. In the position selected by the artist for this relief, the block had a slight overhang, so that the figure swelled forward gently. When seen from the side, the curve appears as taut as a strung bow. It swells up to the extreme point, the maternal belly, then falls away at either end and sinks slowly into the rock, in which the feet seem to melt. The upper part of the body curves gently backward, and the head, resting between two rock projections, seems to be reclining as though on a cushion.

Giedion also comments, concerning the notched bison horn, "This position recalls the belief, current among some African tribes, that a horn filled with blood is the highest symbol of fertility."

A second bas-relief figure, identified as the Quadrille Woman, is less complete, being broken off from the pelvis down. She also has traces of red ochre, and, while less realized than the Venus of Laussel, has similar characteristics: even more voluminous bulging sack-like breasts, belly with navel, wide buttocks, and a partially destroyed genital triangle. Her left arm is raised somewhat like the Venus's right arm and appears to be holding something. Her right arm, hanging by her side, also appears to be grasping something. Her most distinguished features are the vertical and horizontal furrows covering her face.

A third block has the relief of a standing man. The upper part of his body is turning to the right with the left shoulder advanced. The outstretched left arm is still partially intact, but the right is only a short stump. Scholars have conjectured that he is either an archer or a spear-thrower. His head is badly damaged and it is unclear if it was ever completely sculpted (the same can be said about the head of the Venus of Laussel, the left side of which can be read as long hair; looking at the edge of the right side, which would have been her face I have fantasized a fish face). There are two deep horizontal lines above the male figure's hips which look like a belt or girdle. In comparison to the heavy-set female figures, the male is slender. His outlines are firm and sensitively rendered.

A fourth figure, gouged in another block, is one of the most mysterious in Upper Paleolithic art. The image is about 8 inches high, and appears to depict two figures, with a head above and a head below, mirroring each other, or, in Paul Balm's phrase, "resembling a playing-card." The most precise description of the figures, or figure, is still that of Dr. Lalanne, Laussel's excavator. He describes the possibly interlocked figures as follows:

> One of the figures is a woman, recognizable by her large, pendulous breasts.... The belly is represented by a strong, central projection.... The thighs are raised. The arms extend the length of the body and the hands appear to be beneath the lower limbs. The second figure...is in an opposite position but symmetrical to the figure already described. Only the chest is carefully sculpted; the rest of the body disappears beneath that of the woman.

Conjectures by Giedion and others as to what is depicted include copulation, childbirth, a standing Venus figure making use of an earlier unfinished figure, an androgynous figure, two half figures joined at the waist, and a person standing waist-deep in water.

Comparing Giedion's shadowed black and white photo with Bahn's smaller but color photo (presented, it appears, upside down in *Journey Through the Ice Age*), I decided that the best interpretation is copulation: a woman sitting, knees raised, on a man whose lower body is beneath hers and thus, in the engraving, invisible. This interpretation is not without problems, as the lower figure consists of only a head and upper chest. But the lower figure's head is roughly the same size as the upper figure's, suggesting that it is not that of an infant being born.

A fifth bas-relief of a female figure holding out a basket-like object was illegally sold to a German museum soon after its discovery, and then destroyed during the bombing of Berlin in 1945.

Such bas-reliefs seem to appear, out of the Cro-Magnon night, as liftings into view of the newly emergent human, out of a morass of perception crossing perception. Sub-conscious trophies, breakthroughs, wrestlings of minds amazed, in random exploration of what is and what is not. Hamlet at 30,000 B.P. Out of this vise, the earliest metaphors break through.

ROUFFIGNAC & COMBARELLES

Before discussing the first two caves we will visit, I'd like to make a few remarks about the difference between portable and parietal Upper Paleolithic art.

Thousands of carved and engraved pieces, called "portable" or "mobilary" objects have been discovered from the Upper Paleolithic. These include spears, harpoons, spear-throwers, spatulas, beads, pendants, discs, figuringes, engraved plaquettes, painted stones, flutes, and bullroarers.

In contrast to portable art—worked off materials that appear to have been part of an everyday, survival world—deep cave art involved the exploration of an interior and foreign landscape. By drawing in the recesses of a cave, the boundaries of the familiar were extended, and an insideness was engaged, an insideness that with its bizarre and marvelous rock formations may have appeared to be the earth's equivalents of corporeal insides.

Other contrasts abound. Portable art is concentrated and restricted to an object's often very small surface, one that is sometimes round, thus partly unseeable as a person carves. Much portable art was done on material that was once alive, and while such may give a carved piece of deer antler a unique soulful feeling, the antler is also an element of an animal that is assimilated by humans, one that is part of—as well as used by—their bodies.

Cave art takes place on a surface that is relatively flat, sometimes vast, stationary, and not directly related to survival. The size of a figure is often up to the drawer's discretion. While caves are organic, their still and very dark presence is on a much different order of organic life than fauna and flora. At the same time, cave walls form a seamless congruity with the outside world. Cave art is also unframed, and seldom reflects any awareness of horizontality or verticality (in contrast to, say, Egyptian art, which includes the right angle and architecture).

While a ground line is suggested by wall surface contrasts in Lascaux, Upper Paleolithic figures do not seem to ever have been presented in a landscape (other than schematically in a few portable objects). Perspective is utilized in a few caves, but there is no background in the sense that we would say a portrait or a still-life has a background. Many of the animals seem as still as the stone on which they are depicted. Such has led one writer to propose that the "models" for the depictations are dead.

The decoration of Lascaux, for example, required scaffolding, considerable advance preparation (collecting pigments miles away from the cave, heating ochre dioxides to change their colors, fashioning brushes, burins, lamps, etc.), work coordination and, undoubtedly, some kind of apprenticeship. While the paintings and engravings had no visual background, they certainly had an aesthetic one, and a tradition, in that they evolved out of earlier, less sophisticated techniques and images. We are probably closer in time and aesthetics to Lascaux today than the painters of Lascaux were to early Aurignacian engravings within walking distance of the cave.

*

We will visit Rouffignac first. It has an electric train which conveys visitors to the decorated areas to be visited (a justification for the train is that Rouffignac is immense: more than five miles of galleries). It is also a cave of whose paintings the authenticity was seriously disputed in a controversy of the mid-1950s. Speleologists ultimately lost out to archeologists, including the formidable Abbé Breuil and Hallam Movius Jr. of the Harvard Peabody Museum, who in arguing for Rouffignac's authenticity settled the matter for that time.

Today, while most of Rouffignac's paintings are considered authentic, a small but significant number are disputed. There is the frieze of 3 rhinoceroses—speleologists claimed that two of them appeared between September and December 1948, and the third by Easter, 1949. And on the Great Ceiling, there are 11 ibexes, the only ones in the cave, which are drawn as stiff, squarish animals. Such ibex drawings are not to be found elsewhere in Upper Paleolithic image-making. Some people also contest the authenticity of one mammoth there that, again, appears out of character for Upper Paleolithic images.

A book published in 1953 based on visits to the cave in the 1940s showed the rhinoceros frieze, but at the same time did not mention any paintings in the text. When the author was queried, he said that the paintings were not mentioned because they were of recent origin. As early as 1907, Rouffignac had been visited and documented with no mention of paintings. Between the discovery of Font-de-Gaume in 1901 and that of Lascaux in 1940, no one commented on Rouffignac as a cave with paintings (and the area during those years was crawling with speleologists and archeologists). Then in June, 1956, two archeologists—Louis Nougier and Romain Robert—returned to Rouffignac, discovered around 230 paintings, and declared them authentic. In their report, they quoted from a 1575 document that mentioned "paintings in many places." To further complicate matters, Paul Bahn points out that Nougier and Robert were wrong, and that there is not a single mention by anyone of paintings in Rouffignac until the mid-twentieth century.

Breuil's argument for authenticity is mainly based on stylistic comparison, which we now know is shaky. However, in the mid-1950s, Breuil's word carried enormous weight. Movius, in backing up Breuil, commented that certain paintings were faded precisely as one would expect from weathering, inasmuch as they were located near a hole that wind went through. Evan Hadingham mentions that there was a chemical analysis of pigment samples based on the 1956 discovery. He gives no details and one is left to assume that the analysis supported authenticity. Recently, Bahn wrote that the multiple analyses and tests called for had never taken place. In a letter to me, he mentioned that the graffiti entangled with some of the animals on the Great Ceiling has been cleaned off by the owners so that it is no longer possible to tell if it was under or over the paintings. Bahn said that the only hope now is to test the organic material, if there is any, in the paintings. In the 1960s, Leroi-

Gourhan accepted absolutely the authenticity of Rouffignac and proposed that the Great Ceiling was comparable to the Altamira ceiling and the Salon Noir in Niaux.

In my opinion, the animals on the walls look ancient, but on all of our visits to the cave in the 1970s and 1980s, many of the animals on the Great Ceiling looked "funny." Some looked like stiff, schematic copies of other animal depictions, though I've never been able to identify which specific paintings they may have been based on. It is possible, of course, that such models do not exist and that the suspect animals on the Great Ceiling were done on the basis of a generalized memory of what Upper Paleolithic animals should look like.

In all fairness, it should be pointed out that there are nearly inaccessible places and sub-levels of Rouffignac that have paintings. One wonders whether forgers would have gone to the trouble of placing paintings in such places. And Leroi-Gourhan points out that it is possible in caves to pass certain details time and time again without seeing them. Some engravings in other caves are so subtle that a right-hand light will expose them while a left-hand light will make them disappear.

Rouffignac is also known as "The Cave of 100 Mammoths" (there are actually around 150). This huge and majestic animal, whose hump was ten feet above the ground, lived in the glacial steppe and tundra. As a catch, it represented an enormous reserve of meat and fat. It is said that a single mammoth kill could by itself support a group of 25 people for 43 days, and if such meat constituted only 50% of their diet, those days can be doubled. Mammoth tusks provided a large supply of ivory, from which Paleolithic people made all sorts of implements. In the Ukraine, cabins built entirely of mammoth bones have been excavated and reconstructed. The end of the Würm glaciation, 10,000 years ago, brought about a terrific climatic upheavel and Europe became covered with thick forests. The mammoths, needing a cold climate, migrated north and are said to have died by the thousands in the enormous snowstorms triggered by the rise in humidity caused by the post-glacial thaw.

The second most prominent animal in Rouffignac is the rhinoceros, of which there were only a dozen in all of Upper Paleolithic art until the discovery of 65 in Chauvet. Like the mammoth, the wooly rhinoceros is extinct. However, we know quite a bit about them as whole carcasses have been found preserved in the ice in Siberia, with even the stomach contents intact. They were up to 11 feet long and 5 feet high, so powerful and dangerous as to nearly be invincible. They fed on steppe plants, branches, and leaves, and because other game was plentiful and much easier to obtain, they were probably seldom hunted. Until Chauvet, the most notable rhinoceros depiction was the one in the Shaft at Lascaux.

The Rouffignac train will take us into the two main corridors, the north corridor, called the Breuil Gallery, and the northwest corridor with the Great Ceiling.

In the Breuil Gallery, on the left hand wall, there are a number of engravings of horses, bison, and mammoths. On the right hand wall are a number of black paintings: the frieze of rhinoceroses all facing in the same direction, and a frieze of mammoths arranged in two facing groups.

Only at the Great Ceiling will we be allowed to get off the train and walk around (the original floor here was 6 feet higher than the current one, which was deepened to allow visitors to stand under the Ceiling and view the animals). According to Leroi-Gourhan, the Great Ceiling contains 15 mammoths, 11 ibexes, 9 bisons, 7 horses, and 3 rhinoceroses. A total of 45 animals. In contrast, Ann Sieveking finds 37 animals here, and John Pfeiffer finds "over 60." As seems typical at Rouffignac, no one seems to agree with anyone else!

When we ride through the various corridors, we will see cave bear wallows. Bears appear to have been in Rouffignac as early as 40,000 years ago. The walls and even the ceilings are sometimes covered with claw scrapings, leading me to write in one poem, "bear claw hut rain," with the thought that bear claw lines may have been seen as hut or rain shapes by Cro-Magnon.

While there are very few man-made signs in Rouffignac, a gallery we will not visit is covered with thousands of crisscrossing finger-traced meanders in the soft, reddish clay, suggesting thousands of individual acts of participation.

Rouffignac is dated—only stylistically at this point—at around 13,000 B.P., between the Middle and the Late Magdalenian.

Jean Clottes has written that "Radiocarbon dating is an important method for obtaining accurate dates for fossils and artifacts made of organic material. At death, the quantity of carbon-14 present in each living organism starts decreasing at a regular rate. It is possible to arrive at the age of death and obtain a date by measuring the amount of radiocarbon left in the sample. There is, however, a statistical uncertainty linked to the date. 20,000 B.P. ± 300 means that the organism died between 20,300 and 19,700 years before 1950; moreover, the chances of the date's being within this range is 67%. To have a 95% chance of accuracy, one must double the uncertainty."

Our second cave is Combarelles. Based on the 1984 carbon-14 dating of bones in archeological layers from a midden at the entrance to the cave, the art inside has been dated between 13,680 and 11,380 B.P. The cave itself is a 300 yard tunnel whose walls are as furrowed as elephant hide, making it, one would think, extremely resistant to engraving. Combarelles, however, is a nearly totally engraved cave, with over 600 figures and signs now identified (there are also 2 red tectiforms, 2 painted animals, and a negative hand print in black, suggesting that engraving was done by choice).

The floor has been lowered by a yard to enable visitors to walk comfortably through tunnels that are hardly wider than an adult's outstretched arms. We will thus have to go through Combarelles in groups of five, not only because it is difficult for more than five people to cluster around a guide pointing out a difficult-to-identify engraving, but also for preservation reasons: human warmth provokes condensation on the walls which in turn produces a white pulverulence (or dustiness) in the calcite deposits on the walls. Because the number of visitors is limited per trip and by day (100 as of 1996, and 70 as of 2004), the cave is able to clean itself out at night, and in guide Claude Archambeau's opinion will not face the serious deterioration problems that nearly destroyed Lascaux in the early 1960s—which I will go into when I discuss Lascaux.

Claude and his wife, Monique, now retired, were the main guides and caretakers at Combarelles for many years. Monique did her Ph.D. dissertation on the cave in which she determined the chronological situation of some 50 human figures, describing them in detail and arguing that they are regularly associated with the horse—the most frequently depicted animal in Combarelles. Over the years, the Archambeaus have discovered many new engravings unknown to other people who have commented on Combarelles. Sieveking, writing in the late 1970s, stated that there are 250 engravings. André Leroi-Gourhan's apparently detailed map of the cave identifies only a small portion of the figures.

While Combarelles has been described as "serpentine," it is less undulant than angled. We will walk for around 70 yards before seeing any engravings—the first of which is a geometric human face. At this point, engravings of all sorts begin to swarm the walls, crisscrossing the natural furrows and fissures (which makes them without proper lighting very difficult to make out). While I cannot be sure what we will be shown, I will mention several memorable engravings and assume that you will see at least one or two of them. To see everything in Combarelles would take years.

After Lascaux—with 364—Combarelles has more horses than any other Upper Paleolithic cave, around 120 I believe. The horse is the most frequently depicted of all animals throughout Upper Paleolithic art (the bison is the second, and unlike the horse, is sometimes associated with hybrid and proto-shamanic imagery). The most frequently represented species appears to be the Przevalski horse (so named after the traveler who discovered it in 1881) which today is found in the wild only in Mongolia.

The Przevalski horse, which came close to extinction in the 1950s, is small and broad-backed, with a fat, low belly and short legs. The brush-like mane only rarely falls to one side. The coat is short in summer, long and thick in winter, pale yellow to bluish grey. This animal must have been difficult to hunt because of its strength, speed, and aggressiveness. In Combarelle's first area of engravings, on the right-hand wall, there is a mammoth with two trunks, its body outline partly buried in the scarred rock.

A bit further on, to the left, there are three headless female figures in profile, one with strokes down through her buttocks who will remind you of the female profiles on the slab from La Roche Lalinde in the Les Eyzies Prehistory Museum. According to the Archambeaus, there are around 100 human or humanoid figurations in Combarelles—considerably more than Monique included in her study—the largest number on the walls of any Upper Paleolithic cave.

Shoftly after the three female figures comes the first turn in the engraved area of the cave. There are more humanoids at this point, including a somewhat obscure frieze showing an ithyphallic male possibly in animal disguise leaning toward a woman also possibly disguised as an animal; superimposed on the rear portion of the male figure is a smaller hominid whose gender is impossible to determine.

At the end of this short passage, one makes a right turn into what is called the Middle Gallery (one is now walking parallel to the first area of engravings, called the Front Gallery). Near the end of this gallery, on the left, is a lioness following a lion whose tail can barely be made out. The lioness's head is one of the masterpieces of Magdalenian engraving. On the basis of such engravings, S. Giedion declared that "the richest find of engravings showing a structural treatment of the body surface is to be found at Combarelles."

A little further, at the second turning (which serves as the rear section of the Middle Gallery), to the right, is a remarkable engraving of a reindeer with lowered, outstretched head, apparently drinking from a fissure in the wall. The reindeer's antlers leap up like flames. There is a mastery of outline from the tip of its muzzle to the root of its tail. As I stared at it years ago, the fissure became a void, and the composition a Magdalenian vision of the engraver and the animal drawing nourishment from the unknown.

On the right wall of the rear section, there is one of Combarelle's 19 bears. This one gives the impression of being hung, like a hide, on the wall, or sort of shuffling along, head and tail down. It is generally described as a cave bear because of its bulging forehead (in contrast to the European brown bear with a flatter forehead).

The rear section then turns again to the left, becoming the Inner Gallery, an area not open to the public: it has no wire-mesh walkway and once when I visited the floor was rocky and waterlogged. In this gallery, there are a number of humanoid heads in profile, seemingly bending forward. All are animalized, or beast-featured, leading to one theory that male depicitons in Upper Paleolithic art are generally masked (there are exceptions to this throughout cave art, including Combarelles itself: at the beginning of the engravings there is an isolated male head facing the viewer, with staring blank eyes).

However, none of these so-called "masks" have discernible fasteners or indicators of something placed on or around an otherwise human head. During the exploration of Chauvet in 1994, a figure was discovered with a bison head and a human body bending over a black downpointing triangle—as if the origin of the Minotaur was incipient at 30,000 B.P.

In 2002, the Italian scholar Massimo Bacigalupo published a selection of drafts of *The Cantos,* from Ezra Pound's manuscripts, typescripts, and magazine publications. In this selection, he included the following poem, apparently a rejected version of what is now Canto II which was pointed out to me by Robert Creeley in 2005:

> Dissatisfaction of chaos, inadequacy of arrangements,
> At les Eyzies, nameless drawer of panther,
> So I in narrow cave, secret scratched on a wall,
> And the last reader, with handshake of departing sun

drifts from sorrowful horizon, patient thus far, now
impatient
e tu lettor, with little candle long after,
have pushed past the ruined castle, past the underbrush
tangled and netted
past the ant-hive, in narrow dark of the crevice
On the damp rock, is my panther, my aurochs scratched
in obscurity.

While this fragment appears to be undated, it is probably a response to Pound's walking tour through the Dordogne in 1912. The engravings in Combarelles were discovered in 1901 and it is probably this cave that Pound visited and responded to. I think his "panther" is the engraved lioness in the second section of the cave. Pound refers to the cave as "narrow," and since Combarelles is indeed quite narrow, this is another reason for believing that the poet was there.

FONT-DE-GAUME

Discovered by Denis Peyrony in 1901, Font-de-Gaume is a narrow and very high "corridor-sanctuary," about 165 yards long. The ensouled area, which begins 65 yards from the entrance, consists of a Main Gallery with Two Side Galleries. Many of the paintings have deteriorated and are now difficult to "read" (prompting Giedion, in the late 1950s, to tell readers that for Font-de-Gaume they should rely upon the reconstructions—actually, elegant drawings—by the Abbé Breuil, a complicated matter I will discuss later).

Calcareous deposits line the walls, proliferating into some of the paintings, giving them a cloudy, white overcast. There is, in addition, some graffiti, easy to recognize as such, but depressing to contemplate. Since Font-de-Gaume had an open, accessible entrance for hundreds of years before the paintings were discovered by Peyrony, the graffiti was probably done by visiting local people who either did not even see the paintings or, if they did, had no idea of their significance.

Deterioration is, of course, after Lascaux, associated with tourist access and over the past few years such access has been, in a few cases, increasingly restricted—even in Combarelles which has no paintings to speak of. A few years ago, 700 people were permitted to visit Font-de-Gaume; in 1996 this figure had shrunk to 200 people per day. Combarelles is now down to 70 a day in groups of 5. None of the caves open to the public in the Lot and Ariège Departments has of this date placed a limit on the number of visitors.

Font-de-Gaume is recognized as a Late Magdalenian cave, based on stylistic comparisons, with its paintings spanning 13,000 to 11,000 B.P. It has many tectiforms and bison—80—among its 200 animals and signs.

The Upper Paleolithic bison (*Bison priscus*), which became extinct with the spread of forests at the end of the last glaciation, had a height of 6 feet 6 inches, a hump at the shoulder level, long horns, and a powerful jaw with pronounced forward-jutting beard. In winter it was covered with thick, dark, woolly fur which moulted in the spring, leaving in its place a much lighter-colored coat (possibly depicted by the red swath across one of the hindquarters-crossed bison in Lascaux's Nave). Every killed bison represented a windfall for an Upper Paleolithic tribe: 1,000 to 1,500 pounds of excellent meat, fat to be used in the preparation of skins or as fuel for lamps, the skeleton for bones to be engraved, or used as winter fuel, and of course the skin for clothing, boots, or floor coverings.

The bison at Font-de-Gaume are painted on the remains of deep engravings and on a well-scraped surface. Some have massive, mammoth-like humps that give them a distinctive Font-de-Gaume identity (in contrast to some of the bison in the Salon Noir of Niaux, in the Pyrénées, which are humpless and quite streamlined). The Font-de-Gaume bison are outlined with a fine, engraved line, reinforced by a heavier line of black paint, and then colored in with red, or a darker tone of mixed red and black. Font-de-Gaume and Lascaux are the only caves in the Dordogne with polychromatic paintings.

The dorsal lines of the Font-de-Gaume bison are often determined by an undulating crevice in the rock. The animals are positioned on the wall in such a way that they appear to pull uneven surfaces into an undulating pattern. In a half dozen figures a specific contour in the rock is used to develop the animal's body—as if the entire body mass is stimulated by the appropriation of the contour. In one case a deep crevice is used as an outline of the back of a bison's forelegs and their fusion with its body. In another, a bison's belly is stretched to an unnatural length by wrapping it across a long, horizontal fault. While these bison in profile make use of flatly uneven or slightly curved wall space for the most part, the contour appropriations throw, on one hand, a visual torque into the entire body (making it seem to writhe and bristle at the same time that it is static), and, on the other, evoke an inward, dimensional depth. All in all, the multi-directionality of these various stresses result in an intense, specific and generic bison presence.

There are 19 obscure signs in Font-de-Gaume known as "tectiforms." The word comes from the Latin, "tectum" meaning "roof." Those in Font-de-Gaume generally have a tent-shape, possibly representing a dwelling or hut (the Abbé Breuil referred to them as "spirit houses"). They also look like squat arrows pointed upward, attached to a solid horizontal base (curiously, several such signs appear in de Kooning's 1950 painting *Excavation,* to be found in the Chicago Art Institute).

Painting or engraving a tectiform on a bison strikes me as similar, in one respect, to engraving a vulva across an engraved horse neck, as one finds on a slab from Abri Cellier, now displayed in the Les Eyzies Prehistory Museum. Such a juxtaposition implies a narrative relationship. One could call it a proto-metaphor. Something appears to be equated with something else, as if to imply that horse head power is equal to vulva power, or that in Font-de-Gaume such a bison is a tectiformal bison, or even a tectibisonform.

Most of the 19 tectiforms to be found in the cave do look very much like huts, or lean-tos, and are put directly onto the bodies of the bison—one bison has three tectiforms—or placed around them. One possible way to read such bison/tectiform combinations is to think of the bison bones as material to be used in man-made shelters. While no evidence for such has been discovered in the Dordogne, sites with communal dwellings constructed on a frame of mammoth bones have been unearthed in Russia and the Ukraine.

It is also interesting to note that concave wall surfaces appear to have been chosen for bison compositions at Font-de-Gaume in contrast to the convex ceiling formations used for bison at Altamira in northern Spain.

Another comparative point: the animals in Font-de-Gaume, for the most part, are static and peaceful—in marked contrast to the leaping, trotting, and falling animals of Lascaux and Pech Merle.

At the conjunction of the Main and second Side Gallery, there are a few compositions worthy of attention. On the right wall of the Side Gallery there is a bounding horse whose hind legs and rump are formed by stalactitic folds. Giedion suggests that it is a stallion in pursuit of a mare. However, it appears to me that the animal has a distended belly. Does such distension indicate pregnancy, making it a mare? Or is this distended belly part of a stylistic convention?

On the wall of the Main Gallery facing the Side Gallery is a reindeer whose head has apparently worn away. A fine, running line across the reindeer's body separates the dark and light portions of its hide. Such refinement and shading is traditionally associated with the Late Magdalenian. Thus the bison following this reindeer, whose interior shading seems less sophisticated, is placed by Giedion in the Middle Magdalenian.

Another fascinating scene near the headless reindeer: two long, black, curving antlers appear with a hump and back line moving horizontally away from them. The antlers belong to a stag which is bending over and nuzzling the head of a doe kneeling before him.

On the left, a little further along the Main Gallery, is a small chamber called the Apse, or Chamber of Small Bison. Its recessed, arching dome appears to have been rubbed, or primed, with red ochre before the animal outlines were painted. It contains the remains of three aurochses, some quadrangular and tectiformic signs, and around a dozen small bison with exaggerated manes and beards. Cloudy calcite formations make the animals hard to see: some of them have been completely opaqued by the calcite. Oddly enough, a few of the bison are enhanced by the calcite, which one can imagine swirling about the animals like a blizzard.

Beyond the Chamber of Small Bison there is an extensive terminal fissure, which progressively narrows. Because of the squeeze, potential claustrophobia, and possible smearing of paintings, nonprofessionals are not taken beyond the bison chamber. The paintings in the terminal area lack the finesse of many of the paintings in roomier areas of Font-de-Gaume, but they are all interesting in their own way and some are very hard to identify. Besides several bison, bovines, and horses, there is a stag, a rhinoceros, and a feline. There are also two schematized human profiles and a hominidesque "ghost." Right before the dead-end there are 7 red strokes.

If you have seen rather elegantly drawn animals from Font-de-Gaume in books on prehistory, chances are you have seen the Abbé Breuil's copies, originally published in 1910 by the Prince of Monaco, Prince Rainer's father, who was a great supporter of prehistorical research. Breuil was a talented artist, and based his drawings on tracings (no longer done, as they can damage the art) done in La Mouthe (1900), Altamira (1902), and Marsoulas, Font-de-Gaume, Combarelles, and Les Trois Frères in the following years.

While we owe Breuil a real debt of gratitude for all this work, it has become increasingly evident that a Breuil copy is a Breuil version, and much more subjective than may appear (in a way that literary translations often reflect a modeling or reshaping of the original material by the translator, making it conform to what he feels it should become in the second language). Breuil's versions, in fact, are more in evidence, via illustrated books, than the originals themselves.

Because Breuil believed that Upper Paleolithic "art" was based on hunting magic, he tended to concentrate on animals as individual forms, filling in missing parts at times and rounding out shading to offer, as in the case of his Font-de-Gaume bison, bloom-like, elegant creatures. When he came upon lines that seemed to have no relevance to animal outlines, he often left them out (calling them "parasitic lines," as if they had maliciously attached themselves to, or were infesting, otherwise intact and "healthy" animals). He would sometimes lift several predominant figures—such as the bison-headed man dancing behind two capering or fleeing animals in a Trois Frères engraving—out of a complicated composition involving lines, whole and partial figures, as if he were releasing clear-cut forms from a kind of sketchbook redundancy (it would be like reducing a Giacometti drawing to a single outline, and treating the overdrawing and redrawing as superfluous). Today, in contrast to what new techniques in copying tell us, Breuil's drawings look too perfect, too clean. In contrast to his aesthetically refined work, contemporary drawings of Upper Paleolithic paintings and engravings often show the Cro-Magnon creator as being unsure of himself, of redoing line after line, and of being at the mercy of poor lighting or of an already-fractured wall surface that resisted his intentions.

Utilizing infra-red and ultraviolet lamps, Alexander Marshack's and Jean Vertut's photography have picked up layers of paint below the final layer, sometimes indicating that a painting was retraced/repainted again and again. It seems that earlier paintings were reinvigorated by newcomers to a cave who put their fingers or burins into a power source, as it were, and recirculated its mystical electricity.

Vertut, the foremost photographer of European cave imagery, who died suddenly in 1985, aged 56, pioneered an effort to recreate the ambience of the cave environment; he sought to capture three-dimensional space that could not be registered in flat photographs. In the 1960s, he photographed the clay bison in Le Tuc d'Audoubert using four lamps, and in the 1980s re-photographed the same bison using six lamps to enhance the three-dimensional rendering. Via steroscopic photography Vertut was able to display not only the bison but the low-ceilinged chamber in which they were positioned. Finally, he documented them in photogrammetry, and then via a computer he helped construct a model of the bison for an exhibition at the Musée de l'Homme in Paris.

LASCAUX

Lascaux, the most famous of the decorated Upper Paleolithic caves and, until the recent (1994) discovery of Chauvet, unquestionably the most beautiful, is part of a karstic network. It is hollowed out of limestone and consists of an upper level (the accessible, decorated part) and probably a lower level which is today impenetrable. Even before it was painted, Lascaux was very beautiful. It is under a layer of impermeable marl which has prevented the formation of stalactites and stalagmites. Most of its paintings are on surfaces covered with coarse, glistening, calcite crystals. The engravings, and engraved paintings, are on bare, ochre-colored, granular limestone.

Lascaux was discovered on September 12th, 1940, primarily by 17 year old Marcel Ravidat and 15 year old Jacques Marsal, both of whom—Marsal especially—became the caretakers and guides of Lascaux. Several days earlier, Ravidat and other friends had discovered a hole created by a toppled juniper. The boys dropped some stones into the hole and heard them hit far below. On the 12th, Ravidat returned with Marsal, equipped with a lamp made from an old oil-pump, and a big knife. He widened the hole so that he could squirm in a few yards, at which point he tumbled to the cave's floor into what is now known as the Rotunda. With Marsal and two other boys he explored the cave and discovered the paintings.

For many years a story was told in which it was said that Lascaux was discovered by Ravidat's dog, Robot. There is some basis for this, as during the first trip Ravidat had been drawn to the toppled juniper hole by the barking of Robot who had become entangled in its brambly overgrowth. However, it appears that Robot was not around when the boys went down through the hole.

The most recent dates for the decorating of Lascaux come from Norbert Aujoulat's 2005 book on the cave, *Lascaux / Movement, Space, and Time.* Aujoulat was in charge of Lascaux from 1989 to 1999. The oldest date is 18,600 B.P. based on the 1998 radio carbon dating of a reindeer antler at the foot of the Shaft. A second set of dates from the late 1950s, based on pieces of charcoal taken from the Shaft and Passageway, yield 17,190 B.P. and 16,000 B.P. dates. The most recent date, 15,500 B.P., calculated in 1951, is also based on charcoal taken from the Shaft. Except for a bit of charcoal found in the head of a horse from the Rotunda, no paintings in Lascaux have been found that contain charcoal. We must keep in mind that charcoal dates are based on when the wood was burned, not when it was applied to the wall in a painting.

The cave is dominated by large aurochses. However, in southwest France no aurochs bones have been found between 26,000 and 11,000 years ago. Aujoulat states that temperature fluctuations could have resulted in north-south migrations, possibly explaining the elusive presence of aurochses in the Dordogne. Paul Balm, noting stylistic resemblances between some Lascaux figures and those of Spanish Levantine art, dated between 10,000 and 7,000 B.P., proposes that some of the Lascaux art may be Mesolithic.

Following the extremely cold Solutrean period, the landscape of the Early Magdalenian had changed completely, with the onset of a mild, fairly humid climate comparable to that of the Dordogne today. In the sheltered bottoms of valleys hazels, limes, walnuts, oaks, and junipers grew. There were grass prairies, salmon and trout in rivers swollen by melting glaciers, and pools with aquatic birds. Mammoths and megaloceroses (giant elk) seem to have disappeared (there are none depicted in Lascaux), to be replaced by great herds of herbivores. Reindeer continued to migrate and provided the Magdalenians with virtually all of their essential needs: 88% of the bones found in Lascaux are reindeer and every bit of that animal could be made use of, including antlers, skin, offal, meat, tendons, ligaments and bones (there is, however, only one reindeer depicted in the cave).

The Magdalenians of Lascaux were smaller than the big Cro-Magnons of the earlier Aurignacian period. Along with the aforementioned fauna and flora, they had access to wild boars and hares, as well as currants, strawberries, and blackberries. It appears that they frequented Lascaux during the summer, bringing plants into various areas perhaps as stuffing for skin-covered cushions.

There are 605 identifiable animals in Lascaux (including one humanoid): 364 horses, 87 aurochses, 90 red deer stags, 3 red deer hinds, 20 bison, 35 ibexes, 7 felines, 1 bear, 1 reindeer, 1 rhinoceros, and possibly 1 musk ox. There are also over 400 identifiable signs (most caves have no more than a few dozen), which include straight, parallel lines, star-shaped signs, branching shapes, nested convergent lines, tectiforms, claviforms, quadrangles, and composites. There are also over 100 dots, often arranged in undulating rows. In terms of fauna, there is a discernible "Lascaux style," especially in the depictation of horses: swollen bellies, small heads, short, lively legs, with coats often indicated. The most well-known are referred to as the "Chinese horses," presumably because they resemble horses in classic Chinese paintings.

Below the calcite-crystal-covered surfaces, there is a brown ledge which acts as a kind of ground level for the paintings in the Rotunda and the Axial Gallery. While the ground on which the animals move is never directly indicated, it is implicit throughout part of the cave via this ledge, which gives the illusion of multidirectional processions of animals (that is, they do not appear to be arbitrarily placed like paintings on the walls of an art gallery). One recurring theme is the association of large bovines (aurochses or bison), and troops of small horses strung out in a line, walking, trotting, or frisking in the opposite direction.

One should keep in mind that image-making in the Dordogne region originated prior to 30,000 B.P., so that the transcription of three-dimensional nature to a two-dimensional plane was ancient history for the Lascaux Magdalenians. Unlike the Aurignacians of their region, they appear to have been intent upon making species recognizable, anatomically accurate, and, at times, fantastic. To do this they developed (or possibly inherited *and* developed) several methods of perspective. They sometimes depicted the head and body of an animal in profile but drew horns and/or hooves in a three-quarters frontal view (what the Abbé Breuil called "semi-twisted perspective"). Sometimes hooves are depicted in a circular manner, as if observed from above; at other times, the ungulae are split pincer-like as if seen from below. A three-dimensional effect is created by the superimposition of figures—some overlap the silhouettes of their neighbors, putting them on a closer plane to the viewer. Another three-dimensional effect is created by allowing a strip of calcite to show between the body of an animal and one of its legs, backgrounding that leg in contrast to the other leg which has no strip of "distance," as it were, between it and the body to which it is attached.

There is a sureness of execution in Lascaux that argues strongly for the idea of masters and apprentices with coordinated painting activities. It appears that scaffolding was constructed in those areas where paintings or engravings were created beyond human reach (some are 13 feet from the ground; the Lascaux Magdalenians were around 5 feet tall). In the Axial Gallery scaffolding holes have been found packed with incrusted clay and traces of wood chips.

The principle pigments used in the paintings were a wide range of iron oxides (ochres, haematite, black and grey magnetite), silicates, manganese, black ochre, and charcoal. Most of the pigments had to be gathered in their natural state—as deposits containing coloring matter in quarries and outcrops—sometimes as far as 25 miles away from Lascaux. By heating iron oxides it was possible to change their original colors. At 1,832° F, ochre gradually darkens and changes from yellow to yellow-brown, to red, to red-purple, and finally from red to black (a fascinating variation on the medieval alchemical series of transmutations, from black to white to yellow or red). Lascaux research indicates that the best binding agent was water of the cave itself, rich in salts and dissolved calcium. Crayons made of dense, compressed coloring matter were probably used for drawing outlines. In the past, it was thought that figures were probably filled in by dabbings or spoonings, or by brushes made of animal hair and vegetal stems tied together. We know they had mastics strong enough to fix flint to handles, so it seems unlikely that putting a brush together would have been a problem. The Abbé Glory, who worked in Lascaux in the 1950s and 1960s, found 158 fragments of mineral pigments and 20 bone tubes containing colored powder.

Michel Lorblanchet, an archaeologist who has reproduced some of the paintings in Pech Merle, however, believes that the painted figures of Lascaux were essentially sprayed—by mouth or with a tube. Tubes produce denser and tighter marks. Occasionally a swab was used, which produced an imprint with a very clear edge. Lines were sometimes prolongations of dots. Stencils held a few inches away from the wall appear to have been used to delimit an area of color.

Natural, modified, and shaped lamps were used for lighting. Glory found 23 palettes made of limestone or schist, 4 crushers, 1 pestle, 2 pots, and 60 lamps with charcoal. All were turned over, so that surfaces with soot or paint smears faced the ground. Lamps and palettes were always found in close approximation. Fuel appeared to come from the fatty tissue of large animals. Lichen, fungus, and especially juniper were used as wicks. A painter would have needed several lamps going at once to illuminate a working area (another argument for coordinated activities). Even with minimal lighting, a modern visitor sees much more of a gallery than would have been visible to Upper Paleolithic people.

*

I have gone into some detail about Lascaux for two reasons: there is much more information on Lascaux than on any other decorated cave or site. Secondly, a significant amount of the information on Lascaux can probably be applied to other caves for which we have much less information. While the kinds of animals depicted vary considerably, and while no wall surfaces that I know of are the same as Lascaux's, painting as an organized effort, tricks in perspective, the use of pigments and lighting, all took place under similar conditions for most of the caves discussed here. A lesson that one learns from the Lascaux archive is that Upper Paleolithic imagery, at its best, is an extraordinary mixture of keen observation, playful fantasy, selected details, and mannerisms associated with a particular location. While it was done by people we think of as hunters/gatherers, it seems to have represented, especially in the long Magdalenian period, the culmination of thousands of years of apprenticeship and experimentation. From what we now know, this "art"—which was quite possibly not an art at all if judged by modern or even medieval standards—seems the far point of an advance in the conscious organization of experience and communication. Leroi-Gourhan is said to have commented near the end of his life that he believed the people at Lascaux came very, very close to having an alphabet. The combinations of figures and signs probably communicated instantly to those present at Lascaux while its walls were being "ensouled."

As many of you know, the world nearly lost Lascaux. By the early 1950s, Ravidat and Marsal spent most of their time underground orchestrating the flow of tourists that quickly became international—up to 2,000 per day. While archeological excavations continued, the cave's floor was altered to accomodate tourists, making any further research there impossible. By the late 1950s, the carbon dioxide emitted by the visitors filled the cave and the temperature more than doubled. Water vapor condensed and ran down the walls. So a machine was installed to dehumidify the air, and pipes were inserted in the new floor to channel in outside air. It had not been realized that the visitors were also bringing in pollen and algae which the new air machine also dispersed everywhere, leading to the proliferation of whole colonies of algae (subsequently referred to as "the green leprosy") on the walls in the paintings. At one point, the "falling horse" at the rear of the Axial Gallery was said to be disappearing in a prairie of greenish algae.

The cave was closed to the public in 1963. Antibiotics and diluted formalin eradicated the "green leprosy." However, the increase in the levels of carbon dioxide, humidity and temperature caused by the presence of the visitors had also led to the development of opaque crystals of calcite on the walls (known as the "white disease") and it was deemed necessary to try to return the cave to its previous, undiscovered condition—which meant closing it to the public for good. Slow air currents were reintroduced, a low temperature was maintained, and the carbon monoxide (which continually seeped into the cave via the Shaft) was pumped out. At this point, Lascaux seems to have been stabilized. However, many paintings are not as bright today as they were upon discovery.

Work on the replica of the cave known as Lascaux II began in the early 1970s and was completed in the early 1980s. It opened in 1983. The replica is situated in an enormous concrete block frame sunk into a hill about 200 yards from the original cave. The two sections of the cave reproduced in the replica are the Rotunda and the Axial Gallery—which represent about one-third of the total extent of Lascaux and contain the majority of the paintings.

Aujoulat reports that in 2001 the technician in charge of supervising the site reported mould in the air locks of the entrance. This mould was identified as a fungus. At the same time, he noticed that a white blanket of fungus filaments was spreading out on the cave's floor and along the ledges of all the decorated sections. Quicklime spread over infected areas temporarily stopped the proliferation of the fungus. At this point, all special visits to the cave were canceled and they have not, to my knowledge, recommenced.

Later, still in 2001, dark, circular patches of fungus appeared from the air locks toward the Apse.

In 2002 and 2003, the mould, despite treatment, continued to proliferate. A new program commenced that involved cleansing surfaces. Sediments deposited on ledges, which had become collection gutters for organic material, were removed.

As of 2004, the last date Aujoulat gives, a clear improvement was recorded. He also notes that there is no way to determine if such improvement is permanent or temporary. As I mentioned earlier, as of 2007 there were new and very serious problems with the cave, including large black spots on many of the paintings. As far as I know, no one in France has taken responsibility for what could be a catastrophic situation. Attempts to get UNESCO involved have been rebuffed by those in charge of the cave.

*

The Rotunda measures about 30 feet across and is 100 feet deep. It is somewhat horseshoe-shaped, with the curved end of the shoe at the far end of the entrance; it is penetrated at more or less the furthest point of its curve by the entrance to the Axial Gallery, a gently winding narrow corridor about 60 feet long which turns abruptly and becomes an impenetrable tunnel (the "falling horse" which is upside down is wrapped around this turn). The Rotunda (I prefer this name over "Hall of the Bulls" because of its association with the alchemical *rotundum*) is dominated by one of the great friezes in art: four colossal aurochses, the longest of which is over 18 feet. The two on the left face each other; the two on the right face left. Fragments of two more aurochs have been found indicating that originally there were six aurochses in The Rotunda.

The aurochs is the ancestor of most breeds of domestic oxen, notably of the fighting bulls of Spain. Another way to describe it would be to call it a large, longhaired wild ox. The prehistoric aurochs often measured 6 feet 6 inches at the shoulders and weighed up to 2,800 pounds. The first historical mention of the animal is by Julius Caesar who called it an urus; much smaller than the prehistoric aurochs, the *urus* became extinct in 1627. In prehistoric times, it appears to have been less hunted than the bison, not only because of its ferocity, but because its habitat of grasslands and marshes was less favorable for hunting than the bison's steppes.

Among the aurchoses in the Rotunda are a number of much smaller animals: horses, red deer stags, an almost totally concealed bear, and a cow and her calf. At the beginning of the procession, far left, is a grotesque or hybrid creature, curiously known as the "Unicorn" even though it has two long, antennae-like horns (but no ears). It has squat rear limbs, a swollen, sagging belly, and six oversized jaguar-like spots. It seems to be bumping up against the rump of the horse in front of it. Across the creature's hind-quarters is the thin red outline of a small horse; there are possibly two more earlier-drawn animals under this creature now blurred beyond recognizability. It has been called a Tibetan antelope, a Russian rhinoceros, and the skin of an animal patterned with eyes concealing two hunters. If you block out the tip of its snout, its profile becomes that of a bearded man.

The Axial Gallery is painted on both walls and curved ceiling. As one enters, looking up, the animals in the compositions seem to be revolving around the dome-like corridor, the drastically foreshortened animals abstracting out into a kind of Magdalenian "action painting." Once one is inside the corridor, the compositions seem to be arranged in two compartments, with a slight bottleneck between. On the north or left-hand wall, one discovers the so-called "Cow with a Collar," with a black head and neck, and a beautiful ochre body modeled on the rock wall. In the second compartment, the most spectacular figure for me is the Great Black Aurochs preceded by a ghostly red horse with a black trident-shaped sign across it. At the end of the Axial Gallery is the upside-down horse I mentioned before, its legs beating the air, the lower part of its body wrapped around the wall as it turns and narrows into the terminal tunnel—as if the horse were being sucked into the blackness.

Walking back toward the Rotunda, one passes, on the south wall, two ibexes confronting each other, and a large black cow that looks as if she is skidding to a halt before a trap-like sign. Under the skidding cow, a procession of five ponies trots along right above the imaginary ground level. Just before reaching the Rotunda again, there is a magnificent roaring stag, with large, fantastic antlers.

This is the extent of Lascaux II. In addition, two frescos that are not part of the replica are reproduced at Le Thot, a small prehistory museum and animal park several kilometers from the cave.

*

Were we in the original Lascaux, after returning to the Rotunda, we would walk past the two largest aurochses on the left, and turning left again pass through an airlock into the longest gallery in the cave (about 210 feet), made up of four sections: Passageway, Apse (bulging off to the right, and leading to the entrance of the Shaft), Nave, and Chamber of the Felines. The Passageway was originally covered with calcite on which polychrome figures were painted. Sometime later, erosion occurred, and the calcite fell off in patches, causing most of the painted figures to disappear. The bare walls were then covered with engravings, most of which are very difficult to see today (they are more like scratches than engravings in terms of depth). The Apse has also suffered from erosion; it is even more engraved than the Passageway—over 1,000 small horses, deer, aurochses, ibexes, and signs are packed next to each other, and across each other, with no apparent design around the walls and ceiling.

The Shaft today is around eighteen feet deep and contains the most spectacular narrative scene in Upper Paleolithic art: a bison with its entrails hanging out, its rump crossed by a spear, hovers over a bird-headed ithyphallic male figure who appears to be falling backward. Below the man's outstretched right arm is a bird-headed staff and a hooked sign with a cross at its base. Slightly below and to the left of the falling male figure is a woolly rhinoceros—its tail raised. Behind its anus are six black dots arranged in pairs, as on a die. There are two essays in *Juniper Fuse* with abundant commentary on the Shaft "scene." I have with me a short essay on this scene I will be happy to share with you one evening after dinner.

I mentioned before that there are more than 400 identifiable signs in Lascaux. Related to signs and dots are finger tracings, handprints, and hand stencils, none of which occur in Lascaux.

People have attached varying meanings to signs ever since the discovery of the caves. The meaning is adjusted to fit the interpreter's theory of the meaning of cave art in general. For the Abbé

Breuil, whose all-over theory was hunting magic, all long and angular signs were arrows, and claviforms were clubs. For Leroi-Gourhan, whose theoretical approach was based on gender pairing, all long signs were male, i.e., phallic, while solid signs—ovals, triangles, squares—were female, vulvar. When Breuil could not recognize a symbol in a sign—as in the case of thousands of wandering lines that do not appear to be directly related to the figures they cross or surround—he declared that they were of no value. As I mentioned earlier, he called them "parasite lines" and generally ommited them in his tracings. For Leroi-Gourhan, these same indeterminate lines were referred to as "unfinished outlines, and the product of inferior artists." The problem with such negative evaluations is that no one today is in a position to declare that these lines were meaningless to their makers or to the people who saw them at the time they were made.

Using microscopic techniques in the 1960s, Alexander Marshack proposed that lines across animals earlier described by Breuil as spears were actually ferns or grasses. In some cases, Marshack seems to be right, but as usual no theory holds for everything in Upper Paleolithic art. There are many marks on animals that cannot be read as vegetation any more than they can be confirmed as lances.

While most of the hunting magic hypothesis that Breuil subscribed to has been dismissed, an expert on animal drives in North America has recently proposed that much of the artistic layout in Lascaux constitutes a diagram depicting an animal drive. For Thomas Kehoe, rows of dots and the rectangles represent drive lines, blinds, and corrals. The barbed signs near certain animals are interpreted as brush barriers which help to funnel animals into a corral. The so-called "Unicorn," for Kehoe, is a man draped in hides to enable him to sneak up on the herd. All of this is fascinating, but it assumes that the cave was decorated by a single group of painters all with a common end in mind, and it does not address the most complexly decorated area in the cave—the Apse—nor the cave's single most mysterious composition—the "scene" in the Shaft.

COUGNAC

Cougnac is actually two caves, discovered in 1952 after an amateur dowser named Lagarde declared that there was a vast cavern under the earth two kilometers north of Gourdon. Jean Mazet investigated and discovered one cave filled with a fairyland paradise of stalactites and stalagmites (with no imagery) and another cave, thirty yards away, with a couple of dozen figures and as many dots, lines, and tectiforms. The most impressive work in Cougnac is set forth on a thirty-five foot long wall. The mural, which gives the impression of having been constructed in panels, includes 3 megaloceroses (until the discovery of Chauvet, with 5, the most in any Upper Paleolithic cave), and 2 humanoids which are painted on the body of one of the megaloceroses and a mammoth respectively. Unlike most of the decorated Upper Paleolithic caves, the painted area of Cougnac is open and convenient (Paleolithic people, it is believed, broke many of the columnar formations in front of the mural, creating a space that would have accomodated a crowd).

After showing us some signs—including 6 so-called "brace-shaped" signs—the guide will take us around to the mural. I am not happy with the term "brace-shaped," as such a term evokes a shaped piece of metal, a bitstock, or a buckle, all of which were unknown to Cro-Magnon. Over my work desk I have a photo of a wolf spider charging across a dining-room table toward the camera. The spider image reminds me of these particular signs—which is to say they look like schematized versions of something moving toward the viewer, like an insect or arachnoid with multiple legs, its head like a little turret raised above. I will have more to say about these arachnoid forms when I discuss Pech-Merle.

Of the 3 megaloceroses depicted in the mural, 2 are male and 1 female. The megaloceros, or giant elk, is one of the most magnificent antlered animals ever to walk the earth. They were all over Europe during the Upper Paleolithic and became extinct at the end of the Würm glaciation. Their antlers, resembling enormous hands with the fingers held apart, had a span of up to ten feet and weighed up to 150 pounds (for years the skeleton and antlers of a megaloceros have been on display in a glass case in the National Museum of Prehistory at St.-Germain-en-Laye). The megaloceros lived on the great glacial prairies and fed on grass and broad-leafed bushes. At Cougnac, there is no firm evidence of the depictation of horses (which is quite unusual—Cougnac is the only major cave with no horses). One gets the impression that in Cougnac the megaloceros may have replaced the horse.

To the right of the shoulder of the largest megaloceros, over the beginning of its belly, is an upper-body-less humanoid (traditionally called female on no evidence at all) pushing forward, as if running, but without feet. This figure appears to have been struck, while in motion, by three long, curving lines, one in the crack of the ass, one in the loins, and one in the lower back. If we read this scene as representing literal assault, it would seem that the figure was struck from behind by projectiles. However, there is no indication of an assailant, and no sign of pursuit or combat. It is perhaps significant that also depicted on the side of the megaloceros is a small stag, an ibex, and the dorsal line of a bison (or possibly a horse). The four figures on the megaloceros's side, taken as a unit, remind me of the nodal points of a constellation. Were one to draw lines between the four, the image of a slightly flattened diamond would emerge.

I mentioned that the lines apparently striking the running figure are curved. This may also be significant, as they are probably too long for arrows (and they have no feathers or vanes), and they are not straight enough for lances. Looked at carefully, they seem to be coming out of the figure's body more than they seem to be going in.

Drawing on a range of shamanic lore, Giedion proposes that the lines are magic projectiles involved with the initation of a shaman, during which the initiate may be symbolically tortured and dismembered. Sometimes, it is said, shaman ancestors pierce an initiate with symbolic arrows until he or she loses consciousness and falls to the ground.

Until quite recently, all the art in Cougnac had been attributed to the Early/Middle Magdalenian, around 14,000 B.P. Very recent carbon-14 dating reveals that the female (or second megaloceros) is 25,120 years old, and that the large male (the one with the struck figure) is 19,500 years old. In other words, six thousand years after the female was depicted, the large male was added. A black fingermark in the cave has been dated at 13,810. If these new datings hold up, then we have a multiphasic decoration for Cougnac spanning over 10,000 years.

The new dating also raises questions about the figures drawn on the male megaloceros. If the humanoid can also be dated at 19,500 B.P., then it should be read in conjunction with the megaloceros. Like the mammoth under a tectiform at Bernifal, one could propose that this is a scene involving a megaloceros and a wounded humanoid. If it turns out that the humanoid is dated later or earlier than the megaloceros, then it may be reasonable to treat the figure as everyone has done up to now—simply as a wounded, truncated figure, more or less in isolation. Again, we have a total of five figures here: the megaloceros, and within its bounding line the humanoid, the stag, the ibex, and the dorsal line. While the composition is not as dramatic (in our terms) as the "scene" in the Lascaux Shaft, it evokes to me a constellation, or a blazon—with more potential information in it than in the so-called "blazons" in the Apse at Lascaux. Perhaps the composition is a statement relating to megaloceros lore. However, these figures do not seem to interact; they are all in the same vicinity and at the same time in isolation—as are most of the animals in Upper Paleolithic compositions. The difference here is that four figures are contained by the outline of the megaloceros's body.

Multiphasic decoration raises new questions. To what extent should the datation intervals affect how a composition should be read? Imagine an Egyptian sarcophagus visited by Picasso who sketches in a bull in a previously unworked space. Do we say that because Picasso comes from a different culture, in time and in mind, that his addition is, in effect, graffiti? Or do we notice that the presence of the bull adds to the information concerning the soul bird or the dead king's soul painted earlier on the object? We live in an aeon of the multiphasic—juxtaposition of the dissimilar in the collages of Max Ernst or Jess Collins are read as complex interactive maps which argue for the simultaneous presence of the erudite and the vulgar, the sacred and the profane. If we think of Upper Paleolithic images as the manifestation of a newly forming world psyche, then perhaps "additions" should be accepted as "stages" in the evolution of a composite image.

Some fifteen feet to the right of the large megaloceros is an even stranger composition: draped across the side of the head and shoulders of a mammoth is another naked humanoid, with penguin-wing-like arms. He appears to be falling forward while twisting his snout-like head around. I say "he" because there is some suggestion of a penis. The figure has a short tail, and is struck in the chest, the back, the thigh and the stomach by seven or eight mostly-straight lines. The hybrid, grotesque nature of the figure makes an even stronger argument than in the case of the humanoid or megaloceros for shamanism. Below the pierced humanoid is the heavy outline of a small mammoth, depicting only head, back, trunk and chest. It seems to be aligned with the humanoid.

In contrast to the cartoonish ibexes on the ceiling at Rouffignac, the ibexes in the Cougnac mural are well-conceived and drawn. Curves and undulations of the rock wall have been incorporated in their outlines, as well as the fleece dangling from the stomach of one. The positioning of such an animal seems predetermined, as if it were starting to emerge on its own and needed only an artistic bounding line to release its semi-submerged form.

There is also said to be a third humanoid to the left of the mammoth with the pierced humanoid. Mazet, Cougnac's discoverer, describes the figure as follows:

> The oldest figure is that of a human being in brownish coloring. The head is bowed. The feet hover in the air like those of a bird wounded to death and about to plunge down to earth. The face which ends in a duck's bill is that

> of an animal. The body is pierced by three arrrows. Two are in the breast, one in the back. The figure appears to be wearing a kind of mantle reaching to its feet.

Mazet appears to be the only commentator who has seen this figure. I have seen some smudges and marks where Mazet claims it is, but that is all.

PECH MERLE

The cavern known as Pech Merle was discovered in 1922 by André David, a boy at the time (it is worth noting here that other major caves were discovered by teenage boys, including Lascaux, and Les Trois Frères). After two years of clearing out a tight, subterranean tunnel, David discovered paintings 417 yards from the entrance.

Pech Merle consists of a network of passages about a mile and a quarter in length, 130 yards of which are decorated. In the center of the decorated area, there is a high, vaulted hall-like space with immense and fantastic columnar formations. Until the discovery of Lascaux, Pech Merle was the most beautiful and magical of the French caves, one for which such terms as "sanctuary" or "cave-temple" seem appropriate. Until recently, it was thought to have been decorated in two phases, the earliest being around 17,000 B.P. and the latter at 13,000 B.P. Recent carbon-14 datings of charcoal from one of the spotted horses revealed a date of 24,640 B.P., suggesting that like Cougnac, with which it has stylistic affinities, the decorating of Pech Merle also took place over a span of some 10,000 years.

The current entrance, after a steep flight of steps, puts the visitor directly into the main decorated chamber which, because of the amount of rock formations, fallen boulders, and alcoves, appears labyrinthine. It is basically oval in shape, with murals as well as isolated figures and signs around the outer walls surrounding the interior formations. Before commenting on several of the most interesting areas of Pech Merle imagery, I want to mention that, after we descend the steps, off to the right is an area called Le Combel, which is not shown to most visitors, as seeing the paintings involves stooping low and crawling through some tight openings. Le Combel has lots of large ochre red dots, and several paintings of fantastic animals. There is a poem on this area in *Juniper Fuse.*

The first set of paintings we will see are to be found in a shallow recess around 21 feet long and 7.5 feet high. An extraordinary panorama of animals unfurls in staggering bursts of momentum and calm, displaying the Upper Paleolithic line at its finest. This mural is variously known as "The Large Black Fresco" or "The Chapel of the Mammoths." On the extreme left, a knot of animals seem to be tumbling into an abyss: two aurochses fall head-downward followed by a mammoth whose trunk and long body-hair sweeps across the hind-quarters of another backward-sliding aurochs. Slightly above this scene, as if sprung out of it, another mammoth appears to be leaping up and away so that its body is stretched across the rock face in a bizarre elastic arch. The French poet André Breton visited Pech Merle in the 1950s (he had a home nearby in St-Cirq-Lapopie), and upon doubting the mural's authenticity, the director of the Surrealists tried to rub away the color at the tip of this mammoth's trunk. He was not only reprimanded but fined.

To the lower right of this assembly is a mammoth depicted solely by the outline of its dome-like head and hump. The creature is facing left, but the shower of red dots across its head and where its body is implied to be creates an illusion of eyes looking backward. An indescribable ghostliness permeates the creature. To the upper right of this mammoth is another assembly centered by the outline of a large, still horse, whose lines are intersected by the outlines of a mammoth and two bison. Above this close-knit group are the dorsal lines of a mammoth and a bison, floating like mountain ridges on the wall. No animal erases another. They overlap and interpenetrate in curving, graceful lines that on one hand resonate with emptiness and, on the other hand, evoke animals becoming mountains becoming animals simultaneously coming in and passing out of view. This interplay of emptiness and substances, and their mysterious reciprocity, calls to mind the Buddhist doctrine of *sunyata* (emptiness) and *tathata* (suchness, or materiality), formulated thousands of years later.

At the lower right-hand side of the mural are two more mammoths, hoofless, legs intermingling with the long, hanging hair of their pelts. They have a curious ascendant feeling, as if rising like corporeal steam directly out of the earth. They offer an asymmetrical sense of balance with the left-hand side of the mural's animals in descent. From time to time the drapery-like stalactitic formations in Pech Merle suggest the shape of long, trailing mammoth coats. Like the straggly, intersecting bear claw scrapings on the walls of Rouffignac, such formations may have stimulated Upper Paleolithic people to see living forms in the contours and surfaces of organless stone.

The Lot-based paleo-archeologist Michel Loblanchet memorized every mark in the Black Fresco and then reproduced it on an equally smooth panel of similar dimensions in another cave, lit by a lamp in his left hand. Each figure took between one and four minutes to paint. The whole Fresco required about one hour, including sketching with a stick.

Seemingly unrelated to the Black Fresco, and dated much earlier, on a nearby ceiling—some twenty feet up, and very hard to read—is a complex tangle of finger tracings. Making use of the drawings by the Abbé Lemozi who worked in Pech Merle in the late 1920s, there appear to be three female figures (all in profile) in this entanglement, two of which are associated with animals. I have made copies for you of two of these figures (reproduced in Giedion's *The Eternal Present*). The first is headless (her neck is capped, indicating that her head was not simply left out), and her body (with large buttocks that recall certain Venus statuettes) appears to be resting on the back of a completely drawn mammoth. The second female has long, drooping breasts and tiny, pointed arm-stubs. She appears to be pregnant. She may be bird-headed, but if so, the beak is pointed to the rear—leading me to think that the "beak part" might be her hair. Winding across her body is a huge, serpentine form that in context is definitely phallic.

On the far side of this columnar hall, one of the most interesting figures is a male who was described in the 1920s as "an archer armed with bows, equipped with a mask, and his arrows or javelins." Because this figure is so difficult to see (one must crouch and then look up at the underside of the slab he is sketched upon), I have copied for you a photo of him from Giedion's book. He is more pierced by arrows (or magical forces) than carrying them. As at Cougnac, the arrow-like lines are curved, but here they enter and emerge from the body at four points, and look more like thongs or strands, as if the figure is strung up or caught up in some large network. He has a muzzle-shaped or bird-beaked profile, miniscule arms (resembling the flippers of one of the Cougnac figures), a long tail and a dangling penis. Touching his head is the extended outer vertical line of what is referred to as a "brace-shaped sign" by Leroi-Gourhan, a "large and curious symbol" by Evan Hadingham, and a "distinctive geometrical sign" by Jean Clottes. This sign is nearly identical to the "brace-shaped" signs at Cougnac, which I suggested look more insectile than metallic or geometric.

In an essay called "Companion Spider," I envisioned this strung-up man in conjunction with a schematized spider, having previously proposed that the labyrinth is one of the oldest and most complex designs of the creative process, a design that draws upon spiderwebs with the female poised at the center. In the Cretan maze, which appears to be a variation on the web with its centered female and intruding male, the Minotaur is found at the center, and the role of the male spider is played by Theseus. In the bitter conflict at the center, spider copulation is replaced by a life/death Minotaur/Theseus struggle. See page 80 in *Juniper Fuse* for Anton Ehrenzweig's perceptive commentary on labyrinth as metaphor for the creative process. At the end of my essay, with the Pech Merle image in mind, I wrote: "The male's body is slack, as if strung upon the lines passing through. Caressing the figure's head is what appears to be the tip of one leg of a schematically drawn spider. Might the traversing lines be magic projectiles, as in shamanic dismemberment? I take this bird-headed figure to be an initiate depicted at a crucial stage of his transformation."

In the same area of the cave with this figure is another set of partially concealed figures that are unfortunately even more difficult to make out. Leroi-Gourhan has readable photos of them in *Treasures of Prehistoric Art* (five are reproduced on page 164 of *Juniper Fuse*). Here is a brief description of these figures: at the top of the rock face, there appears to be a small leaping bison, head and forelegs merged into a single line. Below it is an enigmatic figure that may be an obese female leaning over; she is blurred and part of a scattering of twenty red dots. Below these dots is a schematic outline of a small mammoth, and several more figures that appear to be hybrids: leaping bisons that are also obese female figures. They look as if they are studies exhibiting the transition from bison outline to that of female outline. For example, it is impossible to tell if one is looking at schematized bison forelegs or pendulous breasts. If we read them as women, they appear to be further examples of the obsession in Upper Paleolithic image-making with female figures in profile, footless (like most of the Venuses), with pushed-back buttocks, moving forward as if leaning or dancing. Sometime such figures have no heads at all; here the heads are like curved hooks. Leroi-Gourhan, in a statement that is now contested by other archeologists, wrote that what he called "the bison-women of Pech Merle furnish perhaps the most striking evidence of the abstract character of Paleolithic art."

The last mural-like image complex we will see in Pech Merle is on a low stone wall, around ten feet long, and six feet high. Two horses are painted in broad black outlines, their bodies (except for heads and necks) sprinkled with black dots. The necks and heads are solidly filled in with black. Facing in opposite directions, the horses' hind-quarters are superimposed on each other. The horse to the right—with charcoal in it that carbon dates at 24,640 B.P.—seems to have been placed where it is because the upper right-hand corner of the rock wall is vaguely horse-head shaped. Thus the painted bird-head-shaped horse head fits nearly inside the rock's outline. The effect is that the rock shape becomes the aura of the tightly-tapered painted head. There are also black dots below both horses' very filled-out—possibly pregnant—bellies.

Across the back of the right-hand horse a fish of the pike family has been sketched in red (it is quite faded, but there). This "red theme" is picked up by a smattering or red dots interspersed with the black dots. Six left and right hands, stenciled in black, snugly frame the animals. In the body of the left-hand horse there are four small horseshoe shapes. According to Michel Lorblanchet, who has also recreated this entire composition, all of it was produced by spitting pigment.

The visual impact of this composition is more fantastic than realistic: in contrast to their swollen bodies, the horses have tiny, pointed heads which are treated as a tapering of their cowl-like manes and necks. They could hardly begin to walk on their stubby, stick-like legs. The dots do not seem to indicate pelts, but, like the hands, give a magical emphasis to the horses. Taken as a whole, the composition is somewhat abstract, with the swaying tube-like bodies dislodged from naturalism by the framing hands and the plethora of black and red dots.

BERNIFAL

There are around 140 caves in the Dordogne with some form of marking or image-making, from the sumptuously-decorated Lascaux to a nameless cave Caryl and I were taken into by Christian Archambeau whose sole decoration, on the back wall, was a red dot. In the Les Eyzies area alone, there are around 70 decorated caves and rock shelters, and 11 of these are to be found in the valley of the Petite Beune River, not far from Les Eyzies. Very few of these caves have been identified as of Upper Paleolithic significance.

Only one of these—Bernifal—is a cave of special significance. It is deep, though not really large (the lesser sites are mostly daylit shelters). Caryl and I begin to visit Bernifal in the late 1970s when it was partially waterlogged, thus difficult to walk through. At the time it was an unlisted cave. In the 1980s it began to appear on lists of caves open to the public and its floor was drained. We are going to assume that while the floor may be wet in places you will not have any problems in making your way through Bernifal during our one hour visit with its farmer-owner who is also the guide.

You may initially feel that Bernifal is not a cave with significant holdings. Abbé Breuil called some of its figures "scraps," and wrote that "they are too mediocre to be dwelt on here." I should mention here that Breuil had set up a criterion for what was of value in cave art based on a theory that has now been for the most part discredited. So what he considered insignificant in the 1940s may be, viewed from new perspectives in the 1990s, quite relevant.

There has been very little documentation of Bernifal—the meager information I will draw upon here comes from Breuil's *Four Hundred Centuries of Cave Art,* Leroi-Gourhan's *Treasures of Prehistoric Art* (which does not include a map in Bernifal's case), and Ann Sieveking's *The Cave Artists.*

It appears that the cave contains 10 mammoths, 5 or 6 horses, 3 bison, several deer, and possibly a bear. Several of the mammoths have triangular eyes, a feature also found in Font-de-Gaume. In Leroi-Gourhan's system of gender pairing, in which a spear is symbolic of a phallus, and a wound symbolic of a vulva, one of the Bernifal bison is used as an important confirmation of his theory. He writes that it "is marked on its side, not with a 'wound' and 'arrows,' but an oval vulva in double outline and two pairs of short strokes." Breuil's earlier drawing of these signs depicts two parallel lines and a slightly-round chevron with two parallel lines inside of it (reproduced by Sieveking in her commentary on Bernifal). Is Leroi-Gourhan reshaping this "female sign" to support his gender pairing theory? I can't say, as the one photograph of this bison I have seen (in *Treasures of Prehistoric Art*) depicts the sign unclearly. While visiting the cave, I was able to make out, I think, the bison all three authors have in mind but I saw no signs on its body. Situations like this occur again and again in Upper Paleolithic cave art.

Perhaps the most fascinating aspect of Bernifal is the relatively large number of strokes, dots, tectiforms and lines that accompany the animal figures. There appear to be over a dozen tectiforms in Bernifal—with the exception of Font-de-Gaume, more than in any other French cave. Most of the Bernifal tectiforms appear to be bundles of lines, with the downward slanting ones resembling insect wings and they are placed on mammoths.

The cave photographer Jean Vertut used infra-red film when photographing a red tectiform in Bernifal. The photo reveals (according to Paul Bahn) that the sign was painted not in continuous lines but as a series of dots from which the color had run. Leroi-Gourhan views such tectiforms as deriving from triangles which he associates with the female pubic triangle or delta, and thus considers them as one of the five female signs—triangles, inverted triangles, ovals, rectangles, and claviforms (key shapes)—to be found in Upper Paleolithic art (the fact that tectiforms can consist of lines of dots—as in the Vertut photograph—is not taken into consideration).

In the 19th century, the earliest theory of the meaning of tectiforms and other signs referred to them as artists' signatures. While this theory is no longer applicable, and while no alphabetical system that we can recognize today as such appears to be part of the

Upper Paleolithic record, the medieval "doctrine of signatures"—the outward marks by which internal characteristics were supposed to be indicated—comes to mind. Might the so-called tectiform have indicated to Cro-Magnon people internal characteristics of mammoth or bison?

Might the insect-like tectiforms indicates fly life, which appears to be parthenogenetic, on an animal corpse?

Most commentators today retain such terms as tectiforms, scutiforms (shields), claviforms, and aviforms (birds), but only as rough guides to particular shapes. We simply do not know if they are object-specific, gender-referential, or conceptual in some other way. I sense that all signs in Upper Paleolithic image-making are responses to something that is physical, even if in combination with a recognizable figure they create an additional, or third, meaning.

Bernifal was discovered by Denis Peyrony in 1902. Breuil thought the cave was Aurignacian because it had some dots. This is a curious dating, since Bernifal's tectiform and animal affiliations are similar to those at Font-de-Gaume which is solidly dated as Middle-Late Magdelanian.

SAINT-CIRQ

Saint-Cirq is a small cave, no more than 30 square feet in size, between Les Eyzies and Le Bugue, discovered by the owner whose property it is on, Noel Brousse, in 1952. Very little has been written about it. It is mainly known for a large engraved male figure which in certain ways is unique.

We will have seen by the end of our trip a representative number of male figures in caves (along with a few on portable objects in the museums we will visit). If the primary female figures are the so-called "Venus" figurines (of which around 140 are now known), the closest to an equivalent in the male category, in my opinion, would be grotesque or hybrid figures who we can associate with magic ritual and in certain cases with an early kind of shamanism. Unlike the continental spread of "Venus" figurines, these male figures are much rarer. I would estimate that 25 to 30 might fall into this somewhat blurry category. The most famous are the so-called "Dancing Sorcerer" of Les Trois Frères in the Ariège (a human armature made up of wolf, horse, owl, and stag attributes), and the bird-headed ithyphallic male floating with outstretched arms under the enraged, disemboweled bison in Lascaux's Shaft. Several of these hybrid male figures are bison-headed. Below the "Dancing Sorcerer" in Les Trois Frère's Sanctuary one who seems to be playing a musical instrument (or smoking a very long cigar) hops along behind two fleeing animals with a young woman figure seated inside him, leading me to the perception that the hybrid is the engine of anima display.

Besides hybrid male figures there is also a range of grotesque to semi-grotesque figures, some bending forward, some in frontal and profile views, "ghosts" (detached spectral schematic heads), and phalluses. Like nearly all of the female figures most of the male ones are either masked or given indistinct faces. Very few have what we would call an "expression" on their faces. Such is what makes the Saint-Cirq male figure pretty unique.

There is no record I have been able to find of the figure's exact size. I remember him as being around 12 to 14 inches from head to feet. He is engraved on a stone section that may be natural or cut into by the Cro-Magnons who decorated the cave. I mention the shape of the stone as from one angle it is extremely feminine, with breast-like outcroppings above a narrowing torso-like area that extends down and outward, somewhat like hips and legs. If we see this stone as the apparition of a female body, the male figure, bending over (if seen as standing) or somewhat curled (if seen as lying on his side), is placed diagonally across the stone's "stomach," with his legs, and long drooping penis, down in the "genital area."

His belly is distended and he appears to be completely naked, with small curving arms extending toward the stone's edge. His face is as naturalistic as we will find in Upper Paleolithic male depictions: there is something infantile about it, the mouth seems pursed, the eyes probably closed. There are no indications of hair anywhere on his body that I can spot. If the stone into which he is engraved is sensed as having feminine characteristics, it is possible to think of him as a fetus, but one with a long and bending (thus by implication semi-erect) penis—or might it be an umbilical cord? The mind races: is he the form asleep in the material? Early indication of animus or homunculus? He has been christened "the sorcerer" in the handful of books that mention Saint-Cirq. Leroi-Gourhan, who stylistically places him in the Late Magalenian (around 12,000 B.P.), questions such an identity as do I.

According to Leroi-Gourhan there is, lower than the male figure, and to his left, a bison head with eyes, ears, and horns, along with a triangle and a few abstract lines. To his right Leroi-Gourhan finds a small engraved horse with a double arc running from shoulders to forelegs and belly. I do not recall having seen these figures. They are probably there but they may be so hard to spot that under the circumstances we will be shown the cave they will not be visible. Were we to get within inches of them with special lighting their outlines might become "readable."

The area with the male figure is in the back of Saint-Cirq, with another engraved area nearer the entrance, an area considered to be worked much earlier than the deeper one. These engravings are not clear but are visible. Close to the entrance is a small bison, and some deep cut lines thought by the Abbé Breuil to represent a reindeer head. Opposite of these figures are the traces of a group of horses.

GARGAS

Near St.-Bernand-Comminges, in the Central Pyrénées, Gargas was explored near the end of the 19th century by Felix Regnault who discovered over 150 negative hands outlined in red and black (an additional 80 were discovered in following years). From 1911 on, archeologists such as Cartailhac, Neuville, and Breuil continued the excavations and undertook a study of the engravings. The Gargas imagery has never been dated by carbon 14 method, so all dates are stylistic guesses (the only paintings in the cave are the hand negatives, which lack charcoal, making a dating impossible; the hundreds of engravings, of course, cannot be dated either). The general consensus is that both the hand negatives and engravings are probably Gravettian. Bone and antler fragments discovered in the cave have been solidly dated at 26,860 B.P.

Hands charged with symbolic meaning appear in quite different cultures around the globe. The hand—the upper body part that extends the furthest—determines the distance at which many people see most clearly. It is also the body part that shapes those things which give human beings a power beyond their innate strength: tools, weapons, all artifacts. While the many finger tracings in soft cave clay (including Gargas) are not dependant upon tools, the development of Upper Paleolithic image-making is contingent upon the gradual improvement in fashioning burins and blades throughout the Paleolithic. Primary contact with cave walls (and floors, to some extent) was made by hands—at first a groping or just touching hand, later by a hand holding a flint, ochre crayon, or crude brush. What we see on cave stone is the legacy of the hand.

The hands at Gargas I have said are negative impressions, leaving the wall bare where hand volume is indicated Occasionally in Upper Paleolithic image-making one finds positive impressions where a hand, covered with red or black pigment, is pressed against cave stone. Red ochre and black manganese could often be found in the rock crevices of the caves.

The Abbé Breuil noted that 124 of the 150 that he counted were left hands. Of these, 76 were surrounded by black, 48 by red. The red ochre produces shades that range from dark red to orange-like yellow. At one point, there are a number of finger marks.

We are not sure how the coloring was applied. One way, as I have suggested, is to blow powder through a tube onto a humid wall. Another way would be to spray liquid paint from one's mouth.

Almost all of the negative hands at Gargas are deformed. In some only three fingers remain—in other only the middle finger remains. Some of the hands look like bizarre gloves. Others do not look like hands, but grotesque variations on the shape of the hand. In one, a wrist indication seems to be holding an infant hand to the wall, as if—my wife Caryl once commented—a mother were saying, "Look what has happened to my baby's hand!"

You have already seen hand negatives around the spotted horses in Pech Merle. They also appear in a half-dozen Spanish caves (one, Fuente del Salin, located just across the Pyrénées from Gargas), including Altamira. The question that has come up again and again in regard to especially the Gargas hand negatives is: on what basis are they deformed? Is the deformation based on holding the hand probably palm upward against the wall and bending the fingers? Or are the fingers (and thumbs) actually missing? And if missing, because of ritual mutilation or through disease (frostbite, gangrene, or Reynaud's disease (which usually only attacks the fingers)?

The most concise and up-to-date assessment of the problem can be found in Paul Bahn's *Journey Through the Ice Age.* While a case can be made for bent fingers, such would allow the powder or pigment to infiltrate behind them, but on the basis of the hand and fingers shapes this does not appear to be so. Also, some of the hands are so truncated and deformed, they do not look natural.

One study proposes a pathological condition (instead of mutilation) on the basis of the fact that virtually all the hands, show abnormality. Other studies, according to Bahn, argue that no known pathological cause can account for the phenomenon.

While the hand debate remains unresolved, what is certain is the visual impact of the hands. Some, alone, isolated in a shrine-like niche, face the viewer with the force of an Upper Paleolithic mandala. Others, in overlapping groups, as if moving like ragged clouds up and across a wall evoke a tragic chorus, in Giedion's phrase, "eternally crying out for help and mercy."

Some of the hand negatives in Gargas have disappeared as a result of natural erosion and present-day vandalism. The last time we visited Gargas we were informed by the guide that more hand negatives had disappeared due to the fact that the chamber where most of them are to be found is imperfectly sealed from outside elements.

When visiting Gargas I have always been so absorbed in pondering the hand negatives that the engravings in the cave have not stuck in my mind. The animal figures—all engraved, none painted—begin in the cave's second chamber, after the hand-filled first one. There are several bison, a horse, and some meandering lines. One enters Gargas at ground level, where the first chamber with the hands is. As one proceeds, one climbs. After the first set of animal figures there are some dots and lines. Another frieze of red hand negatives appears, with the finger marks I mentioned earlier. Near the end of the fourth chamber is a small alcove that is literally filled with animals, animal parts, and meandering long lines. Some of this material is disfigured by 19th century visitor graffiti. It is so hard to make out that when Regnault discovered the painted hands he did not even notice the engravings. In preparing this lecture I went back to the Abbé Breuil's *Four Hundred Centuries of Cave Art* which has some of his Gargas drawings that he made in the early 1900s.

Much of the meandering lines and animal parts seem to have been done either in the dark or under lighting conditions in which no more than a few inches of any composition could be viewed. The animal parts are topsy-turvy, deer heads rear up out of a long waving meander, bovine legs attached to nothing canter across a dorsal line that on inspection seems to belong to an otherwise invisible horse. It is a melee that I associate with the extent to which the Gravettian landscape was swarming with animal life (the abundance of which, no longer existent anywhere on the planet, partially accounts for the time it appears Cro-Magnon people had to establish the first sense of virtual reality in the world). The engravings at Gargas are less impressive than elsewhere (mainly Les Trois Frères and Gabillou) and very hard to assimilate without the hours, and weeks, of study that someone like Breuil had at his disposal nearly a hundred years ago, when a professional would be left alone in such caves for as long as he cared to spend there. Breuil took his lunch in with him, and devised pads filled with grass to lie on while he worked tracing and drawing ceilings and other hard-to-reach slanting walls. Now, given the heightened concerns about cave preservation, we are lucky to have an hour in Gargas or Niaux. Unlike modern paintings and ancient portable objects cave paintings and engravings are seldom decontextualized and relocated in a museum. Photos of the painter Francis Bacon's studio reveal that where he worked looked like it had been hit by a hurricane years ago and had never been cleaned up. I fantasize how interesting it would be to see his grotesquely beautiful, violent, semi-dismembered portraits where they were conceived and resolved or abandoned. As the poet Charles Olson wrote in 1950, in a poem called "These Days":

> Whatever you say, leave
> the roots on, let them
> dangle
>   And the dirt
>
>   just to be clear
>   where they come from.

NIAUX

The cave of Niaux—the Upper Paleolithic imagery of which was recognized in 1906 by Commandant Molard—is in the eastern Pyrénées, 10 miles south of Foix. There is some evidence that it was visited by T.S. Eliot in 1919 and that it is the source of Eliot's comment, in his essay "Tradition and the Individual Talent," that "art never improves." We can imagine Eliot, standing with kerosene lamp in Niaux's Salon Noir, facing a bristling bison drawn in manganese, charcoal, and cave water, adding: "but the material of art is never quite the same."

Caryl and I recall our first visit to Niaux in 1978. We approached the cave via the one lane hair-pin-curving road that loops up a limestone spur rising more than 1000 meters above the Vicdessos, the little river that runs alongside the road below. We rounded a bend to suddenly face a 150 foot high triangular cavity seemingly clawed out of the rock. It looked like either the entrance to, or the exit from, this world. In a postcard photo of this teepee-shaped entrance, the visitor cars parked out on the porch seem to be the size of bugs.

Of the 30 or so Upper Paleolithic decorated caves in the French Pyrénées, only a few are open to the public (such caves as Les Trois Frères, Le Tuc d'Audoubert, and Le Portal are privately-owned and seldom visited). Of the open ones, Niaux is the most spectacular. The paleo-archeologist André Leroi-Gourhan concludes his section on Niaux in *Treasures of Prehistoric Art* with these words: "Niaux is the only cave that vies with Lascaux in the quality of execution of its works and in the vastness and vigor of its compositions. Elsewhere we find excellent pieces and amply developed sets of figures, but nowhere, except on the Altamira ceiling, the same expressive power. Stylistic analysis reveals the perfect unity of the decoration."

Niaux is actually two caves: Niaux and the Réseau Clastres. Niaux is a monumental corridor-cave, with very little imagery until one is nearly 700 meters inside. At this point, one encounters a wide intersection. To the right, some 135 meters beyond, is the famous Salon Noir, the goal of our visit, and the most important decorated area of the cave. Straight ahead, some 100 meters beyond the intersection is a wall with signs and a vertical bison; another 100 meters beyond this wall is a bison vividly engraved into the clay floor with some red signs on the nearby wall. Beyond that is another branch off. To the left is a lake which can only be crossed under exceptionally favorable circumstances. To the right a corridor leads to another underground lake which was not drained until 1970, opening up another corridor over a kilometer long and containing three more lakes (or "siphons" as they are known to archeologists). This is the Réseau Clastres, which is not a prolongation of Niaux, but a neighboring cave, probably frequented by the same Magdalenians who decorated Niaux. It is now believed that the Réseau Clastres was entered by still a third cave, the Petite Caougno ("Little Cave"), the entrance of which is now blocked.

The Réseau Clastres ("The Clastres Network") is named after one of Niaux's guides from the 1950s, and because of the lakes we will not be visiting it. Five animal figures were discovered in it—3 bison, 1 horse, and 1 weasel (or stone marten), all painted with black lines. Nearly 500 footprints have been found as well, a third of them belonging to children (the gender cannot be determined).

In the early 1990s, Jean Clottes (the main French paleo-archeologist to have studied Niaux and to have written about it—unfortunately his study has not been translated) arranged for Caryl and me to be taken all the way through Niaux, including the Réseau Clastres. Such a visit involved fording 4 lakes. When we were checking our lamps, the guide, Yanik La Guillou, asked: "Have you high rubber boots?" Since we did not, he offered us some plastic trash bags he happened to have in his car trunk. At this point, Caryl decided to stay in the car and read.

I pulled on my bags and proceeded to wade each lake up to my thighs. At the far end of the Réseau Clastres—after scrutinizing the only weasel in Ice Age imagery—Yanik and I started back. I saw him leap up, catch the lower edge of a hole, and slip through. When I tried it, I couldn't catch hold. For the first time in a cave,

I panicked, then shouted: "Yanik, can you help me?" For a moment there was silence. Then his arm arched through the hole and helped me up. Had I been alone…

Returning through the final lake, my trash bags broke. I sloshed back through Niaux to our car where Caryl, reading *The Abyss,* looked up and laughed.

While the outer entrance to Niaux is immense, upon leaving daylight one passes though a narrow hallway which dramatically expands into a gallery the size of an airport hangar. In contract to most of the caves we will visit, Niaux has no interior lighting or walkways. In the past, visitors carried kerosene lamps which stained the entrance hall walls with blacking. For the past 15 years, portable electric lamps have provided a flexible and harmless source of light (we will, however, probably be asked to leave our lamps on the ground at the point we turn toward the Salon Noir—every effort is now made to protect the paintings from unnecessary exposure to light).

Niaux's interior has been scoured by powerful streams issuing from glaciers which filled the valley during the coldest phases of the Ice Ages. The walls of the cavern are polished smooth by the abrasion of fine sand which now lies in heaps along the corridor and in the side chambers.

At the intersection that affords access to the Salon Noir there is an extraordinary panel of signs which the early archeologist Cartailhac likened to inscriptions. They make me think of a backstage power panel in a theatre where the lighting, curtains and stage apparatus are controlled—as if this is the control panel for the Salon Noir! Leroi-Gourhan has the most complete description that I have been able to find:

> At Niaux, engravings were made only on sandy or clayey surfaces… The hard rock of the wall has not been scratched, and instead of a tangle of unfinished outlines, we find here a host of devices painted in black and in red. These include no animal outlines; there are exclusively

> signs, and these can be divided into three categories: 1) dots and strokes, either isolated or disposed in single or double rows running in every direction; 2) three, possibly four, claviform signs; 3) miscellaneous signs—a circle, a "wound" made of two converging lines, and a two-pointed "coat-of-arms." There are nearly two hundred dots and strokes. Thus, apart from miscellaneous signs, the group consists of paired signs like those we find at other locations in the cave—claviform/stroke, claviform/dots. What seems to me remarkable is the absence of unfinished animal outlines. The function of the panels of scrawls and unfinished outlines remains unclear; they are often in the only cave areas that suggest repeated visits. Studying them one cannot help thinking that, whereas the other decorations in sanctuaries were rarely retouched, these panels repeatedly receive new figures, often clumsily executed, which sometimes form inextricable tangles.

It should be noted here that since Leroi-Gourhan made his observations in the late 1950s and early 1960s, photographic techniques have improved to the point that over-painting and retouching have been discovered in a number of caves.

The partially circular chamber known as the Salon Noir (the Black Salon) is at the top of a long slope (and at the highest point in the cave). If we enter from the left, there are some engravings on the ground to see, two groups of them. One consists of 4 bison, 1 horse, and an ibex (the main animals depicted in the cave). Another group includes an ibex and a curious five-lobed sign which appears to be unique in cave imagery. It reminded the Abbé Breuil of a clenched fist. Under this "fist" is an aurochs, accompanied by paired signs.

Leroi-Gourhan, perhaps overly-preoccupied with special categories in cave art, identifies six panels, or painted areas, in Niaux's Salon Noir. While there are unpainted areas that can be thought of as interstices between painted ones, "panels" implies a sense of organization that has not been communicated to me on my half-dozen visits. I have experienced this area as a curving, irregular roving assembling of some 80 Ice Age herbivores, half of which are bison, followed by a lesser number of horses, and then an even smaller number of ibexes. According to Clottes, there are 104 animal figures in the entire cave (more recently, Bahn states there are 120). Along with the above-named animals, there are several aurochses, fish and deer (not including the figures in the Réseau Clastres).

In the Salon Noir the animals are always shown in profile (with the amazing exception of a stag-head-shaped hole high on one wall to which barbed antlers have been added, creating in effect a stag head facing the viewer). A few are headless, intentionally it appears (given the fact that there are headless animals in at least 9 caves, this may be a motif we have yet to make sense of). Some Niaux animals appear to be wounded, with "V"-shaped wound signs, or protruding arrows or spears. I say "appear to be," as Alexander Marshack has claimed that some of the weapon signs on Lascaux animals reveals themselves to be, in infra-red photography, long grasses.

The Niaux animals hover the walls like suspended pelts—in only one case does bison hoof placement indicate ground level. In contrast to other caves (the leaping, skidding, and trotting animals of Lascaux, for example), Niaux beasts seem to be absolutely still. While some are superimposed, such does not seem to indicate a narrative relationship (again, in contrast to Lascaux, where in the 18 foot deep Shaft there is clear narrative involvement in a "scene" including a bird-headed ithyphallic man, a disemboweled bison, dots, shamanic paraphernalia, and a rhinoceros).

Since the animals are presented in outlined profile they appear to us to be more drawn than painted, even though they have been painted in black manganese over what appear to be charcoal sketches. There seems to be little concern over their actual size (none are life-sized: the largest animal is a 1.4 meter long horse).

Some appear to have been rapidly and schematically done, while others have a lot of detail. The bison seem to have different "expressions," due to differing treatments of eyes, horns, or nostrils.

Many caves have, along with animals in outlined profile, partial animals, animals that are not identifiable, or wandering lines that might be a dorsal line or simply a non-representative line. The cupola-like ceiling in Lascaux, called the Apse, is a veritable *Finnegan's Wake* of lines, clusters, sprays, animal parts and complete animals punning on and off each other. In the Sanctuary at Les Trois Frères, spiderweb-thin flint-incised animals and lines superimpose and tangle to create a vision of the earth as a swarming pelt of animal powers, in which bison-headed men appear as tiny flecks. Not so at Niaux. At Niaux, more than in any other cave with the possible exception of Font-de-Gaume where the bison appear to be unmoving, I feel the presence of an early laboratory or sketching station, where animals have been projected out of Cro-Magnon heads to be studied as images in contrast to their living earthbound counterparts.

Not only has outline been mastered in the Salon Noir, but perspective (generally associated with the Renaissance) is indicated. Sometimes the leg of an animal closest to the observer is foregrounded via great detail while the opposite leg is backgrounded via a simple sketch. The texture of animal coats is indicated, now heavier, now lighter, now crossed by lateral strokes to indicate mane or beard. Certain hooves are beautifully handled. S. Giedion compared them to sketches by Raphael.

There also appears to be very little deterioration in the Black Salon paintings (however, in the late 1970s, inflows of water damaged around a dozen figures before the flows could be rechanneled). At 800 meters from daylight, such paintings are free from fluctuations in temperature, and the immense amount of space in the cave diffuses what humans carry in on them, including a higher temperature than the caves are used to. In the much smaller and concentrated space of Lascaux the throngs of visitors doubled the temperature in the early 1960s.

Concerning the dating of Niaux's imagery, Paul Bahn has written: "The Salon Noir previously thought to be extremely homogenous, has at least two phases. In the past, the whole of Niaux's decoration was assigned on stylistic grounds to about 14,000 years ago; however, charcoal from two bison figures in the Salon Noir has been radio-carbon-dated and produced strikingly different results: one bison was dated to 13,850 years ago, as expected, but the other produced a date of 12,890 years ago. In other words, Niaux's decoration seems to have been built up in at least two separate phases, while Cougnac—whose famous Megaloceros panel was confidently thought to belong to a single phase—may had had at least three or four episodes spanning many millennia."

Bahn also mentions that the Scanning Electron Microscope has shown that the wood charcoal used for Niaux figures was a resinous wood similar to juniper. One of the reasons that I titled my study of cave imagery "Juniper Fuse" is because most of the wick remains found in Lascaux were juniper, and the uprooted tree that enabled the Montignac teenagers to dig their way down into the cave was also juniper.

Finally, Bahn discusses the pigment analysis undertaken by Clottes and his team at Niaux. A number of mixtures have been detected: "B" in which biotite has been used as an extender, "F" in which feldspar was added, and "T" involving talc. Extenders would have been added to black manganese not only to make it go further, but also for other advantages: adding biotite, for example, makes paint spread easily when wet, and in the case of red ochre, produces a darker shade. It also improves adhesion to the wall, and stops the paint from cracking as it dries. No one knows exactly how these mixtures came to be. Extenders may have been naturally present in clays with the pigments, or may have been added to mixtures through becoming detached from the grinding instruments used.

It seems that in the Salon Noir most of the animal figures were first sketched in charcoal, with manganese paint added on top employing a biotite extender. At other points in the cave, namely in the Rèseau Clastres, paintings were done without preliminary sketching.

In the past it was assumed by everyone that the binding medium was some sort of fatty animal product. However, Claude Couraud did a series of some 200 experiments in two caves using a variety of pigments and binding substances (including fish glue, Arabic gum, gelatin, egg white, bovine blood, and urine). He determined that fatty and organic substances were totally unsuitable binding agents because they failed to adhere to humid walls. The only substance which was good for fixing and preserving the pigments on a rock face was water—especially cave water, rich in calcium carbonate. I believe that it has now also been decided that the binding agent at Lascaux was water from the cave itself.

Discussing the great compositions in Upper Paleolithic art, S. Giedion writes: "The major preoccupation of prehistoric art, from beginning to end, was the attainment of an every greater mastery of the outline. Within the outline the essential features of an animal must be captured with the utmost economy. So it is not altogether surprising that something highly unusual in art occurred: line drawings took on a monumental character… the large animals in the Salon Noir are the product of the Magdalenian in its full maturity, in complete command of the tools at its disposal."

V

SPELUNKIN' WITH CLAYTON: AN INTERIVEW

Jared Demick

There is no one else in American poetry like Clayton Eshleman. In fact, he might just be an endangered species. While many poets are happy to go catatonic in the writing workshop's sheltered claustrophobia, Clayton's spent decades wrestling with our psyche, trying to emerge from the battle with some shred of the soul. There's nothing polite or comforting about his poetry. It's sheer savage brilliance, dazzling in its illumination.

When looking at Clayton's list of work, one wants to say "prolific." However, I'll go with "mind-warping." To date, he has written enough books to build a house with and has been published in over 500 magazines and newspapers. He has edited two landmark literary journals *Caterpillar* and *Sulfur,* magazines that helped to keep the American avant-garde spirit alive. His extensive research of Upper Paleolithic cave art not only made him a spelunker of caves, but also a spelunker of human nature. And if there was ever a Mount Rushmore for translators, Clayton would be on it. His translations of César Vallejo, Antonin Artaud, Aimé Césaire, Michel Deguy, and others are that good. Don't listen to your Mama, believe the hype. It's enough to make a Southern belle fan herself and exclaim, "Good gracious. . ."

When American poetry threatened to become lame, Clayton roared a gigantic NO!!! That's gotten him into *The Jivin' Ladybug* hall of fame. Then we also discovered he's that rarest of creatures: a nice human being.

Jared: Unlike many poets, your poems cannot be easily divided. Themes, allusions, and images constantly return in them like recurring chords in a jazz solo. This got me wondering, do you see the poem as the destination of a poet's journey or as the map tracing the imagination's quest for greater comprehension?

Clayton: While I am aware that since the late 1970s, images associated with the Upper Paleolithic crop up occasionally in my poetry, and that for many years civil materials, pertaining to the American government with its nose in everyone's business, are always just around the corner, I would like to think that I do not reuse the same images. As for your question, the response would have to be: both. Map and destination. A lifework is a map filled with destinations, a map that is also a palimpsest. My poetry is also contoured with evocations of material from poems I have translated by Vallejo, Artaud, and Césaire.

Jared: Is the imagination a physical entity?

Clayton: No more than Satan is. I believe that imagination is the central function of man and the basis of all art. In poetry imagination is a kind of conductor who directs not only the orchestra but the pit, mediating between the critical faculty and spontaneous subconscious input. A mental dance, as it were, which also includes the handling of dead ends, blocks, and what the alchemist Fulcanelli calls, "the bitter conflict at the center of the labyrinth."

In the creative process, one is in the dark much of the time, and of course the end product can never be seen until it is suddenly upon one. Therefore I think the writing of poetry corresponds to being in a labyrinth. At the point I enter the poem, I leave the material world of my workroom and enter a multifoliate maze of decision making which at some point either realizes itself or peters out. This would be that "bitter conflict," when the Minotaur is defeated or destroys the operation. Then: one must get out. This is closure. I like to end a poem with a line or two that completes the process and could also be the beginning of a new undertaking.

Jared: Over the years it seems that your poetry has become increasingly political. I am thinking of bitterly funny lines in *Under World Arrest* and *An Alchemist with One Eye on Fire* such as:

"'Norman our huggable Desert Storm Teddy Bear...
plush and loveable...ready to storm into your home
and right into your heart'"

Is there a motivation behind this increasing political engagement?

Clayton: The complete stanza from which your quotation comes is as follows:

"Wipe out the trauma of war
Turn it into entertainment
The Disneylands on which our fancy feeds
'Norman our huggable Desert Storm Teddy Bear...
plush and loveable... ready to storm into your home
and right into your heart'"

I had come across an ad from The House of Tyrol (a direct mail Georgia retailer) for a Teddy Bear based on "Stormin' Norman" Schwarzkopf, the commander of the Coalition Forces in the Gulf War. I think the complete stanza is self-explanatory.

I have felt for many years that one "wing" of my poetry must be written by someone let's call Citizen Eshleman, who reads and listens to the news, and suffers the impotence of not being able to directly interfere with the overseas horrors our government has been perpetrating since the late 1940s. I think that this "wing" must be accommodated with other "wings," must not be allowed to take over, and must not turn into agenda-speak. That is to say, it must remain part of my imaginal process at large.

In the 1940s, nearly all major American poets writing at that time failed to respond to the opening of the Nazi death camps (Reznikoff and Oppen are the primary and noble exceptions). And no one to my knowledge wrote about our failure to bomb the camps or to provide haven for fleeing Jews.

I would like for someone reading my poetry fifty years from now to see that I was actively engaged as a citizen in my work.

Jared: My co-editor Angela once said to me, "I like how Clayton makes up words in his poems. They're very striking." We got to talking and wondered if you felt that language is unsuited for the deep psychic explorations in your poetry?

Clayton: I would like to think that all levels of language, from the arcane, the archaic, the scientific, the vulgar, and the made up, are welcome, at any particular moment, in the poem. I do this very spontaneously. The made up occurs when a more conventional expression seems trite or misleading. I think the poet must have real respect for language *and* no respect for it at all. One role of poetry is to keep language rich, unpredictable, and spontaneously adhesive to the heat of the moment in composition. I am most interested in what happens to my mind as it pokes, sniffs, roots about, bumps into, sails through the resistance and release of language.

Over the past couple decades, I have written many poems responding to art or artists. In a poem called "Michaux, 1956" I make up some words to evoke in language images in Henri Michaux's drawings in which one cannot tell if the lifeless is squirming alive, or a living organism is in its death throes. Thus the following line:

"Black sand dense on white ground. Mites. Mites in mitosis. Mitochondria. Misible mites. Mitomitosalchondrialmaze."

Jared: Unlike many translators, you develop complex and involved relationships with the poets you translate. For example, your decades-long devotion to giving César Vallejo's warped Spanish a proper English voice is truly astounding. Do you see translation as a sort of apprenticeship? If so, what do you learn along the way?

Clayton: A good answer to this question can be found in "A Translation Memoir," which follows my translation of *The Complete Poetry of César Vallejo.*

While I was living in Kyoto, Japan, in 1963, my friend Will Petersen, a lithographer, visited one afternoon and told of having just left a Bonsai gardener who, he said, was now doing wonderfully inventive work. For some reason, I asked Will: "How old is he?" Will responded that the man was in his early 70s—and that he had only recently completed his apprenticeship! Such information set me back on my heels. At that time I was a 28 year old who, like millions of other young Americans, thought that, with some luck, and ingenuity, I could make a name for myself in art. Will's story led me to the realization that I too was going to have to go through an apprenticeship if I really wanted to count on poetry to guide my life. So I rather impulsively decided that I should commit myself to the toughest poetic task I knew about at that time: a translation of the eighty-nine poems that made up Vallejo's 1939 European collection of poetry, *Poemas humanos.* I intuited that I would learn something from attempting to translate the *Poemas humanos* that I could not get elsewhere. And I also thought of my work as a potential offering to others who did not have access to the original Spanish.

Blake writes somewhere that the most divine act is to set another before you. One does this in love, and Whitman proposes that adhesive love, the love of comrades, is deeper and of greater human service than romantic love. In my translational apprenticeship I set Vallejo before me—as gate, and as obstacle. He has become my adhesive poet comrade for my whole writing life.

Also, in 1963 I did not know how to proceed, in poetry, on my own. By working on Vallejo I worked on myself in a way that I could not at that time do directly. Of course, given my distress and the translational difficulties I faced, at times I thought that by working on Vallejo that I was evading working on myself. Vallejo was my wall. By slowly burrowing through that wall, by not going over or under it, I positioned his work in my being (and also turned him into a figure in my own poetry).

Jared: Who would you choose as a bodyguard down a dark alley, Vallejo or Artaud?

Clayton: Actually, I would probably choose my friend Mark Moore, who is a black belt in Aikido, or poets Hugh Seidman and André Spears who are black belts in Karate. Vallejo would be useless as a bodyguard. Artaud would undoubtedly scream so hideously the assailant would scram. Or I might enlist Wallace Stevens, who I understand held his own in a drunken fist-fight with Hemingway once in Florida.

Jared: I was wondering if we could talk about your long-time research in the Upper Paleolithic cave art in France. What's it like being in those ancient caves? Do you feel a connection to our ancestors when face to face with their art? What's your favorite cave and why?

Clayton: *Frustrating* is the first word that comes to mind for being in many of the Ice Age painted caves in France open to the public. Why? Because one is always with a guide, who has been in the cave hundreds of times before, and for whom being in the cave is just another job. There are a few exceptions, like Jean Pierre Vanzo, at Font-De-Gaume, who is clearly moved by being there, and draws the tourists in to a focused reading of the beautifully conceived bison there. And of course the grand exception would be Jacques Marsal, one of the 1940 discoverers of Lascaux. Marsal stayed on to become the principle caretaker and guide of the cave (until the late 1980s when he became ill and died).

My first grand experience in an ensouled Upper Paleolithic cave was in fact Lascaux in the spring of 1974. I was completely unprepared for the impact of The Rotunda, the crystalline-white walls of which are covered with polychromatic aurochses, ponies, and stags. Marsal led us down into this area, in the dark, and told us to stand there for a few moments. He then turned the dim lights on, and we were suddenly surrounded by this cavalcade of creatures which in their own way remind me of the animals encircling the pond with bathing maidens in the central panel of Bosch's *Gar-*

den of Earthly Delights. Much of the art of Lascaux must have been planned in advance with specially heated ochre and manganese minerals, and executed by trained artists.

I like the Combarelles cave a lot too. There furrowed elephant-hide-like walls are covered with some 600 often crude engravings, including 50 or 60 humanoids. I say "humanoids" instead of "humans," since most are sketchy and extremely grotesque, and give the impression, unlike the animals in Lascaux's Rotunda, of being done in the dark by ordinary men, women, and probably children, responding to the stimulation that sensory isolation in caves can create.

Jared: In *Juniper Fuse,* you mention how Rimbaud's attempts at finding the unknown "I" were aesthetic rather than psychological. That got me thinking, do you believe that most modern writers have used the novelty of aesthetic innovation to avoid probing deeply into the soul? In other words, a change of thought presentation instead of a change of thought?

Clayton: For readers who are interested, my comments about Rimbaud and others are on pp. 82–83 of *Juniper Fuse.*

My point there is that while Rimbaud sought to make himself into a seer, his journey did not involve the sort of interior dismemberment that at least some shamanic novices go through. I think aesthetic innovation *can* involve "probing deeply into the soul," but that modern and contemporary poets do not gain access to "the unifying womb of things," which, to me, suggests tapping into the tribal subconscious with archetypal formations that have been experienced by medicine men/women or shamans in the past. One must also keep in mind here that artists are obsessed with a product, a much different goal than that of a novice shaman.

I think of Blake at this point. He might be the grand exception here, in as much as he seems to have determined that the old mythical universe was dead and that a new set of myths had to be constructed to accommodate revolutionary shifts in the mind.

This meant new gods and goddesses, and nothing less than the invention, with some Biblical aid, of a personal cosmogonic mythology. From a shamanic point of view, Blake attempted to redirect "the tribal subconscious" into a vast re-visionary network that he believed responded to the psychological and social world he lived in.

Jared: How can the poet learn to abandon the ego?

Clayton: Rimbaud makes another appearance. His "somebody else" is a more dimensional sense of the ego, complexed with material from his subconscious. I would propose that one reason we may feel that a particular poet's work is great is because he comes at us with more heft and metaphoric density than we associate with daily ego-oriented consciousness. To say that a great poet dreams awake suggests that he is able, in composition, to draw upon his subconscious, and in that way brings to bear on writing irrational formations.

However, "dreaming awake" is not quite right, because when we dream we are passive receptors (very few people, in my experience, are able to direct their dreaming while they are asleep). I would like to think that the full blast no holds barred version of "somebody else" involves a multifoliate traffic between all of a poet's mental states, including rational scrutiny of this traffic as he directs it and picks it off while aligning it.

Jared: Why do you think some artists shy away from their deepest, darkest work? I am thinking of Neruda here, how he went from being the poet of submerged darkness in *Residence on Earth* to the poet of perpetual light in the later odes.

Clayton: Interesting you bring up Neruda here. He was on my mind too, while I was completing the poems in *An Alchemist with One Eye on Fire*.

Based on what I know of his poetry, the first two *Residencias en la tierra* are the most mysterious and engaging works of his career. However, I find them more moody than "dark". In the third *Residencia,* much of which is compelled by the Spanish Civil War, one sees Neruda moving toward "universal voice," or "voice of the people," a perspective that reaches its peak in certain sections of *Canto general.* At the point Neruda merges his voice with that of the common man, or makes that claim, I begin to back off, and suspect that a doctrinal agenda is right around the corner.

Which turns out to be true, for the longest of Neruda's poems, published a few years after the 1950 *Canto general,* is *Las uvas y el viento,* a dreadfully superficial work that includes birthday songs to Stalin (this in the early 1950s!).

The "perpetual light" you refer to in the *Odas* (all three volumes of which were also published in the 1950s) continues the journalistic poetry of *Las uvas y el viento,* but the focus has shifted to common things, such as socks, tomatoes, conger eels, onions, and César Vallejo. I think, keeping your terms in mind, that politics knocked the brooding darkness out of Neruda. Politics forced him to the social surface and though he occasionally wrote fine poems in the 50s and 60s ("Sueños de Trenes" from *Estravagario* is one of them) he never regained the dream-like, metaphoric thickness one finds in the first two *Residencias.*

Neruda is of course just one example. Very, very few poets can hang in there with "their deepest, darkest work" for very long. Baudelaire and Artaud are among the few exceptions.

Jared: Will it be possible for modern humans to reconnect with their origins?

Clayton: It depends on how you mean "reconnect." The writings of the anthropologist Wade Davis are saturated with articulated experience based on contact with tribal and nomadic peoples. At the same time, Wade lives in Washington, and works for the National Geographic Institute as an "Explorer-in-Residence."

Your question, however, seems more aimed at humankind than at any particular person (I thought of Wade Davis because he is, in my estimation, a marvelous bridge figure between many different worlds). In that sense, I would say no. Humankind is drugged on the conveniences associated with modernity and religion and, like lemmings, we will follow them right over the cliff. Let's see what we do without oil—that might be a good test of how much regenerative stuff we have left in us.

Jared: You and your wife Caryl seem to have a close working relationship. How has she affected your work and vice versa?

Clayton: I began to read things I was working on to Caryl in 1973 and by the late 70s she had become a terrific responder, orally and textually, to what I was attempting to do as a poet and essayist. She has functioned as my editor now for many years, and because of her input I have repeated myself less than I would have without her. She has made me a more careful reader of my own work and has constantly noticed botches and glitches in drafts and in revisions. My poetry owes her more than I can express.

Because of certain health problems, Caryl has not had the energy to pursue an art of her own. So she has very generously offered me imaginative input that under different circumstances would have been channeled into her own workings.

One of the ways in which I have responded to her gifts to me, is by helping her do certain things, from grocery shopping to shopping for clothing. For many years I have also done, with the exception of desserts, all the cooking.

Jared: You've mentioned to me that you and Caryl will be going on another trip to France to continue your cave explorations. What do you hope to accomplish on this trip?

Clayton: We don't really *explore* caves anymore. With the exception of a visit I made to the recently discovered (and magnificent) Chauvet cave at the beginning of 2004, my exploratory work ended in the 1990s, at the time I finished my research on *Juniper Fuse.* These days we visit caves we have been in many times with the small groups we take to the Dordogne and Lot regions, every June, sponsored by the Ringling School of Art and Design in Sarasota. We enjoy these trips. They enable us to return to southwestern France and help others appreciate what I have come to call "the back wall of imagination" (there will be a long essay on the researching and writing of *Juniper Fuse* in the September issue of *APR*).

The commercial scene is much greater in Les Eyzies de Tayac, the town we always stay in, than it was in the 1970s when I began my research. What was then a sleepy village with a single street and a half dozen stores now has a tourist focus, with pizza joints, rock shops, boutiques, souvenir stands etc. The new national prehistory museum is expected to bring in a half million people per year.

However, the ancient Dordogne can still be sensed in spite of these changes—especially the magnificent rock walls that line the Vézère River and the town. They are the place's signature and probably the force, along with the images in the caves, that made me feel, in the late 1980s (when I finally got my cave book in focus), that I had *come home,* had found my true *home* there. So when I am in the Dordogne, I try to see around the tourists and shop-keepers and keep focused on those primordial images that changed my life.

Jared: What other new projects are on the horizon for Clayton Eshleman?

Clayton: A new collection of essays, prose poems, notes, and interviews will be published this coming October by Black Widow Press as *Archaic Design.*

Because this has been a big year for readings—I did around fifty between November 2006 and April 2007—I have not tried to finish many new poems. I have a lot of things in drafts that I want to spend the summer with after we return in late June from France. Some examples:

—poems contemplating bizarre figures on Mayan vases (based on Justin and Barbara Kerr's marvelous roll-out photos);

—a work on tent caterpillars;

—a word sarcophagus for my mother;

—working with notebooks filled with jottings made in the three major Madrid museums (2006) and the British Museum (2007);

—a poem to be called "Tjurunga," in which I create my own out of my foundational experiences as a poet (the idea for which came from Barry Hill's book: *T.G.H. Strehlow and Aboriginal Possession*).

I have been thinking about expanding my translation of Artaud's writings from his 1945–48 period, *Watchfiends & Rack Screams,* to include additional texts published in *Conductors of the Pit* and *Sulfur #9*.

There is an "Eshleman Reader" in the works for Black Widow Press in 2008. This will mean re-reading a great deal of what I have written and translated, and selecting around 350 pages of poetry, essays, and translations.

Over the past two years I have been assembling pieces from *Sulfur* magazine for "A Sulfur Anthology." I am sure no press is going to publish an anthology of more than 600 pages, yet at this point the smallest compilation I am happy with, based on *Sulfur's* 11,000 pages, comes to 2000!

Jivin' Ladybug, 2007

Jared Demick is a Ph.D. student in American literature at the University of Connecticut. He is currently writing a dissertation about the uses of nonstandard English in American popular culture ranging from urban slangs to Chinese pidgin English. He is also the editor of *Jivin' Ladybug* (http://jivinladybug.com), a website devoted to the arts.

KAM: A good deal of your poetry is inspired by visual art. "Meditation on Marwan's Faces," for example, is fascinating. Where does your mind as a poet overlap with the mind of the painter, and where does your poetry intersect with the painting? Could you elaborate on the process by which you compose a poem about a painting? What goes on in your mind while translating a visual expression into words?

CE: As I recently wrote the painter Mary Heebner (with whom I collaborated on a portfolio of poems and images, *Deep Thermal*, simplemente maria press, 2007): "I am interested in what I see in paintings as well as what the paintings see in me. I try, facing works of art, to inhabit a "between" in which a reciprocal distillation can occur. I found in certain of your watercolors a resonating psychic stimulation and attempted to improvise on the words, narrative nodes and associational 'chains' they flushed forth."

I don't know that my "mind as a poet" overlaps "with the mind of [a] painter," since I am almost always responding to a painting and not what was on the painter's mind when she or he was creating the painting. I often carry a notebook with me when I go to museums or art galleries and when a work stirs interesting sensations, I open the notebook and follow out those words or phrases based on such sensations, attempting to keep my eyes on the painting at the same time that I respond to its stimulations.

On June 1 (my birthday), 2004, in Paris, I spent several hours at a Matta show, with paintings and drawings from 1936 to 1944, in the Malingue art gallery. After about a half an hour of looking, I began to write rapidly in my notebook, drifting around the gallery, from painting to painting (or drawing to drawing), letting Matta's metaphoric deep space constructions, which evoke the cosmos as well as the recesses of the mind, impinge and flush out language. A couple of my phrases—"convict of light" and "panic suction of the sun"—are translations of Matta titles. Matta is indescribable in the way that the best work of Arshile Gorky is, and thus a delicious challenge to articulate, since any words one find seem to come out of a collision between one's own tapped subconscious and his anti-illustrative forms.

That is one way to proceed. Another is to take a painting like Bosch's *The Garden of Earthly Delights* or Caravaggio's *The Beheading of St.-John the Baptist* and study it for months, reading what others have written about it, taking notes, and in those ways arming oneself with an arsenal of material to bring to bear on a piece of writing. In the case of Caravaggio, my wife Caryl and I traveled to Valleta, Malta, for a week to study this gigantic painting which is in the CoCathedral there.

I also enjoy responding to African masks and sculpture. Such are usually anonymous and relate to cultures I know very little about if anything at all. There is a powerful transpersonal force that comes through many of such pieces and it is a great challenge to come up with language that somehow expresses what I see and feel.

In the winter/spring of 2004, I spent several days each week in Chicago, teaching two creative writing workshops at Columbia College. I walked to the Chicago Art Institute each week and over the semester took around 50 pages of notes while in the African section of the museum. I will copy out some of my notes, and follow them with a poem that they in one way or another inspired.

Chicago Art Institute, February, 2004

Snakes wrapping the arms of a headless 14th century Western Sudan terracotta figure—snakes as interface between inner & outer, as bonding rings, uroboric ongoing, more than ornament or cosmetic, living clothing, abyssal caresses.

Nyama, a vital force that strengthens the spirit (Mali, Dogon)—jaw and neck seem "attached" as if under the control of another force—the nyama?

The figure's body encrusted with animal blood, millet porridge, plant juice and oil.

"sealed by a mirror..."

Clinton as Nkonde figure, his back filled with Republican nails and blades.

The mask as reabsorption of the lost particulars of being, replacing the bald human face with its wilderness eyes, beard and skin. The mask freezes movement, arguing infinity as sleep, or as *cuitlacoche,* the "sleeping excrement" of being, that once attached to humankind enables a doubling to manifest, nothing and its double, while the interstices (areas between mask, skin, and human) swarm with pupae.

Mali Bamama *boli* recalls the headless Montespan bear. *Boli-wise,* one wonders if blood and grains were applied to the bear's surface. The *boli's* wrapped wooden core evokes the fiber art of Judith Scott—do her wrappings harness energy? What charge does she project in her labyrinthine fiber turns? The *boli's* surface also evokes the cow cud my father brought home from the Kingham slaughterhouse where he worked.

Rake tines rising from the back of a Ntomo mask, as if to project brain energy into the atmosphere, and vice versa, to impale descending antagonistic hexes.

A Senufo angel bearing in one hand an oxen yoke and in the other a barking snake.

Upper Paleolithic line superimposition appears to be captured in some masks by a synthesis of animal parts in harmony and dissonance (in one Senufo crocodile mask:

snout of hyena, twisted horns of a ram, slender curving horns of antelope). Via such intersections forces intermingle, share veins.

These are one morning's notations. About six months later, after re-reading them, as well as visiting the Dapper Museum of African Art in Paris, I composed the following poem:

WITCHERY

Realm of co-penetration, grotesque, affirmative,
I offer you what grows from my chest
in tumor splendor, gnarled, polished, wet.

I protect you with my navel blades,
my nipple nails, my kidney mirror—
dead mirror in which cloud fungus is trapped.

Steel pins puncture my thigh, belly and throat—
they enable me to pray with torturous force.

Mask reabsorbing the lost particulars of being,
mask replacing the bald human face with wilderness eyes,
mask sharing veins with its plant juice doubles,
mask whose interstices swarm with pupae.

If, over my tall blue pearled neck, I stare in terror, it is be-
    cause
foxes have gotten inside me,
foxes are tearing apart my death.

Pitch-black head breaking out in red currants, in spikes,
    in blisters,
head a field sprouting buds, pebbles, studs,

head issuing a living waving horn,
head asleep, head replete, head whose dream matrix pos-
tulates
the prayer of all things: to emerge at once.

KAM: As a poet, what is your view of American involvement in the Middle East? What's your vision of a true dialogue between East and West? Do you think it's possible?

CE: I hang my head in shame over the "American involvement in the Middle East." Any open and honest research on American foreign policy of the past fifty years will explain why 9/11 occurred—if it was solely the work of Arab terrorists. I am not convinced that it was. There are too many unexplained aspects of what happened at the World Trade Center and the Pentagon, and the official report carried out by the Commission is a humiliating sham. But assuming for the sake of your question that the Bush administration was not in on the attack, the proper response, in my opinion, would have been to send a tactical force in to where those responsible for it were based and to have destroyed them and their base. What we have done in Iraq, and I am including the terrible sanctions, is unforgivable. The Israelis should have been forced, years ago, to withdraw to the 1967 borders; a Palestinian state should have been made possible. The thing that gets me about Bush—I mean there are many things, but this one in particular, is that the man is without conscience. If he could feel shame, he would either have not done what he has done, or having done it would have torn himself apart by now.

America has hundreds and hundreds of military bases throughout the world. And the occupation of Iraq is clearly a permanent one. I do not see how a true dialogue could take place "between the East and West," as you put it, until America stops dominating the planetary direction of life.

KAM: What has haunted you daily for as long as you can remember?

CE: Many things haunt me daily. Iraq. The quality of life for Palestinians. People on death row who are innocent. Americans in prison for marijuana possession. Female genital mutilation. People being thrown out of hospitals because they are too poor to pay for care. On an ontological level, I am haunted by the irreconcilable gulf between desire and the fulfillment of desire. That paradise remains mental. I am haunted by being infested with absence. As a poet I am haunted by the fact that there is hardly any relationship between what I intend in as poem and how some hypothetical reader is going to read it. But I do know definitely that I will die. So I am not haunted by immortality or heaven or God. And: I feel I have lived my own life, and not someone else's. So as I twist on knowing the extent of human cruelty, I have a little relief in the gratitude I feel toward the forces within and around me that have enabled me to live the life of a poet.

2007

Khaled Al-Masri is Assistant Professor of Arabic at Swarthmore College. He has published a book in Arabic on the fiction of the prominent Iraqi author Gha'ib Tu'mah Faraman. Additionally, he has edited twelve Arabic translations of English novels, including *Housekeeping* and *Gilead* by Marilynne Robinson and *The Known World* by Edward P. Jones. His English translations of Arabic poetry have appeared in *Banipal.*

JACKET #36 INTERVIEW

Clayton Eshleman in conversation with Ian Irvine, late 2007 to early 2008

Ian: Clayton, you seem to have been enormously productive these past few years, and across all areas of your public profile as a writer. There is certainly no sense that you're slowing down either in terms of publications or public engagements/ performances. Similarly, in terms of quality it appears to me as though you're at the height of your powers as a poet, translator and essayist. Are their any reasons for (secrets behind!) your remarkable productivity at the moment?

Clayton: Completing *Juniper Fuse* in the late 1990s released a lot of energy. I also retired in 2003 and soon realized that I had been quite depressed in the classrooms at Eastern Michigan University for the past decade. I was trying to teach students how to write poetry who had read hardly anything at all and were mainly in my classes, as far as I could tell, out of curiosity. My best students were painters.

So, getting out of the classroom made me feel like a lion let out of his cage. I completed a number of projects involving essays and poems, and the following year, when I got a contract from the University of California Press for *The Complete Poetry of César Vallejo,* I began translating Vallejo's first book — the only collection of his poetry I had not previously translated — and revising all of the rest of my work, with a great deal of joy.

There is something about an accumulating focus that pays off. I had insisted on dealing with my background in the late 1960s and early 1970s, so that early life traumas were written into and through, and cleared, for the most part, by the time I began my research, in 1974, on Ice Age cave art, for the book that turned out to be *Juniper Fuse.*

I had also taught myself, by the mid-1990s, to write first drafts of poems and then turn them over and leave them alone for a year or so before doing any revising. I had discovered that when I attempted to revise immediately I destroyed the most original parts of a poem. I was like an animal mother turning on one of her cubs. After a year or so, I could re-approach poem drafts and inspect them as if I had not written them. This has enabled me to protect what was most original about such beginnings, and to revise on that basis.

Ian: In my first encounter with your poetry back in 1983, i.e. the poems in *Hades in Manganese,* your incorporation of terms drawn from the technical vocabulary of Ice Age archaeology really stood out: 'A wheeled figure stabs and sews/ the infancy in our grain to the skin of the ground./ Wheeled wall master who mends in manganese ...' Just how important was your engagement with the caves to your development as a poet?

Clayton: To my knowledge, the lines you quote there, from the poem *Hades in Manganese* have no technical archeological language. I think those lines are imaginal improvisations off what I saw initially in the paintings on certain Ice Age cave walls. I think the "wheels" on my "wall master" came about via my attempting to engage the acrobatic drawings and engravings in such caves as Pech Merle and Lascaux. Lines swirling and superimposing evoke a wheel-like motion, or a wheeling of the mind as, like an ice-skater, the engraver or painter's hand cuts and feints across the wall.

I became aware of Upper Paleolithic cave paintings in my late thirties, at a point when I had worked through a lot of my own personal early life, and was looking for new challenging material. The cave paintings, with no historical context, turned me from my personal life to transpersonal materials and that was both exciting and demanding. The caves and their ensouled decorations took me out of myself, and made me utilize my imagination in a way I had not done before. The cave images also humbled me as they empowered me. They also gave me a back wall, not a Greek or even Neolithic one, but a true back wall, where that truly revolutionary move from no image of the world to an image seems to have taken place.

Ian: Much of your poetry projects an aura associated with elements drawn from primal spiritual traditions. This aura is supplemented by your use of imagery etc. related to Upper Paleolithic cave art and also from more contemporary art. It strikes me that whatever happens to be unfolding in the foreground of your work is often positioned in a kind of unique communion with a vast repository of archaic and modern imagery. You seem to describe aspects of this in terms of your 'compositional method' in the notes to the poem 'Spirits of the Head' (in *Reciprocal Distillations*) [1] when you write that the poem arose out of 'over a dozen pages of notes'. Could you comment on both the layered visual quality to much of your post-70s poetry and its relationship to your way of composing poems.

Clayton: I think that the main benefit from research for a poet (in the case of *Juniper Fuse* it involved library work as well as cave crawling) is that it builds up a file of materials that cling to the underside of consciousness, and can be brought into play when, in composition, one needs a hoist to move the poem along into another dimension or sounding. I also try to open myself to what I call "lateral entries" while writing, so that the focus can be bombarded left and right by images that, at a glance, do not seem to have anything to do with the ongoing core meander, but may turn out, when viewed in terms of the whole composition, to extend the focus into a more complex, or as you put it, "layered" presentation. I am not talking about "automatic writing" here, or "free association" (whatever that is). I attempt to keep a rational "shit detector" beeping slightly above my head to the left, while I write, so that trash (clichés, sentimentalities, repeats, nonsense) is immediately phased out of the composition. Thus I'd say I work in a state of qualified spontaneity. The "layered... quality" you speak of probably refers to the conjunctions that occur in my lines, where what I am probing is intersected by materials from the research arsenal.

Ian: Another aspect of your poetry is the impression you give the reader of a kind of metaphysical/sacred (or at least 'visionary'/ 'magical realist') view of our place in the cosmos. In your recent poem 'Some of Her Names', for example (in *Reciprocal Distillations*) [2], you write: 'As a poet my *cor,* my heart, is under Cerridwen'. In some of your poetry you seem to express a deeply immanent, embodied spirituality informed by mythopoetic feminism and archaic spiritual traditions. Do you see your work as a poet as 'spiritual' or 'religious' — if so, in what ways?

Clayton: My poetry is not "religious," as it is not based on a point of view involved with organized religions. I was raised as a Presbyterian Christian but most of that stuff fell away when I discovered poetry in my early twenties, as a student at Indiana University in the late 1950s. Poetry became my practice, my way of orientating myself to my life as well as to the world around me.

I disagree with Gary Snyder here who has written that a poet needs religion in order to learn how to live. While poetry, fundamentally is without moral strictures, and irritating "do thises" and "don't do thats," it is such an all-embracing way of being that a sense of meaningful living emerges via what one teaches oneself while writing. I should acknowledge here the work of Wilhelm Reich. I was in Reichian therapy with Dr. Sidney Handelman (who was a student of Reich's) in NYC in the late 1960s, and at that time I read many of Reich's books. I was extremely impressed by his ideas concerning Self-regulation and its relationship to orgastic potency (see pp. 39–41 in *Companion Spider*), which I saw, along with Research and Experimentation, as one of the poet's "powers."

Ian: It seems to me that your poetry has a great deal to say about humankind's relationship with the animal and plant worlds. Arguably your work on Upper Paleolithic cave art uncovered a kind of pathogenic psychic 'splitting off' ('fracture?') between humankind and other non-human forms of life on earth. The poem 'Fracture' (1983) seems important in this respect, at one point you write: '... crying the oldest cry// that earth is responsible for our deaths/ that if we die collectively/ we will take the earth with us *if we can*.' [3] How do you see our current global environmental crisis given the archaeological material you've researched over the past few decades?

Clayton: The human immortality compulsion is one of the filthiest flies in our ointment. César Vallejo has written (see p. 355 of *The Complete Poetry of César Vallejo*) that "the sorrow of men... lies in never being certain of death." Not being certain of death but of seeking to deny death via solutions provided by organized religions, all of which I find odious (Tantrik Buddhism seems to be the least odious). I think that one reason people are cruel to each other is because acts of cruelty screen one off from one's own mortality.

The planet suffers, as always, the human immortality hang-up which says, in effect, that life in the here and now, existent life, does not in the long run count for anything. As you may know, American Evangelicals are on record of having stated that it does not matter what we do to the earth (in fact, they say, the quicker we ruin life on the planet, the better). The same people heap abuse on Arab suicide bombers who can't wait to get into their own form of paradise supposedly filled with sloe-eyed virgins.

There are other factors involved in human cruelty that I cannot nail down under the rubric of religion. I think human beings were cruel before there occurred what we call "religion." For a monotheistic God to exist, you needed a social structure with a king or imperial leader. Before the Neolithic, before agriculture, there is no evidence of what we call "war;" hunter/ gatherer tribal units appear not to have been hierarchically organized. However, I do not think we can assume that such people were not cruel to each other, especially to strangers.

Becoming human, thousands of years ago, appears to have involved separating the human out of the animal continuum, a blessing and a curse if there ever was one. Cro-Magnon people seemed to have revered animals in ways that one still finds traces of in indigenous peoples today.

At the point that the connection between semen and pregnancy was discovered (very early I think) then the stage was set for our two-tiered system of women being inferior to men. The male became the "star," the creator, with women relegated to being hot houses for his progeny.

Ian: In doing a web-search on your work (and also in reading more generalist texts on US poetry) three terms are repeatedly used to describe your core poetics: 'deep imagist', 'American grotesque' and 'ethnopoetics'. How useful are any of these terms to describe the unique poetics you've developed during your life?

Clayton: "Deep Image" emerged out of the evolving poetics of Robert Kelly and Jerome Rothenberg in the mid-late 1950s. Statements on it can be found in issues of *Trobar* and *Poems From The Floating World* magazines. This term was mainly a provocation and a sighting, and not a "movement" proposal. Both poets dropped the term after a few years. Curiously, it was then picked up by Robert Bly and James Wright who simplified it and are still today, by some, thought to be its founders. I was just finding my way into poetry at the time Robert and Jerry were involved in "Deep Image" (an American crossbreeding of Surrealism, Projective Verse, and depth psychology, to my mind). I found their thoughts about it fascinating but I was never part of it in a procedural way.

"American grotesque:" I am not sure where this term comes from or exactly what it refers to in American poetry. Perhaps it is a play on Mikhail Bakhtin's term, "grotesque realism," elaborated in his book *Rabelais and His World*. If so, then I do feel it is relevant to my work. I read the Bakhtin book in 1972 when I was finishing the writing of *Coils*. Bakhtin confirmed in his discussion of "grotesque realism" certain strategies that in my manuscript I felt uncertain about. His vision of the open body, blended in with animals and the world, or degradation as involving both burying and sowing simultaneously, confirmed the breakthrough farewell to my "given" Indianapolis world, which I viewed as racist, sexist, and rancidly repressed.

"Ethnopoetics:" Another Rothenberg formulation which I am very sympathetic with, but am not directly a part of. I suppose you could extend my work on the deep past, and connect it with ethnopoetics, but such is an association, not a link. Back in 1966, I was suspicious of what Jerry was up to, when he was asking American poets to transform ethnographic or missionary versions of tribal poetries into a kind of Williamsesque speech-oriented American poetry. I recall sitting in the living room at Paul Blackburn's flat on East 7th Street in NYC, which I had rented for the summer of 1966, staring at a missionary version of an African hippopotamus chant and feeling absurd. The chant, in the version given me, was not only stilted and probably filled with translation errors, but it was just one aspect of a charged, sensual rite involved with dance, color, smells, food, and the environment. So I told Jerry that I did not know how to do anything with it, and did not became involved in his initial ethnopoetic project.

Since then I have decided that in spite of my objections to the "hippopotamus chant" situation, that Rothenberg's project was an honest and imaginative attempt at a grand inclusion of the world's poetries relative to 20th century American poetry. In terms of the continental USA, as demonstrated in the Rothenberg and George Quasha anthology of the mid 1970s, *America A Prophecy*, the ethnopoetic push brought to bear on poetry written for the most part by white heterosexual males, indigenous and folk poetries heretofore excluded and confined to such categories as Folklore and Ethnography. I recall Helen Vendler's fury in her review of *America A Prophecy* in *The New York Times*. She could not tolerate such inclusiveness. Imagine! Sitting Bull cheek to jowl with Marianne Moore!

Ian: In 'Prologue to Origins' contained in Vol. 1 of *Poems for the Millennium* the editors state that it is impossible to understand 20th century radical poetries 'without mapping at the same time some features of the old worlds, brought newly into the present & viewed there as if for the first time ...' It seems clear to me that in some senses your attempts to plot the origins of the imagination back to Upper Palaeolithic cave imagery represent perhaps the exemplary case of what Rothenberg and Joris were describing. If as they put it 'the new seeks out the old', the 'old' you went in search of was very old indeed. I wonder how you now view your decades long commitment to this project given that your major work on the 'origins' theme, *Juniper Fuse* has just recently been published? Do you have a sense of closure?

Clayton: *Juniper Fuse* was published by Wesleyan University Press in 2003. The book is going into a second edition this winter.

For the most part, my work on Upper Paleolithic imagination is complete. I stay up on archeological publications in the field, because my wife Caryl and I lead a yearly tour to the painted caves of the Dordogne every June, and I want to be able to respond to clients' questions.

In 2004, I was given permission to visit the Chauvet cave, discovered in 1994, in the French Ardèche. Chauvet appears to be as important as Lascaux. I wrote a poem about the lions on the left wall of the end chamber that is included in *Reciprocal Distillations.*

Ian: Any Australian reader of *Juniper Fuse* would be immediately struck by the great silences one encounters at every point of your tentative poetry and archaeology-based reconstruction of the subjectivity of Upper Paleolithic humanity. "I wonder if she will pass through// the Aurignacian assembly./ I'd like to hear the speeches/ as she defends her ogre intelligence." [4] Given the immense antiquity of indigenous Australian traditions, not to mention the fact that much Aboriginal rock art remains intimately connected to living spiritual and cultural traditions the question arises: how might contact with living guardians of our indigenous traditions impact on your work? I know that you've been interested in visiting Australia for some time now and wonder what it is you might be seeking here were you to make a visit?

Clayton: As you know, I have read Barry Hill's *Broken Song,* and written a six page poem, which I regard as a kind of summation piece, called "The Tjurunga." I hope to publish this poem in an Australian magazine, and I would be very interested in the response.

I would love to visit Australia and made an attempt a couple of years ago to get enough readings and honorarium to cover a one month trip. Were I to come, I would try to arrange to see rock art sites and to have some contact with indigenous people — especially artists and writers. I keep thinking that there will come along, one of these days, the indigenous equivalent of the French poet Antonin Artaud: a man or woman who will tear away the communal residue of two hundred years of colonization and reveal the psychic force within.

I have an old friend in Los Angeles, the scholar Ronald Gottesman, who collects contemporary indigenous paintings from Australia. He has visited, in Australia, the artists he collects, several times. This has been a remarkable experience for him.

I would also like to visit Australian museums and wineries, and to meet non-indigenous artists and writers. Besides my own poetry, I would like to read my translations of César Vallejo, Antonin Artaud, and Aimé Césaire.

It would also be very interesting for me to show some slides of European Ice Age cave art to indigenous Australian artists and talk with them about their response!

Ian: You've had some fairly critical things to say about neo-formalist trends in US poetry (its promotion of a return to 'traditional' ideas of poetry). There is the sense that your critique comes out of your long engagement with traditions of experimental poetry. Is there still a 'mainstream' in US poetry and a clearly defined *avant garde,* or is the situation more complicated these days as you seem to be suggesting in your article "A Wind from all Compass Points"?

Clayton: While the boundary between the conventional and the innovative is always hazy, I think it is definitely possible to understand that poets like Robert Kelly and Billy Collins come from two essentially differing viewpoints concerning the art of poetry. The difference is one between an alchemist (Kelly) and an entertainer (Collins).

The lineage of American poetry that interests me the most is the one that begins with Walt Whitman's extraordinary breakthrough, nearly Cro-Magnon in its originality, and continues in the early part of the century with the work of Ezra Pound, William Carlos Williams, and Gertrude Stein, to name three. In the 1940s, Charles Olson appears, and, in the 1950s, Robert Duncan, and those two poets carry forward aspects of early 20th century innovative strategies. Hart Crane and Wallace Stevens, both poets I admire a great deal, especially Crane, are outside the directions I just indicated, but they are both very special, very original, and so I don't care what lineage they belong to. Crane is our Arthur Rimbaud. Stevens has an extraordinary mind but is also passionless and suffocatingly proper.

I do not believe that poetry is sentimental thinking done up in classy wrappings and ribbons. It is about the extending of human consciousness, making conscious the unconscious, creating a symbolic consciousness that in its finest moments overcomes the dualities in which the human world is cruelly and eternally, it seems, enmeshed.

It looked as if in the late 60s, as part of the alternative culture explosion, that innovative poetry was going to move to the fore, and cease to be foregrounded, as it always has been, by poetry that reinforces the status quo. But this did not happen. The energy of the 60s suddenly crashed, in 1970, with the Manson murders and the death of Charles Olson. Two new things occurred: the university creative writing degree programs began to proliferate (there are now over 300 of them) and a new and relatively uncommunicative experimental poetry, Language Poetry, proposed itself as the new American avant-garde. Powerful poets of my generation like Robert Kelly, Gustaf Sobin, and Jerome Rothenberg were, in the eyes of the handful of critics writing about the "new," leapfrogged by the Language Poets. The writing degree programs are not interested in poetry on an international scale, and the poets emerging from them, with jobs on their mind, have proven to be, in some cases, quite talented, but in nearly all cases, not original or commanding.

Two primary enemies of poetry are education and entertainment. The university system in creating young professor-poets out of graduate students focuses on a poetry that can be easily bricklayered into the educational curricula.

But back to your question: sure, there is always a mainstream American poetry and it is never very interesting, from my point of view. The current one "stars" such poets, for example, like Collins, Louise Gluck, Derek Walcott, Mary Oliver, and Robert Pinsky, all talented writers who have never made me change my mind about anything. Collins has replaced Allen Ginsberg as the famous populist poet. This is very sad. At his best, Ginsberg was a miraculous bridge figure, wise, available, courageous, risky, and politically savvy. Collins is none of these. Ditto Dana Goia and Ted Kooser.

Ian: Some commentators on post-WWII US poetry suggest that a crisis in language (as un-problematically 'transparent to reality') was at the heart of poetic postmodernism and that it gave birth to what we might call certain 'non-linear' poetries. Others have suggested that a more significant strand in postmodern US poetry was the attempt by many post-war poets to breakdown Western ethnocentrism and expand the range of possible poetries in multiple directions. Commentators on your work seem to see it as representative of in particular the second type of poetic postmodernism. How do you place your work in relation to the larger poetic and cultural trends of the mid to late 20th century? In what sense do you feel your work gives voice to a post-modern poetics?

Clayton: I have read internationally from the late 1950s on, and feel more connected in a comradely way to poets I have translated, especially Vallejo, Césaire, and Artaud, than most English-language poets. Translating creates what I call an "assimilative space," opened up by doing many versions of a single poem, and spending hours with dictionaries, especially English-language ones. Thus Vallejo, for example, permeated my mind in a way that Pound or Williams never did.

This is not to dodge your question, but to offer it a perspective. My work does relate to that of Charles Olson's in its concentration on the archaic. In a way, you could say I took a lead from Olson's 1953 notes on paleo-archeology and cave art, and developed what he only touched on. I also feel a kinship with the poetry of Robert Duncan of the late 1960s on, and Denise Levertov's political poetry from this period too. The last thirty years of Adrienne Rich's and Gary Snyder's poetry means a lot to me. But no one has touched me a deeply as Vallejo, whose broken lantern glass I will carry in my stomach until the day I die.

I should also mention William Blake here. His Herculean attempt to create a new realm of mythology for the West engaged me deeply when I was in Kyoto, Japan, in the early 1960s. In an effort to dynamite my blocked ego I created some of my own godforms in a long poem called "The Tsuruginomiya Regeneration." I was not able to complete this poem and abandoned it in the early 1970s, using some sections from it in my book *Coils*.

If my language turns out to be as inventive as I hope it is, if my work on the origin of image-making connects poetry to the earliest kinds of mental travel, and if some of my translations turn out to be energy deposits for poets to come, then I guess I will have contributed to a late 20th century/early 21st century extension and enrichment of consciousness.

Ian: As a follow up question: where do you feel we are currently headed in terms of the main thrust of poetic innovation?

Clayton: Who is "we?" All English-language poets, including Australian and the English? The question is too general. I am not well-read in either contemporary Australian or English poetry.

In terms of American poetry, the younger awarded and widely-published mainstream poets, nearly all of whom have been through the university writing mills, appear to be involving a kind of non-sequitur Language Poetry to which is added displays of self-sensitivity. Among my younger contemporaries, I admire the writing of John Olson, Rachel Blau DuPlessis, Anne Waldman, Andrew Joron, and the late Tory Dent, to name a few. I mention others in the essay you have cited, "Wind From All Compass Points," which is in *Archaic Design*.

One of the notions I have come to believe is that ego consciousness is inadequate to write poetry. So one thrust of poetic innovation in our times is the work of Will Alexander, whose poetry seems to be driven by a revolving bicameral psyche, and take place in a trance-awake dream state.

The challenge for American poets writing today is not only to explore their imaginations but to simultaneously hold themselves open to information and feelings about being Americans and part of a system that has been thrusting an armored nose in other peoples' business since the end of World War II. One must pick up on what is in the air, not merely information, but the ways in which imperialism creates psycho-linguistic micro-climates that are willy-nilly tapping into all of us. Adrienne Rich's new collection of poems, *Telephone Ringing in the Labyrinth* (which I finished a review of this morning) is one capable response to the challenge I am sketching out here.

Writing poetry is an essentially affirmative activity, but affirmation, as such, only makes uncommon sense when its feet are relentlessly being held to the fire by negation. There are social negatives as well as one's own intrinsic dark. Cid Corman wrote a two line poem years ago which goes:

You are dead.
Speak now.

That is also part of the furnace of our challenge.

Ian: It strikes me in reading your poetry and essays that you have spent a great deal of time exploring what we might call the deep psyche or the collective psyche. A number of psychologists have also influenced your work over the years — most obviously James Hillman and Wilhelm Reich. Where do you stand these days in terms of the various depth psychologies that were developed in the 20th century? Are alternative psychologies still inspirational to you?

Clayton: While in Japan, I read Joseph Campbell's tetralogy, *The Masks of God.* That was my introduction to world mythology and, as an introduction, it was useful. Today I find Campbell often superficial, and much of his cross-cultural mapping suspect.

Jung is a much deeper vault, and anytime I get involved with a mythical figure or event, I always consult my *Collected Works* of Jung's writings to see what he has to say. Jung's contrast of the ego with the self, and his thinking about individuation, has fed me for years. I probably should have sat down at one point and read him straight through. But I haven't. I have cherry picked, as they say, here and there.

I met Jim Hillman while living in Los Angeles in the 1970s, attended a number of his lectures, and at one point, in Dallas, Texas, interviewed him (the interview appeared in *Antiphonal Swing,* my first collection of prose, published in 1989). He is a very smart guy and a fine writer. He has been obsessed with getting "image" back into an archetypal psychology, and probing mythic cores that connect with poetry. My attention was first called to Hillman by Robert Kelly and Robert Duncan, two poets with their own vast encyclopedic files. Hillman's book, *The Dream and the Underworld,* was very useful in offering me a perspective from which to regard cave art, to study it as a psychic phenomenon, and not as literalistic "hunting magic." Hillman himself has not studied the deep past (his back wall is Greek) but he has a broad sense of the European underworld.

Ian: When I read your poem 'Hardball', for example (out of the collection *Under World Arrest*) [5], and even some of your more recent poetry concerned with the consequences of the extension of US hegemony abroad I am struck by the link between your understanding of acts of injustice and oppression ('personal' and 'structurally engineered') and neo-psychoanalytic (especially Reichian) critiques of what we might call the fascist/authoritarian character type. It seems to me that a poetic assault on the authoritarian character type has been a long-term subtext/theme in your work. Did this arise with your early readings of Reich or did it come from somewhere else?

Clayton: I wrote "Hardball" in a state of anguished fury and tried to jam words together to the point that they cracked or melted. The first half of the poem is stronger than the later half. It is very difficult to follow the first half assault with convincing reflection.

Up until I went to Peru in 1965, I was what we call "apolitical," meaning supportive of the status quo, and thus, actually quite political, though I didn't know it. In Lima, I had an adventure with the American State Department and that, plus my utter shock and bewilderment over the extent and depth of Peruvian poverty, made me wake up and start to regard peoples' lives as politically contoured. At this point, Vallejo's *Poemas humanos* took on greater resonance. It is a masterpiece of political awareness realized in non-agendafied innovative language.

By the time I moved to NYC in the summer of 1966, I was ready for Reich — not only the Reich of *The Function of the Orgasm,* but of *The Mass Psychology of Fascism* and *People in Trouble.* In 1967 I became very involved with Angry Arts, an organization of some 500 NYC-based artists and writers protesting the American invasion and occupation of Vietnam. I organized the "poetry wing" of Angry Arts. A couple dozen of us rented flatbed trucks which we parked in hostile neighborhoods in the Bronx, Harlem (where people turned out to be supportive of us) or before the Metropolitan Museum of Art. With megaphones, we read our angry poems about the horrors our government was perpetuating in Vietnam. At one point, I met with a doctor who had just come back from Vietnam with some photos of napalmed children. *Ramparts* magazine ran a few of his photos, but some were so ghastly they would not touch them. I ran two of the most horrible in the 3rd issue of *Caterpillar* magazine. Our Angry Arts poetry group had these photos blown up in poster form, and we rolled them up under our suits and went in to high mass at the arch-conservative St Patrick's Cathedral, with the idea of standing up at a certain point, taking out our posters, holding them over our heads and marching out. Alas, we had a stool-pigeon in our midst and the plain-clothes cops hidden among the congregation were waiting for us. At the moment we stood up, they pounced. I was on the cover of *The New York Times* the following morning, along with another poet being hustled down the cathedral steps by a cop. We all spent the night in jail.

Ian: When I first read the poems 'Iraqi Morgue', 'Dead Reckoning', 'One if by Land, None if by Void', 'From a Terrace', 'A Ferocious Fold' and others in the *Alchemist* collection I was fascinated by the incendiary mixture/cocktail of visionary language *and* political directness. In 'Autumn 2004', for example, we come across the lines: "Dick Cheney's mouth/ slides on circular-saw teeth, with rakers,/ to rip out the throats of words… " [6] Is this visionary, political directness a general feature of the US poetry scene at the moment or are you in some senses a lone voice?

Clayton: While I like to think that my political, or civil, poetry bears my own stamp, I am in no sense a lone voice now. Since the beginning of the 20th century there has always been some American political poetry. However, if you look at the work of the major poets of the Pound generation, there is a sad lack of response to Nazism and the Holocaust. This absence is most embarrassing in

Pound and Stevens. Charles Reznikoff, almost alone, of that generation, addressed the Holocaust in his 1975 collection, *Holocaust.* Of a slightly later generation, Muriel Rukeyser wrote potent political poems at many stages of her career.

The Vietnam War forced both Duncan and Levertov into a political dimension, as I have mentioned earlier. In fact, fine poems aside, their correspondence contains, at points, a remarkable meditational exchange on the role of the poet during wartime. I highly recommend *The Letters of Robert Duncan and Denise Levertov* to Australian readers. Of this period, Michael McClure's *Poisoned Wheat* is also a fiery political poem.

Today, five years into the Iraqi invasion and occupation, many American poets have been moved to express their distress over what our government is doing. The poets whose names first come to mind are Adrienne Rich, Anne Waldman, Amiri Baraka, Ed Sanders, and Jayne Cortez. Jerry Rothenberg wrote a powerful middle-length poem in the late 1980s, called *Khurbn,* documenting a trip he made to what was left of the death camps, where some of his family members perished, in Poland.

I am, however, one of the few poets to question in poetry the so-called "official version" of what happened on 9/11. A year after the attack, I wrote "The Assault," which accuses the Bush administration of complicity in the destruction of The World Trade Centers and the attack on the Pentagon. It can be found in *Archaic Design.*

Ian: In your prose introduction to *Alchemist* you write: "American poets today, facing the possibly comprehensible mindset of neocon conquest, *amor-fati,* and the need to find out for oneself, must assimilate such vectors and figure out ways to articulate them. If we cannot accomplish this, then our distinction may become that of being the first generation to have lived at a time in which the origins and the end of poetry became discernable." [7] I wonder, have the recent crises (from the perspective of an outsider admittedly) in US relations with other nations, and within the US itself helped birth a new 'poetic' of historical significance among contemporary US poets — i.e. one capable of addressing the destructive side to the Neo-Con 'vectors' you allude to?

Clayton: Unless one is willing to spend hours daily visiting websites, watching television, and reading newspapers and books, it is very, very difficult to gain a comprehensive sense of what is actually going on, as far as our government, at home and overseas, is concerned. It is probably harder now, than ever before, because of the Bush administration's secrecy and stealth. I give the news about two hours daily, and I know that I am aware of only a fraction of what is actually going on. The amount of governmental dissimulation makes me question anything I read or hear and such subsequently makes it difficult to be bold in working with such matters in my writing.

It is also an up-hill battle to, as they say, wrap one's head around the true facts of what our government is up to because of the self-censorship that is built into all of us. We have been educated for decades that America is a democracy that supports freedom everywhere. We know this is false — have known it for years — yet the propaganda entangles itself with the American landscape which, with jarring industrial and urban exceptions, is still without the conflicts taking place in so many countries. Speaking for my own generation, I believe there is an attitude in me concerning America that was fashioned during the Second World War (when I was a child). Younger American writers may be less imbued with such formations. I would be foolish not to recognize these traps and make myself aware of their subconscious *and* conscious force.

Ian: Given your long history promoting, translating etc. poets living and working under socially repressive regimes — as evidenced by the recent up-date to your 1988 anthology of translations, *Conductors of the Pit* (2005) — what advice would you give to poets and other writers/ intellectuals on the receiving end of what Pen

International has described as an increasingly global attack on freedom of expression — often under the banner of defending the public against 'terror'?

Clayton: As an American writer who can still write and publish what he wants to, I don't think I am in a position to give advice to writers in places like Burma, Russia, and China. I met the Chinese poet Bei Dao in 1993 and have since watched what he has been up against with the Chinese state. And Bei Dao is hardly what is generally called a "dissident writer."

Here, for the most part, people do not pay attention to what writers say about the state of the union. Of course there are exceptions: immediately after 9/11, Susan Sontag, in *The New Yorker* magazine, said, in effect, "what did we expect? We have been provoking those people for decades." While she was harshly criticized (I think mainly for not merely expressing sympathy with the victims' families), nothing happened to her.

Ian: Earlier this year a book containing your translations of the complete poems of Vallejo was published. [8] His work has haunted you — often in an almost literal sense — for many decades and you've written extensively, over the years, about the role he's played in your development as a poet and writer generally. I'm struck, in particular, by the idea you have that becoming a poet involves, at times, subordinating one's ego and entering into an apprenticeship that involves giving something back to poetry/literature. Could you discuss how you see your long commitment to translation, editing and teaching at this point in your life?

Clayton: I have translated off and on, sometimes full-time for months, ever since I was a student at Indiana University in the late 1950s. I have only translated poets whose work I thought had something to teach me (I have translated no prose at all). And I have always been aware that in doing so I have, on one level, been shoveling some of their coal into my own furnaces. That is, in moving Spanish or French into English I was creating half-way houses, texts that were no longer "theirs," but also texts that were not truly my own, texts that I could influence myself with — in contrast to being influenced by poets who write in English. So in the kind of translating I do, there is a trade off: I create what I believe is an accurate translation that absolutely respects the integrity of the original. I can offer this text to a monolingual American reader and assure him or her that what I am offering does not misrepresent the original. In this way, I have provided a useful service, in exchange for which, while translating, I have planted in my mind many seed-ideas and sensations that may be of use in work-to-come. There is a community involved here, of the living and the dead, and it includes as well the unknown reader/poet who may take some charge from my translations and build it into his or her own work. I see this as part of the readership I would like to think I am in touch with.

At this point, I do not have any new translation projects. I may edit a larger edition of my Artaud translation (*Watchfiends & Rack Screams,* 1995), but that will not involve doing any new translations to speak of. My co-translator Annette Smith and I were very close to a "Complete Poetry of Aimé Césaire" in the early 90s, having translated all but some seventy or so pages of his poetry. There is a possibility that we can complete this work in the near future.

I don't plan to edit or teach anymore — other than in brief residencies, which I am happy to do. Although you do not bring her up in any of your questions, I do want to mention that since around 1973 Caryl has worked as my companion-editor, and has read all of my work, usually in an early stage, commenting astutely often on what she finds there. I think I have improved as a writer for one reason because of her honest and intelligent commentary.

Ian: In viewing your recent output as a poet, translator and essayist it strikes me that you seem to have completed or wound up at least three long-term projects — winding up *Sulfur,* publishing a definitive translation of Vallejo's poetry and publishing your theories regarding Upper Paleolithic cave art and the origins of the imagination. However, these endings seem to have birthed new and fascinating projects — almost by some law of energy transference. Could you talk about your up-coming projects and answer the question: is one lifetime enough for a poet such as yourself?

Clayton: Black Widow Press will publish *The Grindstone of Rapport,* in 2008, which is a 600 page "Eshleman Reader," with a selection from the past 40 years of poetry, prose, and translations. I spent a couple of months editing it this summer.

I also have a longish (sixty-five pages) work in poetry and prose on Hieronymus Bosch's *The Garden of Earthly Delights* that I researched at The Rockefeller Study Center in northern Italy in 2004, and completed here in Michigan just this year. This summer I worked a manuscript of short poems called "Anticline," around seventy pages, some forty pieces. I think that I will add the Bosch poem, called "Tavern of the Scarlet Bagpipe," to "Anticline," for a book to be published in 2010.

I have quite a bit of unpublished early writing that I don't know what to do with. It is not up to my current standards, so I am hesitant to try to have it published. There is, for example, a journal with over three hundred entries, called "Heaven Bands," that was written between 1968 and 1972. It is one of those workbook projects, full of dead ends, clumsy configurings, and statements I no longer agree with! I think it would be impossible to rewrite it and end up with more than a fraction of it.

I would like to go very deep into the ocean, really deep, down into one of those trenches. Were I to luck out, and someone offer me a ride, I would love to try to write what I see and experience in the abyss. An oceanic descent would be an extension of my work on the European Upper Paleolithic, as would a visit to some Australian rock art sites. After the European cave paintings, on the basis of studying photographs, I think indigenous Australian rock art is the most imaginative in the world.

Ian: Are we likely to see you 'down-under' in the near future?

Clayton: If I am invited in such a way that my and Caryl's expenses could be covered for a month, I would love to come.

Notes

[1] "A Note on the Poem 'Spirits of the Head'" in *Reciprocal Distillations,* pp.5–11, 2007.

[2] 'Some of Her Names', in *Reciprocal Distillations,* pp.30–33, 2007.

[3] 'Fracture', in *Fracture,* p.37, 1983,

[4] From 'The Aurignacians Have the Floor', p.25 of *Juniper Fuse* (2003) and *Hades in Manganese* p.88, 1981.

[5] 'Hardball' can be found in *Under World Arrest* p. 132, 1994.

[6] 'Autumn 2004' can be found in *An Alchemist With One Eye on Fire,* p.49, 2006.

[7] ibid, pp.6–7.

[8]César Vallejo, *The Complete Poetry* (2006).

Ian Irvine is an Australian-based poet and writer. His work has featured in many print and online publications, both in Australian and overseas, including the anthologies *Best Australian Poems* (Black Inc. Books, 2005), *Agenda* 'Contemporary Australian Poets' (2005), and *Fire* (UK) 'Special International Edition' (2008). He is the author of three books and holds a PhD for his work on the phenomena of chronic ennui and alienation. He currently coordinates a writing program and has been working to develop a unique transpersonal-relational poetic. He first encountered the work of Clayton Eshleman in an Auckland bookshop in 1983.

Jacket Magazine, #36, 2008.

CLAYTON ESHLEMAN IN CONVERSATION WITH PAUL HOOVER AND MAXINE CHERNOFF— *SULFUR* AND *NEW AMERICAN WRITING*: A TRIALOGUE

PH: Clayton, you've edited a literary magazine for most of your life as a poet, first *Caterpillar* and then *Sulfur*. What caused you to found the magazines when you did, and why did you decide to suspend publication of those influential magazines when you did?

CE: I started doing Caterpillar Books after I moved to NYC in 1966 and discovered that I could cover more ground with a literary journal than with undistributable chapbooks. So, *Caterpillar*, initially subtitled "A Gathering of the Tribes" (which I soon dropped), began in the fall of 1967. I wanted to do a magazine based on Cid Corman's *origin*, but one that was bigger and more burly, taking on more "fronts" than Cid had engaged. I sensed, correctly I still feel, that I was part of a new generation "coming on board" at the time, and there was no magazine around that was going to let us gather and do our thing in one (hopefully) noisy space.

I stopped *Caterpillar* with its 20th issue, in the spring of 1973, then living in Los Angeles. Caryl and I were preparing to go to France for a year.

As for *Sulfur*: in 1981 I was a poet-in-residence at Cal Tech, in Pasadena, and once more, there was nothing around that was up to my vision of what I thought a literary journal could be. I recalled that Charles Olson had sold the idea of *The Black Mountain Review* to the administration at Black Mountain College as a promotional flag for the school, so I approached Roger Noll, an economist who was the Head of the Humanities Division at Cal Tech, and suggested that a literary journal would tell the world that Humanities were alive and well at Cal Tech. It was a little far-fetched (as was Olson's proposal) but Roger liked the idea, and found money to start and underwrite *Sulfur* for five years.

In contrast to *Caterpillar* (20 issues in 6 years), *Sulfur* had a long life for a non-institutionally-based magazine — 46 issues, 19 years (I lost Cal Tech's backing in *Sulfur*'s third year, something we can discuss if you like). Caryl and I moved to Ypsilanti, Michigan in 1986, when I became a Professor in the English Department at Eastern Michigan University. EMU gave us a little support, and we edited issues 17 through 46 there, coming out bi-annually most of the time. By the late 1990s, we had realized everything that *Sulfur* had set out to do, and we were ready to do other things. We had also lost our National Endowment for the Arts grants (of which we had 13), so that made doing the magazine more difficult, including no longer paying contributors. So we stopped it with a big double issue, #45/46, in 2000.

Paul and Maxine, tell us about the origin of *OINK!*, and how it evolved (if that is the correct word) into *New American Writing.* In what ways is *NAW* a different kind of magazine than *OINK!* (one of the great all-time literary journal titles, in my opinion)?

PH: James Leonard, Dean Faulwell, and I founded *OINK!* as a quarterly in 1971 when we were graduate students in the Program for Writers at University of Illinois Chicago. We had already been meeting at Dean's Belden Street apartment every Monday evening to discuss our poetry; those meetings turned into editing sessions. The title and focus was influenced by Dada, Surrealism, and the New York School. The first issue contained our own work and a satire Dean wrote on the poetry of Robert Bly. We were great admirers of Ron Padgett's *Great Balls of Fire* and the Berrigan-Padgett collaboration *Bean Spasms.* Dean was a lecturer in the German Department at UIC and older than Jim and I, so he was our leader. We produced three issues quickly. Then Dean moved to California, where he founded the short-lived *BOINK!* Jim dropped out following number six, and Maxine and I produced 13 more issues of *OINK!* In 1985, we ceased publication, only to revive the magazine as *New American Writing* in 1986. The final issues of *OINK!* had largely the same poetics as the first issues of *NAW,* and we consider it to be the same magazine with a different title. Its 30th anniversary was celebrated at the National Arts Club in NYC in 2001. I was surprised to note recently how many poets from the first issue of *NAW* still appear in its pages. However, it's fair to say that *OINK!* had more of a New York School emphasis and that since the mid-80s *NAW* has published a balance of innovative work, with New York School and language poetry among the major threads.

As we were preparing *OINK!* double issue 9/10 (1974), Jim Ramholz gave us the following information, which we placed on the final page: "OINK is the Romanized spelling of לנו (auinak), meaning 'thine eyes,' which is found in Isaiah 1, 20: "Thine eyes shall behold Jerusalem at peace, even thy habitation. The 'peaceful habitation' refers to the Sephira on the Tree of Life called Kether, the Ancient One, who is hidden and incomprehensible." All true, according to an online search. Odd coincidence that, in Robert Graves' *The White Goddess,* the words *porcine* and *porcelain* relate to the whiteness of flour and of a pre-Christian female deity. Of course, we knew nothing of this when we named the magazine. We had intended to be as arbitrary and undignified as possible!

MC: We stopped *OINK!* for a year because we were having twins, but we never wanted to end it. Although it was quite a departure, we felt that we wanted to make a bigger claim with the new title. With the appearance of the first issue, distributors who hadn't represented us before suddenly took us up. In both magazines, we have published well-established and emerging writers. Also, *NAW* has come to have more of a focus on translation.

Tell us how you put together an issue of *Sulfur* with regard to your own editorial focus and how you selected and collaborated with contributing editors, for instance in your intellectually robust back pages.

CE: Initially, Robert Kelly and I were going to co-edit *Sulfur.* We edited the first issue together, but then Kelly disappeared. By the third issue, Michael Palmer, Jerry Rothenberg (only for several issues), and Eliot Weinberger had become Contributing Editors;

they could include anything of their own they wanted to, as well as solicit work. Slowly a Correspondents group was assembled, and with #20 Rachel Blau DuPlessis also became a Contributing Editor. Correspondents were welcome to contribute, but were not asked to solicit work. The editorial shape of the magazine constantly shifted through the first twenty-five issues (for a while John Yau was the art editor listed as a Contributing Editor). When I had a piece that I did not know what to do with — to accept it or reject it — I sent it to three other editors (including Correspondents) and let them vote it in or out. DuPlessis, Palmer and Weinberger were all terrific to work with — each made a substantial contribution to the magazine as contributors as well as editors. I never held material over. Everything that was accepted went into the next issue. I tried hard to get a few unknown people into each issue. Especially with Rachel and Eliot I worked hard to include archival material (Pound, Williams, Crane, Olson, Dahlberg, Leiris, Artaud, Oppen, Loy, for example). It still amazes me to what extent each issue came together and usually cohered. This was remarkable because many of the editors and correspondents had differing aesthetic viewpoints (an argumentative discussion of Language Poetry by Weinberger, Charles Bernstein and Michael Davidson took place in #20).

The Commentary section (roughly 40 pages per issue) was by far the most complicated aspect of the magazine to edit. Since we paid very modest contributor fees, it was hard to assign books for review unless someone took it on him or herself to do a review, meaning it was very hard to place books objectively with a reviewer. Occasionally, I asked people to take charge of the Commentary section (such as Dennis Phillips and Jed Rasula) and to give me X number of pages of reviews for a particular issue. The Commentary part of *Sulfur,* while dynamic, was uneven, and of varying quality. In spite of such complications, I kept it going because I feel that a literary journal without commentary is more of an anthology than a journal. I think a journal must constantly express, and test, its viewpoint, and praise especially accomplished books that otherwise might not even get reviewed, and also include polemic e.g., Weinberger's sardonic review of Frederick Seidel in #1, Jerry Rothenberg's blast at Harold Bloom in #3 or Gerrit Lansing and Don Byrd's negative evaluation of the Tom Clark Charles Olson biography in #29. In the late 1990s, I asked Dan Featherston, Roberto Tejada, and John Olson to provide *Sulfur* with several short reviews each for each issue. We chose books together. While this worked out pretty well, I think earlier Commentary sections in their own ways were just as interesting.

Having briefly made a case for reviews in a literary journal, I wonder on what basis you have not included them in *New American Writing.* I assume you disagree with my position in this regard, and I wonder why.

MC: At times we have published special sections containing interviews and considerations of writers — #19 has a Clark Coolidge feature that was a double issue with John Tranter's online magazine, *Jacket* (issue 13, April 2001) and #25 a Nate Mackey section — but we've largely considered it our aim to publish the work and let the discussion of the work enact itself outside of the issue. We have always looked at the Commentary pages of *Sulfur* with great interest but have decided to let the poems in *OINK!* and *New American Writing* seek their own judgment. Also, given that Paul and I have chosen to do all aspects of the magazine ourselves (aside from rare but occasional help from an intern), it seemed that our focus on poetry was adequately large for us to pursue without engaging others for reviews, comments, etc.

PH: *OINK!* and *New American Writing* have never published a review, not once in 36 years, and perhaps only three of our issues, in the 1980s, contained authors' notes, largely because Ned Rorem, a contributor of that time, convinced us to include them. The leanness of the *NAW* format was probably inherited from *OINK!*, which for many issues was that of a 32-page chapbook (or as many 8.5 x 14 sheets as were needed to print "two-up," wrap with a cover of the same size, bind with a special long-armed stapler, fold in the center, and crease the spine with the side of a coffee cup). We have published essays and interviews. We enjoy reading reviews in other magazines. But the machinery and politics of the review section, and authors' notes as well, seemed a distraction. In this way, we were consonant with the Beat attitude that an intellectual stance was at odds with the real work of writing. The Beats and New York School only rarely produced "thought pieces" on their poetics; it was the Projectivist, or Pound-Olson, tradition that very effectively did so. Maxine has written reviews of fiction on assignment for the *New York Times Book Review,* as I did briefly for the *Chicago Tribune,* and I began to write essays in earnest in the 1990s (*Fables of Representation: Essays,* 2004), but we have largely avoided writing reviews. All by way of saying that we came to commentary late, for me with the enormous work required of preparing the anthology *Postmodern American Poetry* (1994).

Clayton, your vision as a poet is distinctive, as is the character of *Sulfur,* the magazine of yours that we know best. Can you elaborate on the evolution of your vision as a poet and translator as it relates to your vision as an editor?

CE: Could you focus this question more specifically? Are you referring to vision as a viewpoint, or in the sense that one would say: William Blake is a visionary? I think you may mean the latter in regard to my own poetry but probably the former in regard to *Sulfur.* If you can tell me what is in back of your question, I will have a go at it.

PH: You do have aspects of the visionary in your work, the "companion spider," the caves, and so on, but I meant the relationship of your vision as a poet (or kinship in poetics) with those you have included in *Sulfur* — Césaire, Artaud, Vallejo, Celan, Will Alexander, Jerome Rothenberg, James Hillman, and so on. But I would love to hear your response to both sides of the question.

CE: In both of my magazines I have tried to address the range of my interests in art and in literature. There is virtually no fiction in either *Caterpillar* or *Sulfur* because I have read very little fiction since leaving Indiana University in 1961. I'd like to think that my magazines have backed not only poetries that are compatible with my own but poetries that argue with my own. Ron Silliman, at the beginning of his career, appeared in *Caterpillar* in 1969 and I imagine that a strong 300 page selection of Language Poetry could be assembled from the pages of *Sulfur.* While I do not feel much connection between Language Poetry and my own work, I recognize that Language Poetry raises pertinent questions about what poetry is and can be today; therefore, it was important to include some of it. Ditto a poem by Jorie Graham, which she sent in unsolicited. I am not much of a fan of Graham's work at large, but "Le Manteau de Pascal" is a terrific poem and I was happy to include it. On the other hand, I rejected one of Donald Hall's baseball poems because I did not think it contributed to the complex mix I tried to achieve in each issue. By running a lot of archival materials, *Sulfur* tried to keep a sense of many generations still being pertinent to poetry today. In fact, I think someone should apply for a Guggenheim Fellowship to investigate and make a check-list of the archival holdings in university special collection libraries. I suspect that some of the most interesting writing of the 20th century is to be found there.

I see the poet as a figure who, while based in his own poetry, extends his vision into translation, prose commentary, and into long research projects (mine being translating César Vallejo and researching the origin of image-making via the Ice Age painted caves). To some extent these concerns are borne out in *Sulfur.* I published writers like James Hillman and N.O. Brown because I feel that their visionary scholarship is absolutely pertinent to what poetry can be. Both men have given me ideas to think with and against. I think Will Alexander was hardly published when we met in 1981. Along with Linh Dinh, Will is one of the most important of the magazine's "discoveries," in my opinion the most extraordinary American poet to appear in the past several decades.

I have to say here too that I had no direct control over at least 40% of the material that went into *Sulfur.* So while I feel that the magazine backed up my vision of what is valuable in contemporary poetry, there was a lot of action there that contested or even contradicted it. I like to think of poetry as a simultaneous synthesis and melee and to some extent my magazines have supported this notion.

I found this question difficult to respond to, so I am going to turn it back on both of you! Tell us how your magazines have supported or argued with your visions of what your own work should be.

MC: I presume that all editors move within their own interests as they select poems for their magazines. Over the years our magazine has been consonant with our interests but, for example, in the years I wrote only fiction, roughly from 1990–1999, *NAW* remained a poetry journal. Even while I was a fiction writer, I identified myself more closely with my first literary incarnation as a poet. Also, it seemed that with an actual market for it, fiction could do fine without us, but there was a need in poetry for a magazine such as ours that published different aspects of the innovative in poetry. Because Chicago, the location for our journal until 1994, was outside the major centers of poetry on both coasts, local grievances were unimportant to us as we looked for important poetry of various "schools." Once, to the dismay of both, we published Carl Rakosi next to Barrett Watten. Neither man was fond of the other at the moment, but we wanted to enact conversations in our pages that went beyond the local. That, I think, should be a goal of editing, to include more voices and be open to possibilities.

Another interest that developed in us first as editors and now as practitioners was for translation. This began with *OINK!* 12, which had a section on class-conscious Latin-American poetry. It contained some wonderful Cuban poets, among others. In more recent years we've done major Brazilian, Russian, Chinese, and Vietnamese sections. To some degree these special features have paralleled our travels as writers. More recently, as Paul has come to co-translate Vietnamese poetry and Paul and I together the poems of Hölderlin, we've turned a keener eye to translation in general.

PH: I looked up Linh Dinh in our files. We first published him in *New American Writing* 16 (1998), a story.

The "vision" question is difficult, because, as in Heisenberg's Uncertainty Principle, the measurement of a phenomenon changes and risks freezing it. Some years ago I sent some poems to *Conjunctions,* and Brad Morrow sent me a note of rejection saying that his publication was of the Olson/Duncan line of practice, whereas my own was of the Pound/Williams. That's cutting it fairly fine, but we can sense the distinction — my work had a "voiced" quality that was too close to Williams for his comfort. The best magazines have a distinct poetics, or taste, but they should feel as if they are always opening rather than closing. Poets and editors should always be in discovery mode.

As with *Caterpillar* and *Sulfur,* there are no dicta nailed to our magazine's doors. An early issue of *OINK!* contained an Oulipo-esque poem by Bruce Andrews; another, published in 1974, contained the following poem by Billy Collins — yes, the Billy Collins, then in the process of founding a journal called *The Mid-Atlantic Review:*

BACKSPIN

It's a pingpong ball
        language,
Each word white spherical
                spherical   hollow
      hollow   white
and
     (dropping your paddle
     stepping back)
            the same.

This is a different Billy Collins than the one writing today. His humor and conceptual framings now float on more sustained, languorous rhetoric.

To attack the question directly, our earliest influences were Surrealist poetry and New York School adaptations of it. We had an attraction to prose poems, especially the violent humor and fictiveness of Michaux and Edson. Michaux's, "My King," in which the narrator keeps his King under his bed, now and then slapping his face until the snot flies, was, along with the paintings of Chicago Imagist Roger Brown, the tapestry we stood in front of as poets and editors. Those interests may be hard to locate in our own most recent works of poetry, as well as in *New American Writing*, but the "deep play" of mind that drew us to poetry in the first place is still there. The most recent issue of our magazine, no. 25, opens with the poem "Remorse" by Jorge Luis Borges, translated by Terese Coe. The first stanza is: "I have committed the vilest of any crime / a man can commit. I have not been happy. / Let the ruthless glaciers of forgetfulness / come wrench me out and lose me." No king is shoved beneath the bed. But there's a backlit melodrama of light and shadow figures that's our idea of a good time in language. The work of Vallejo has so much linguistic drama, it's like standing on a carpet of lightning strikes.

Clayton, what other emerging poets than Linh Dinh and Will Alexander are you proud of having brought forward? Secondly, as you now reflect upon *Caterpillar* and *Sulfur*, in what ways did they contribute to changing American poetry?

CE: Before responding to your question, Paul, I want to comment on something that Maxine brought up: the juxtaposition of Rakosi and Watten. That's smart, in my opinion, and an editorial move I first became aware of in the 1960s reading Henry Rago's editing of *Poetry* (Chicago), where I once discovered a Charles Olson facing James Wright. Rago was one of the finest eclectic editors of any American poetry journal, and after he left *Poetry* (Chicago), it ceased to be, and has never again become, interesting. I mentioned publishing Jorie Graham's poem earlier; in *Sulfur* we published a number of poets most people would not associate with the magazine: for example, C.K. Williams, Charles Simic (a very interesting poem dedicated to Clark Coolidge), and Hayden Carruth. As you two know, keen editing means keeping open to anything of interest that comes in, regardless of who it is by. Anyone can exceed himself, and it is one of our responsibilities to not edit on the basis of names.

Your mentioning of Watten's being upset over appearing next to Rakosi reminds me of an odd incident: when Jed Rasula was editing the Commentary section for *Sulfur,* he was also working on a PhD at UC-Santa Cruz, which was taking up most of his time. At the end of one summer, he sent me around twenty contributions for the next issue, commenting that he had probably accepted some pieces that should not be published and that I was free to edit them as I saw fit. This put me in a situation I didn't much care for, but I still had to deal with it. One piece was a twenty page lecture by Barrett Watten. Watten was apparently discussing one of his own books, but he did not mention its title, and I found the piece utterly incomprehensible, so I returned it to him, with a brief explanation as to why we would not run it. Two weeks later, I heard not from Barrett but from his friend Lyn Hejinian whose letter began: "*Sulfur* is now the enemy."

Paul, you ask what emerging poets I am proud to have brought forth. I don't know in most cases whether these were first publications, but *Caterpillar* was at least one of the first magazines to publish David Henderson, Hugh Seidman, Frank Samperi, Carl Thayler, Max Douglas, Thomas Meyer, Charles Stein, Ron Silliman, Richard Grossman, Michael Burkard, Rae Armantrout, and Lauren Shakely. With *Sulfur* and its 46 issues, the list is much longer. I am particularly proud of being one of the first, at least, to have published Mary Caponegro, Gerald Burns, Andrew Robbins, Aaron Shurin, August Kleinzahler, Craig Watson, Diane Ward, Martha Ronk (at the time: Martha Lifson), Rafael Lorenzo, Robert Fitterman, Andrew Schelling, Geoffrey O'Brien, Norma Cole, Chris Cheek, Ammiel Alcalay, Susan Wheeler, Roberto Tejada, Daniel Tiffany, Karen Kelley (her "The Red Snake We Woke" in

#26 was one of those great blasts out of the blue editors live for), Phillip Foss, Myung Mi Kim, George Kalamaras, Martine Bellen, Pam Rehm, Dan Featherston, Heather Ramsdale, Wang Ping, Garrett Kalleberg, Tina Rotenberg, and Dan Beachy Quick (at the time: Dan Quick).

Here it makes sense to include, for young writers reading this, the following: occasionally a young would-be contributor to *Sulfur* included with submission a cover letter in which she briefly discussed what she had read in the magazine that had moved her to want to contribute to it. Such letters got my attention, and made me read the accompanying submission more carefully than I probably would have had it come in with no cover letter or a generic one.

Here is another story: I accepted some new poems by John Ashbery for #19 shortly after his *Selected Poems* appeared. Sven Birkerts, who had already written a couple of book reviews for *Sulfur,* asked if he could review the Ashbery book, so I sent it to him. The review he submitted was a total rejection of Ashbery's work. Absolutely negative. I suddenly realized I was going to be printing new Ashbery poems in an issue in which a review dismissed all of his poetry! The easy way out was to reject the Birkerts review, but since I had approved it in the first place, to do so smelled of censorship. So I was in a pickle. I then decided to send the review to four *Sulfur* editors (Palmer, Rasula, Coolidge and Weinberger). I was pretty sure they would all come down on it (they did, with even greater ferocity than I anticipated!) and that by running their responses along with the Birkerts review (and Ashbery's poems), I would have handled the situation as well as it could be handled under the circumstances. I wrote a little note explaining what I had done. The results: Birkerts wrote me that he felt like Saint Sebastian filled with *Sulfur* arrows, and, understandably, he never contributed again. Ashbery, who I had thought would have been at least amused, was, in fact, infuriated at me for having run the Birkerts period, and has never spoken to me again.

MC: People and their feelings! We've had moments of difficulty with authors, but mainly they're personal and often petty: poet X had six pages but you gave me only two, and so on. Or, "Now that I've published you, of course you want these poems for *NAW*." Like you, we take pride in publishing many writers early or even at the complete beginning of their careers, including a few you name: Susan Wheeler, Elizabeth Robinson, Linh Dinh, Noelle Kocot, Elaine Equi, Connie Deanovich, Mary Jo Bang, (the last three were Paul's students), as well as early Bruce Andrews (early *OINK!* issue, David Sedaris, C.S. Giscombe, and many others. Certain people we were delighted to find who were already published but new to us such as Caroline Knox, John Olson, Aaron Shurin, Andrew Joron, and Phillip Foss. Our consistency is also notable. Many poets included in *OINK!* are also found in all stages of *NAW*, again and again. Those people are too numerous to name. One person I am delighted to have published is Tymoteusz Karpowicz, a Polish poet now in his eighties, who emigrated in the 1970s under huge pressure from the Polish government, who hadn't published his work for 17 years because of its "surrealist" and "experimental" tendencies. When he wanted to leave Poland, he had to requisition, in triplicate, every one of his 7,000 books to leave the country. Some of them, seen as "national treasures," were not allowed to leave the country and became property of the state. He's one of the most inventive and playful poets I can name, and I wish he had received more of the post-1989 attention that has gone to Eastern European poets, because he is far more advanced than most of them. We published him in *OINK!* before he moved to Chicago to teach Slavic languages at University of Illinois Chicago, and produced a special section on his work in a recent *NAW*. He had lost an arm in the Polish resistance and had a prosthetic one with a black glove on its hand — no kidding. Everyone should make it a point to find his work. He deserves a major book of his wonderful, complex poems.

PH: I would add Sharon Mesmer to Maxine's list of young poets whom we were the first to publish. She appeared in *OINK!* 19, 1985, with its Joe Brainard cover, along with the poets and writers Ned Rorem, James Laughlin, Jacques Prevert, Philippe Soupault, Barrett Watten, Carl Rakosi, John Godfrey, Ron Padgett, Marjorie Welish, Maureen Owen, Bob Perelman, Bernadette Mayer, Lewis Warsh, William Corbett, Kenward Elmslie, Geoffrey Young, Tony Towle, August Kleinzahler, and Carla Harryman. We were among the first to publish Peter Gizzi and Kimberly Lyons, and we helped to introduce John Tranter, as well as a number of foreign poets, by means of Tranter's Australian supplement in *NAW* 4 (1988), Ric Caddel's "26 New British Poets" in issue 8/9 (1991), Wang Ping's translations of contemporary Chinese poetry in *NAW* 21 (2004), Todd Swift's extensive feature of young Canadian poets in issue 23, and Nguyen Do's "Nine Contemporary Vietnamese Poets" in the same 2005 issue.

Regarding consistency, we have long been identified with New York School practice, but language poetry has been a large part of the discussion, too. The first issue of *New American Writing*, 1987, contained the work of Alice Notley, Bill Berkson, Barbara Guest, Ann Lauterbach, Marjorie Welish, Kenward Elmslie, August Kleinzahler, Caroline Knox, Geoffrey O'Brien, Rosmarie Waldrop, Charles Bernstein, Nick Piombino, Ron Silliman, Bruce Andrews, Stephen Ratcliffe, and William Fuller, who for years had the distinction of being Chicago's only language poet. In fact, he should be added to our list of discoveries. The New York School & language poetry "dialogue" is a major part of what *New American Writing* has offered; it's a particular signature of the innovative that has, in a sense, "come true." We had nothing to do with the invention of either approach, but our magazine was one of the major forums (*Sulfur* and *Conjunctions* were others) where the two forces jostled for attention, and in that jostling revealed their relation more than their difference. That is, the inherently expressive nature of language poetry, both as personal expression (Lyn Hejinian) and poetics (Charles Bernstein), was in dialogue and competition with the inherently self-conscious, ironic, and abstract aspects of the New York School, as seen especially in Ashbery and Guest and their heirs. In that dialectic, the dark side of the mirror conversed with the reflective.

Clayton, it has been announced that your Vallejo translation, *The Complete Poetry,* is on the international shortlist for Canada's distinguished Griffin Prize. Congratulations. Also, the great poet Aimé Césaire, whom you translated, recently died at age 96. This seems the proper occasion to ask to reflect on your larger experience as poet, editor, and translator.

CE: To write the unsayable, and to translate the untranslatable — aren't these the two grand challenges for any poet or poet/translator? As a student at Indiana University in the late 1950s, I was simultaneously involved in working on poems, starting to translate Neruda and Vallejo, and editing the English Department literary journal *Folio.* I have practiced that triadic discipline ever since. I have found that working on poems is mainly working on self, the subconscious as warp, consciousness as woof, while keeping self positioned in the actual world. Much of what I have learned about language itself has come through translation. I have spent much more time with my 2nd Edition *Webster's International Dictionary* (the best one I know of) as a translator than as a poet. And translation has constantly over the years swept me away from myself, locking me to the minds of those poets I have translated and, by doing so, have challenged and deepened my own base. Editing *Caterpillar* and *Sulfur* enabled me to construct an ongoing active mosaic of poetry and translation, and how the contemporary might mesh with archival materials, artwork and commentary. Over the years, this triadic discipline has operated in a fugal manner, one "theme" relentlessly intersecting another. I have tried hard to keep poetry as the core activity, seeing translating and editing as extensions of it. I guess the concern here is to not finally register as a "jack of all trades," or a "man of letters." To be a mental traveler, in a combined Blakean and shamanistic sense — that has been my lifelong goal.

MAXINE CHERNOFF is the author of six fiction collections and ten poetry books, including *World* and *Evolution of the Bridge,* both from Salt, and *Among the Names* and *The Turning,* both from Apogee. Chair of Creative Writing at San Francisco State University, she co-edits *New American Writing.* With Paul Hoover, she has translated *The Selected Poems of Friedrich Hölderlin,* to be published by Omnidawn.

PAUL HOOVER's most recent poetry collections are *Poems in Spanish* (2005) and *Edge and Fold* (2006). Les Figues Press will publish his book *Sonnet 56* in 2009. With Maxine Chernoff, he has edited and translated *Selected Poems of Friedrich Hölderlin* and, with Nguyen Do, the anthology *Black Dog, Black Night: Contemporary Vietnamese Poetry.* He has also edited the anthology *Postmodern American Poetry.*

Jacket Magazine, #36, 2008.

20 QUESTIONS FOR ROBERT KELLY

Introduction

Robert Kelly (1935–) was born in Brooklyn NY. He attended City College and Columbia University and, in 1960, with Jerome Rothenberg, formulated the "Deep Image" concept of poetry. He has taught literature and writing at Bard College since 1961, where he is now the Asher B. Edelman Professor of Languages and Literature. He lives with his wife, the translator, Charlotte Mandell, in Red Hook, New York. He is probably the most prolific American poet of the 20th and (so far) 21st century, being the author of over sixty collections of poetry, several novels, four works of short fiction, and two theoretical/critical books. He has also published The Garden of Distances, *a collaboration with the Tyrolean painter Brigitte Mahlknecht, and* Shame / Scham, *a collaboration with the German poet, Birgit Kempker. His most recent full-length collection of poetry is* Lapis *(2005).*

The range of Kelly's interests and formal competence is enormous. He is inventive in the way that Picasso was: he can improvise intelligently and imaginatively on anything that strikes his ear, heart, or gaze. Kelly thinks of the poet as a scientist of holistic understanding, a world scholar to whom all data whatsoever are of use. Considering his achievement up through the mid-1970s, Guy Davenport wrote (in Vort 5, *a special issue of the magazine dedicated to Kelly's work): "No American poet except perhaps Wallace Stevens has his sense of balance in a line. What Eliot and Pound slaved over Kelly seems to have an innate gift for balancing out… And he prefers a multiple subject. He has the Chinese sense of bringing diverse things together into a stark symbol, and is happiest when he himself can't quite see the meaning of the sign he's made. Thus his poems are mysteries to be pondered, something to dream on rather than to puzzle out. To understand in our times has sadly come to mean to dismiss; Kelly moves in the opposite direction. I should think that he would be interesting to the philosophers (had we any), for he seems to me to be a man determined to think deeply and carefully about Being itself (perhaps the one subject that pervades his poetry)."*

For readers new to Kelly's writing, I suggest the following: in 1981, Jed Rasula edited The Alchemist to Mercury, *200 pages of poems not collected in Kelly's Black Sparrow Press volumes, fourteen of which were published between 1968 and 2005.* The Alchemist to Mercury *includes the 17 page poem "The Exchanges," which is an excellent piece with which to dig in. Black Sparrow Press published a* Selected Poems *(1960–1993), in 1995, called* Red Actions. *It is a fine overview. In it, I recommend, especially for someone new to Kelly, "Last Light," "In Mahler's Sleep," "The Centerfielder," the sections from "Postcards from the Underworld" and "A Stone Wall in Providence," and then, to move into a more complex register, "Man Sleeping," and "The Door." Kelly's single, finest book, in my opinion, is the long poem* The Loom *(1975), which is a symphonic display of all his talents. It is also extremely readable, and filled with lyrical meditations out of which fantastic narratives (Kelly calls them "Recitals") erupt.*

CE: How would you characterize the primary innovative events in the American poetry of the 1960s? How have such events developed or vanished over the past thirty years?

RK: The poem is the shaping of time, it is shaping by language (words plus silence plus intonation) of our experience of time. So the poem is a score, a language mise-en-page for the reader as performer. The reader as performer. A peak shared by unlikely mountaineers: O'Hara, Blackburn, Mac Low — all demanded an alert performing of the page from the reader, otherwise nothing would make sense. That score idea has diminished in recent years — you need it for O'Hara, but not for Ashbery. You need it for Blackburn but not for Creeley, who has a different sense of compelling music. Or maybe just a simpler music, more simply scored.

But innovation is such a slippery word, a promo word, shiny easy packaging kind of word. Every time two words rub up against each other in a proposition, or in a public space (which is always what language is) where propositions arise, imply, kiss, depart, then that's new. Innovation is what we do all the time. So I would say, in terms of your question, that the innovative events of the (late 50s and) 60s, those individual sudden awarenesses of what could be done—like MacLow's The Pronouns, Olson's Maximus, Spicer's whole work utterly lyric yet utterly remote from sentimentality, Duncan's Pindar and the prose-rhythmed Structure of Rime, Blackburn's Journals, Creeley's miraculous breath alone as music, his suspensions, Ashbery's gorgeous lyrical disconnects, Berrigan's sonnets, Lansing's symphonic essays cloaked in poem raiment—all that is still with us. Look at Mackey's miraculous polyphonic Gassir workings. Nothing has been lost, as impetus. The only thing that strikes me as having vanished is the page itself—the page as the stage on which the poem acts. That tradition, stemming from Mallarmé and Apollinaire, climaxing in Pound and Olson, has drifted out of sight now—partly I'm sure from the technology of web 'pages'—the page now is of infinite length, so there is no longer a rectangle (golden or otherwise) within which our words disport themselves. Now it's the endless going down—as if Kerouac's teletype roll were the defining trope for all computer poetry and internet poetic presence. The words run towards us frontally—there's not much lateral thrust in contemporary work. And the oral delivery of poetry has literally no space for the lateral gesture, it's all ongoing-through-time, therefore linear—in a way that written poetics had escaped half a century ago. Much contemporary practice—on screen or podium—is essentially retro, restoring (or confining) poetry to the linearity and literalness in time of ancient spoken poetry. That is a real achievement, a presentness and gift. But there's also the loss of something we used to know and practice not so long ago: the sideways maneuver, the quick shunt from the margin that carried us *out of time.*

CE: In a recent interview, thinking of the future and what you might hope for poetry in it, you wrote: "Perhaps poets will reach towards a kind of star-like, radiating continuity, something that makes the poem in front you continuous with all your experience." Could you open up that statement and concretize it with some examples?

RK: If I can just get the reader to keep reading past the end of the line, edge of the page, her eye will presently engage with the world. Then a new line begins again, summoning him back to the book. In this shuttling forth and back the weaving of that continuity will occur. Continuity in Sanskrit is *tantra,* a word that also means loom, and weaving on the loom. The star-like radiating (I had forgotten this phrase, and thank you for reminding me) means to me that the poem has to be, or be read as, an event in the space of the world. No aesthetic isolation—no more than a cathedral is isolated from the marketplace in which it stands, the beggars on the steps, the weary tourists taking photos. The poem has to be like that, accessible from within life, and at the same time offering a way out. Through the portal of the cathedral, you enter sacred space. Where another kind of tourism takes its pilgrim course. You ask for examples, and I'm answering with architecture. Sorry. I have the poets reaching towards that continuity—more a stance for them, a way of gesturing as men and women towards the men and women who read them. I'm not talking about performance here, or performance space—that can get lost in the abyss of Entertainment or Education. I'm talking about an attitude in the language and gesture and urgency of the poem or text itself, one that invites the reader to work with it, dance it might even be with it, interact, bringing the reader's expectations of form and story to a text that proposes to deny them both in aid of some more intense transaction, a more pungent giving. The poet needs to leave space for the reader to enter. "I am the Door," said Jesus, the great poet who instructs us in John's Gospel. The poem must be the door. Examples? Dickinson. Olson. Ashbery. Language civil in its permission to engage.

CE: You once wrote, in 1973, that "short poems don't teach a poet how to live." I wonder if you still believe that today. If so, how do you understand your statement relative to the poetry of Bashō, Cid Corman, and Robert Creeley?

RK: Basho did not look to poetry to learn how to live. For better or worse, he had the fierce light of the Buddha's teachings to help him with that. Creeley did not write short poems, in my sense of 'short'—and to my mind Creeley was richest, best, when he gave himself the time to go onward. Time to go onward. Poetry doesn't in general teach how to live, does it? Doesn't it rather speak, out of living, a word that only living knows, but only the poem can speak? Poetry reveals, tells, even shows. But only life teaches how to live. Poetry listens.

CE: Please comment on the following words:

craft

RK: Once I called craft "perfected attention," and somehow that phrase caught on a while, long enough to be quoted. I think it's true enough as stated; I could gloss it: listen. Listen all the time. Listen especially to the spaces between words, the friction that rubs there, word against word, sound eliciting sound—from such attentions, propositions speak, images arise, truth happens. That is the truth: truth happens. As we speak. What the poet has to do is constantly look away from the poet's own intentions, own meaning, and focus intently, intently, on what's going on with the words in front. The words that alone can speak what you really mean.

bonobos

RK: I don't know much about these simians and their postulated linguistic gestures. In fact, I have trouble with all the apes and monkeys. I want to look away. I am Darwinian enough to see them, like ourselves, as products of evolution. But I am sad when

I look at them, because they seem to be descended from us, from humans; they have continued evolving in directions I find comprehensible but immensely sad. They are my lost children. Of course they'll retain some linguistic enterprise (as we retain coccyges and appendices)—vestiges of what they were. I think we should look away in modesty and pudor from the simians, and leave them to the sensuous journey, so different from our own, on which they have perhaps willingly embarked. We can't help them except by carefully refraining from harming them by hunting, imprisonment, vivisection. Vivisection of any creature is hellish—of a simian it's a blasphemy.

Atlantis

RK: Well, I've had a lot to say about this in many places, most recently, and most explicitly in a long review of Peter Lamborn Wilson's book on *Atlantis* (Shivastan Press), which I think is the best and briefest of all books on that subject. I have only one contribution to the idea or practice of Atlantis—it is this. Consider how so much of the ancient scriptural and mythological material that has come our way over the past few thousand years often has to be understood in rather a special sense—typically, backwards or upside down from the 'plain' meaning. (I have been working secretly for years on a Project Achorei that reads Genesis and Exodus that way—hint: Cain means strong, Abel means vain, empty. Hint: we are born from women's bodies—when Genesis shows the opposite, it is teaching us how to read the rest of sacred history.) Back to Atlantis. I know how to find Atlantis, the real Atlantis. Follow this thought experiment: the sea level changed. But the sea did not rise, it sank. Atlantis did not sink invisibly below the waves. It rose invisibly to be part of the land—it is hidden in plain sight to this day. Now find that hill on which the seven terraces of its citadel once rose.

Bugs Bunny

RK: His is the voice of my childhood as much as any other—Bugs's sassy sagacity, decency and teasingness, struck me as plausible armor in a Fudd world, full of softy dopes with guns. Here he was, impossibly long ears, in and out of every hole. But those tiresome carrots. I ask you, did you ever try to eat a carrot? No wonder they call them crudités in the Old Country.

closet

RK: Ah, my closet. I love the word, the thing, the environment. I'm very, very claustrophobic—so in all my life, par exemple, I've only twice ventured into a cave, and the last one was a pretty modest cave indeed. But in the closet: fear turns into desire, as Dante says. The closet, stuffed with tender garments and floored with weird obstacles—boots, vacuum cleaners (maybe even your old Kirby), boxes of ornaments—what a place this is to experience the fear, and inside the fear find oneself, the only breathing entity (you hope) inside the closet, alone. What a place of discovery! And the only thing to discover there is yourself—body and soul, time sense, space sense, trusting the hands to touch and know, trusting the nose. Total darkness. For a kid living in a crowded small apartment, the closet was heavenly silence and solitude. The smallest, tightest place became a glorious and innocent Mohave of silence. (This is the paradox, I come to know now, that is the heart of poetry. The smallest is the largest: a poem is a topological solid whose interior is larger than its exterior.) (As an aside, I'd refer here to the collaborative work I've done with the German poet Birgit Kempker, exploring the trope of the closet [*Ein Kollabor*] and shame [*Scham/Shame*].)

CE: Around 1980, I believe, you lost a lot of weight, some 200 pounds as I recall. What effects has this regenerational act had on your life and work? I recall that you once wrote that doctors had told you that you would not reach your 35th birthday. Your weight loss at 45 must have been a tremendous second life confirmation.

RK: The real affirmation was passing 35—and right after my 36th birthday—as you well know, we were together in Los Angeles, you in Sherman Oaks and me in Altadena—I began *The Loom,* the longest single stretch of poetry I've ever done. And it was with a "Look, we have come through!" (DHL) attitude that I began it. I felt freer than I had ever felt in my life. I was in the clearing now, and all my time was free.

Then, as you say, losing all that weight in 1979–1980. That was affirmation too. Suddenly, the greatest thing (something most people will never experience), suddenly I was invisible. That is, I looked like anybody else. Talk about freedom! All my life I had been cynosure, collected every stare and many a rude remark. Now there I was, mid-40s, healthy, and indistinguishable half a block away from any other tall white male. I could walk down a street all to myself, and people passed with the celestial civility of inattention! It was wonderful. I still enjoy it. Even thirty years later I still expect to see those eyes swivel towards me. And they don't. And if they do, it's because someone knows me.

CE: One of your salient self-commands is "write everything," which has appeared in *Finding The Measure, The Loom,* and *Kill The Messenger.* How are we readers to understand such an admonition? What role does it play in the size of your body of work?

RK: Write everything. It came to me that way, the way certain words or sentences do, coming from on high, or from down low, it's not up to me to decide about that, just to listen. Listen and think it through. You call it 'self-command,' a phrase with a whole other range of meaning, but I can accept it here—certainly a command to myself, but I'm not sure if it was, is, a command from myself. Doesn't matter. To me, the command (and that's what it does amount to) to write everything meant this: when something comes to mind, deal with it. When a word or phrase comes into mind or mouth, deal with it. Deal with it = write it down. Inscribe it, and work with it. Work with the words that are, as Olson said, before us, there, on the paper, under hand. With the same fidelity that Jackson Mac Low addressed the results of his chanceful procedures and strategies, I try to address *the words that begin.* So what comes to mind becomes the matrix, casual, random to whatever degree the neuronal processes of a human are random, the matrix from which poems come. Another thing that 'write everything' means is something trivially like Keats' great articulation of Negative Capability, in this case, meaning never to resist the words under hand if they say, or seem to be saying, something "I" don't like or don't believe or don't want. "I" have no business in that stage of the poem. If the poem is ever going to be greater than the poet's self-awareness. If the poem is ever going to be *itself.*

Incidentally, write everything doesn't mean write *anything.* So I don't think my obedience to that stern command has much to do with the size of the body of my work.

What it does influence though is the variegation of my work, all the kinds of writing that come to me to want to be done. Let me tell you an anecdote. In a London pub once, standing around with some English poets, a man just introduced to me said Aha, so you're the Kelly who defeated Eric Mottram! I asked what on earth he meant, I loved Eric, no way I'd fight with him, let alone defeat him. No, no, the man said, Eric wanted to write a study of you and your work, but you do too many things, write too many kinds of thing, and he felt baffled and overchallenged. That did not make me feel happier. But it's something that comes from my obedience to the Write Everything command – this past summer, I suddenly found myself writing a play, obedient to a title that spoke into my head: *Oedipus After Colonus.* And so it had to be written, and I had nothing but the title to go on.

CE: In your poem on one of Messiaen's Symphonies, "Turangalila Meditation," you write:

The fat space of the cathedral chants her dark
litanies, the cool grey stone light of the Lady Chapel
lets me sit down. There is rest here. The traffic
is not far. I hear it
through the ideal blue of the ogival windows,
glass stained color of consciousness, love her,
everywhere I have gone was for her sake

In other poems in *Kill The Messenger,* you wrote: "Love means to find / your original religion," and "Eros was my master." Here we have a cluster of vectors: love, religion, and Eros. The "her" in the cathedral appears to be the Virgin Mary (in contrast to a living woman). Tell me about the role women play in your poetry.

RK: Novalis says somewhere: My Beloved is shorthand for the Universe. Something like that. Never, never the Virgin Mary *in contrast to* 'a living woman.' The blue robed Madonna in the window is a picture, 'ill-silenced by the [glass] itself,' of a living woman. The woman to whom such constant (do you find it tiresome? some do, maybe I do too, from time to time, but who am I? My views are not the point.) references gesture is the woman who stands before me. To whom it wants in me to speak. That's all. There's no definition I could give of woman, or prescription for how or what she is or should be. Every woman is different. And there is no essential woman, any more than an essential man. Dozens of genders and thousands of sexes, but only one you. Everything I have spoken was for her sake, this 'you' to whom I speak. The living woman. You (as Whitman, no woman in mind, surely, wrote), you who are holding me now in your hands.

CE: The title—*Kill The Messenger*—puzzles me. According to the book's title page, the full title appears to be: "Kill the messenger / who brings bad news— / the world is only / description." How do you intend this title to be read? Didn't Bruno bring bad news?

RK: And those who thought that the news Bruno brought was bad news, they up and killed him for bringing it. But for us, he brought very good news indeed: we can change the sky, can change the stars that preside over our birth—the way Robert Duncan used to say that you can't pick your parents but you can pick your grandparents—as he chose Baudelaire and Brahms to be his.

My point in choosing that title was not so much the killing as the *only*: "the world is only description." The world we describe (to ourselves, to other people, and obviously to posterity) is the only world there is. The world (to amplify Wittgenstein) is whatever has been asserted to be the case. How we describe the world conditions utterly how we live in it. And how we live in our minds and souls and hearts as we do go on living in the described world—Rilke's 'interpreted world'.

CE: In your marvelous 1993 poem, "Man Sleeping," you write:

> No one will relinquish money, a revolution
> is shattering mirrors only,
> doesn't change the endless empire of Light,
> every blood-slimed sliver of the glass still reflects
> the intolerable injustice of this one-life universe.

One might conclude from such a statement that you do not believe we can change the way things are. And it is also true that you have written "We are silenced by the way things are." But as I understand your body of work, its primary drive is to change the way things are. Are poets locked into an impossible situation in this regard?

RK: The situation is possible. An effective outcome is unlikely. But we must work for it. Changing the base—Stalin denied that linguistic (poetic) change could affect the working mind of society. I think it can. The marxisant poets of the 80s (Language poets, etc.) soldiered on, fueled by that great hope. I don't know any poets nowadays who still evince much in the way of hope (other than for venal entitlements of job and fame). But hope is still one of the 'theological virtues'—the three virtues (*strengths*) by which we speak God into the world. Faith, Hope, Love. Yes, my body of work is driven by that hope, to change the way things are, to open onto an otherness from which our own true instinct towards kindness and love might welcome a nurturing breath from a harmless world. I am a child trying to talk my way out of punishment. I am trying to talk the killer out of killing us. I am trying to beguile the monarch into listening to my stupid poem instead of killing anybody at all. A one-life universe is unjust, is terrible. We must live again. The poem must give us the will to want to, the gumption to get around to life.

CE: Michael McClure wrote (in the early 1970s) that "It is conceivable that the most colossal example of vanity that can be found in history is held by the peoples of contemporary North America." How does this statement reverberate, or not, to you today?

I recall in this context lines from a poem in your 1998 book, *The Time of Voice*: "o my country / how I long to love you, / be love-worthy, be factual, / be a face / of liberty / and let love in..." What would have to happen for you to be able to love the United States now?

RK: America. How can I answer. I love the skin and rock and skies, and the people of us, our ways, our folkish madness. I do not love our masters. I do not love the word democracy as it is used to hide from us the fearful (in both senses) oligarchs who rule us. I don't think it has much to do with the United States. It is the world, or the world now. We are complicit in a vast nightmare of enslavement, indifference, control. Sony/BMG hurts the world as much as Monsanto does—mind-control by mass music, lifestyle compulsion through image-manipulation (Entertainment is the largest single industry in America, and sculpts the world more than the Pentagon has managed to do). I do not like war, and think it is always evil. We have lived for more than a century with that evil. Even the Civil War was evil—our bloodiest war yet, and some other way had to be found. And the War in Iraq is the vilest evil we have yet contrived. We sink, we sink lower – and I say we only to the extent that we tolerate (and god forgive some of us, actually endorse) the vileness of our masters. We know not what we do. If some states seceded, some states whose populations abstained from war and mass imprisonment of minorities, then those states could be the Re-United States of righteousness, and those I could love. But for the moment, I can only love America. Which was before our politics. And will be after. America in eternity. You know it too. Every honest word is an act of contrition. Every word is a pledge of allegiance.

CE: When we read Zukofsky's translation of Catullus, are we reading Catullus? Or Zukofsky? Or something else? What do you consider to be the value of homeophonic translations?

RK: Answering the last part first: the value of all procedures and constraints used by the poet. Procedures and constraints are powerful tools, but they are tools to build the house we have in mind—especially the house we have in mind but don't know it, or don't know it's there, or how it's shaped. I mean that homoeophonic translation (or any other strategy of compelling words to appear where none, or others, were before), is finally of greatness and power when it succeeds in shaking something out of the poet's head, shocking the poet into seeing what was never there: letting her shout out with full conviction what she didn't know, a second before, that she meant at all. And now she'll stake her life on it, because that is what one does, in fact, in the poem, throw a handful of grit into the machinery of eternity and change, hopelessly change, the pattern of the real. Any poem does this, and the more it changes and defies and renews and challenges the reader's expectation, his habit of attention, the better the poem does its work. When I hear Celan or Hoelderlin *as* English, I am hearing that most wondrous music, a song nobody sang. So, to answer: neither

Catullus nor Zukofsky. No One's Song we hear, like Celan's famous No One's Rose. But it's Zukofsky's ears we bless, his 'lute' for letting us hear.

CE: Here are a few names for you to respond to:

Miles Davis

RK: Damn braces, bless relaxes, said Blake. Davis relaxes, I guess, irritates me. Too smooth, too crossover, too popular, too smoky, too clean. I feel I ought to say something, at least, given your question. to bring jazz in. Not that I know much about it. Fats Waller when I was a child, Parker when I was half-grown, a one-night stand with John Birks Gillespie in San Francisco, Don Cherry on Tenth Street, Ornette all the time. But that's not a life with jazz—it's moments of vivid interruption during my Mahler life, Bellini life, Biber life, Strauss life, Bach life.

Richard Pryor

RK: Blank. I really don't know him. Sorry. I gather he's a comedian, from seeing ads. Never saw him in a movie or on tv. You maybe are just teasing me with this reference, since I think you know how notorious I am for not being fond of narrative film, but for loving 'experimental' films. As far as I'm concerned, and I know I'm eccentric here, there really is in film a place for story, but only when it makes its way to the viewer by eye (Atom Egoyan, say, or Tarkovsky, or the supreme Sokurov) rather than by dialogue (Truffaut, Cassavetes) or narration. Think of the way Pasolini, who is a powerful writer and poet, nevertheless does it all in film *by eye.* What a great being he was. Right up there with Brakhage and Bergman. Anyhow, my heroes of comedy are the purely visual: Keaton, Tati, Lloyd, Chaplin.

James Baldwin

RK: You're the second person to ask me about him today. With his quiet, tenebrous anxieties so elegantly summoned, aired—he's the one who taught, told, most of us, the white audience, what we needed to know, so little wanted to know. About race, yes, but not just race but all the shades and infamies and tendernesses of human difference. And he did so with a beauty of style, a parlando eloquence, unstoppable flow, that made us listen. Made me listen. Thanks for reminding me of him.

Gaudi

RK: Greatest underappreciated sculptor of our time, maybe the truest one. Instead of sculpting objects (Moore, Lipchitz) or environment/atmospheres (Smithson, Serra), he sculpted vast invisible art works that stand solid in the sky as buildings. We call it architecture, and smile, and walk in and out. But he gestures in the sky (Sagrada Familia) or on the ground (Parc Guell) and the gestures last. He's wonderful. He made the angels smile.

Joan Mitchell

That grand era of art, the body gesture lifting to the sky, intercepted, "ill-silenced" by the canvas itself. She was I suppose the last of them, the painters who threw themselves into the marks the body's gestures make on surfaces, the self as fresco, sudden, vivid. In my mind, she inherits a little of the excitement I felt around Kline and de Kooning in The Old Days, that the mark can be enough, the gesture can hold space intact, the gesture can be mark, And the mark can be read. I haven't followed her work particularly, which I suppose means something. It pleases me to look at it, but it has not yet drawn me to build a house in the mind around her way of work.

CE: How do you understand "improvisation" in poetry?

RK: All poetry is improvisation. It is listening to the voice in the head (no bets on where that voice resides, or where it is coming from, or what 'from' could possibly mean), listening: to the first thing that comes to mind. Then following up on that, riffing on that, sometimes with a formal intention, sometimes (better) just the intention towards form.

So called jazz-poetry misses the point. Poetry is there already—doing it 'with' music or 'to' music just hides either the real poetry or the inept imagination of the performer. Poetry is the other side of music. And in any case, poetry is doing what jazz is doing, but with greater freedom—no chart, no time signature, no dance floor packed with rowdies. It is improvisation at its purest. Something out of nothing.

CE: Write me a poem here called "Moments with Shostakovich"

RK: Here is the poem, I wrote it as soon as I read the question – so it's the first question answered of all these. Thanks (as they say) for asking!

MOMENTS WITH SHOSTAKOVICH

for C.E.

I am fourteen it is New York
he is walking towards me, his sallow
face his glasses the two goons beside him
keeping him in line, the world's
greatest composer (Strauss has died)
walking towards me towards me,
I stand in awe but try not to look
impressed, I am a kid, as a kid
I am always performing for myself
just like the poet I would become

or am I, I am I am a poet Williams
said was he speaking for me then
there with the Waldorf-Astoria
then the classiest joint in America
hovering over D. D. Shostakovich
walking towards fat little Robertus
Jacobus whose heart filled immensely
with the authenticity of this
unbelievable occasion, me with him
on this very street in my own town
forever I am real! this is now! this is
the real thing the real world, I am in it
at last, here he comes the man
whose music lives in my head
we share space, I belong to the world!
By now they had passed, maybe
he was smoking, I probably was,
maybe he caught my adoring eye
maybe he saw it was all too full
of self-importance to see him,
too busy with I-am-with-Shosty
to actually be with him, there,
on the grey street, a frail unhappy
looking man between his two
apathetically vigilant bodyguards
and they too might like him have
looked at me then looked away.

Actually, a few months ago I wrote a number of pieces 'listening through' some of the Shostakovich preludes and fugues. That was part of a big cycle of compositions, working also through Biber sonatas, Bax orchestral works, and most of the Mozart piano concertos. At the moment, I am working on a text 'listening through' Franck's Prelude, Chorale and Fugue as performed by Robin Freund-Epstein, towards a live enactment with her of music and text next spring. But I'm very happy that you made me write a new

Shostakovich poem, one that, as you see, breaks into the stifled air of my childhood, to reclaim a memory that's important to me. A child, even a child, is in the world.

CE: Christopher Wagstaff has written: "Robert Kelly shares the view that in poetry something of permanent and ultimate importance to man is revealed." If you agree with Wagstaff, tell us something about the revelation of permanent and ultimate importance in poetry.

RK: I do share that view (but with whom am I said to share it?). I think it is in language that the importance (permanent is a hard word, ultimate harder, but important, yes, has import for us, big import), and poetry—which I keep defining as the shaping of time by language alone—preeminently allows language to do its work, work from its depths, which are our own depths, caverns to which we have—as you have shown us vividly in your poetry as well as in *Juniper Fuse*—access only, or perhaps most fully, in language: the linguistic consequences of what happens to us in the abyss, what we come out spouting and sometimes get to write down. It happens down there. So we have to write it down. (Prepositions, aren't they the purest words?)

CE: You have often mentioned the word "lust" in your poetry, especially in *The Loom*. You have written that it is more important than truth, that there is a purity in it, that you yourself are lust, that your lust is faithless, that it monopolizes, and that "What I have made / I made from lust / for eternal conditions, / open systems." How does lust operate in poetry?

RK: Once I wrote something like this: Fear/and lust/ Trust/ nothing else. I mean simply we know it when we feel lust, we know it when we feel fear. These feelings are guides. I by no means intend to endorse either as operators in a situation. No, they are criteria from which we can decide our actions. We blunder fearfully when we *deny that we feel* lust, or deny that we feel fear. I'm not saying (I'm not Blake) indulge the lust, indulge the fear—do as you will with them, and it is right and good sometimes to turn away, and sometimes not—but know that they're there, working in you. So lust is something that turns us towards the world. That is wonderful. What is terrible about lust is that what it focuses on becomes the Figure, and all the rest of the poor world just the Ground. This gestalt effect of lust is the danger—while seeming to grant more ("I want, I want!") it confers always less and less. The more you grasp, the more you let fall away. So I speak of trusting those feelings as signposts—not as destinations.

CE: In his 1990 book, *Words With Power,* Northrop Frye writes: "Blake was, so far as I knew and still know, the first person in the modern world to see the events of his day in their mythical and imaginative context. He realized that the old mythical universe, in its ideological form as a rationalizing of traditional authority, was dead, and that it was time for a new emphasis in mythology that would accommodate the revolutionary movements he saw rising all around him."

In responding to this statement, I wonder if you would keep in mind another of Wagstaff's perceptive comments on your work: "Unlike many contemporary poets, Kelly views mythology as something which arises up out of the human mind and hence as something quite different from poetry. Because mythology presents a certain world-view or picture, it cannot embody the basic forms of experience in as immediate a way as poetry can. As Martin Heidegger points out, poetry exposes one to 'divine lightnings' rather than to world-views."

RK: I really don't know what Chris means when he says that mythology is quite different from poetry. It is only different in the sense that the fruit is different from the tree, yet they can both be called 'apple,' yes? This one is a very important question—let me try to do something with it. What comes to mind: mythos and logos started out as two words in Greek, each meaning roughly the same: 'something spoken—a word or words together making up a story or an argument.' Over time, the mythos word (I think Pindar may be the first to use it this way) drifts away and takes on the restricted meaning of 'story—not necessarily factual,' while logos tends to be restricted to 'statement of fact.' The former eventually gives us myth, the latter logic. But look at: mythos/logos and what you really get is 'story/telling.' That's what mythology is – there is no myth except what is told. All the gods we know arise from telling—whether the telling of poets or the telling of 'prophets.' And Frye certainly is right about Blake, if we understand him to mean (leaving aside the tendentious remark about revolutions 'all around'—there was only one) that Blake was the first poet willing to let myth arise out of his own telling, the first one who allowed a full-blown mythology to be told 'in his own words.' But thank God not the last: what else are The Cantos, Maximus, Paterson, The Changing Light at Sandover, but myths of our day, of our telling. And in them our gods move, swift and enigmatic and confusing as ever—no clear sign ever from Zeus, the Greeks said, and our gods are no more explicit. And no less energetic in the workshops of the heart and mind. If Heidegger's lightning flashes are indeed divine, they light up—moment by moment, flash by flash—the only world there is. As poems do, in their own moments. Their flashes. Which are, alas, seldom as long lasting as the whole poem might be. The flash shows the god. The duende, we used to call it back in the 50s, stealing Lorca's thunder to make our own lightning with.

CE: In *The Time of Voice,* one poem is titled "Every Language is a Second Language." Does one write poetry to break out of second language into first language? Is the language shamans tell us they hear, and converse with animals in, a first language?

RK: No, shaman talk and beast talk are second language too. First language is what happens to our skin and eyes and mind in the world, the hurt of happen. The touch of hand. The wind. We can name all those things later, but when they happen, they are first language talking to us, and we speak that language by moving, touching, tasting. I mean the movement from perception into language is far greater in its abstraction, its terror, than the movement from English to Japanese or Tibetan. My title, its idea, is to keep people firmly aware of how remote all language is from the healing joyous horror of primary sensation.

CE: At one time you wrote: "Dreams are dragon-snorts, / worth little." At another: "dream is translation from dreamless sleep into waking." What is your position on dreams at this time?

RK: There have been periods (I'm in one now) when I dream obsessively, oppressively, and wake relieved by morning light. Other times I go months without dreaming (i.e., to soothe the science brethren, without remembering a single dream). In those times, I feel nostalgic about dreams, and come all over Breton-like about the magistry of the dream state, and its wisdom. Right now, I dread the dream because it imposes on the awakened dreamer the responsibility of taking notice—interpreting, maybe, or reporting it to spouse or friend or counselor, or just writing it down, or just carrying the heavy thing through the day, stubbing against odd corners of dream remnants that show up through the day. The converse of Freud's famous phrase (*Tagesreste*) is also true: the day is a remnant left over from dream.

I also have felt for years that in addition to all the other ways dreams have been received or understood (messages from the gods, from the collective unconscious, from the personal unconscious, scraps of the day, somatic impressions symbolized as narration—cold feet dream of snow), there remains for us to explore the possibility that dream is an authentic *language:* that is, like any natural language, a social event, that we dream in a community. I infer that we owe it to that community to report our dreams; our dreams are for the other, are the words our nights speak to the community. Dreams are the News of the Night, and need to come to us every morning. I have some other notes on this in my old book of essays, *In Time,* and some more, along with other people's responses, and community dream experiments, in Lynn Behrendt's interesting and ongoing *Annandale Dream Gazette* online.

CE: In "On Discourse" (1973) you posed the following question: "What is the other side of *this* place?" At that time, you did not respond to this question. Would you do so now?

RK: You have given the answer. The other side of this place is now. Now has been waiting for us all along. Are we ready for now yet? Maybe I should ask you.

finished 4 October 2007
published in APR, *2008*

LETTER TO THE *APR* EDITORS

17 September 2008

dear Editors: Steve Berg invited me to be an *APR* "columnist" in July of 2006. When I asked him about a contract, he wrote that no one ever had a contract for such at *APR*. He informed me that the "column" was all mine for nine contributions over a period of three years and that I was to have "complete control" over what I would write. He told me that while editors might make suggestions, I was under no obligation to take such suggestions or even respond to them. He said that even if what I offered was "considered to be outrageous," I would not be "pressed for changes." In earlier correspondence he had told me that *APR* had no problem in printing work that had been published elsewhere. This turned out to be true; *APR* subsequently ran several poems of mine that had already appeared in books.

In 2007 and 2008 I sent *APR* four "columns" which were published in Vol. 36 #1, 3, and 5, and Vol. 37 #1. They were:

1) "A Translation Memoir:" a detailed year by year description of my 48 year translation saga that led to the 2007 publication of my translation of *The Complete Poetry of César Vallejo* by U of Cal Press. Berg had expressed a deep interest in this project, had published 14 of my translations in the May/June issue of *APR*, and had asked me for names of potential reviewers for the book, stating that he wanted to run an article-length review. I gave him a list and nothing came of it..

2) "Six Introductions:" 6 brief articles on Gary Snyder, Michael Palmer, Will Alexander, Christine Hume, Jeff Clark, and Andrew Joron. While Snyder and Palmer are now quite well known, I offered this set to *APR* because I thought it would introduce some readers to the work of the other four.

3) "The Back Wall of Imagination: Notes on the *Juniper Fuse* Project." I spent 25 year researching Upper Paleolithic cave art in southwestern France in an attempt to assimilate the origin of

image-making as it seems to have occurred during the last Ice Age. My book on all this, *Juniper Fuse: Upper Paleolithic Imagination & the Construction of the Underworld* was published by Wesleyan University Press in 2003. The article I sent in as my "column," a companion to "A Translation Memoir," goes into great detail concerning how I worked through this long "saturation job." I thought it would alert any young poet to the possibilities and ramifications of the big poetic project.

4) "20 Questions for Robert Kelly:" Kelly is, from my viewpoint, one of the finest 20th century American poets. To my knowledge, his work has never appeared in *APR*. So I spent several months rereading his poetry and put together a wide-ranging questionnaire, which he carefully responded to.

During this period, I also encouraged Michael McClure to send work to *APR* (which was published) as well as Gustaf Sobin's daughter to send the magazine some of Gustaf's René Char translations (which also appeared).

In short, I felt during this period that I was being a responsible "columnist" as well as a good friend of the magazine.

In the winter of 2008, something went haywire between *APR* and me, and this is the reason that I am writing this up.

I have always admired Wallace Stevens' "Adagia," a collection of aphorisms, sightings, notes, and quotations, and decided to assemble one of my own. I pulled material from books of others as well as my own, and added new unpublished material. "Tesserae" is a "gists and piths" autobiography of my thinking on poetics, politics, cave art, translation, reading, and human experience over many years, including the words of others that have meant a lot to me. I have never seen anything like it in *APR*.[1]

---

1 "Tesserae" is now called "Erratics," a different version of which was published by Hunger Press in 2000. The final version of "Erratics" is the penultimate piece in *The Price of Experience*. Since no one at *APR* bothered to respond to my letter, I now regard it as public information.

After sending it in, January 2008, I received the following letter from Managing Editor David Bonanno:

> We don't want to use "Tesserae" as your next column. It is all your own work and some of it previously published. That doesn't fit into any of the editor's definition of what a column should be. Sorry.

This rejection of course flew in the face of everything that Berg had previously written me about my "column." As for it being "all [my] own work," such was true of three of my four published contributions. As for "some of it [being] previously published," that was true, but Berg had told me that *APR* published work that had appeared elsewhere, and had already published some of my own previously published poems. When I queried Elizabeth Scanlon about the matter (Elizabeth had edited all of the poetry and prose of mine that had appeared in the magazine), wondering why the letter came from Bonanno, she told me that Berg had made the decision but had asked Bonanno to be the rejecter.

I wrote Elizabeth that while I felt that I was entitled to an explanation (for a rejection that contradicted the terms on which I was invited to be a columnist), that if "Tesserae" was being rejected on the quality of the writing in it, I would accept this decision and place the piece elsewhere. I thought this was being more than generous on my part since according to my original arrangement with Berg, even if it was "outrageous" (which it was not) it was to go in.

So, for my next "column," I submitted a three-way interview with Paul Hoover and Maxine Chernoff on editing literary magazines. Between the three of us, we have edited four magazines (spanning some twenty-five years). We thought it would be interesting, especially for young writers, to learn what we had gone through, and learned, as editors. From my viewpoint, *New American Writing,* the current Hoover/Chernoff magazine, is one of the very best of our time.

Several weeks passed. Then I got a one line letter from Berg asking me if I had read "Franny." No mention of my "column," just this off-the-wall question. We exchanged several one sentence messages in which I asked him when my "column" would appear, and he continued to tell me to read "Franny." Finally, I said I would, and again requested that he respond to my "column." Here is the letter he sent me:

> I have read through your piece on certain magazines various approaches to editing and I don't see how the reader truly interested in poetry and literature in general could possibly involve himself in the list of magazines and editors etc that make up your essay. as an historical document it does not belong in *apr*'s pages but in a section at the back of a book on the ideas behind and activities of those magazines and their editing. I really am surprised at how much effort you put into the project of self-promotion that informs much of what we receive from you. you will of course despise these remarks—or as you once wrote to me many years ago about your work and *apr*—"never again"—I am still in favor of running your column but I would like to see some writing for people who are devoted to reading good work. we could discuss many possible topics, sometimes I ask columnists if they would consider writing about such-and-such. for example if I asked you which modern long poem you thought supremely important—asphodel, four quartets, the bridge, paterson, esthetique du mal, etc etc would you be interested in writing about it?

This is a very insulting letter. Two of my published "columns" were on other poets, and in the case of the Kelly interview, my only role was that of creating and asking pertinent questions. I suppose that anything anyone writes in the first person can be misconstrued as "self-promotional," but there is a huge difference between addressing the convolutions and complications of a 48 year translation saga (an essay that after appearing in *APR* resulted in a half-dozen letters to me of reader appreciation) and, as we used to say, "tooting one's own horn." In his letter Berg contradicted everything he had told me when he invited me to become a "columnist" two years ago.

Paul Hoover and I sent our trialogue to *Jacket* magazine. John Tranter immediately accepted it, posting it two days latter.

Berg's letter ends by treating me as if I were one of his students, needing help with term paper ideas. While I do not "despise" his remarks, I find them condescending, dishonest, and proof that the arrangements he made with me two years earlier meant absolutely nothing. I suspect that I was fired by Berg because my contributions were becoming too strong as an alternative direction in the magazine. I also suspect that other *APR* "columnists" have been dismissed during their agreed-upon work period because in one way or another they piqued the double-crosser Steve Berg.

VI

HENRI MICHAUX: *MOVEMENTS* [1951]

Against alveoli
against glue
against glue one another
against the soft one another

Cactus!
Flames of blackness
impetuous
dagger mothers
battle roots shooting through the plain

Race that rolls
crawling that boils
unity that swarms
lump that dances

One defenestrated flies off
one torn apart from bottom to top
one torn apart throughout
one torn apart never again retied

Man buttressed
man bounding
man rushing down
man for the lightning operation
for the tempest operation
for the assegai operation
for the harpoon operation
for the shark operation
for the shatter operation

Man not according to the flesh
but by the void and evil and intestinal torches
and gusts and nervous discharges

and reversals
and returns
and rage
and quartering
and tangling
and taking off in sparks

Man not by the abdomen and gluteal plates or vertebrae
  but by his currents, his feebleness which straightens up under
  shock, his starts
man according to the moon and burning powder and the
  kermess in himself of the movement of others
and the squall and the rising wind and the never orderly chaos
Man all flags flapping, clapping in the wind whispering from his
  pulsions
man who thrashes a parrot
who has no articulations
who breeds nothing
goat-man
crested man
spined
abridged
tufted man, galvanizing his rags,
man with secret props, spreading far from his degrading life

Desire barking in the dark is the multiform form of this being
Impulses scissored
forked
impulses radiating
impulses around the whole compass dial

In noise
in roaring, if one gave it a body!...
In the sounds of the balafon and in the ear-splitting drill
in throbbing adolescents who don't yet know
what their breasts want which is as if they're going to burst
in jolts, in rumblings, in outpourings

in blood tides in arteries suddenly switching direction
in thirst
in thirst above all
in thirst never quenched
if one gave it a body!...

Soul of the lasso
of seaweed
of the jack, of the grapnel and of the wave that swells
of the sparrow-hawk, of the gnu, of the sea-elephant
the triple soul
the eccentric soul
the energumen soul
soul of electrified larva coming to bite at the surface
soul of blows and of teeth grindings
soul always out of plumb toward a new straightening

The abstractness of all weight
of all languor
of all geometry
of all architecture
abstraction realized: SPEED!
Movements of quartering and of inner exasperation more than the movements of walking
movements of explosions, of refusal, of stretching every which way
of unhealthy attractions, of impossible desires
of the sating of flesh struck on the nape
headless movements
What good is a head when one is overwhelmed?
Movements of folding and coiling up on oneself while expecting better
movements of inner shields
movements of multiple spurts
residual movements
movements in place of other movements that one cannot display but which dwell on the mind

of dust
of stars
of erosion
of crumblings
of vain latencies…

Feast of stains, gamut of arms
movements
one jumps into "nothing"
efforts turning
being alone, one is a crowd
What incalculable number is advancing
increasing itself, extending itself, extending itself!
Goodbye fatigue
goodbye economical biped at the bridge abutment station
the scabbard torn off, one is somebody else
any somebody else
no longer to pay tribute
a corolla opens, bottomless dive…

The stride henceforth has the length of hope
the leap has the length of thought
one has eight paws if one must run
one has ten arms if one must stand fast
one is deeply rooted, when its necessary to hold on
never beaten
always returning
the new revenant
while appeased the master of the keyboard feigns sleep!

Stains
stains to obnubilate
to reject
to unshelter
to destabilize
to be reborn
to scratch out

to make memory shut up
to restart

Crazy baton
boomerang ceaselessly returning
returning torrentially
through others
to take off again…

Gestures
gestures of the ignored life
of the impulsive life
and happy to squander itself
of the jerky, spasmodic, erectile life
of perfunctory life, of life no matter how
of life
Gestures of defiance and of retort
and of escaping from bottlenecks

Gestures of excess
of excess
especially of excess

Gestures one feels, but which one cannot identify
(pre-gestures inside oneself, much grander than the visible and
practical gesture to follow)

Tanglings
attacks that resemble dives
swims that resemble excavations
arms that resemble trunks

Joy of the motor life
that saps meditating on evil
one does not know to what kingdom belongs
the bewitching ovenful that leaps out
animal or human

immediate, without pausing
already off again
the next one already coming
instantaneous
as in thousands and thousands of vertiginous seconds
a slow day completes itself
Solitude practices scales
the desert, the arabesques
the multiplication
the indefinitely reiterated

Signs
signs not of a roof, of a tunic or of a palace
not of archives and of the dictionary of knowledge
but of torsion, of violence, of jostling
of kinetic envy

Signs of the rout, of pursuit and of transport
of thrusts antagonistic, aberrant, dissymetrical
signs non-critical, but deviating with the deviation and racing
with the race
signs not for a zoology
but for the figure of unbridled demons
accompanists of our acts and contradictors of our reserve

Signs of ten thousand ways to be in balance in this moving
world that laughs at adaptation
signs above all to snatch one's being from the trap of others'
tongues
set to beat you, like a carefully adjusted roulette
which allows you only a few happy rolls
and ruin and defeat in the end
inscribed from the start
for you, for everyone

Signs not for a backward return
but to better "cross the line" each instant

signs not like one reconsiders
but like one pilots
or, as may occur in dense congestion
when an unconscious automaton, one feels as if piloted

Signs, not for being complete
but for being faithful to its transience
not for conjugating
but for regaining the gift of tongues
one's own at least, for, if not oneself, who will utter it?

Direct writing finally for the unwindment
for the alleviation of forms
for the decongestion of images
of which the brain-public square in these times is especially
glutted

Lacking aura, at least scatter its emanations.

Note: This poem is taken from Henri Michaux's book, Mouvements, *published by NFR/Gallimard (under the collection,* "Le Point du jour"*) in Paris, 1951, with 64 drawings and a Postface. Bernard Bador and I translated it together in 2010/11. I have been looking at Michaux's drawings and reading his texts for decades. In 2005, I wrote a poem called "Michaux, 1956" (see* The Grindstone of Rapport / A Clayton Eshleman Reader, *pp. 207–209), my testament to the artist's antic and teeming lines, verging on doodles but so possessed by figures emerging out of the void that they might as well be new forms of life, sprinting about in oceanic deeps, or like unidentifiable insects, boring into our dreams.*

At that time, in the poem cited above I wrote: "There is in Michaux an emergent face/non-face always in formation. Call it 'face-before-birth.' Call it our thingness making faces. Call it tree bole or toadstool spirit, anima mundi snout, awash in ephemerality, anti-anatomical, the mask of absence, watercolor by a blind child, the half-disintegrated faces of souls in Hades pressing about the painter Ulysses-Michaux as, over his blood trench of ink, he converses with his hermaphroditic muse." For readers interested in looking into Michaux's art, I highly recommend Emergences / Resurgences, *published as* Drawing Papers #14, *by The Drawing Center in New York City, with a text superbly translated by Richard Sieburth.*

AIMÉ CÉSAIRE'S LOST, FOUND, SCATTERED BODY

While co-translating *The Collected Poetry of Aimé Césaire* with Annette Smith in the late 1970s/early 1980s, I met with Césaire twice on my own, each time with a list of words that we needed his help with. We would meet in a café near the Sorbonne in Paris. The third time the poet agreed to respond to questions, in the summer of 1982, Annette and the scholar A. James Arnold joined us, and Césaire invited us to his son's apartment where he stayed while representing Martinique in the French National Assembly. Because this would be our last discussion with him about his work, after responding to our questions (which would occasionally send him to the book shelves to check an arcane word he had not used for many years), we asked him to read us a poem. Sitting under a painting by Wifredo Lam, he chose "Corps perdu" ("Lost Body") and read it to us in a measured, solemn voice.

"Lost Body" is the title piece of a collection of ten poems Césaire published in 1949 (in an edition including thirty-two etchings by Picasso). As Arnold, who regards "Lost body" as one of Césaire's most powerful poems and the finest example of his demiurgic manner, has written: "'Lost Body' is located at the watershed that slopes in one direction toward the origins of negritude and in the other toward the modifications necessitated by a hostile political and economic situation."

*

Lost Body

I who Krakatoa
I who everything better than a monsoon
I who open chest
I who Laelaps
I who bleat better than a cloaca

I who outside the musical scale
I who Zambezi or frantic or rhombos or cannibal
I would like to be more and more humble and more lowly
always more serious without vertigo or vestige
to the point of losing myself falling
into the live semolina of a well-opened earth
Outside in lieu of atmosphere there'd be a beautiful haze no dirt
    in it
each drop of water forming a sun there
whose name the same for all things
would be DELICIOUS TOTAL ENCOUNTER
so that one would no longer know what goes by
—a star or a hope
or an underwater retreat
raced across by the flaming torches of aurelian jellyfish
Then I imagine life would flood my whole being
better still I would feel it touching me or biting me
lying down I would see the finally free odors come to me
like merciful hands
finding their way
to sway their long hair in me
longer than this past that I cannot reach.
Things stand back make room among you
room for my repose carrying in waves
my frightening crest of anchor-like roots
looking for a place to take hold
Things I probe I probe
me the street-porter I am root-porter
and I bear down and I force and I arcane
    I omphale
Ah who leads me back toward the harpoons
    I am very weak
I hiss yes I hiss very ancient things
as serpents do as do cavernous things
I whoa lie down wind
and against my unstable and fresh muzzle

against my eroded face
press your cold face of ravaged laughter
The wind alas I will continue to hear it
nigger nigger nigger from the depths
of the timeless sky
a little less loud than today
but still too loud
and this crazed howling of dogs and horses
which it thrusts at our forever fugitive heels
but I in turn in the air
shall rise a scream so violent
that I shall splatter the whole sky
and with my branches torn to shreds
and with the insolent jet of my wounded and solemn shaft

I shall command the islands to be

*

Now I will try to key in the transmutational power of "Lost Body:"

It opens with seven percussive lines, like the blasts of a conch, in which the assertive speaker forces objects and phrases into verbal display. Suddenly there is a shift in tone and implied social position. He is now a black lackey whose colonial status will remain subliminal until it is more clearly formulated as a "street-porter" twenty-five lines later. The speaker's desire to "lose himself" is a psychic as well as a social statement. He wants to enter a magic plenitude as well as to forget who he is, a complex that is heightened by the wish, to "no longer know what goes by."

Now, in a womb-like "underwater retreat" the speaker, totally passive, not only fantasizes being mollycoddled by "merciful hands," but loses all sense of having any substance. We have reached the nadir of the poem: the speaker's desire to be "without vestige" has become so successful that he is no longer in contact with a past.

Then, in a sudden swerve, before completely losing consciousness, the speaker metamorphizes again, attempting to regain the assertiveness expressed in the poem's initial blast. In a Rimbaldian sense, he makes himself monstrous, at once "street porter" and "root-porter," doning a headdress-like assembly of tentacular "anchor-like roots. It is as if the near loss of consciousness has made the former "conch man" much stronger and more dimensional (offering some potency to the cliché: "you must be lost to be found"). Again, he forces an adjective ("arcane") and a noun ("omphale") to function as verbs. In her trenchant commentary on the poem, the scholar, Ronnie Scharfman, addresses this moment: "All these urges unite in the wonderful neologism 'j'omphale…' The subject/verb stands rooted to the middle of the page like an umbilicus, surrounded by space on either side, curiously tight and vulnerable at the same time… The umbilical cord is, after all, the first root and also the first experience of severance, *déracinement,* castration."

At this point, in a deft forecast of the poem's detonational conclusion, the speaker prepares to meet "the harpoons." But before doing so, in another one of the work's subsidings, before the next climax, he commands the monsoon wind (from the poem's second line) to lie down with him, to press its derisive "face" against his own. This is certainly the strangest moment in this peristaltic lyric, evoking for a split second the denouement of Ingmar Bergman's *Persona,* in which the two women's faces fuse. It is as if the speaker has finally gathered the strength to face what the "ravaged laughter" of the wind contains: the core negation of his being, the inescapable image of the "nigger."

If the wind itself calls him a nigger, then he is an eternal fugitive. For a moment Césaire's entire body of work buckles with the dilemma that Northrop Frye sighted writing about William Blake's "The Four Zoas:" that true humanity might only be discovered in madness or apocalypse. The severity of this moment is registered in the wrenching ending where the nigger, although rent apart by the white devil's hounds, destroys the sky and re-creates, primal islands, in one paroxysmic, ejaculatory gesture. Such an ending not only recalls the Egyptian self-fecundating primal god Atun "copulating in his hand," but Hart Crane's great lyric, "Lachrymae Christi," in which a Nazarene/Dionysus who is crucified, torn asunder, and burned at the stake is beseeched to reappear whole. Both poems confront the reader with a radical vision of creativity that is bound up with an assimilation of such destructiveness as to render it, in the same moment, sublime and absurd.

A decade earlier, Césaire's 1055 line *Notebook of a Return to the Native Land* was based on a parthenogenesis in which the poet gave birth to himself while exorcising his introjected and collective image of the black. In "Lost Body," which lacks the socio-political survey and commitment to a political career that the *Notebook* contains, the process of self-birth is compressed into 56 lines.

Césaire's vision of Eden also includes its nightside, a dyad that is incredibly difficult to maintain, for a vision of paradisal wholeness and existent human suffering in the present negate each other. A significant part of the energy in his language is generated by his attempt to transform the language of the slave masters of yesterday and the colonial administrators of his own day into a kind of *surfrancais,* as in *sur*real, a supercharged French that in its own fashion is as transformational as Surrealism attempted to be of bourgeois, patriarchal French mentality.

"Lost Body" is Césaire's most jarring rollercoaster ride of the negritudinal self, turning and being turned by inner and exterior self and social forces. Poised on a complex dramatic peak between the mythologically-immersed poetry of the 1940s, when the poet was working out the heroic dimensions of negritude, and his later-life confrontations with "le nègre," or nigger, stripped of revolutionary political optimism, "Lost Body" moves with the speed and finesse of John Coltrane's "Giant Steps," through the "changes" that sound the affirmation/negation turbines of a realized poetic career.

Aimé Césaire's Martinican fingers taking our pulse forever.

Note: The quotation from A. James Arnold comes from his book, *Modernism & Negritude,* Harvard University Press, 1981, p. 235. The quote from Ronnie Scharfman is from her book, *Engagement and the Language of the Subject in the Poetry of Aimé Césaire,* University of Florida / Humanities Monograph #59, 1980, p. 80. This paper was read at the Aimé Césaire Tribute, October 10, 2008, at New York University, as part of the international symposium, "Slave Routes: Resistance, Abolition, & Creative Progress." It was then published in *Callaloo* #31, 2008.

GLOSSES ON THE FIRST 12 POEMS IN LAURA SOLORZANO'S *LIP WOLF*

1: The swan of poetry, neck-twisted, found dead in its cistern, a sister swan, a "you" desolate, divided, numb—yet miraculously alive, near-form, a beautiful filthy thing covered, a kind of self-tearing nourishment. Approached, this Muse of poetry tautens, twists, reburies itself.

2: "You" is matrix, the force in nature that self-conceives. Parthenogenetic, it contains its own prize (like a piñata it hides its prize and must be broken open). "You" as the poetic word, the poet's shadow (or the shadow's poet), if spoken unspoken, mouth loss, cow mute.

3: The speaker is also "you-less," alone, masticating fable and monster, assimilating the spectrum of her livingdying, chewing language as her mortal immortality. She is a mill in grind with measuring, nibbling the fuse of the flower as well as its signature.

4: The bee-work of language at the mercy of the speaker's body, vaporous as a cloud. The tension in poetry overturns, a desert as well as a savior, a savior who is hollow, at home. The speaker begs for a rootedness, something cloud-ungraspable. In the language hive she experiences the explosions of her own excavations.

5: To hold "you" as a house contains statues, orgasmic couplings, this is the task. To come to form in the face of all she sees and experiences. Such is the price of a realized "you," the price of experience. "You" thingifies as it burns. Its nature is one of combustion and salvation. To fuck until she bursts is to fabricate a torso, a curve in the pruned and burning disintegration.

6: The speaker discovers that the "you" she has made contact with has not experienced the torrent of touching fully. She also discovers that this "you," so fully without, is knotted within, in the thimble tightness of her own life material. At this point "you" is still incompletely activated, is still nut-hard, uncracked, refusing to be broken into imaginal vectors.

7: The speaker drives into an obsessive naming, a female Adam calling out essence via identification. She breaks out of herself, but her lake is lunar, and the goal of her pursuit keeps on shape-changing. "You" as the "combined object" of the subconscious, the ungraspable and multifoliate rain ray.

8: How make "you" speak? The Muse as a medusa the poet is to give birth to, deadly and devouring. In the delirium of birth, "you's" members are glimpsed: spine, finger, forehead, all dough, all stuff to be transformed in blundering digital blindness.

9: Once the speaker was pregnant, her brain not her own. Suffering physical pregnancy (versus imaginal bud-forthing) she experiences self-devouring as giving birth. A cavern of masks, she bore her ton, her cubic tangle, this "you-less" gift.

10: Between "you" and the speaker is a centrifuge of time and space, a particle flow of the seen and unseen, motherhood stuffed with participation, a cave haven for all the contradictions she encounters in the grand "between," the unrelenting exploding pregnancy of life between the target and the aiming.

11: The process of fulfillment now kicks in. "You" identified again and again transforms under touch. Such transformation is now experienced as an antiphonal filling and vanishing, for the speaker herself is also in a state of transformation. She is "other" to "herself," and thus released in the playful chemistry of thingness and being. "You" bald, "you" tearful, "you" fulfilled in momentary cessation of the hurricane of becoming.

12: "You" has been called out, named, 80 times, and is now malleable, no longer prudish nor meek. "You" is vein ink debating itself in the fire in love with the fire that is the poem. A filled void, musicalized, in mouth loss sexual exuberance. Not a timid lip but a wolf lip, de-smothered, de-upchucked, an unceasing flute celebrating its narcissian rivers. The precipice **reached.**

Note: The Mexican poet Laura Solórzano was born in Guadalajara in 1961. She has recently been translating essays on the painter Orozco, and teaching at the Centro de Arte Audiovisual in Guadalajara where she continues to live. I met her work in Lobo de labio (translated by Jen Hofer as *Lip Wolf,* Action Books, 2007). The twelve paragraphs above are instantaneous responses on a 5th or 6th reading to the first twelve numbered poems in that collection. Other books by Laura include: *Semilla de ficus,* Ediciones Rimbaud, Mexico, 1999; *Boca Perdido,* Editorial Bonobos, Metepec, Mexico, 2005; and *Un rosal para el señor K,* Prefacio de Ricardo Castillo, Anaquel 3, Universidad de Guanajuato, 2006. This gloss was published on the *Action Now* blog in 2010.

ORGANIZED NOMADISTORMS OF BROKEN OASES

In late 2008, I was invited to participate in Week Three of the 2009 Summer Writing Program at Naropa University. The theme for my week was identified as "Polyvalent/Rhizomic Identities" and described in the following way: "The rhizome is a tuber system that moves horizontally and shares a paradigm with *Indra's Net* and the world wide web. We are all polyvalent hybrids, capable of moving in multiple directions simultaneously. On a genetic level we are composed of dominant and recessive genes. How does this translate in our writing and in our work as writers? Walt Whitman contained multitudes. From some point of view, we are all hairy bags of water. How does one identity serve another? We'll honor the brilliant scholarship and vital translations that Clayton Eshleman has done of Peruvian poet César Vallejo."

Unsure exactly what to make of all of this, I wrote to my old comrade Pierre Joris and began to explore with him what I thought "rhizomic identity" might be. Branching off from the writing of Gilles Deleuze and Felix Guattari in their book *Rhizome,* Joris has mounted a new poetics on the concept which he lays out in his book, *A Nomad Poetics.* Here, after quoting Joris's proposal, I would like to set forth our exchange, illustrate how such theory might relate to Joris's own recent poetry, and then briefly reflect on the rhizomic, Pound's *Pisan Cantos* and Olson's *Maximus Poems.*

JORIS: What is needed now is a nomadic poetics. Its method will be *rhizomic:* which is different from collage i.e., a rhizomatics is not an aesthetics of the fragment, which has dominated poetics since the romantics even as transmogrified by modernism, high and low, and more recently retooled in the neoclassical form of the citation—ironic and/or decorative—throughout which is called "postmodernism." *Strawberry Fields Forever.* A nomadic poetics will cross languages, not just translate, but write in all or any of them. If Pound, Joyce, Stein, Olson, & others have shown the way, it is essential now to push the matter further, again, not so much as "collage" (though we will keep those gains) but as a material flux of language matter. To try & think, then, of this matter as even pre-language, proto-semantic, as starting from what Julia Kristeva calls the *chora,* which she defines as "a temporary articulation, essentially mobile, constituted of movements and their ephemeral stases." And then to follow this flux of ruptures and articulations, of rhythm, moving in & out of semantic & non-semantic spaces, moving around & through the features accreting as poem, a lingo-cubism, no, a lingo-barocco that is no longer an "explosante fixe" (Breton) but an "explosante mouvante."

Concerning "crossing languages" Joris elsewhere writes: "We will write in foreign languages (real or made-up ones) in order to come to the realization that all languages are foreign. And those that are not are uninteresting in their self-reflecting egoism. All languages are creolized by what Edouard Glissant has called the chaos-world. The first need thus is to have done with the prison-house of the mother tongue i.e., why should one have to write in the mummy/daddy language, why should that oedipal choice be the only possible or legitimate one...." I will return to these points later. Here it is also important to bring in a bit more of the Deleuze and Guattari theory, especially their rejection of the "tree": "The rhizome is an anti-hierarchical means of organizing knowledge and of recognizing intersections and engagements between seemingly disparate ideas and things. Botanically, the rhizome is a branching that has no 'center.' All segments are fertile. Any segment broken off from the rest may serve as a new starting point, a new origin of life. As a heterogeneous composition, it brings all manners of materials into productive contact with one another. In contrast to the tree: knowledge organized around and branching out of a central 'truck.' In the arboreal system, 'trunk' is understood as origin, source of authenticity or authority. Its branches are mere iterations or representations of their own content."

ESHLEMAN: To think of the rhizome in the sense that Deleuze and Guattari are describing takes me back to the origin of the metaphor at around 30,000 B.P.: juxtaposition of a vulva and a horse head engraved in a limestone slab (the two equal in size, slightly overlapping, and 'punctuated' with three cupules, one before the horse head, one as the horse's eye, and one in the center of the vulva). The metaphor and the meander (the basis for Aurignacian "art" which was rediscovered by Jackson Pollack in the 1940s) seem to me to be the rootstock of imagination, or the fold between no image of the world and *an* image.

JORIS: That is indeed very accurate both to the thought of the rhizomatic and in relation to your work on caves & beyond. "Metaphor," however, may be a difficult one as metaphor is easily (always if you believe Derrida who writes marvelously about it in his essay "White Metaphor"), a hierarchical, vertical situation, an attempt at transcendence. I wonder in the case of the cave material and Pollock if "image" isn't the better word. What Pollock produces is an image in process that is finished when the energy, physical and psychic, that he pours in, runs out ("a painting is never finished, it is abandoned"). In the cave work what is absolutely fascinating for me is the mass of drawings, one next to, over, or across another, with something of an implied equivalence between them. Not one of the cave drawings, not one of Pollock's squiggles or canvases is "it" i.e., THE metaphor for art, life, the godhead, the masterpiece-that-says-it-all. Your "juxtaposition of a vulva and a horse head" doesn't necessarily seem to create a metaphor, but is a complex image, with no need to elevate them into what could only be some sort of abstract transcendental unity.

ESHLEMAN: I feel that metaphor is neither vertical nor horizontal. How is "love is a red, red rose" hierarchical? It is an intensification, a sensualization of an otherwise abstract term—love—that is often involved in an idealistic, hierarchical system. The literal is hierarchical. The Bible read literally results in the saving of believers and the burning of non-believers, total lowering, total raising. I think of metaphor as fusion ("my eyes are fix'd / in happy copulation"), as a new creation, a third. God is an absolute, a one, not a metaphor. The shaman is a metaphor (as is "I," as Rimbaud astutely stated) because he is a fusion that participates in both the human and the animal realms.

Deleuze and Guattari we must keep in mind (I am thinking, having not read them, knowing them only via scattered quotations) are secondary thinkers whose work places them in the middle of something else. Aurignacian meander "systems" have many beginnings and many ends. It strikes me that primary thinkers involved in what we can call the autonomous imagination make use of arboreal metaphors as well as rhizomic ones; that is, a creative project determines its own vectors, designs, limitations, signatures as it moves out, or in. You also wrote that a truly open field has no up/down, front/back. But rhizomes themselves send out tendrils, or rootlets up, and below, as they themselves project horizontal movement. So they are somewhat tree-like in this regard.

JORIS: I think the difference here is, to use Deleuze and Guattari again, that trees cannot transform their individual (hierarchical) parts (roots/trunk/branches) into each other (they are fixed, in that sense), while rhizomatic plants can & do all the time. But you are right in saying that major artists use both—though their tree or hierarchical structures are often what is or remains the least interesting (Dante is a great poet despite the Christian hierarchy that is structurally and in every other way the core to his poem; same goes for most of, though not all of, the religious art of the Renaissance—which we appreciate in spite of the doctrinal underpinnings).

ESHLEMAN: Gerrit Lansing's early book is entitled *The Heavenly Tree Grows Downward*. How do you understand this? One approach would be to say that Lansing is interested more in the rootwork of the tree than in its foliage. Years ago, I thought he was plunging the tree into the earth and reversing its flow. But now I think that the direction he is interested in is underworld, root realm, and the nourishment of earth to root, versus branch to air. However, all this may be moot, as the tree in its full environment draws upon air and earth. The first World Tree is in Le Combel, a section of the Pech Merle cave; it is a stalagmitic formation with a vulvar fissure in its base and breast-like pod shapes above (daubed with black manganese by Cro-Magnon people between 18,000 and 16,000 B.P.) This Tree can also be thought of as the first Black Goddess. There is a photo of this amazing figure on p. 211 of *Juniper Fuse.*

JORIS: Gerrit comes out of a very hierarchical (the magical, hermetic, etc) tradition. One could see his tree as an attempt to exactly reverse this, to upset the apple-cart (which is still keeping an inverted hierarchical order of the universe going). I think the poems are often better than what the title's indications/limitations propose.

ESHLEMAN: Northrop Frye calls Blake's "The Marriage of Heaven & Hell" an *anatomy* because it is made up of varying literary genres. This thought crossed my mind while I was working on "Notes on a Visit to Le Tuc d'Audoubert" and helped me understand the overall form of *Juniper Fuse* as a giant *anatomy.* It occurs to me that William Carlos Williams' *Paterson* (with his father/son hierarchical title) is a marvelous example of an anatomy in a way that must be related to rhizomic theory. From Paterson:

> a mass of detail
> to interrelate on a new ground, difficultly;
> an assonance, a homologue
>   triple piled
> pulling the disparate together to clarify
> and compress...

You wrote that one aspect of rhizomic theory as you understand it is a poetics that will cross languages. Lucky you with four. As a monolingual Hoosier I have tendril forays into Spanish and

French but cannot write in either. By the way, I think there are many Englishes. The English I write in is not "the mummy/daddy language." However, according to my father, who kept a meticulous Baby Book record of my first two years, at two I wrote in "mummy/daddy language" my first poem: "Bok *old* Mamma, Tak-a *new* Mamma."

Did Deleuze and Guattari consider Artaud to be a rhizomic writer? I wonder, since Artaud was so body-centered (the screaming body, ceaselessly attacked, and in constant self-defense). I envision Artaud as a kind of St.-Sebastian nailed to the World Tree. While his writings, and drawings, are punctured by disconnects, detours, dead ends, and mythic grabs, he has always seemed to me as one who fought to maintain a central core (for had he lost it, he would have been dispersed into incurable insanity).

JORIS: This abstract transcendental unity may also be behind Artaud's desire to be done with the judgment of god—who is nothing if not a hierarchical "metaphor" (for whatever you want to have him say)—and whose "body without organs" seems to be primarily an attempt to get rid of the hierarchy of organs (hierarchy is necessary for the demonic—no demonology without strict hierarchies of "fallen angels"—and it is demonic possession that Artaud fought all his life).

*

From the mid-1990s on, the words "nomadic poetics" and "oasis" have provided focal energies for Pierre Joris's poetry. While he seems to have settled on American-English, his 4th language, for poetry, he is also fluent in Luxembourgian, German, and French. The latter two languages often flicker through his American. One meaning of his nomadic drifting is an openness to crossing languages. His nomadic poetics involve turbulent opacity, the poems composing, recomposing, decomposing before the reader's eyes.

The poem as a sand storm? Here I also think of the water-filled tunnel leading to the Upper Paleolithic Chauvet cave opaque with kicked-up silt by the diver-nomad-poet swimming through.

In line with nomadic drift, the poem becomes a poem-oasis, or "poasis (punning as well on *poesis,* from the Greek word for "making," generally understood today to mean "the making of poetry"). "Nomadic poetics" and "poasis" suggest that for Joris the world has become a symbolic desert, evoking Jerome Rothenberg's term, "The New Wilderness," an update twist on T.S. Eliot's vision of "The Wasteland." Joris's "desert," however, is hardly empty; there is an electric friction in his writing, a ragged palimpsest of words seeing through or being blocked by other words. In our correspondence, I proposed that Pound's *Pisan Cantos* struck me as the primary predecessor example of rhizomic procedures for our age, and that Pierre's poem "Winnetou Old" was somewhat beholden to the Cantos. Pierre disagreed with my latter point and wrote me back the following:

> I don't think "Winnetou Old" goes directly to or from *The Cantos,* though obviously the C's were essential to my sense of poetry from early on. WO in fact arose from a strange mass of shapeless near automatic writing, some 20 pages or so, that came out of the blue in an Indian restaurant in Tooting at the tail-end of a solitary boozy lunch. It then took me a few months to puzzle out those non-lineated prose ramblings & find a way of setting them up on the page. And yes, there is some Dante and some Italian connectivity (though the latter is radical politics of the opposite sort of Pound's—as the Bridgadi Rossi were still active at the time I wrote it). The core figure, who weirdly disappeared in the main, was a narrating voice, half-hallucinatory, that was "Winnetou," the Karl May fictive Mescalero chief who came to me, returning as a rundown contemporary old Indian, the kind you could meet in

most towns along RTE 66 in New Mexico or Arizona. I figured there was also some Castaneda & some Artaud in there or in the voice I was hearing.

With Pierre's words in mind, I returned to *Poasis* and re-read "Lemur Mornings," at 24 pages the longest poem in the collection. While this poem moves faster with less contextualization than other poems in the book, its "flux of ruptures," "warp speed," and "constant destabilization of view point" is typical of the writing in *Poasis.* Here is the beginning of the first of eight (relentlessly vertical on the page) "Lemur Mornings:"

caught may in coattails
aztec drudge goddess
pianola payback hogs
these last testamentary folds
quadrants drive & divide
blindfold trees new
greenage acres the ford
uptime brought to you
carries over the noise
the disc monthly
microsoft conjunctions
smudge the stellar
meals the spillover
a major backup snuggles
close & wet & warm
child's play a haystack
shoves a needle home
carry-over from winter
tour yacking on the frozen
tundra radioactivated
mink coats coatliqueued...

The methodology implicit here is glossed in another poem, "Animals to the Point:"

do not come to a point
flow, keep moving
the sound from just
below to just above
modulate the
unending lines,
start again in
the middle, nel
mezzo sing it anew,
sparrow,
finch,
do not come
to a point.

The writing in "Lemur Mornings" is apparently automatic writing moving so fast that in comparison a draft of some lines from *Canto* 74, described by Richard Sieburth as "rapid… swift, heavily enjambed verse units; in the onrush of inspiration…" reads almost stately. It yields its meaning in a way that, in contrast, makes the Lemur passage appear to be, as Joris puts it in another poem, "shoveling / sand & mica into our eyes…" Here is the Pound:

infantile synthesis
    in Barabas
minus Hemingway—
  minus Antheil—
  ebullient
by name Thomas Wilson
Mr. K said nothing
  foolish
in one whole month
  nothing foolish
if we weren't dumb
we wdn't be in *here*

When typing up his notebook material later, Pound lengthened some of these 12 lines, turning them into 5, which also made them more available. The reading problem here is one of referentiality; one needs Sieburth's notes to learn that Wilson and Mr. K are Pound's fellow prisoners at the Disciplinary Training Center outside of Pisa.

In archeology, a "core meander" is the initial line of an engraving; lines that follow, attached to or in relation to the core meander, are called "branch meanders." As a language nomad (on a jet-powered camel), we can think of Joris's writing in "Lemur Mornings" as meanders bereft of their core, or as unmoored branch meanders that occasionally intersect with the poet's main fire source, the poetry of the Rumanian Paul Celan who chose to write in German and to consciously syntactically disintegrate it. As Celan's sterling and primary American translator, Joris has been drenched in the Rumanian's often nearly opaque densities, and it is a mark of his strength that his work shows not a copycat indebtedness but an assimilated transformation of his tormented predecessor.

Pound is a predecessor for Joris in a different way. The elegiac and autobiographical *Pisan Cantos,* identified by Sieburth in his excellent Introduction to the 2003 New Directions edition as Pound's "nomadic poem of exile," fulfills all the requirements of Deleuze's and Guattari's (and by extension, of Joris's) literary rhizome: "recognizing intersections and engagements between seemingly disparate ideas and things… a branching that has no 'center'… Any segment broken off from the rest may serve as a new starting point… it brings all manners of materials into productive contact with one another." The fact that Pound wrote most of the *Pisans* while he was in a tent ("gripped by hoar frost" he writes) is a fascinating if minor aspect of that journey. As for Joris's call for the poet to write in foreign languages, Pound writes in Greek, Latin, Provençal, Italian, French, Spanish, and Portuguese in the *Pisans*. Sieburth again: "Unlike the motif of descent in the earlier Cantos, however, the anamnesia enacted by the *Pisans* is far more internalized or subjective, turning as it does on the poet's free-associational excavation of the various buried strata of his own personal past." And: "it is a particular feature of Pound's schizopoetics (as Deleuzians might call them) that the positions of self and other, subject and object, remain ever unstable, ever convertible."

There are of course some significant differences between what is to be found in the *Pisans* and *Poasis*. Joris is, from an American viewpoint, a sharp liberal thinker with no manic hatreds to expunge. Joris's *Poasis* is also, if not exactly dominated by theories of others, constantly aware of what he has made of them and, to my reading at least, never transgresses against what one might call a rhizomic viewpoint. He writes not as an expatriate prisoner (who in 1945 feared for his life) but as a free intellectual who has been based in America, with academic affiliations, for decades.

Any reader aware of Charles Olson's "Projective Verse" essay may by now have realized that one of its primary commands—"ONE PERCEPTION MUST IMMEDIATELY AND DIRECTLY LEAD TO A FURTHER PERCEPTION"—attributed by Olson to Edward Dahlberg, could be formed based on a careful reading of the the *Pisan Cantos* which Olson read in manuscript in 1946. I read such a command as an attempt to keep poetic movement in an appositional swiftness and away from description and narrative tied to memory. There is a fine example of the fruits of such a practice in a late *Maximus* poem, "As of the Parsonses or Fishermans Field or Cressys Beach or Washington, the Capital, of my Front Yard?" I have in mind the following sequence:

Gassire's
fate to
I FA—to
s-i-n-g the
root of
the Well of the
Liquid of the

Eagle's mouth:
Teonanacatl is also
God's body...

Gassire is the hero of a folktale from Niger who is told that his lute will only sound when it absorbs his pain, blood, breath, and the lifeblood of his son. In Dahomey, a man seeking to see into the future visits a sorcerer who "draws the FA"—fruit stones are thrown like our dice and the way they fall enables the sorcerer to make a prediction. The Well of Mimir is located beneath the Nordic World Tree, Yggdrasill. Odin, turned into an Eagle, let fall from his mouth drops of magic mead and in this way humankind received the gift of poetry. "*Teonanacatl*" is the Nahuatl sacred mushroom and means "God's flesh." So here we have a kind of metonymic syncretism utilizing four mythic systems, a brief rhapsody of "stitched song." The risk here is Poundian: if the nodes do not light up, the dramatic presence will be weak, and the reader's only thoughtful response will be to turn to the reference texts.

After reading the Olson *Selected Letters* in 2002, I wrote to the editor, Ralph Maud: "One of the things that struck me, with some of the intellectual letters, is the way Olson's mind acts when it gets excited. It reminds me of watching a stone being skipped across a pond—hit hit hit pong! The associations come in so fast that each is touched upon, struck, followed by a ricochet, and so on. This is one version of 'one perception must lead directly to the next,' but in a version that often seems to me to work against thinking. In contrast, some of the best poems seem slower than the above procedure, with quick decisive moments, but with enough of the image or material offered for the reader to grasp before being taken forward. 'The Librarian,' for example, or 'In Cold Hell...' I am wondering what if anything accounts for such speed. Is this vertical thought (as Olson once proposed)? An attempt to discharge a contellational moment so that all nodes are present at once?"

[2003-2010], *ActionYes*, 2011

ERRATICS

Introduction: Fifteen years ago I discovered a cache of worksheets that I had abandoned in the early 1990s. Going through them, I found fascinating passages and lines in poems that as poems did not work. Rather than losing this material with everything else, I typed it up. I think there must have been a hundred or so entries, one to five or six lines each. Since there was no continuity, I put the cut out pieces in a lettuce dryer, spun it, and ask Caryl to pick them out one by one. Her random pick determined the order in which they appeared. I called them "Erratics" after the boulders one finds in fields, provenance unknown. Hunger Press published them as a chapbook in 2000.

A couple of years later, I reprinted them in a revised form in My Devotion, *Black Sparrow Press, 2004. Several years after that, I again edited them and added a few of the sightings, aphorisms, and probings that had appeared in some of my books. I also added some quotations of writers and artists whose insights have stayed with me over the decades.*

This is now the final version of "Erratics," the form of which is once again determined by Caryl's random pick (other than for the first and final entries). This last entry is Northrop Frye's penetrating statement on Blake's figure of Enion, from "The Four Zoas," whose lament is the epigram to The Price of Experience. *The first entry concerns the multifoliate spider experience in 1962 that has invested my poetry with a daemon familiar.*

The challenge of such notations is to avoid the traps associated with aphorisms: clichés, truisms, commonplace. Here, while many of the entries reflect each other, the random pick creates a shifting galaxy. My aim has been in this labyrinth of tesserae to register the focal points, and the gists and piths, that have supported my poetics over the years. Such are set against a backdrop of speculations on the origins of image-making initially worked out in my book Juniper Fuse: Upper Paleolithic Imagination & the Construction of the Underworld.

*

1]: 1962, Kyoto: There was a gorgeous red, yellow and green Aranea centered in her web attached to a persimmon tree in the Okumura backyard. I got used to taking a chair and a little table out there under the web where I'd read. After several weeks of "spider sitting" the weather turned chill, with rain and gusting wind. One afternoon I found the web wrecked, the spider gone. Something went through me that I can only describe as the sensation of the loss of one loved. I cried, and for several days felt nauseous and absurd. When I tried to make sense out of my reaction, I recalled César Vallejo's poem "La araña"—"The Spider"—which I first read in Bloomington, Indiana, in 1958, right at the time that I had started to get serious about writing poetry. Like the death of the Kyoto spider, the poem had gone right through me. I could not get it out of my mind for months:

The Spider

It is an enormous spider that now cannot move;
a colorless spider, whose body,
a head and an abdomen, bleeds.

Today I watched it up close. With what effort
toward every side
it extended its innumerable legs.
And I have thought about its invisible eyes,
the spider's fatal pilots.

It is a spider that tremored caught
on the edge of a rock;
abdomen on one side,
head on the other.

With so many legs the poor thing, and still unable
to free itself. And, on seeing it
confounded by its fix
today, I have felt such sorrow for that traveler.

It is an enormous spider, impeded by
its abdomen from following its head.
And I have thought about its eyes
and about its numerous legs…
And I have felt such sorrow for that traveler!

A week later, I decided to motorcycle out to northwest Kyoto and visit Gary Snyder. Gary was not home, so I had tea with Joanne Kyger and, late in the afternoon, started the half-hour drive back home. Riding south on Junikendoori, it appeared that the motorcycle handlebars had become ox horns and that I was riding on an ox. A lumber company turned into a manger of baby Jesus and kneeling Wise men. I forced myself to stay aware that I was in moving traffic. Looking for a place to turn off, I spotted Nijo Castle with its big tourist bus parking lot. Getting off my ox-cycle, I felt commanded to circumambulate the square Castle and its moat. I saw what seemed to be Kyger's eyeballs in the moat water. At the northwest corner, I felt commanded to look up: some thirty feet above my head was the spider completely bright red, the size of a human adult, flexing her legs as if attached to and testing her web. After maybe thirty seconds the image began to fade…

In my spider vision, the green and yellow of Aranea's abdomen disappeared. The visionary spider was all red.

I had been given a totemic gift that would direct my relationship to poetry. Out of my own body, I was to create a matrix strong enough in which to live and hunt.

2]: Robert W. Brockway: "It is very doubtful that we have any myths that could be traced back to the last Ice Age, although Wilhelm Schmidt, Mircea Eliade, and other scholars have made such claims. Both, for example, think that the creation story of the animal who dives into deep water to bring up the stuff of which the earth is made originated in central Asia and was brought to the Americas in Paleolithic times."

3]: A squirrel peers, traffic-confused,
through its Jurassic periscope
darts out
flattened anthem.

4]: As an early form of Ariadne, Arihagne ("the utterly pure") was a spinning hag or sorceress who enjoyed intercourse with the labyrinth and its grotesque inhabitant. When patriarchal consciousness overwhelmed matriarchal centering, Ariadne became a "maiden to be rescued," who "falling in love" with the hero Theseus gave him a "clew" or thread that would enable him to get in and out and, while in, to slaughter the sleeping Minotaur. The labyrinth, without its central hybrid, was thus emptied of animality.

5]: The uroboros is hardly "prior to any process, eternal" (Neumann à la Jung), but rather a major arrest of movement drawing into its vortex an overwhelming preoccupation with mother-goddessing the earth (carrying in its wake the attribution to women of many of the horrors to be found in nature). Of relevance here is a little poem by Charles Olson excluded from *The Maximus Poems:*

the IMMENSE ERROR
of *genderizing*
the 'Great Mother'

incalculable
damage

6]: Reality is a feminine wall
soft and cloud-like, a white Hermitage with a skeleton
of steel.

7]: In the beginning was touch, walls everywhere, signed by finger or palm. Hand negative, color radiating out, hand-embedded wall turned altar, negative hand. "The Spaniards would cut an Indian's hands off and leave them dangling by a shred of skin and they would send him on saying 'Go now, spread the news to your chiefs.'" Among such spirit hands I wander today, my hands swinging, horror momentos, at my side. This hand is an outline of Hispaniola on which I locate My Lai.

8]: Hans Peter Duerr: "In order for [these night travelers] to understand their own essence, they had to descend to that place, to return to the uterus of she who gave birth to everything, the place of origin not only of humans, but of all creatures of nature…

This act of insight was at the same time also an act of love, which would have represented incest with the mother if at the place of origin incest itself had not been dissolved together with the barrier to incest. There is no sin at the place of origin. Where there are no longer any norms, no norms can be violated. Knowledge of the place of origin means: dissolution of the separation of things from each other…

In later times, in the classical Greek period, people spoke of 'knowledge of memory.' This is actually a watered-down form of what in archaic times was a factual leaving behind the 'world of separation' and a return to the unifying womb of things, which knew no knowledge and no object of knowledge, no above and no below, no animals or people, no men or women….

Archaic humans… possessed the insight that one had to leave the world, that one could become 'tame' only if before one had been 'wild,' that one could only live in the true sense of the world if one had proved one's willingness to die…

In order to be able to live within the order, in other words, in order to to be consciously tame or domesticated, one had to have lived in the wilderness. One could know what *inside* meant only if one had once been *outside.*"

9]: In contrast to the rich pantheon symbolized by the double helix/dyadic Kundalini, a starker variant on the vertically-streamed center is presented by the erect phallus that appears to grow out of a foundational vulva (see the portable object from La Placard, in *Juniper Fuse,* p. 235). Rather than appearing as an aperture in a phallic shaft or as a triangular hole near the base of a World Tree, this vulva seems to produce her own phallus. To put it idiomatically, this is a hole that grows into a pole.

10]: I keep recalling the Ashbery/Yau reading at the LA La Cienega Palmer Gallery in 1985—the audience staring into the sliding vortices of the words, vaults within vaults. An audience transfixed, unhearing—or hearing the mumble of art, freed from the coiling umbilicus of the street. I wanted to shout: Johns! Don't let them escape the street here! I could hear moments of imagination in the poems, but they wavered, blips in a magma of spectator distance, art as a curtain pulled across a doorless wall. A fringe to finger, while the "real" ceremony, outside the gallery, shifted gears in the city's storied guts.

11]: Quasimodo: Each stands alone on the heart of the earth
transfixed by a ray of sunlight:
all at once
evening.

12]: Aleister Crowley and, later, Kenneth Grant, sought to hang intercourse with the cocoons of an alien grandeur, as if the act provides magical access to extra-terrestrial worlds. Before we dismiss their fractal claims, we must spend more time running our fingers over the runic engravings on the inner side of the gold and leaden gate that occasionally opens just a crack in orgasm.

13]: In Tantrik sexual magic, the two ingredients of the Great Rite can be *sukra* (semen) and *rakta* (menstrual blood). The sulfurous red ingredient in alchemical gold-making probably at times was this female essence (the *rubedo,* or precious red "stone" that sweats blood and turns the world to gold, and is also a conjunction of a whitened queen and a reddened King—such a blending could be seen as a *pinkening*). Some images of the labyrinth have not a Minotaur but a rose at the center, a sign that a transformation has taken place. Seven days, across her period, the Old King is dissolved, rinsed of himself, his selves, lost in her "bath," her anabasis.

14]: Robert Kelly: The Subjective
is not the opposite of the rigorous.
It is the most rigorous, the most difficult.
The precise subjective is what the philosophers are too
lazy & too generalizing to labor, scientists too
frightened to search out.

The Objective is p.r. for the Generalization.
Objective Order, so-called, is mental artifact,
Consensus, "collective consciousness,"
"lethargy of custom (STC"

The "objective" is a consolation prize for those
who've lost the real.

15]: Jake Page: "For some American Indians, the continent of North America is known as Turtle Island. Even more widespread is the theme of the earth diver, the figure who must dive into the depths of the primeval, undifferentiated world of water and bring up the makings of earth to provide a place for the creatures to live. Thus was primal order created from primal chaos, the void. The earth diver is common among the Inuits and the Athapascan people of the Arctic and far north; among many tribes of the Plains, the southeast, and the Northeast; as well as among many tribes of California and western Arizona. It is a common theme also in central Asia, Mongolia, and Siberia, as well as among the Ainu of Japan and some of the northernmost peoples of Europe. This suggests that the essential features of this version of creation are something those who would become American Indians brought with them."

16]:

Faceless Laussel turns to her held up, notched, blood-filled horn.
Drink from your own core.

17]: One must look long and hard at coitus to escape intellectual inhibition. Coitus: bridge and windmill, furnace and vault into which the dreamer is dipped and held, as if by animal tongs, or tongues. Most poetry appears to be inhibited in this regard relative to psychoanalytically-oriented ethnography (Róheim, Ferenczi, Klein—all Hungarians!). Paradise from a creative viewpoint means: no fear, rather, fearlessness; anything, is, can be, material.

18]: Corman:	Hamill:
wild seas (ya to Sado shoring up the great star stream	High over wild seas surrounding Sado Island, the river of heaven
summer grass warriors dreams ruins	Summer grasses: all that remains of great soldiers' imperial dreams
cruel! under the helmet cricket	Ungraciously, under a great soldier's empty helmet, a cricket sings
quiet into rock absorbing cicada sounds	Lonely silence, a single cicada's cry sinking into stone

Two American poets translating haiku from Bashō's *Oku no hosomichi*: Corman (translating with Kamaike Susumu): language as enactment, the reader interprets. Hamill: language as interpretation, the reader abandoned. Corman/Kamaike are deft where Hamill is pleonastic and imprecise (crickets don't sing; cicadas don't cry). In a haiku-like poem of his own, Corman writes:

> The cicada
> singing isn't;
> that sound's its life.

19]: Sunday afternoon. I squat in my mother's arch, eating, the black beckons, so in I go, crawling to I know not where. The terror within my own shoulder space is exceeded by the instinct that I might fully crawl out of the frame my mother dimensioned me with—but to continue is finally to return, doubled back on my umbilical possibility, and it is on the way back that I scratch on the wall what might be thought of as the observation that since I ceased being an animal, I have not know what to do with myself.

20]: Ah, the seltzer of self, the carbonated, carboniferous antiquity of the ever-evaporating self!

21]: My basic exercise in Reichian therapy (1968) was to lie on my back, naked, knees raised, legs falling out and being brought back together in coordination with breathing amply in and out (at "out" the knees flopped to the side—at "in" they came up together) AND to stay in eye contact with Dr. Sidney Handelman while one of us talked. The more I stayed in eye contact while doing this kind of breathing, the more I felt my body—which led me into severe emotional corners. After a year of this exercise, with all its consequent meanders, I started to feel a streaming sensation in my feet and fingertips which, into the second year, gradually passed through my body to the point that near the end of the therapy in 1969 a bracing streaming would take place throughout my entire body immediately upon commencing the exercise. To be naked on one's back, knees raised, under the searching eyes of a clothed adult, evokes what is earliest in us, our infancy, being suffused with feeling, inducting and responding.

However, some of my success in Reichian therapy went to my head. For several years afterwards, I was inconsiderate of others and insensitive to their as well as my own foibles.

22]: Carlos Castaneda: *Sunday, April 15, 1962* As I was getting ready to leave, I decided to ask don Juan once more about the enemies of a man of knowledge. I argued that I could not return for some time, and it would be a good idea to write down what he had to say and then think about it while I was away.

He hesitated for a while, but then began to talk.

"When a man starts to learn, he is never clear about his objectives. His purpose is faulty; his intent is vague. He hopes for rewards that will never materialize, for he knows nothing of the hardships of learning.

"He slowly begins to learn—bit by bit at first, then in big chunks. And his thoughts soon clash. What he learns is never what he pictured, or imagined, and so he begins to be afraid. Learning is never what one expects. Every step of learning is a new task, and the fear the man is experiencing begins to mount mercilessly, unyieldingly. His purpose becomes a battlefield.

"And then he has stumbled upon the first of his natural enemies: Fear! A terrible enemy—treacherous, and difficult to overcome. It remains concealed at every turn of the way, prowling, waiting. And if the man, terrified in its presence, runs away, his enemy will have put an end to his quest."

"What will happen to the man if he runs away in fear?"

"Nothing happens to him except that he will never learn. He will never become a man of knowledge. He will perhaps be a bully, or a harmless, scared man; at any rate, he will be a defeated man. his first enemy will have put an end to his cravings."

"And what can he do to overcome fear?"

"The answer is very simple. He must not run away. He must defy his fear, and in spite of it he must take the next step in learning, and the next, and the next. He must be fully afraid, and yet he must not stop. That is the rule! And a moment will come when his first enemy retreats. The man begins to feel sure of himself. His intent becomes stronger. Learning is no longer a terrifying task.

"When this joyful moment comes, the man can say without hesitation that he has defeated his first natural enemy."

"Does it happen at once, don Juan, or little by little?"

"It happens little by little, and yet the fear is vanquished suddenly and fast."

"But won't the man be afraid again if something new happens to him?"

"No. Once a man has vanquished fear, he is free from it for the rest of his life because, instead of fear, he has acquired clarity—a clarity of mind which erases fear. By then a man knows his desires; he knows how to satisfy those desires. He can anticipate the new steps of learning, and a sharp clarity surrounds everything. The man feels that nothing is concealed.

"And thus he has encountered his second enemy: clarity! That clarity of mind, which is so hard to obtain, dispels fear, but also blinds.

"It forces the man never to doubt himself. It gives him the assurance he can do anything he pleases, for he sees clearly into everything. And he is courageous because he is clear, and he stops at nothing because he is clear. But all that is a mistake; it is like something incomplete. If the man yields to this make-believe power, he has succumbed to his second enemy and will fumble with learning. He will rush when he should be patient, or he will be patient when he should rush. And he will fumble with learning until he winds up incapable of learning anything more."

"What becomes of a man who is defeated in that way, don Juan? Does he die as a result?"

"No, he doesn't die. His second enemy has just stopped him cold from trying to become a man of knowledge; instead, the man may turn into a buoyant warrior, or a clown. Yet his clarity for which he has paid so dearly will never change to darkness and fear again. He will be clear as long as he lives, but he will no longer learn, or yearn for, anything."

"But what does he have to do to avoid being defeated?"

"He must do what he did with fear: he must defy his clarity and use it only to see, and wait patiently and measure carefully before taking new steps; he must think, above all, that his clarity is almost a mistake. And a moment will come when he will understand that his clarity was only a point before his eyes. And thus he will have overcome his second enemy, and will arrive at a position where nothing can harm him anymore. This will not be a mistake. It will not be only a point before his eyes. It will be true power.

"He will know at this point that the power he has been pursuing for so long is finally his. He can do with it whatever he pleases. His ally is at his command. His wish is the rule. He sees all that is around him. But he has also come across his third enemy: Power!

"Power is the strongest of all enemies. And naturally the easiest thing to do is to give in; after all, the man is truly invincible. He commands; he begins by taking calculated risks, and ends up making rules, because he is a master.

"A man at this stage hardly notices his third enemy closing in on him. And suddenly, without knowing, he will certainly have lost the battle. His enemy will have turned him into a cruel, capricious man."

"Will he lose his power?"

"No, he will never lose his clarity or his power."

"What then will distinguish him from a man of knowledge?"

"A man who is defeated by power dies without really knowing how to handle it. Power is only a burden upon his fate. Such a man has no command over himself, and cannot tell when or how to use his power."

"Is the defeat by any of these enemies a final defeat?"

"Of course it is final. Once one of these enemies overpowers a man there is nothing he can do."

"Is it possible, for instance, that the man who is defeated by power may see his error and mend his ways?"

"No. Once a man gives in he is through."

"But what if he is temporarily blinded by power, and then refuses it?"

"That means his battle is still on. That means he is still trying to become a man of knowledge. A man is defeated only when he no longer tries, and abandons himself."

"But then, don Juan, it is possible that a man may abandon himself to fear for years, but finally conquer it."

"No, that is not true. If he gives in to fear he will never conquer it, because he will shy away from learning and never try again. But if he tries to learn for years in the midst of his fear, he will eventually conquer it because he will never have really abandoned himself to it."

"How can he defeat his third enemy, don Juan?"

"He has to defy it, deliberately. He has to come to realize the power he has seemingly conquered is in reality never his. He must keep himself in line at all times, handling carefully and faithfully all that he has learned. If he can see that clarity and power, without his control over himself, are worse than mistakes, he will reach a point where everything is held in check. He will know then when and how to use his power. And thus he will have defeated his third enemy.

"The man will be, by then, at the end of his journey of learning, and almost without warning he will come upon the last of his enemies: Old age! This enemy is the cruelest of all, the one he won't be able to defeat completely, but only fight away.

"This is the time when a man has no more fears, mo more impatient clarity of mind—a time when all his power is in check, but also the time when he has an unyielding desire to rest. If he gives in totally to his desire to lie down and forget, if he soothes himself in tiredness, he will have lost his last round, and his enemy will cut him down into a feeble old creature. His desire to retreat will overrule all his clarity, his power, and his knowledge.

"But if the man sloughs off his tiredness, and lives his fate through, he can then be called a man of knowledge, if only for the brief moment when he succeeds in fighting off his last, invincible enemy. That moment of clarity, power, and knowledge is enough."

23]: There is an archetypal poem, and it most ancient design is probably the labyrinth. One suddenly cuts in, leaving the green world for the apparent stasis and darkness of the cave. The first words of a poem nose forward toward a confrontation with what the writer is only partially aware of, or may not be prepared to address until it emerges, flushed forth by digressions and meanders.

Poetry twists toward the unknown and seeks to realize something beyond the poet's initial awareness. What is seeks to know might be described as the unlimited interiority of its initial impulse.

24]: Since the hidden is bottomless, totality is more invisible than visible. Insistence on a totality in which life is totally visible, is the anti-dream, Hades deprived of his cave, Satan attempting to establish a kingdom—or death camp—solely on earth.

25]: The human is initially indeterminate, unclosed. The open Aurignacian vulva evokes a simple labyrinth with an exit and stresses, sexually, torsion. It seems possible that an early intercourse/pregnancy association was torsion (underscored by the fire drill) and that the subsequent uroboros belongs to agricultural peoples, with stress on the enclosed seed, the male as "star" i.e., patriarchy in contrast to an earlier more mysterious "open" union, in which the female was both place-of-fire and phallus (the so-called "Venuses" fit neatly in the palm).

26]: The alchemist Fulcanelli: "the picture of the labyrinth is thus offered to us as emblematic of the whole labor of the Work, with its two major difficulties, one that path which must be taken in order to reach the center—where the bitter combat of the two natures takes place—the other the way which the artist must follow in order to emerge. It is here that *the thread of Ariadne* becomes necessary for him, if he is not to wander among the winding paths of the task, unable to extricate himself."

27]: As species disappear, the Upper Paleolithic grows more vivid. As living animals disappear, the first outlines become more dear, not as reflections of a day world, but as the primal outlines of psyche, the shaping of the underworld, the point at which Hades was an animal. The "new wilderness" (the term is Jerome Rothenberg's) is thus the spectral realm created by the going out of animal life and the coming in, in our time, of these primary outlines. Our tragedy is to search further and further back for a common nonracial trunk in which the animal is not separated out of the human, while we destroy the turf on which we actually stand.

28]: Robert Kelly: "The typical mistake of religion has been to assume that what the priest does at the altar is somehow transmittable to me, poor dumb me sitting in the pew, kneeling there with my mouth open, that somehow some magic that he can perform in Latin or with his hands or in Mithra with a cut bull can transform me. And the superstition that lies there forgets that I must do something too; even if the magic part works 10 minutes later my transformation falls off me just as I dry out after coming in from the rain. It may be real rain in that church, maybe there's real blood, but somehow my habits are sufficient to drain that out again, purify my animal nature. I think the poem gets harder in that way that a religion, if it were a real thing, would be a hard thing because it would inevitably be personal, it would inevitably be something *you* have to do & *I* have to do. That if I'm given a poem which tells me the whole thing I have no work to do with it. It can't save me then. I don't know exactly what I have to be saved from, but let's allow salvation for a moment—I can't be saved unless I do it myself. And I think poems become hard exactly as religion fades away—because we've got to get the sense that nothing is really easy. There's a certain kind of person who will inevitably go to *The Cantos* or *The Maximus Poems* or some other ballbuster & make that his destiny for a year or two years, who recognizes however dumb he is when he starts out, there is something in this complexity that if he just goes through it, if he follows the dance or the pattern or climbs the rock, he will have passed through a process which is not just a process of perception or critical judgment but a process of transformation."

29]: Orgasm
        drops me
   for a few seconds
              out, and it is my business to know
   the "no nature" of this out,
   which I suspect today
   is the concretization of *sunyata,*
   the body   gong of the void
   the soul   in reverberation
   clambers back to its bone,
   its Cro-Magnon loam,
   for also, in orgasm, all bones are
      on loan.

30]: The poem: a tumor-entangled, umbilical sight-line.

31]: Magenta globes of orchids, enfolding
   snow white blossoms. Scarlet dots in stipple
   on a daffodil ground, the fury of Eden,
   cobra sprung, liver brown.

32]: Weston La Barre drawing on Emile Durkheim: "Supernatural projections can derive only from the secular historical reality-states of society. There was no High God at Les Trois Frères because there were no secular political structures."

33]: Anton Ehrenzweig: "Any creative search, whether for a new image or idea, involves the scrutiny of an often astronomical number of possibilities. The correct choice between them cannot be made as a conscious weighing up of each single possibility cropping up during the search; if attempted, it would only lead us astray. A creative search resembles a maze with many nodal points.

From each of these points many possibly pathways radiate in all directions leading to further crossroads where a new network of high- and by-ways come into view. Each choice would be easy if we could command an aerial view of the entire network of nodal points and radiating pathways still lying ahead. This is never the case. If we could map out the entire way ahead, no further search would be needed. As it is, the creative thinker has to make a decision about his route without having the full information needed for his choice. This dilemma belongs to the essence of creativity."

34]: Infants who, unlike Australopithecus,
could no longer cling to the mother's body hair.
So, a baby sling
out of animal tendon, at the beginning of the Pleistocene.
Perhaps the earliest sling,
with the baby as its shot.
Cobble or skull cradle, subsequent spear-thrower,
tension point on the bow thong against which
the notched arrow presses—

did a baby sling
carry first mind away
from the jaws of *Dinofelis barlowii*?

35]: *Looking at Hans Bellmer drawings:*
Nippular door knob
A woman vomiting a thermometer
The pelvic gaze
Oneiric orgy on a scaffolding enfolding Baudelairian lampreys
Possession as permutational symmetry
Lingual oysters roving in a sole
Under a café table sprouting bat wings: Hydra's smile-sewn skull

Masturbating the fifth and lowest breast
Inside the scrotal pile-up: The Holy Crater
Pulling open her belly brickwork to inspect the fetal lounge

36]: I look at a reproduction of Hiroshige's "Plum Garden, Kumata," and sense paradise. Nascent white plum blossoms dot a persimmon raw silk sky, over moss-green grass without depth or blade. It is not Whitman's grass. It is, relative to Whitman, inorganic, artificial (as the grass in paradise would have to be)—yet because of the shade, one feels change, but of such slowness that permanence almost holds. The actual and the visionary—not a churning visionary, more a delicate tilting of the actual toward the visionary—coincide, have lost seam, are in relaxed and radiant fusion.

37]: I have thought more about poetry while translating César Vallejo than while reading anyone else. Influence through translation is different from influence through reading masters in one's own tongue. I am creating an American version out of a Spanish text, and if Vallejo is to enter my own poetry, he must do so through what I have already, as a translator, turned him into. This is, in the long run, very close to being influence by myself, or better, *by a self I have created to mine.* In this, I do not feel that my poetry reflects Vallejo's. He taught me that ambivalence and contradiction are facets of metaphoric probing, and he gave me permission to try anything in my quest for an authentic alternative world in poetry.

I think the key lesson Vallejo holds today may be that of a poet learning how to become imprisoned, as it were, in global life as a whole, and in each moment in particular. All his poetry, including the blistering Eros that opens up a breach in the wall separating mother and lover in *Trilce,* urges the poet to confront his own destiny and to stew in what is happening to him—and also to believe that his bewildering situation is significant. To be bound to, or imprisoned in, the present, includes confronting not only life as it really is but also psyche as it really is not—weighing all affirmation against, in an American's case, our imperial obsessions and our own intrinsic dark.

38]: No one has returned from death—other than Saint Generalization.

39]: William Blum: "No American should be allowed to forget that the nation of Iraq, the society of Iraq, have been destroyed, ruined, a failed state. The Americans, beginning 1991, bombed for 12 years, with one excuse or another; then invaded, then occupied, overthrew the government, killed wantonly, tortured... The people of that unhappy land have lost everything—their homes, their schools, their electricity, their clean water, their environment, their neighborhoods, their mosques, their archeology, their jobs, their careers, their professionals, their state-run enterprises, their physical health, their mental health, their health care, their welfare state, their women's rights, their religious tolerance, their safety, their security, their children, their parents, their past, their present, their future, their lives... More than half the population either dead, wounded, traumatized, in prison, internally displaced, or in foreign exile... The air, soil, water, blood and genes drenched with depleted uranium... The most awful birth defects... Unexploded cluster bombs lie in wait for their children to pick them up... An army of young Islamic men went to Iraq to fight the American invaders; they left the country more militant, hardened by war, to spread across the Middle East, Europe and Central Asia... A river of blood runs alongside the Euphrates and Tigris through a country that may never be put back together again."

40]: Wallace Stevens, why did you describe revolutionaries as "hairy-backed... hump-armed... serpent kin... in clownish boots... a little sly"? Why did you write to Latimer in 1935: "The

Italians have as much right to take Ethiopia from the coons as the coons had to take it from the boa constrictors"? Or to say to Cole, at the 1952 National Book Awards: "This is the poem that mentions the womb. I can't even pronounce the filthy thing."

41]: Derrida like a virus in Artaud's texts, autocatalytically spreading here and there. After two hours, the standing-room-only audience wandered out of the MOMA auditorium. Only a handful, I am convinced, understood anything Derrida said. But come they did, to view the appearance of a "holy man" on Hotel Artaud's shit-smeared balcony.

42]: I met a man who told me everything about man. As he spoke, I wandered ebony corridors, obsidian shafts. His fingers were stained with breasts. He claimed that he issued from everyone and that the JFK assassination was the gateway to Atlantis. Oh no you don't, I said, as he gripped the right wing of my girdle, I'm not your toucan, not your marble.

The man who told me everything about man was windy, empty clothes, a meaty ramrod with sucking porticoes. He told me everything is what a man thinks he is. He said that man is a projective demon, whose tendrils shoot their foragings back into the bottomless need to be his own mother.

On Atlantis, he continued, there were no men. Kennedy was preparing to reveal this. Men are post-Atlantic; that is, they only, and vaguely, remember a time… a time when…

man was an egg dipped in blood,
man was a Sunday outing.

43]: When headhunting was suppressed among the Toradja of Celebes, there was intense anxiety lest the ancestral spirits, no longer fed with a "harvest" of enemy heads, would perforce eat the villagers themselves. Try "war" instead of "headhunting" in this thought: when war was suppressed there was intense anxiety lest ancestral spirits no longer fed with a harvest of souls would perforce eat the living themselves. Does war, then, at base, exist as soul food for the dead?

44]: The lack of a Sisyphean load
drives me horizontal.
I wander, accidental acolyte,
the San Christobal de la Casas zócalo,
weighing the USA-shadowed blocks, the timidity of the
 pizza.
Is my lack a new load?
Could be, white spectre that I am
Could be, white spectre of I am

The work is self-
indented meaning in a world that denies worlds.

I stand within I, as in shuttle exhaust,
an atom in the fulgurating lift off.

45]: Kenneth Rexroth: "Jerome Rothenberg is one of the truly contemporary American poets who has returned United States poetry to the mainstream of international modern literature. At the same time, he is a true autochthon, only here and now could have produced him—a swinging orgy of Martin Buber, Marcel Duchamp, Gertrude Stein and Sitting Bull."

Rothenberg, our Polynesian navigator through the ethnosphere.

46]: As far as poetry is concerned, "the bitter combat of the two natures" can be understood as the poet's desire to discover something new or unique versus the spectral desire of tradition to defeat the new and to continue asserting its own primacy. It is a "bitter" combat because the realization which writing a poem may provide is inevitably partial. The Minotaur is at best crippled, never slain, and the poet never strides forth from the labyrinth heroic and intact. At best, he crawls forth "wounded," as in the cry of César Vallejo in his poem "Intensity and Height"; more often than not, he never emerges at all. The poet never leaves this site of combat with a total poem because such a poem would confirm that the discrepancy between desire and the fulfillment of desire has been eliminated. But since my desire is ultimately to create reality and not merely to observe it, I am bound to be defeated if reality is at stake in my poem's ambition. As I emerge from the poem, regardless of what I have realized while in the poem, I am back in the observable biological continuum, and part of it, part of its absolute mortality.

47]: Sheela-na-gig, the witch in the wall—she takes off! And like a falcon returns, fence-sitting hag, the *hagazussa* bridging culture and wilderness: the mind in paradox, holding against dualistic split-offs. Sheela gapes, Sheela shows through, the back wall void shows through her cunt. I am one with her because, fundamentally, I am a zero, a zero that counts 0 0 0 0 0 all the way back to the om-matriculated other.

48]: EMILY: What the fuck are you doing in my hopscotch?
ANTONIN: I'm fighting the zodiacal hyenas that created these traps!
EMILY: Have you a problem with my British sky?
ANTONIN: Have you a problem with my organless body?
EMILY: Rimbaud is making mincemeat of us in Abyssinia.
ANTONIN: Rimbaud stopped writing poetry because he got close enough to paradise to learn that he could not get in.

49]: Artaud in a phone booth
between the Marquis de Sade and Savonarola,
trying to dial belladonna as they burrow into him—

de Sade to draw out his sphincter,
Savonarola to wringer his heart

sadona   de dada   arola
savosartona   rotolaaa

the booth filling with Araudanola's blood.

50]: Theseus, a tiny male spider, enters a tri-level construction:
look down into the poem, you can see the labyrinth.
Look down into the labyrinth, you can see the web.

51]: Hart Crane drank to split open the ayahuasca cantaloupe he thought was packed with god tongue. Or if not tongue, reptilian dictators resting on the lower depths of his brain. Were a split to have occurred, to whom would the dictation belong? To the anacondas or to Crane? Poets warm their livers at the crossroads of a dilemma that draws and quarters imagination. Poets camping there, squatting, as if in disembowelment, reading their entrails for signs—of the Divine?

52]: *The hole that grows*—in a way that is simultaneously transitive and intransitive—may be one of the most fundamental versions of the logos, or story, of the soul which, according to Heraclitus, grows according to its needs—as does, according to shamans, the World Tree. Increasing in height or depth as the gods or shamanic familiars ascend and dive, the soul's end, or purpose, is always beyond our own, a tunnel generating its own light—or crown of flame. It is a hole grounded in both absence and appearance, a convexcavatious abyss. When it rests for a moment in contraction, some of us experience it as a cave or pit. When it expands beyond what the mind can contemplate, some call it the void.

53]: John Lash: "If dyadic perception is truly primary to the primitive (i.e., original, prelogical) perception of the world, nowhere is the evidence more clear than in the mythology of First Parents represented as Twins. In countless symbolic and figurative expressions, primitive intuition discloses what we now designate scientifically as the structure of DNA, the parenting substance of all organic life. The ancestor couple from Maketu in the Bay of Plenty, New Zealand, are limbically entwined like the coils of DNA: as if genes had faces and bodies, so that they might reveal themselves as supernatural entities, which indeed they must have done in the numinous moment of atavistic vision. Likewise the Chinese Adam and Eve, Fu His and Nu Kua, exhibit long, entwining tails, a perfect image of the double helix as a kind of dyadic Kundalini."

54]: Chaim Soutine: "Once I saw the village butcher slice the neck of a bird and drain the blood out of it. I wanted to cry out, but his joyful expression caught the sound in my throat." Soutine patted his throat and continued: "This cry, I always feel it there. When, as a child, I drew a crude portrait of my teacher, I tried to rid myself of this cry, but in vain. When I painted the beef carcass it was this cry that I wanted to liberate. I still have not succeeded."

55]: Poetry from the beginning is posited,
based, on resistance,   it is a work against,
whether with flint or quill
it is to convert one's boring into a lateral spell,

an ecstatic wandering in which one lives
as if weightless on the hunch of a fingertip—
hunchwork   wonderous release of the body
poised on the burin of itself.

56]: Kenneth Grant: "The mystery of non-being lies at the root of all inspiration."

57]: From the glass wall of Lisita restaurant, Nimes, November, late evening:

in light rain, next to a flock of leaves bypassed by the mistral,
an old man lets his black dog pee, reluctantly pulling on the thin leash—

to remain within the winding paths of the task, or risk emergence from
a labyrinth that has confounded but also provided refuge...

observing and notating, one way to travel and feel ok about
dining within the shadow gore of the amphitheatre.

In Memory of Gustaf Sobin

58]: Train whistle through Ypsilanti, sirenical, rusty, as if brakes were being applied to the engine's genitals. Pipe organ constricted while in full expansion. Tabernacle slaughterhouse factory sounds in a single screaming clangor.

59]: Peter Beard juxtaposes dead African animals with celebrities and fashion models. I doubt that he intends a metaphor, but what bawls out at me from these collages is: fashion and celebrity = dead animals. Not "pheasant under glass" but nude model under poached elephant tusk. Marginal graffiti buzzing blow-ups of the unending destruction of African wildlife. And how does one read Beard himself posed halfway out of a dead crocodile's jaws, scribbling in a notebook? The final grounding of Jonah's emergence? Karen Blixen juxtaposed with a flayed leopard; Francis Bacon's whipped, creamy flesh by African children's bulbous bellies. We will begin dinner with a giraffe fetus, and follow with caviar, driftwood, and someone's legs.

60]: Winding through my language,
the delicate tentacle of an infant's mouth seeking
a maiden camel
on which to cross.

61]: The beginning of the construction of the underworld takes place in Upper Paleolithic caves. To identify this "place under construction" I use the later Greek word "Hades," and it is there that the first evidence of psyche we can relate to occurs. To be in the cave is to be inside an animal—a womb—but to draw there is to seek another kind of birth: an adjustment to the crisis of the animal separating out of the human—or, the Fall. To be inside, to be hidden, to be in Hades—where the human hides in the animal.

62]: Jackson Pollock reclaimed the Aurignacian floor. His next move might have been to extend the floor to the walls and then move onto the ceiling, an entire interior turned into a subjectile. Jack the whipper. Sawfish dancer from the Torres Straits: "with your strong stick, scar the ground! As you stab and score, stoop and bow your head!" Sekhmet's sistrum strings, cat gut and caul.

Line as acrobatic anabasis. The wall ballet in the Pech Merle cave's "Black Fresco": underexposure of a mountain showing through a bison showing through a deer.

63]: Poetry workshops should be taught by boa-constrictors.

64]: For twenty-five years haunted by Robert Creeley's "For love, I would split open your head and place a candle behind your eyes." The man making a vagina out of the woman's mind and then plugging it with his cock. From which "light" flows. Semen illumination. A projection of this poet's erection-loaded head which he would like to split, to Zeusify an image (one that would address him, confirm him). But in the poem he projects his anguish against "her"—and in the name of "love." But how could he have allowed himself to write: "Because I am parentally organized, I would thrust my cock between your eyes. How else maintain and forever elude my need for primal surprise?"

65]: On the mall TV screen
van Gogh's eyes
digitally eye-droppered.

A mortuary of profit plunges through the heartrock.

66:] To write in accordance with what I know is a dead end. I must do the contrary thing: write in accordance with what I seek to know, and intuit that in the crack between knowing and not knowing there is not merely distraction but vision.

67]: The maggot in every artist's craw is his ensign of life.

68]: When I go to prehistoric Europe for depth, am I not in exile to the possibility of depth at home? Indeed, where is "home?" In a media-transfixed planetary "global village," our constellations mix and link, suggesting that no place is without the spore of home. At the same time, our hearts will always be scored by the primal home, locus of exile. The womb in imagination opens out into a realm of ancestors as, simultaneously, it bottlenecks our fate.

69]: Every artist participates in Ariadne. The transformation of the "given" life into a "creative" one not only involves entering a dark or "inner" life, but generating as well resistance substantial enough to test oneself against and to shape the focus of one's work. Having experienced the bestowal of soul (which is the reality of Ariadne), one must liberate the experience in a creative product, must emerge with more than the claim that something "happened" while "inside."

70}: The bear that comes up from the primal waters with mud, as the first signs of earth, on his paws, is perhaps also a Cro-Magnon cave quester with red ochre on his or her hand—it use in this case: to be utilized on a wall in the depths. The cave descent, which resulted in images being made below, adds a twist, and another realm, to the cosmogonic dive, as passageways and chambers become creational sites. It is now believed that the mixing agent for manganese, ochre, and charcoal was cave water, suggesting that, like bottom mud, the agent for pigment was discovered within the realm of the descent.

71]: Passionate Eros suffuses the mind in layers of storm mergers.

This excites the bears in the void
turning honey into ransacked hives.

Poetry:
Sunyata ryori
Emptiness cuisine

72]: According to Weston La Barre, "God is only the infantile shaman's-eye view of a father one has not grown emotionally into, a child's psychic recreation of his Creator."

For E.M. Cioran, "God is our rust, the gradual decay of our substance: when He penetrates us, we think we are elevated, but we descend lower and lower; having reached our end. He crowns our collapse, and so we are 'saved' forever. Sinister superstition, haloed cancer which has eaten away the earth for ages."

For Wallace Stevens, "After one has abandoned a belief in god, poetry is that essence which takes its place as life's redemption."

For Robert Kelly, "religion is primeval entertainment."

73]: July cloudburst, luciflailing maples, sun-burnt top leaves
shredding patter gnomes, pupa ghosts, fairies in a freckled
pounce—

to be in the rush of the core, *to feel the rout side.*

74]: I write below
a wasp nest
strung to the ceiling,
immense weightless grenade of masticated fiber,
inner walls honeycombed with tiny samurai
frozen this past October—

My work here is to bury
and keep alive
a fertile queen.

75]: People of all races in McDonald's, devouring rain forests a football field a second.
Polytheism turns out to be contingent upon the earth's fertile perpetuity.
The gods are not dead—they are, as is the earth, mortal.
An era called: *the death of eternity*

76]: The delectable atmosphere of *A Midsummer Night's Dream,* nature as fairy-flitted paradise, strands of a shamanic world in which spirits communicate. I adore the tree bed in which Titania and Bottom make love, the bottomless dream in which hybrids mingle with fairy queens. There is something of *Midsummer* in our life and love, a sensual, orgasmic mix. I love you so much at sixty-four. Memorial Day: black kids from next door whiz down the sidewalk in carts and on bikes. We just shared a Veuve Cliquot Rosé, with a few ounces of caviar, and some canapés you invented: slices of smoked salmon on tiny crusts smeared with a caper red-onion butter. A Ulyssean homecoming every time I step outside the shower.

77]: First trip to Kyoto, January, 1962: having pulled away from the train station, our small taxi passed through a thick snow fall alongside a canal. Snow flakes seen against bar and club variegated neon: cherry blossom ghosts.

It was here, at this moment, that I began my own transformation.

78]: The Upper Paleolithic is retrieved spar by spar. All of historical mythology hovers over, a meaning cloud so wanting to drizzle drops onto these mute, analphabetic partialforms. To be drawn into these beveled resonances is to confront the abyss of potential form-to-be, a free-wheeling non-systematic Abyss Board where moves subtract as they add—where I play against the Abyss (like Bergman's Knight played chess with Death)—what can I garner, gain, pick up, before I lose?

79]: The natural spinning mind of the earth weaves itself in personifications throughout our humanity. Biological peril is always central, and sublimated by image-making into "scorpion hopscotch," or the imaginative gambling called poetry. It is possible to formulate a perspective that offers a life continuity, from lower life forms, through human biology and sexuality, to the earliest imaginings of our situation, which now seems to be bio-tragically connected with our having separated ourselves out of the animal-hominid world in order to pursue that catastrophic miracle called consciousness. If the labyrinth is a Double Axe, one might see it as humanity's anguished attempt to center a ceaseless duplicity conjured by the evidence that each step forward throws a shadow step backward. And the haft? Phallocentricity that fuses the menstrual/ovulatory cycles into an instrument of inner and outer ceremony which injures but does not restore.

80]: Robert Duncan: "The drama of our time is the coming of all men into one fate, 'the dream of everyone, everywhere.' The fate or dream is the fate of more than mankind. Our secret Adam is written now in the script of the primal cell. We have gone beyond the reality of the incomparable nation or race, the incomparable Jehovah in the shape of a man, the incomparable Book or Vision, the incomparable species, in which identity might hold & defend its boundaries against an alien territory. All things have now come into their comparisons. But these comparisons are the correspondences that haunted Paracelsus, who saw also that the key to man's nature was hidden in the larger nature."

81]: Northrop Frye: "What is needed for creation is a new bicameral mind in which something supplants consciousness."

82]: Linear time, tunnel time. The "light at the end" to justify this struggle, this now. But such "light" is a haze, a distraction from the here and now. Populate the tunnel with bathing elves, bring in the rats. Let's gnaw to a bask, corrode the stiff sides of the image, build in shelves, rose windows, alcoves with access to the child-devouring Saturns of the heart. Unlike trees, we are adrift in a breath bowl, rootless algae, wings searching for angelic bodies.

83]: To be inside Robinson Jeffers' Hawk Tower is to be inside his knobby, tight mind. Steep narrow steps, embowering a music room for Una—a Beulah haven within the cragginess of Robinson's distancing angel. Tower that is menhir, tombstone, cross. Gigantic honeycomb torched by Yeats. Rocks dragged from the Carmel shore. The weight-lifter finding in the air a berth for his life load.

84]: The body piles at Abu Ghraib,
apple-stacked asses like a gigantic Sadean sexual molecule
male all the way through,
the Caucasian subconscious unleashed on the brown body.

I walk Washtenaw Road,
a pupa in a Hydra-tainted imperial chrysalis.

Controlled demolition of the three Towers.
Controlled demolition of our Constitution.
Controlled demolition of our rights.
Controlled demolition of our environment.
Controlled demolition of our ice.

The missile that penetrated the Pentagon:
the Entry not of Christ
but Pat Robertson into Washington.

It is *Alien* o'clock.
When will the truth explode from Bush's chest?

(2004)

85]: N.O. Brown: "Since the one and solid meaning does not in fact reveal itself, the commentary which does establish it becomes the higher revelation." The ultimate goal of criticism is to backdrop poetry, and to foreground criticism. For the late-comer to manipulate the former so that it appears to be belated. N.O. Brown again: "The proper response to poetry is not criticism but poetry."

86]: The poetry I call conventional or "academic" is that which argues in the long run that one must conform to the outer world—poetry as adjustment, as diminution of metaphorical conflagration. Poetry that exposes the literal but remains faithful to its implications. Poetry that says: you must learn to live with the way things are. All poetry is a desire for "cominglings from head to foot" but many poets end up acting as "as pompous High Priest entering by a Secret Place." In a Fallen (= literally organized) world, conventional poetry carries the day because it reinforces and is reinforced by the institutions that support conventions. Avant-garde temptation is to blow up the Mausoleum of Tradition and to present is swirling debris as art.

87]: Garcia Lorca's essay on the "duende" identifies this diablotin of the blood, or bloodmare, which provokes some of the world's great art as a struggle with a wound that never closes. Is Garcia Lorca therefore caught in Ariadne's turnstile, responding to blood that for thousands of years has mesmerized and enraged men as it appeared in rhythm with the moon and the tides and, without violence, ceased, to only re appear again and again?

88]:

At 4 A.M. suddenly waking up with these words in my mind:
Caryl, you are
the greatest adventure of my life!

89]: N.O. Brown: "Each of us is not a human being, but only the symbol of a human being. We are not individuals; we are pieces—tesserae, tokens, or tallies—temporary repositories of value in a game of chance. Paraphrasing Lucretius: the life that mortals live is not their private property: it is more like a torch transmitted in a relay race. It is a game of chance: *de jeu de l'amour et du hazard;* the dicing table of the gods."

90]: Commenting on Michael Maier's alchemical journeys (specifically his 1617 *Symbola aureae mensae*), Jung speaks of Maier "approaching that region of the psyche which was not unjustly said to be inhabited by 'Pans, Satyrs, dog-headed baboons, and half-men.' It is not difficult to see that this region is the animal soul in man. For just as a man has a body which is no different in principle from that of an animal, so also his psychology has a whole series of lower stories in which the specters from humanity's past epochs still dwell, then the animal souls from the age of Pithecanthropus and the hominids, then the 'psyche' of the cold-blooded saurians, and, deepest of all the transcendental mystery and paradox of the sympathetic and parasympathetic psychoid processes."

Here we have an active, vertical midden image of the personal unconscious down through the collective unconscious based on evolutionary scale. One might conclude that "animal souls" began to intermingle with nascent human souls when Cro-Magnon projected and drew/engraved animal and hybrid images.

91]: Northrop Frye: "The world of nature is a completely callous world, and Enion seeing her children suffering in a life of pain, cannot understand what has happened. She knows only that she can never be comforted as long as pain exists, and that she will not cease to be a wandering and mourning spirit until nature has become again the 'happy garden-state' it once was, and in which the vision of God seeing the sparrow fall with concern for its suffering is not a mere 'augury' of the state of innocence but its realization. She is the 'vain shadow of hope' which finds everything short of a complete apocalypse hopeless. She is the part of our minds which dimly realizes that all pleasure is at least partly a dream under an anesthetic. Something is always suffering horribly somewhere, and we can only find pleasure by ignoring that fact. We must ignore it up to a point, or go mad; but in the abyss of consciousness, to which Enion has been banished, there lurks the feeling that joy is based on exclusion, that the Yule log can blaze cheerfully only when the freezing beggars in the streets are, for the moment, left to freeze. It is a terrible song that Enion sings, and disturbing enough to have in the mind a thought which can lead only to madness or apocalypse; yet we cannot eliminate this thought without sacrificing some of our humanity, and the implication that true humanity can be found only in either madness or apocalypse is the dilemma to which all history proceeds."

* * *

AN ANATOMY OF THE NIGHT

Introduction

"An Anatomy of the Night" is a summational work, much of which was written and organized in 2010 and 2011. I call it "summational" because along with the new writing that makes up over half of the poem, there are also six sections of quotations from the work of Géza Rōheim, Wilhelm Reich, James Hillman, A. Alvarez, E.M Cioran, Djuna Barnes, and James Hamilton-Paterson, and another dozen sections (or passages in sections) made up of poems, parts of poems or prose entries previously published (between 1983 and 2011) in such books as Fracture, Novices, From Scratch, Juniper Fuse, An Alchemist with One Eye on Fire, Anticline, *the unpublished "Heaven-Bands" and earlier versions of "Erratics."*

"An Anatomy of the Night" was generated initially off of a draft of "Undulations," a poem I had written for our painter friend, Linda Jacobson, who works and lives in Venice, California:

Open this red door to the menstrual irrigations of the earth
to the pot-headed lordly and deathless hybrids.
Beware of their shadows consuming the shadow you costume here—
the earth wears fluid robes, liquid land and static sea,
their intercourse: a goddess merging with her serpent in and out,
the sky a bath incestuous, momentary cornfields dissolving urn and tower.
Strewn petals of a yoni gust and blend.
Whitman hunched by his menstrual harp—
"Annihilation is injustice" he strums,"each love, each non-love, are unique.
Think of the bull in its factory stall injected merely to provide
burgers for you sitting on your creviced dot.

How many slaughters since you glimpsed the spider queen's tiara beacon
sweep across the Goya consensus: that the disasters of war
are the genetic inheritance of man's petrified snore."

I turned to Bashō's compote of cicada-absorbed rock,
to Linda Jacobson's vision of a stone's magenta folds,
beholdings in which the moon swims Atlantis-ward through eons of russet doom,
passing chakra by chakra through the serpent panels of our spines
Kundalini now embedded in the easter unfolding of the buried from the slime.
Praise for these radial stages layered with animals and yellow sand,
interlocked stages released by fountains arising from when we were masts.

Earth of the Shahnameh, pink earth quilted with tufts of violet grass,
earth of clouds like entangled, albino eels,
earth of miniver and rose rock alive as coral reefs
in which the dead can be glimpsed, fuscous hands gripped in prayer,
earth of cobalt bird-filled trees, chirping purple blossoms,
all is alive including the death I load into the carousel of my awareness
and here is Bixby Canyon Bridge agasp with 9 eyes,
recalling Ginsberg's tidepool bubble talk high on his old weenie there,
seals like fat brown worms, an azure sky with amber thistle stars
lighting flocks of nuzzling boulders—Ah, two hares:
one enraged by the boldness of a dilated peony,
the other bemused in a bramble refuge lined with dragons.

An Anatomy Of The Night

[1]

The sky a bath   incestuous
dissolving urn and tower
strewn petals gust and blend   Whitman arched by
his menstrual harp,
vermilion moon scarves,   surf resounding,
swim through our serpent-paneled spines,
stages interlocked and released by fountains rising from
when we were masts

Earth
pink and quilted with tufts of violet grass,
miniver and rose
I glimpse Wilhelm Reich
the last night of his life,   November 3, 1957
recumbent on a prison cot

All is alive including the death carousel I load into the projector
of my awareness

Bashō's compote of cicada-absorbed rock
Aphrodite's pudenda served on an orchid of clouds

Graze of the night's hydra-mollusced tongue

[2]

All night long I was Argiope
laying out draglines,   sifting
visual seam for word spore,   dragonizing

my agon,   working
star wreathes into phrase fairs,   excreting
sermon fuel, thread coals,
a shadow self in shaman sores…

The queen's pedipalp tapped my shoulder,
plumbed my marrow flora
"Come,
let us irritate the vessels of the earth—
they shall distill strange wine"

[3]

What is the nature of the night?

Might it be the boundless destruction of existence in the origin of the universe?

Is it an infusion brewed of cosmic darkness, initially articulated by those shamans who, spanning the abyss of the Fall, reconnected, if only in vision, humankind with its animal matrix?

Is earth but a tear in mad Ophelia's mangled target eye as she crawls the Milky Way searching eternally for the right black hole in which to deposit the God-crisis in her being?

O light, you are oasis!

Descending / ascending, a plumb line through our minds, the axis mundi longings to connect that antlered shaman buried in ice with the morning stars all singing hosanna together.

Is there a basic dream?

An animal dives deep into primal waters, brings up earth...
I tumble into a hole, turn my body into a womb; while in this cave
I begin to daub its walls,   out of my body
                    I begin to make a world...

[4]

Géza Róheim:

"The ancestor of the [Siberian] Yakuts is called 'The Lonely Man.' He lives in the center of a plain in a palace with four silver-gleaming corners, forty windows, seven stories. When he comes out of his house he sees the tree of life. Its roots reach down to Hades, its crown pierces the seven heavens. From under its roots foams 'eternal water.' Cattle and game drink or lick the sap which drips from the trees' branches and their youth and strength are restored. The spirit of the tree is a white-haired goddess with breasts as large as leather bags. When she leaves the tree it grows smaller, when she re-enters it it regains its former size. This milk-breasted goddess of the tree is actually the mother of the First Man."

[5]

Le Combel section of the Pech Merle cave contains a Black Goddess stone tree only partially emerged from stalactites, fissures and folds. Possibly as early as 25,000 B.P., Cro-Magnon people identified and marked this proto-World Tree.

Her broad, short trunk has a vertical cleft, widening near the base into a triangular hole. At the top of the trunk, out of the chamber ceiling, pod-shaped stalactites proliferate. Under two of these pods, along the cleft, the stalactitic mass seems to liquefy and descends, icicling across the triangular hole, fusing with the molten stone which appears to be emerging from the hole. Cro-Magnons daubed manganese on a dozen or so of the pods, turning them into blackened breasts, the trunk into a torso, the fissured torso into monstrous trunk-legs and the triangular hole into a seeping vulva.

These people envisioned all of this and more, for they marked both upper sides of her trunk torso and the top of her stalactitic clitoris with large, red-ochre disks: rotating anointments, menstrual suns.

The stone river flowing out of her vulva conjures wise blood, a proto-Styx, life-giving aurr, nectar of blood and honey—her trunk Yggdrasil, the Qabalistic Tree of Life.

[6]

Tracers 1

Midnight: out our bedroom window across the neighbors' driveway through black walnut tree branches into two yellow windows. Nothing moves, moves me deeply. Nothing, dwelling in its still birth. I want a shadow play to silhouette Lilith mounting Adam, a Beanstalk to sprout from Jack-Adam's groin… Two yellow windows thirty yards away… They hang there, ghost garb on an invisible line…

*

I stare into a ceiling where Savior is manacled to Sobibor

*

Haunted by the last line of a poem by the Armenian poet Nigoghos Sarafian: "To die without death, oh Lord, to be taken from it alive, whole."

*

Night as the mingling of those "kissing cousins," birth and death. As the recumbent turns on his side, drawing up his knees, a cradle begins to tremor; as the tremor becomes a rocking, bits of yellowish froth appear, isles of conception in the endlessness of non-existence. Before we were / After we are: reciprocal postings, sped on by sleep.

*

In a letter to Jean Paulhan from the Rodez asylum, Antonin Artaud writes: "To sleep is not to slumber, but to live on the side of the dream, and not like a sleeper giving off the compiled mucus of the dream, but like a fiend seeking itself, contrary to any consciousness of wakefulness, in that sort of terebrant immanence, in that space of unfathomable immanence where our unconscious is woven."

[7]

James Hillman:

"Each dream is a child of Night, affiliated closely with Sleep and Death, and with Forgetting (Lethe) all that the daily world remembers. Dreams have no father, no call upwards. They come only from Night, and they have no home other than in that dark realm.

"From the psychic perspective of the underworld, only shadow has substance, only what is in the shadow matters truly, eternally. Shadow, then, in psychology is not only that which the ego casts behind, made by the ego out of its light, a moral or repressed or evil reflection to be integrated. Shadow is the very stuff of the soul, the interior darkness that pulls downward out of life and keeps one in relentless connection with the underworld.

"What is most dead and buried in each of us is the culture's neglect of Death. Hades only now begins to reappear in ominous new concerns with the limits to growth, the energy crisis, ecological pollution, aging and dying.

"Jung's attempt to darken the Christ figure must be understood in terms of soul-making, in terms of a recognition that only through reestablishing the underworld, which it was Christ's mission to void, could the soul-making of descent and deepening toward death, so basic to the work of psychotherapy, happen at all. I understand Jung's struggle as one between two archetypal obligations: Christianism that denies the underworld, and soul-making that inevitably goes there.

"We must know the archetypal substructures which govern our reactions; we must recognize the Gods and the myths in which we are embroiled. Without this awareness, our behavior becomes wholly mythic and consciousness a delusion. When Christ was the operative myth, it was enough to know his modes and those of the Devil. We had the Christian structure for our reflection. But now that this single model of consciousness has dissociated into the root multiples which lay dormant below it and which are presented by mythology, we cannot get by without mythological reflection upon our patterns of reaction, our attitudes, our fantasies."

[8]

In a North American's thermal, carnivorous dream ground
there are cells in which jaguars are prancing. The jaws of the oldest
 gods,
bearded dragons, arch open. Out of these cuspidors,
skeletal geezers are ceaselessly squirming. They carry long knives,
they're on the lookout for baby jaguar gods. These shades
still roam the Popol Vuh regions of the mind
where the Daughters of Xibalbá are ceaselessly

impregnated by spitting, decapitated heads. Ceaselessly
bearing jaguar sons. Ceaselessly avenging, ceaselessly bearing,
coming into being while losing being…

Look:

a monkey-headed human skeleton is dancing in procession with
Gladys Eshleman, a

dead baby Clayton on her right arm.

[9]

My first "visionary" dream took place in Kyoto, 1963, when my first wife Barbara and I were living and sleeping on tatami in two rooms of a nineteenth-century Japanese house. I was daily trying to imagine what I could make of myself. Since I did not know how to generate imagination, what took place in those long mornings was often the typing out of a line or two on my typewriter, before which, cross-legged, I sat staring at the page. Grinding against latent self in the hope that an expressive self could be sparked or coaxed forth. I often had nauseating headaches and was so tense that one afternoon I passed out while reading William Blake's *Book of Urizen.*

In April of that year, I became aware of the following pattern when I stretched out on the futon to sleep: as I was about to doze off, I would hear a sharp PING that rang in or seemed struck off my forehead between my eyes (was my pineal-eye calling?). At first this "bell" was more frightening than I can describe. In an effort to escape it, I would concentrate on falling asleep. In doing so, a second thing would happen: from about fifty feet away, there was the sound of a window being slammed shut, as if someone with both hands had slammed a window as hard as possible (in our neighborhood there were no houses with Western windows). I curled tighter into myself and awaited the third phase which was a rerun of this "visionary" dream: I was in a twisting tunnel moving at high speed, head first, with a sense of impending collision, as if the only culmination could be a shattering. The tunnel was smoking, and in attempting to see through the fumes, and to get to the tunnel's end before it got to me, I would conjure my father's face. The dream would always end before I reached the tunnel's outlet. I seemed to be in the tunnel a little less time each rerun. It was as if I was on some sort of psychic hamster-belt being run through my paces night after night until a certain charge exhausted itself.

[10]

My natal daemon is the Indianapolis shadow present at birth, which dogged and occulted my existence for some twenty-two years. Upon the discovery of imagination via poetry I began to destroy this daemon. Although I cut it out of my solar plexus in 1963 in "The Book of Yorunomado," its elimination is a lifelong task. The natal daemon in exultation is what Blake calls the Selfhood, the hood worn by the self blinding it to pity and forgiveness as well as to its own annihilation and cruelty.

This hood is like a caul kept on, as if paradise is only in the womb and not a convexcavatious display of metaphoric transformation.

The natal daemon can thus be sent packing but its ashes are never blown off. Its ashes are our bones, our lightness, our ephemerality. Thus the daemon must in banishment also be honored. Without the Indianapolis mother-father conjunction I would not have had the opportunity to engage in mental war.

[11]

What was my dream in my mother's womb?
To know my double Gemini, my Clayton double, Ira?
But I was unnamed then, of the non-named,
tuned into placenta static with the chaos of my pillow.

Did my coming into being dream at all?
If so, it was a fetal fantasy of ingesting mother morays, yes,
the eels of the mother right, the right to be,
a dream of eels wavering upright, in mother left,
wavering and reeling. Was I fearing to be left in mother as an eel?
Or to lose my eel while emerging, to be without eelity,
an ash lemon? No, I did not know this then,
I knew nothing but the daemon moray amassing in my umbilical tail,
the eel passing between my mother and the meander becoming me,
the whelping mortar, placental nog, rich with her tissue,
the gift I was taking in, her life, I was converting into a moray male.

[12]

Sylvia Likens, sixteen-year-old boarder into whose belly Gertrude Baniszewski and her kids, with nails, wrote: "I am a prostitute and proud of it." Chained to a cot in an Indianapolis basement, you are turning sallow lily-white before my eyes, but your awful spongy agony only *evokes* Persephone. You died in an unidentified "underworld" with nameless monsters leeching your brain. What call these spirally eyes I meet blinking awake? Are these Sylvia's eyes, sister whirlpools of my own?

[13]

And how do you see my soul, I asked Nora Jaffe

"It looks to be from Arnhem Land,
a greasy red knot with filaments aspiral.
Now I see maggots on knuckle-bones—
you were entered by one.

It sank into you, a fiery amulet.
Your birth was blank and right-handed,
you're always drizzling or leaking secrets
and you throw out too many loops to the unregenerate.
This ancestor of yours was brought by a German circus to
    Switzerland
and exhibited. Before dying of ptomaine poisoning
he mated with a cage-slosher.
The infant was adopted by the Aeschelmann family
who raised the boy to be a veterinarian specializing in livestock.
While performing a Caesarean section,
he spotted the Virgin's face enwebbed with the fetus
and thereupon renounced earthly labor and delight.
He embalmed the calf fetus and prayed to it,
believing that he had made contact with a nexus uniting
the Virgin with the Beast—an unfortunate association,
for the church elders in Bern interpreted it as satanic,
proposing that Ira Aeschelmann had delivered
nothing less than the Apocalyptic Whore's fetus.
Ira was lucky to be merely banished
and spent the remainder of his seventy-seven years
as a kind of wild hermit, wandering the Alps.
Imprint is all. These circuits now
range in your shadow, ankle-chained but lively,
constantly skittering out of the light."

*

The pepper-dotted room began to undulate.
I thought of the veils within "No one has lifted her veil,"
    revelation,   to draw back the *velum,*
to hear dead Nora through a spiritual gate,
to see the Dogon earth naked and speechless,
without language, a fiber skirt the first word,
speech as plaited fiber,   "speech lattice,"

or Christ nailed on the cross as the arrested word,
vulva as lower mouth issuing red fiber,
a many-colored Isis rainbow, net within which
my fate is entangled, where the Nora spirits can be heard.

Then I saw a black-capped facial netted "full body veil"
sitting, as if on the Kabul bridge, begging.
"No one has lifted her veil" became
"At no time have women not been oppressed."
My heart tore left and right, I tried to peel
the true from the truthful, the rainbow flashed
a central scarlet band—I knew it was the Wawilak Sisters' menstrual blood
circulating within rock python venom.
I saw ripples of albino babies, each with a red or silver balloon,
setting off across the rainbow bridge for
the argentine body of the moon—

the Kabul bridge beggar roared back,
burkha, menstrual never shed,
chrysalis of a monstrous anti-metamorphosis
"sewed up in a hammock, with a small opening so she can breathe"
—are all of us, enclosed in the world of five senses, mummified pupas?
The beggar hissed: "Your bars, spaced and wall-papered, allow some comfort and expanse.
Mine, wrapped around me, nearly cover my eyes…"

I turned and sought sleep's stagnation,
respite from the sear of intersecting planes.

[14]

Tracers 2

Gazing through the dark at the Eden eel, Thomas's "green fuse," Montale's "L'Anguilla," "the spark that says everything begins when everything seems burnt out black." Eel as self-oiling word, cry swiveling in its calling, aisle or ale, no, *eel,* phantom of Monet's Giverny. And in the pond as well: trash, unwanted caskets of desire, wrecked Hopkins' anapests, sludge in which living fossils churn.

*

Met a couple in my dream café who asked me what I'd like to drink. I'll have an iced Lucifer, I said. Then they wanted to show me some "low down" bars—oh, I replied, that reminds me of "the house of blue lights," when I was a teenager in Indianapolis there was a story circulating about this mysterious mansion out in the countryside. At night it supposedly had a single blue light on by the door. Kids would drive out to it, as if moths lured by that blue flame. I drove out there once, and yes, there it was, the mansion inside absolutely dark. Now what to do? Park and neck? What was going on inside? In this dream I saw inside that long-ago mansion: it was run by, ruled by, dogs, or were they wolves? They had captured a woman whose body was now covered with bites. Each time one of the animals mounted her they'd bite her as well. "Our Lady of the Body Covered with Bites."

At the base of the sacred, this holy-dreadful (wholly dreadful) body, the tortured woman, mutilated Coatlicue inside the *Coatlicue* goddess urn.

Things do not add up; they subtract out. In the soul's countryside this animal-clustered "goddess," the blue flame around which, like circling planets, male minds rotate, bowing and scraping, coming in for a nip now and then…

*

Once again wanting to join the yolotl heart-soul dance of the dead as we wind toward November 2. Down our marigold trail, the souls follow, sniffing for me, for you. I am thinking of Aztec excavation, the feeding of hearts to the sun; what does it mean to shovel life into source to maintain life? The Aztecs were still rooted, half-immersed in natural mash, stewing in a venomous instinctual fodder. All was blood and flower flow, Coatlicue, Mictlancihuatl... Día de muertos as the snake of America in 2009 winds through Afghanistan, as our baby snakes burst their eggs in a thousand bases "overseas"— So do I escape into this ancient Día de muertos with armadillo-shell mandolin strummers in a bald and splendid din.

[15]

O night, black wet-nurse of the golden stars!

That inspired by the nebulae in the endlessness surrounding us, poetry might become prodigious, peregrine.

That imagination might engage the wonder of galactic imagery, as, like the En Sof of hydrogen, it bubbles and wanes in me, microscopic doodad.

The poem as test tube. To mix dark rose gas cliffs with swan-snakes of exploding cotton light, orange bonfired skulls wrapped in lit white wire...

And then to descend to those deepest trenches, the ones with siphonophores, copepods, glass octopi, bloody-belly comb jelly and armored sea robins—can we introduce them to Charon as he circles Pluto?

The hell that is man mesmerizes as if to keep the mind mantised on grief and torture, bent upon ourselves, panting after beauty, when like astral sharks we should be cruising the Sombrero Galaxy,

or the Eagle Nebula: trillion-mile-long towers of molecular hydrogen rising, horned and nippled stalagmites trailing belts of turquoise blood,

or the Carina Nebula: scorching ultraviolet radiation shredding pinpoint stars in an amassing flux of blue and rust giraffe necks, layered imploding simian craniums—

Is there interpenetration? Am I inspected not only by the eye of Muriel Rukeyser but by that of a Crowned jewel squid?

> "Press close barebosomed night! Press close magnetic
>   nourishing night!
> Night of south winds! Night of the large few stars!
> Still nodding night! Mad naked summer night!
>
> Smile, for your lover comes!"

Nearly one hundred years after the 1855 *Leaves of Grass,* in *Cosmic Superimposition* Wilhelm Reich, starting with the superimposition of two organisms or energy systems in the sexual embrace, moved to the superimposition of two orgone energy particles in the formation of matter, the development of galaxies, hurricanes, and the aurora borealis.

"Before there was any life, there was the streaming of cosmic orgone energy. When climatic conditions were sufficiently developed on the planet, life began to appear, most likely in the form of primitive plasmatic flakes... From these flakes, single-cell organisms developed over the aeons. Now, the cosmic orgone energy not only was flowing in the vast galactic spaces, but also in tiny bits of membranous matter, caught within membranes and therefore flowing, still in a spiraling fashion, within these membranes, following a *closed* system of flow.

"The fright which overcomes man still in our time when he thinks about himself; the general reluctance to think at all; the whole function of repression of emotional functions of the Self; the powerful force with which man resists knowledge about himself; the fact that for millennia he investigated the stars but not the inside of his own organism; the panic that grips the witness of orgonomic investigations at the core of man's existence; the fervent ardor with which every religion defends the unreachability and unknowability of God, which clearly represents nature within man, and many other facts speak a clear language regarding the terror which is connected with the deep experience of the Self."

[16]

Imaginal love
incorrigibly infected by violence,
the damnation strut in the human,
fuse of extinction   formless horizon:
now the daily telepathy

I listen to Caryl breathe.
               Why cannot her being
bless the world? Bless it to awaken from the doomcraft
                    that is religion—

The dark sloughs its "d" and the ark of dawn,
first in my heart, then in the fuzzy edge of the window
   blind,
reveals Caryl's recumbent profile.

Blind edge, road of awe, world axis that allows me to contemplate her breathing.

[17]

A. Alvarez:

"Nobody knows for certain when man first produced fire mechanically. The archeologists believe there were fire-makers in China 350,000 years ago, in Europe by 250,000 BC, in Africa and West Asia 50,000–100,000 years ago. According to William T. O'Dea, who wrote the most authoritative book on the subject, fire-making by using sparks from flint and pyrites on tinder probably came before the other ancient method of rubbing hardwood against softwood (the hardwood powders the softwood to make tinder and the fiction between the two creates heat), because the latter 'implies a rather more advanced stage of tool manipulation.' What is not in doubt is that, until about one hundred years ago, the only source of artificial light was fire: millennia of fire, scraps of flame in the darkness of prehistory, fragile, easily extinguished, infinitely comforting. For ancient man, whose night was full of terrors, God's first triumph was always a triumph over darkness:

"And God said, Let there be light.

"And God saw the light, that it was good: and God divided the light from the darkness.

"What you see is what you know, and what can be heard of felt or smelled but not seen is terrifying because it is formless. There are only two ways to make night tolerable: by lighting it artificially and by sleep which shuts down the senses."

The first words were mixed with animal fat,
wounded men tried to say who did it.
The group was the rim of a to-be-invented wheel,
Their speech was spokes, looping over
Around, the hub of the fire, its silk of *us,*
its burn of *them,* bop we dip, you dip,
we dip to you, you will dip to us, Dionysus
the plopping, pooling words, stirred
by the lyre gaps between the peaks of flame,
water to fire, us to them.

"The other great prehistoric invention came about when some Paleolithic, lateral-thinking genius noticed that a twig which fell into the grease below a roasting animal went on burning beyond its natural span. From that observation, step by slow step, the idea of the grease lamp evolved: first of a wick immersed in grease, then of a portable container for the grease. The device had been perfected at least 15,000 years ago since the painting in the Lascaux cave in the Dordogne was illuminated by a hundred or more grease lamps.

"Some primitive communities did not bother with making lamps; they simply dried oily fish, stuck them in cleft sticks and lit them. The Indians around Vancouver Island did this to the little salmon-like candle fish, the Penobscot Indians used the sucker fish, the New Zealand Maoris the mutton fish, the Newfoundlanders the dog fish. Oily birds got the same treatment: until late in the nineteenth century, Shetlanders used to catch stormy petrels, thread a fiber wick through them, stick the feet in a lump of clay and burn them as lamps; much earlier, the Danes had done the same with the Great Auk, using a moss wick stuck in the creature's oily belly. The simplest of all natural lamps was the firefly. The West Indians used to put them in wooden cages or even stick them with gum to their big toes in order to see snakes on the path at night. Anything for a light.

"By the time of classical Athens, domestic lighting was commonplace—fragments have been found of more than ten thousand lamps made between the first and third centuries BC—and the Romans were almost as addicted to artificial light as we are now. They set up factories to make pottery lamps in vast quantities both at home and throughout the empire. Even slaves had lamps: they used snail shells to hold the oil and a tow wick. The Romans also invented the candle, another great leap in lateral thinking: solid 'oil' instead of liquid made light truly portable and eliminated the expense of a container.

"Night life as an option democratically available to everyone, as a time when ordinary people can go about their ordinary business, give or take a few qualifications, is a relatively modern invention. Until less than two centuries ago, night was still a time of terrors, evil portents and violence, a no-go area where criminals, hobgoblins and all the other forces of darkness ruled, a time when law-abiding people bolted their doors and huddled together around the fire with only a candle to light them to bed.

"It was not until the introduction of gas lighting in the early nineteenth century that cities began to be illuminated regularly, reliably and on a large scale. London had gas lamps in the streets by 1807, Baltimore in 1816, Berlin in 1826.

"In January 1882, when someone threw the switch for the first street lamps… our perception of the world changed for good. Rayner Banham called it 'the greatest environmental revolution in human history since the domestication of fire.'

"According to the sociologist Murray Melbin, night is the last frontier and since the invention of artificial lighting we have colonized it in much the same way and in much the same spirit as the Americans colonized the West in the nineteenth century. Time is a dimension like space, says Melbin, and people have moved into the realm of night as the hours of daylight have become more congested... As Melbin sees it, night and day will soon be interchangeable; we have transformed our environment, so we will transform ourselves—physically, socially and psychologically—to fit the new 24-hour cycle of work.

"After the physical conquest of night, the search moved on into the inner darkness, the darkness inside the head. When Freud, defining the aim of psychoanalysis, said, 'Where the id was, there the ego shall be,' he was echoing, in his own way, God's first edict: 'Let there be light.'"

[18]

In the summer of 1996 I was left alone, without a light, for a half hour, in Le Portel cave. Not a long time, but enough for my eyes to become accustomed to total darkness. At first I closed my eyes (wondering if it would make any difference; it didn't), and rubbed my eyelids with my knuckles creating the dazzling diagrammatic millrace known as phosphenes. Then I opened my eyes and stared into the dark. After some ten minutes, pinpoints of light appeared like a fine snowfall holding in place. I thought of the three levels of light in the dark I felt myself inhabiting: the light in my head, the light in cave dark, and the stars in the night sky above.

[19]

Herbert Kűhn, a German writer and the author of *On the Track of Prehistoric Man,* visited the Niaux cave in 1949. He believes that Niaux was one of the great religious centers for Ice Age people. At one point, he describes his feelings about The Green Lake, the underground siphon to the left of Niaux's second intersection:

This lake is one of the most sinister things to be found in any of the subterranean grottoes, and when M. Clastres and I had reached it we sat down on a stone by its edge. Black and deathly quiet the waters stretched before us. The absolute stillness by the lakeside is so uncanny that it soon becomes almost unbearable. One is surrounded by premonitions of dread. Life is timeless and, what is more alarming, motionless. So profound is the quiet that one can feel one's very heartbeat. This sitting by the strand of a subterranean lake is a unique experience. There is always movement around us. Something or other is always happening. Even in the depths of the night there is noise. Leaves shiver, some beast will stir. You hear a house floor creak, you see the twinkling of a star, the wind comes blowing or a field mouse rustles in the grass. But by the banks of the pool in Niaux nothing stirs. If I had been alone on that occasion I believe that I would have broken down. Anxiety would have gripped me too tightly. A stillness, an immobility, a timelessness man cannot endure. And I could recollect the relief we felt when a drop of water plopped down from the vault above onto the surface of the lake. Something had happened. A sense of salvation. Faint, circular ripples ringed outward toward the banks. Then again, all was still. So had the underground waters lain throughout the millennia: black, immobile, uncanny, awful.

[20]

Cold gibbons
nested fledglings
the crucified left for dead
cry out as one

or, as No One—if you're cyclopically listening.

[21]

Tracers 3

One day in the Dordogne there was a cool gray September flow through the chestnuts, a leaf flutter so intense no single leaf could be outlined. A dazzling like the sparking milling of cuneiform fragments the backs of my hands release pressed against my closed eyelids—all of which resolves into a doughnut of light, with a cenote-black center, the outer ring of which appears fused to astral dark. Is this the deep cone of the human, Giacometti-wrapped in erasures, restarts and retreats?

*

We continue to be in multiphasic expulsion from a paradise we unconsciously rejected when we separated ourselves from animals. It took thousands and thousands of years but we did create the abyss out of a seemingly infinitely elastic crisis: therio-expulsion—and we have lived in a state of "animal withdrawal" ever since. The pictures from the abyss that flicker our sleep and waking are the fall-out that shouted us into dot and line and from which we have been throwing up and throwing down ever since.

*

Bird spirit flew into Apollo—
animal appeared in Dis.
What was sky and earth became life and death,
or hell on earth and psychic depth,
and I wonder: how has Hades been affected by Dachau?
In the cold of deepest bowels, does a stained
fluid drip? Does pure loss now have an odor
of cremation, a fleshy hollow feel
of human soul infiltrating those realms
Hades had reserved for animals?

Are there archai, still spotted with
this evening's russets, stringing and quartering
an anthrobestial compost? Or are the zeros,
of which we are increasingly composed,
folding out the quick of animal life?
Is that why these outlines, these Hadic kin,
take on mountainous strength,
moving through the shadows of these days?

*

As if the night has tunnels that if tapped could lead one into the recrementitious depths where Cro-Magnon dreams might be envisioned... Were their dreams "open" in a way that ours are not? The open Aurignacian vulva evokes a simple labyrinth with an exit and stresses, sexually, torsion, possibly the earliest intercourse/pregnancy association (underscored by the fire drill). The subsequent uroboros belongs to agricultural peoples, with stress on the enclosed seed, the male as "star," i.e., patriarchy in contrast to an earlier more mysterious "open" union, in which the female was place-of-fire and phallus (the so-called "Venuses" fit neatly in the hand). Did Cro-Magnon people sense life as indeterminate, the human as unclosed? In Western symbolism, the circle is a symbol of death, or the wholeness that must include death... Cro-Magnon "death" as an absence containing a hidden presence to be drawn forth through stone.

[22]

E. M. Cioran:

"Two kinds of mind: daylight and nocturnal. They have neither the same method nor the same morality. In broad daylight, you watch yourself; in the dark, you speak out. The salutary or awkward consequences of what he thinks matter little to the man who questions himself at hours when others are the prey of sleep. Hence he meditates upon the bad luck of being born without concern for the harm he can cause others or himself. After midnight begins the intoxication of pernicious truths.

"Once the shutters are closed, I stretch out in the dark. The outer world, a fading murmur, dissolves. All that is left is myself and... there's the rub. Hermits have spent their lives in dialogue with what was most hidden within them. If only, following their example, I could give myself up to that extreme exercise, in which one unites with the intimacy of one's own being! It is this self-interview, this inward transition which matters, and which has no value unless continually renewed, so that the self is finally absorbed by its essential version.

"Dreams, by abolishing time, abolish death. The deceased take advantage of them in order to importune us. Last night, there was my father. He was just as I have always known him, yet I had a moment's hesitation. Suppose it wasn't my father? We embraced in the Rumanian manner but, as always with him, without effusion, without warmth, without the demonstrativeness customary in an expansive people. It was because of that sober, icy kiss that I knew it was my father. I woke up realizing that one resuscitates only as an intruder, as a dream-spoiler, and that such distressing immortality is the only kind there is.

"For Mallarmé, who claimed he was doomed to permanent insomnia, sleep was not a 'real need' but a 'favor.' Only a great poet could allow himself the luxury of such an insanity.

"The light of dawn is the true, primordial light. Each time I observe it, I bless my sleepless nights, which afford me an occasion to witness the spectacle of the Beginning. Yeats calls it 'sensuous'— a fine discovery, and anything but obvious.

"Much more than time, it is sleep that is the antidote to grief. Insomnia, on the other hand, which enlarges the slightest vexation and converts it into a blow of fate, stands vigil over our wounds and keeps them from flagging.

"'And God saw that the light was good': such is the opinion of mortals, with the exception of the sleepless, for whom it is an aggression, a new inferno more pitiless than the night's.

"I should like to forget *everything* and waken to a light *before time.*"

[23]

November 7, 1970 Methodist Hospital, Indianapolis

Walked into C 743. She was in a single railed bed, picking at covers, trying to sit up—most of her hair gone—moth-eaten stringy clumps sticking out straight—dyed-brown, skull showing. *Acorn, monkey:* these words now cross my mind—then, to my horror, I only saw my mother possibly mad in a short hospital gown, sitting, helplessly picking at whatever, eyes wide, seeing, not seeing, skull-head on tiny shoulders—legs bruised, dark splotches, big feet, large dead toenails, legs like helpless clubs sticking out.

We embraced—I held her a long time, a minute it seemed—two minutes—she was a little crumpled and loosened pack of faggots. I sat down, instant knowledge that she was my mother and also no longer was—but she recognized me and told me, her mouth and face slack and tense at once, that she was surprised and happy to see me. I held her hand. Her grip strong two weeks ago was somewhat gone, but her *fingers* held—sheer bone—her loose skinned wrist mottled brown. I wanted to cry right off but kept almost *savoring* the duality: this was the first time I had never clearly seen her as my mother. In spite of her growing old, aging until now did not essentially change her—even as she grew stiff, and would walk leaning backwards, I still regarded her essentially as I had from childhood, babyhood even, on—but today, at 5:00 PM Death had moved in—was now more than 51%? in and of her. I thought immediately of Sam Abrams' youngest child Joshua who at ten can't talk and has an acorn monkey fidgety muscle gesture look. Death as an interior other, coming alive—no—not *alive,* but as if, as a tree dies, *another* form of its withering emerges—as if dying /withering at a certain point becomes an image which is not simply the *loss* of life. This is horrible—more horrible than if I had walked into the room, saw her head bent over and she had looked up *without a face.* But it was not a blankness either that shook me—I couldn't say she had de-evolved and was now a wild child, or an animal crazed with disease in the woods. Again, that would have saved *me* from seeing *her.* No, it was my mother acting like a child—that is, she no longer had any protocol. She did not cross her legs, she had no underwear on and if I had tried to do so she would not have stopped me from looking at her cunt. Later she ate with her fingers and let me help her to the toilet. I lifted up the hospital gown and helped her sit down. In our whole life together I had never seen her undressed or had been with her while either of us performed a function in the bathroom. She was so out of it, so overtaken by biological ravage, that I had no context in which to place her. The yet that most profoundly resounds is: she was my mother. Death was Gladys Maine Spencer.

I sat down and held her hand. She again tried to get up into a sitting position, seemingly to read the hospital stamp on the sheet edge. I kept holding her hand and at a certain point my eyes were so flushed I let the cry come. I dropped her hand, buried my face in my own hands and wept. Not as long as when I realized in 1966 that I could not live with Barbara and Matthew, and not as convulsively. She patted my shoulder and said: "There, there, don't feel bad." I started to laugh in the midst of my tears, saying "You! You're telling *me* not to cry!" I awkwardly told her that I was crying because she was so sick. Then she said: "The greatest pleasure in my life has been to be your mother." I replied: "I *guess* (and I weighted that word) I've really liked being your son"—which I immediately corrected to: "I've *loved* being your son." Very quietly she said: "I know that." Then her mouth slacked and twitched, and she stared off, eyes wide open, into the dim wall...

I wish I could *render* her state more totally. I was struck by how her *otherness* was so close to that of many young people I've met briefly, when I have thought that they were out of it, drugs or whatever. When I finally made contact with the nurse, a very starched woman in her late 50s, squat and simplistic in the way she acted (telling my mother to be a "big girl"), she seemed just as out of it! After the nurse left, I helped my mother eat some of the smelly hospital fish they gave her. At one point, I looked out of the window and watched in the darkness seven stories below a large heavy black woman slowly cross the parking lot—*it's all dead*—that is the phrase that came to me, as if the nature of life—including the imagination that had opened to me when I was twenty-two—was that of death, as if that which lives and goes on is death. My mother was now a puppet, jerked by the cords of Death.

The shit on her hospital gown didn't upset me, nor did the single tooth that appeared to be the last one left in her mouth. It was when I *remembered,* thought of her as the person I had known more consequently than any other—thirty-five years—that I felt scared and sick. As long as I stayed in touch with what I immediately saw, I felt somewhat numb, as if memory is part of our lives and we repress whole memory out of not being able to stand the discrepancy between it and what we see. It was ok to watch her drowse. I was kind of charmed that she would eat with her fingers and would let me help her to the toilet with its frightening diagonal aluminum bar along the wall for the dying to grasp as they lowered themselves down.

[24]

I put my life into my mother's tomb. Her furniture: frozen animals. The atmosphere? I pulled the WC udder-chain of iron-geared clouds. It began to drizzle aftermath, inner math, registries of Wabash glades. Her bones, milk-soft, were xylophone to my mental tongs.

[25]

Djuna Barnes' Dr. Matthew-Mighty-grain-of-salt-Dante-O'-Connor:

"We are but skin about a wind, with muscles clenched against mortality. We sleep in a long reproachful dust against ourselves. We are full to the gorge with our own names for misery.

"And the tree of night is the hardest tree to mount, the dourest tree to scale, the most difficult of branch, the most febrile to the touch, and sweats a resin and drips a pitch against the palm that computation has not gambled… We will find no comfort until the night melts away; until the fury of the night rots out its fire…

"For what is not the sleeper responsible? What converse does he hold and with whom? He lies down with his Nelly and drops off into the arms of his Gretchen. Thousands unbidden come to his bed. Yet how can one tell truth when it's never in the company?

"For the lover, it is the night into which his beloved goes that destroys his heart; he wakes her suddenly, only to look the hyena in the face that is her smile, as she leaves that company… When she sleeps, is she not moving her leg aside for an unknown garrison? Or in a moment, that takes but a second, murdering us with an axe? Eating our ear in a pie? Sailing to some port with a ship full of sailors and medical men?

"And so I say, what of the night, the terrible night? The darkness is the closet in which your lover roosts her heart, and that night-fowl that caws against her spirit and yours, dropping between you and her the awful estrangement of his bowels...

"To our friends, we die every day, but to ourselves we die only at the end. We do not know death, or how often it has essayed our most vital spirit. While we are in the parlour it is visiting in the pantry..."

[26]

Tracers 4

"It is clear," declared César Vallejo, noticing a black beetle giving head to a caiman virago, "why metaphysical life is so rich with pause."

*

Insomnia: trapped between the black wall inside my mind and the bedroom's darkness. I hang tracer after tracer upon this wall, as if to bring it down, but it regards these tracers as medals, expanding and thickening, proud of its valor...

*

Sudden image of the coal bin in my childhood home's basement where my father, with freshly-cut buckeye switch, took me one Sunday after lunch for having criticized that morning Reverend Ragan's sermon. I peer into the bin to discover in citrus-green light Hart Crane peering back... How do I know it is him? He has cauliflower ears...

*

Jazz improvisation relates to dream improvisation. Chord structure: the life under, directing the dream. No wonder the nighttime interest in jazz, the dream-fractured improvisational lines. "Koko" the ghost of "Cherokee," "Cherokee" the host of "Koko;" out of Charlie Parker's coke haven this mantic anthem. Walking on the gym track, listening to Sonny Stitt inject some "Koko" anti-freeze into my ear drums, I thought of the harp of baby birds plucked by Eve, the birth pangs of absence in every babe.

*

In the neuron orgy
in cranial dark
to know thyself is to give a self to no.

[27]

I was going many ways at once,
a drop of psyche had separated into streams,
each with a febrile image purpose,
ravenous image serpents all heading out hungry for extension,
one must choose
which serpent—or might one choose their knotted source?

One says: dream is a stable place to flail,
to swingle bast from circumstance

One says: dream wisps are image produce
the poet must pestle
or tie, dead giveaways

I am crawling a black alley past sights I cannot bear,
alley intestines, the monster composed of daily news

Last night a nipple was offered—
instead of sucking in the squalor discharge
I wrenched up, banging against
a ceiling roar of celebration

I looked back, the alley now spiraling to a vanishing

I was inside a Horn of Plenty with worm nests for the poor.
Where the fruits of the earth were said to spill,
a slab for the rich
barricaded the cornucopian flow.
Blood issued from the head of Achelous,
his horn ripped off by Heracles.
It is said that from the blood of this rupture
the Sirens were born—

ragged round pit of this tear:
does it mask the Muse's bloody mouth?

It is also said that Sirens were in the meadow with Kore,
bird-footed bearded girls
watching Kore pluck a psilocybin out of a cow-pie and bite
into the pileus

—I turned on the sink disposal and heard Kore's screams

Binder Siren, throttler Sphinx
cornucopia down into Muse eggs where inspiration
and fate separate and combine—

I keep having this fuzzy vision of
a brain termite queen pumping out image tendrils,
and then a creature blowing into it
(Sirens, the night-side of the ancient form of the Muse,
are said to suck the breath of the sick
and are associated with siesta-nightmares)

"muse" akin to *musus,* "animal muzzle,"
a Muse-muzzled succubus crawling across the dreamer
or up through the dreaming,
blowing the dreamer's mind,
mind ejaculating into Muse muzzle,
"psyche" akin to "psychein" = to blow.

[28]

January 31, 1998. 8:16 AM. After writing my Notes, I assumed *From Scratch* was finished and went to bed. I dreamed for hours it seemed, over and over, of being at universities for poetry readings. Each time I showed up for a reading I would discover that I either had no books to read from, or that my books were in foreign languages. At one point, someone handed me a copy of *The Gull Wall.* Gratefully I opened it to discover words in incoherent sentences instantly turning into other words. A 1950s college audience was there, shuffling about, sitting down, getting up, Cokes in hand. After five years, four thousand worksheets, this dream... But are my books incomprehensible—is that the message of this dream? You say that you write for yourself but that you try hard to communicate this self to others. Maybe you try too hard. Nobody wants all anybody else has. Are "alls" poisoned, are some so heavy they feel like nothing? Is my all the empty coal bucket Kafka's bucket rider mounts, or, in my case, a book, there I am, riding my book about, hovering over a reader's condo. Hello, I cry, it's me, Clayton E, I've just completed another book! Another book, the interior groans, oh god he's written another one. But no! This one is the best I've ever done, this one will light up the distant horizon and demonstrate how you are attached, or belong to that which is under you, this one will point you at the looney tunes under all you think, Indiana to Lascaux, one fast drive, a single smoking road.

[29]

I found myself yearning for the flutter folk, cordial nothing, the "is" without organs that so appeals to us.

Keep in change, reap falling—beautiful in the streetlight-lit night air: crystal down, dear fellow particles.

I had to come back to the Midwest to admire the separate isles of lacy structures as they mound on the redbud branch: mirth of the void, mouthlessly ho-hoing us…

What do these empty tree grails make of you? Who is your goddess? Are you the diamond nature?

As if the snow were a ludic mitten endlessly lolling…

As if what is invisible were mating with obliteration…

[30]

James Hamilton-Paterson:

"The famous and fatuous opposition of light and darkness is pre-Socratic in origin, only one pair of many made up of a 'noble' element (right, above, hot, male, dry, etc) and an 'ignoble' (left, below, cold, female, wet). By the sixth and fifth centuries BC the faculty of vision and the attributes of knowledge had run together in the Greek word *theorein,* meaning both 'to see' and 'to know.' Knowledge was henceforth a register of vision. Ignorance therefore becomes a lack of knowledge predicated on objects not being visible, so darkness equals ignorance. In turn, the dark becomes a source of fear as if a knowledge of visible objects were the only defense against terror and anxiety.

The very gradations of sleep itself seem to suggest a vertical descent into annihilating depths, the deepest levels of sleep being those of oblivion. The levels of dreaming, like the levels of the ocean which can support the biggest life-forms, lie near the surface. In any case, by descending into the sea we would expect to meet the monstrous rather than the divine.... Astronauts have claimed close encounters with a Supreme Being, but never deep-sea divers. Nor should we be surprised. Superior beings are by definition on top, while only the inferior can lurk below. The deeps also remind us of where we suppose we originally came from, what we have left behind. Going back to our genetic roots rather than to the sunlit idyll of Eden is a disquieting affair. Did we not abandon our ancestral dark by crawling toward the light?

No; we did not. The sea, to its dwellers, is not a dark place. With exceedingly acute eyes perceiving low levels of light and complex codes of bioluminescence; with sensitivity to sounds, smells, and minute pressure differentials far beyond the spectrum of our own senses, it is as pointless to speak in crude human terms of 'light' and 'dark' as it would be when speculating about what a bat sees. A bat 'sees' with its ears with great precision and at speed. In short there is no such thing as darkness. It exists only in the perception of the beholder. Vision does not depend on light."

[31]

Listening to Caryl sleep,
thinking of the cross-hatching in the 7-mile verticality of her
living
as her mind makes its way across the 40,000-mile mid-ocean
ridge,
across abyssal plains and canyons in tree-shaped networks,
her young life, which she remembers so keenly,
like a die tumbling among arabesques of leafy sea dragons
trailing
kelp blends, green clouds pouring

from the sides of wounded fish, millions of image trains—
I am on one, looking down at the stratified carriers below,
one called Venus's-flower-basket, the passengers:
shrimp, crabs, worms, and clams. Multiple water spindles
containing
water fairy proms, high school friends being reborn,
I am following the course of her sleep
through sea pastures of whirring diamond saws,
she carries away with her, in her trailing skirts,
a web filled with tiny men, radiolarian ooze,
at 800 feet, only the deepest, blackest blue,
the ocean of her sleep breaks over me, light gravel,
sensation of being in a horse's mouth, a deeper breathing is
forming—
the infinite, far from being a suburb of the gods, is an eternal
surpassing, removed from any essential halt.
I see her standing before a glass stairway, a Jacob's ladder
with more steps than she could ever climb in three lifetimes,
they disappear like bubbles in champagne,
now she is struggling against
suctions and pulls, against stretched webs,
she breaks free—what nightmare did she just slip?—
she becomes navigation itself, shining with a pure white flame,
passing over foaming ditches, wheeling ravines,
I imagine her retinue: dwarf plankton, flamingo tongues,
coccoliths giving the water a milk glow, bristlefoooted worms
patterned with colored rosettes, salmon-pink winged slugs,
salps like little barrels, pulsating, a mouth at each end.
How do we do without a head? How present all edges of the
body
equally to the outside world? A poem without subject,
all parts of which surprise and interlock, a poem with twenty
centers,
all muscular and avid, each word dense, full in itself, a nest,
a sound of wood crackling in the fireplace, monkey words
feeling the earthquake coming before I do.

Going through myself,   is it her heart that I am hearing?
—she gasps—silence—rebreathes   ka   ka   ka   ka
suddenly she is other than herself,
rake tines rise from her brow projecting brain energy into the atmosphere,
impaling celestial hexes, they glow pale blue in the dark
like thin upraised arms; I pass slowly through them,
standing in my Protestant canoe, alone, stiff, an erection curving
from a golden pubic beard—behind my back:
the Absolute, straight as a wall.
I am possessed by a sole idea: that snow is ceaselessly falling
obliquely through all of us, on each flake
the population of the Beyond cluster
like minute beardless seals, or albino cougars,
spherical knots of unearthly calm… As my monoxylon
sinks slowly into dead space, the dark is flecked with one-winged birds,
barkless trees, and now I see the full squalor of the sea,
the rubbish of a thousand boats daily fishes up, winnowed,
and thrown straight back—crushed into the netted haul
the new mermaid, limbs twisted among dogfish, whiting and plaice,
a deflated life-sized sex doll, hermit-crabs inside her
red-rimmed mouth. O sea layered into my dreams,
the daily rewound trash, visitations of the dead, Tenochtitlan
thoroughfares, extra-terrestrial spider queens,
cork-screwing flights through kaleidoscopic barriers—
to land by a nightstand and be watched by
two swans,   who are being watched by
two ocelots,   who are being watched by two snakes,   watched by
sixteen triangles,   watched by countless staring eyes.
Cessation of the mirage of the finite—
call it re-embarkation, call it a multiple leaving.
I have for shade a whole spread of hyena shadow,
I am my own ground, slashed, a wild sea of ground.

There is a silent breaking of waves,   spots of light,   sensation of
  fissure,
a flowing furrow,   I see Caryl gliding through
the little curlicues in its flanks,
when I graze her I graze a deep pit of joy.

[December–February, 2010/2011]

ALSO BY CLAYTON ESHLEMAN

Poetry

Mexico & North [1962]
Indiana [1969]
Altars [1971]
Coils [1973]
The Gull Wall [1975]
What She Means [1978]
Hades in Manganese [1981]
Fracture [1983]
The Name Encanyoned River: Selected Poems 1960–1985 [1986]
Hotel Cro-Magnon [1989]
Under World Arrest [1994]
From Scratch [1998]
My Devotion [2004]
An Alchemist with One Eye on Fire [2006]
Reciprocal Distillations [2007]
The Grindstone of Rapport: A Clayton Eshleman Reader [2008]
Anticline [2010]
An Anatomy of the Night [2011]
The Jointure [2012]

Prose

Antiphonal Swing: Selected Prose 1962–1987 [1989]
Companion Spider: Essays [2002]
Juniper Fuse: Upper Paleolithic Imagination & the Construction of the Underworld [2003]
Archaic Design [2007]

Journals and Anthologies

Folio [Bloomington, Indiana, 3 issues, 1959–1960]
Quena [Lima, Peru, 1 issue, edited, then suppressed by the North American Peruvian Cultural Institue, 1966]
Caterpillar [New York–Los Angeles, 20 issues, 1967–1973]
A Caterpillar Anthology [1971]
Sulfur [Pasadena–Los Angeles–Ypsilanti, 46 issues, 1981–2000]

Translations

Pablo Neruda, *Residence on Earth* [1962]
César Vallejo, *Human Poems* [1968]
César Vallejo, *The Complete Posthumous Poetry* [1978] (with José Rubia Barcia)
Aimé Césaire, *The Collected Poetry* [1983] (with Annette Smith)
Michel Deguy, *Given Giving* [1984]
Bernard Bador, *Sea Urchin Harakiri* [1986]
Conductors of the Pit: Major Works by Rimbaud, Vallejo, Césaire, Artaud, & Holan [1988, 2005]
Aimé Césaire, *Lyric & Narrative Poetry 1946–1982* [1990] (with Annette Smith)
César Vallejo, *Trilce* [1992, 2000]
Antonin Artaud, *Watchfiends & Rack Screams* [1995] (with Bernard Bador)
Aimé Césaire, *Notebook of a Return to the Native Land* [2001] (with Annette Smith)
César Vallejo, *The Complete Poetry* [2007]
Bernard Bador, *Curdled Skulls* [2011]
Bei Dao, *Endure* [2011] (with Lucas Klein)
Aimé Césaire, *Solar Throat Slashed* [2011] (with A. James Arnold)

© Tom Wallace

CLAYTON ESHLEMAN was born in Indianapolis, Indiana, June 1, 1935. He has a B.A. in Philosophy and an M.A.T. in English Literature from Indiana University. He has lived in Mexico, Japan, Taiwan, Korea, Peru, France, Czechoslovakia, and Hungary. He is presently Professor Emeritus, English Department, Eastern Michigan University. Since 1986 he has lived in Ypsilanti, Michigan with his wife Caryl who over the past forty years has been the primary reader and editor of his poetry and prose. His first collection of poetry, *Mexico & North,* was published in Kyoto, 1962. From 1968 to 2004, Black Sparrow Press brought out thirteen collections of his poetry. In 2006, Black Widow Press became his main publisher and with *The Price of Experience* has now brought out six collections of his poetry, prose, and translations, including in 2008 *The Grindstone of Rapport / A Clayton Eshleman Reader.* Wesleyan University Press has published five of his books, including *Juniper Fuse: Upper Paleolithic Imagination & the Construction of the Underworld* (2003), the first study of the Ice Age cave art by a poet. Two book-length poems, *An Anatomy of the Night* and *The Jointure,* were published by BlazeVOX in 2011 and 2012. Eshleman has published fourteen collections of translations, including *Watchfiends & Rack Screams* by Antonin Artaud (Exact Change, 1995), *The Complete Poetry of César Vallejo* (University of California Press, 2007) and *Solar Throat Slashed* by Aimé Césaire, co-translated with A. James Arnold (Wesleyan University Press, 2011). He also founded and edited two of the most important innovative poetry journals of the later part of the 20th century: *Caterpillar* (20 issues, 1967–1973) and *Sulfur* (46 issues, 1981–2000). Among his recognitions and awards are a Guggenheim Fellowship in Poetry, The National Book Award in Translation, two grants from the NEA, two grants from the NEH, two Landon Translation Prizes from the Academy of American Poets, and a Rockefeller Study Center residency in Bellagio, Italy. Forthcoming publications include, with A. James Arnold, a cotranslation of Césaire's original 1939 *Notebook of a Return to the Native Land* (Wesleyan, 2013) and *Penetralia,* a fifty-seven-year poetry retrospective (Black Widow, 2015).

TITLES FROM BLACK WIDOW PRESS

TRANSLATION SERIES

A Life of Poems, Poems of a Life
by Anna de Noailles. Translated by Norman R. Shapiro. Introduction by Catherine Perry.

Approximate Man and Other Writings
by Tristan Tzara. Translated and edited by Mary Ann Caws.

Art Poétique
by Guillevic. Translated by Maureen Smith.

The Big Game by Benjamin Péret. Translated with an introduction by Marilyn Kallet.

Capital of Pain
by Paul Eluard. Translated by Mary Ann Caws, Patricia Terry, and Nancy Kline.

Chanson Dada: Selected Poems
by Tristan Tzara. Translated with an introduction and essay by Lee Harwood.

Essential Poems and Writings of Joyce Mansour: A Bilingual Anthology
Translated with an introduction by Serge Gavronsky.

Essential Poems and Prose of Jules Laforgue
Translated and edited by Patricia Terry.

Essential Poems and Writings of Robert Desnos: A Bilingual Anthology
Edited with an introduction and essay by Mary Ann Caws.

EyeSeas (Les Ziaux) by Raymond Queneau. Translated with an introduction by Daniela Hurezanu and Stephen Kessler.

Furor and Mystery & Other Writings
by René Char. Edited and translated by Mary Ann Caws and Nancy Kline.

The Inventor of Love & Other Writings
by Gherasim Luca. Translated by Julian and Laura Semilian. Introduction by Andrei Codrescu. Essay by Petre Răileanu.

La Fontaine's Bawdy by Jean de La Fontaine. Translated with an introduction by Norman R. Shapiro.

Last Love Poems of Paul Eluard
Translated with an introduction by Marilyn Kallet.

Love, Poetry (L'amour la poésie)
by Paul Eluard. Translated with an essay by Stuart Kendall.

Poems of André Breton: A Bilingual Anthology
Translated with essays by Jean-Pierre Cauvin and Mary Ann Caws.

Poems of A.O. Barnabooth by Valéry Larbaud. Translated by Ron Padgett and Bill Zavatsky.

Préversities: A Jacques Prévert Sampler
Translated and edited by Norman R. Shapiro.

The Sea and Other Poems by Guillevic. Translated by Patricia Terry. Introduction by Monique Chefdor.

To Speak, to Tell You? Poems by Sabine Sicaud.
Translated by Norman R. Shapiro. Introduction and notes by Odile Ayral-Clause.

forthcoming translations

Jules Choppin (1830–1914) New Orleans Poems in Creole and French. Translated by Norman R. Shapiro.

Poems of Consummation
by Vicente Aleixandre. Translated by Stephen Kessler

MODERN POETRY SERIES

ABC of Translation by Willis Barnstone

An Alchemist with One Eye on Fire by Clayton Eshleman

Anticline by Clayton Eshleman

Archaic Design by Clayton Eshleman

Backscatter: New and Selected Poems by John Olson

The Caveat Onus by Dave Brinks
The complete cycle, four volumes in one.

City Without People: The Katrina Poems by Niyi Osundare

Concealments and Caprichos by Jerome Rothenberg

Crusader-Woman by Ruxandra Cesereanu. Translated by Adam J. Sorkin. Introduction by Andrei Codrescu.

Curdled Skulls: Poems of Bernard Bador Translated by the author with Clayton Eshleman.

Endure: Poems by Bei Dao Translated by Clayton Eshleman and Lucas Klein.

Exile is My Trade: A Habib Tengour Reader Translated by Pierre Joris.

Fire Exit by Robert Kelly

Forgiven Submarine by Ruxandra Cesereanu and Andrei Codrescu

from stone this running by Heller Levinson

The Grindstone of Rapport: A Clayton Eshleman Reader
Forty years of poetry, prose, and translations.

Larynx Galaxy by John Olson

Memory Wing by Bill Lavender

Packing Light: New and Selected Poems by Marilyn Kallet

The Present Tense of the World: Poems 2000–2009 by Amina Saïd. Translated with an introduction by Marilyn Hacker.

The Price of Experience by Clayton Eshleman

The Secret Brain: Selected Poems 1995–2012 by Dave Brinks

Signal from Draco: New and Selected Poems by Mebane Robertson

forthcoming modern poetry titles

An American Unconscious by Mebane Robertson

Eye of Witness: A Jerome Rothenberg Reader Edited with commentaries by Heriberto Yepez & Jerome Rothenberg

Memory by Bernadette Mayer

LITERARY THEORY / BIOGRAPHY SERIES

Revolution of the Mind: The Life of André Breton by Mark Polizzotti. Revised and augmented edition.